IRELAND

The Complete Guide and Road Atlas

IRELAND

The Complete Guide and Road Atlas

Third Edition

A Voyager Book

The Globe Pequot Press

Old Saybrook, Connecticut

Third American edition published in 1993 by The Globe Pequot Press

First published by The Appletree Press Ltd,
19–21 Alfred Street, Belfast BT2 8DL

Copyright © 1988, 1991, 1993 by The Appletree Press Ltd

Gazetteer : Hugh Oram. Additional Text : Fergus Mulligan. Maps : Engineering Surveys Reproduction Ltd.
Photographs : Bord Failte, Down District Council, Christopher Hill Photographic, Light Fingers, Media Management and Production
Ltd, John Murphy, Northern Ireland Tourist Board, Office of Public Works (Dublin) and Waterford Glass Ltd.
Printed in the EC. The publishers gratefully acknowledge the assistance of Bord Failte and the Northern Ireland Tourist Board.

Library of Congress Cataloging-in-Publication Data
Ireland : the complete guide and road atlas. — 3rd ed.
p. cm.
"A Voyager Book"
Includes indexes.
ISBN 1-56440-180-4
1. Ireland — Guidebooks. 2. Northern Ireland — Guidebooks.
3. Northern Ireland — Maps. 4. Ireland — Maps. I. Title: Ireland guide.
DA980.I55 1993
914.1504'824 — dc20   92-42369
CIP

Third Edition/First Printing

Contents

Introduction

This guide is a comprehensive and up-to-date compilation of facts and ideas to help you plan your holiday in Ireland. The book combines reliable, up-to-the-minute information with background sections on Ireland's history, landscape and customs.

Many visitors are perfectly content to spend their holiday simply exploring the countryside and getting to know the people, but if you have a more specific purpose in making your trip to Ireland – perhaps you're curious to trace your ancestors or eager to participate in a particular festival or musical event – it is well worth consulting our special sections on various aspects of Irish life and culture. Fifteen succinct and informative chapters covering everything from ancient monuments to contemporary theatre will tell you all you need to know and give you essential details of dates, venues, addresses and contacts. We

INFORMATION POINTS

Tourists and other visitors are strongly advised to check opening times for buildings and sites before they set out. Quite often, opening times can vary slightly from those given, although especially with country locations, a certain flexibility is shown. Whenever possible, the telephone numbers of individual tourist attractions are listed; during the peak summer period, most larger towns in Ireland have TIOs in operation, with full access to information on local opening times. If you are using boat facilities, it's worth checking with the local TIO that the boat operator is licensed. Local TIOs will also tell you which accommodation is registered with Bord Failte, a useful consumer safeguard.

The telephone systems in both the Republic of Ireland and Northern Ireland are fully automatic for both national and international calls. In this book, area codes are given in brackets; they need only be dialled when phoning a number outside your own area.

To call a Northern Ireland number from the Republic of Ireland, dial **08** followed by the area code and number.

To call a Republic of Ireland number from Northern Ireland, dial **010** 353.

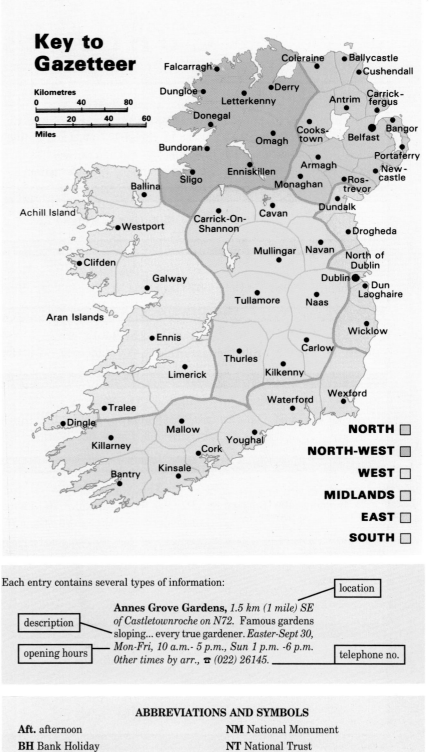

Key to Gazetteer

Kilometres
0   40   80
0   20   40   60
Miles

Falcarragh
Coleraine • • Ballycastle
• Cushendall
Dungloe • • Derry
Letterkenny   Antrim   Carrick-fergus
Donegal   Cooks-town
Omagh   Belfast   • Bangor
Bundoran   Enniskillen   Armagh   Portaferry
Ballina   Sligo   Monaghan   Ros-   New-castle
trevor
Achill Island   Carrick-On-Shannon   Cavan   Dundalk
• Westport   Drogheda
Mullingar   Navan   North of Dublin
• Clifden   Galway   Tullamore   Dublin   Dun Laoghaire
Aran Islands   Naas
• Ennis   Wicklow
Thurles   Carlow
Limerick   Kilkenny
• Tralee   Waterford   Wexford
• Dingle   Mallow   Youghal
Killarney   Cork
Bantry   Kinsale

NORTH ☐
NORTH-WEST ☐
WEST ☐
MIDLANDS ☐
EAST ☐
SOUTH ☐

Each entry contains several types of information:

location

Annes Grove Gardens, *1.5 km (1 mile) SE of Castletownroche on N72.* Famous gardens sloping... every true gardener. *Easter-Sept 30, Mon-Fri, 10 a.m.- 5 p.m., Sun 1 p.m. -6 p.m. Other times by arr.,* ☎ *(022) 26145.*

description

opening hours

telephone no.

ABBREVIATIONS AND SYMBOLS

Aft. afternoon
BH Bank Holiday
By arr. visits by arrangement only
C Roman Catholic
Cl Church of Ireland
EC early closing
Eve evening

NM National Monument
NT National Trust
SO Summer only
TIO Tourist Information Office
☎ telephone number
♿ wheelchair access

also give you some appetising suggestions for places where you might like to eat, drink and be entertained in traditional Irish style – but the choice is yours. There's so much to see, so much to do, that we can't make all the decisions for you! We've even thought of your last-minute holiday gift and souvenir dilemma – our section on shopping is crammed with ideas, both classic and original, for items you'll treasure long after you've returned home. Our further reading list covers a wide range of topics you might like to read up on – we're sure you'll be keen to explore some new aspect of Irish culture discovered on your travels, whether it be the history of poitín or the art of traditional cookery!

Of all possible holiday destinations, Ireland

lends itself especially well to touring. The roads are blissfully quiet and uncrowded, the scenery is spectacular and you'll find no shortage of welcoming guesthouses, farms and hotels. What's more the whole island can comfortably be covered by bus, car or train in the

space of a short holiday. Our self-drive touring ideas have been designed to let you travel through the country's most beautiful spots, both inland and coastal, at your own pace. The suggested routes will take you to lakes, mountains, beaches and famous cities – but feel free to stray from the main roads and thoroughfares when the notion takes you; you'll make your own discoveries and, wherever you end up, you can be sure the locals will give you a warm welcome.

At the heart of the touring guide is our attractively illustrated gazetteer, which you'll find invaluable. Its listings are based around 55 of Ireland's main towns and cities selected on the basis of their cultural, historic, geographic and commercial importance. Whatever attracts you to any of these towns, whether it is a castle, church, art gallery or swimming pool – or even if you just want to know who hires out bicycles or boats – you'll find it here, classed by type. Places of interest and activities in the areas around each of these towns and cities then follow, listed alphabetically.

In the greater Dublin area, the scheme is slightly different: one chapter is devoted to Dublin city, and the surrounding areas are described in three separate chapters – Dun Laoghaire (south), Naas (west) and North of Dublin.

Finally, whether you're travelling by bus, car, train or a combination of all three you'll want to see where you're going, so to make things even easier we've included a large-scale road atlas which is clearly laid out and simple to use.

History

The first people who settled in Ireland were hunters, probably from Scotland, who arrived in Co. Antrim c. 7000 BC. By 3000 BC tribes from the Mediterranean were building megalithic tombs all over Ireland which reveal a high degree of civilisation. The most spectacular are the passage graves at Newgrange, Co. Meath, Carrowmore and Lough Crew, all of which can be visited. The National Museum in Dublin has a collection of masterpieces from this period: gold collars, torcs, dress fasteners and hair ornaments.

The Celts arrived around 300 BC bringing their distinctive culture, laws and customs. The Irish language derives from a dialect of Celtic, and *The Tain* is an epic account of Celtic life at the time.

In the 5th century St Patrick brought Christianity from Britain, establishing monasteries which became not only centres of learning but in effect small towns. Places associated with Patrick include Slane, Co. Meath, where he lit the Paschal fire in defiance of the Druids, Tara where he used the shamrock to convince the high king about the Trinity and Downpatrick where a crude slab marks his grave. Irish monks produced a large number of beautifully illustrated manuscripts, among them the Books of Durrow, Armagh and Kells, which can be seen in Trinity College Dublin. The monasteries of Clonmacnois, Glendalough and Kildare drew scholars from all over Europe. In turn Irish missionaries took education and religion to every corner of Europe. At the same time craftsmen were producing exquisite reliquaries, brooches, belts, and personal adornments made of gold and studded with precious stones (see the Ardagh Chalice and the Cross of Cong

General Post Office, O'Connell Street, Dublin

in the National Museum). This period is rightly known as the golden age.

The wealth of the monasteries and their towns attracted the Vikings, who swept in burning and killing. Distinctive round towers and bell towers were built as a refuge from them. Later the Vikings settled around the coast and founded towns such as Cork, Waterford, Limerick and Dublin. They were finally defeated by Brian Boru at the Battle of Clontarf in 1014.

On his death, inter-kingdom rivalry led to a century of chaos until the Normans arrived from England and brought order and prosperity. They were so well assimilated into Irish society that the English crown decided a reconquest was needed. Ulster put up fierce resistance under Hugh O'Neill and Hugh O'Donnell but they were finally defeated at the Battle of Kinsale in 1601. Their exile and that of the Gaelic aristocracy is known as the

'flight of the earls'. The systematic dispossession of the natives and settlement of migrants from England and Scotland followed. This division of Protestant settler and native Catholic has had repercussions ever since.

The campaign of Oliver Cromwell in Ireland is infamous and lives on in folk memory as the 'curse of Cromwell'. His approach to the Irish problem was drastic: the remaining lands were taken from their owners; those who could prove themselves loyal were exiled to Connacht, while others were put to death. The incompetent James II was deposed from the English throne (for trying to impose Catholicism on the English) by William of Orange in 1688. William then defeated him at the Battle of the Boyne on 12 July 1690. This battle is celebrated each year as Orangeman's Day, a public holiday in Northern Ireland.

James was replaced by Patrick Sarsfield, and the war dragged on until the signing of the Treaty of Limerick, which was accompanied by the imposition of harsh penal laws.

This oppression, coupled with grinding poverty and recurring food shortages, set the pattern for more than a century. A series of revolts at the end of the 18th century culminated in the French invasion of Killala, Co. Mayo. Although initially successful it was finally suppressed with great slaughter.

The Act of Union in 1800 abolished the Dublin parliament and removed power to London. Daniel O'Connell's election to Westminster (which, as a Catholic, he was forbidden to enter) led to the repeal of the more oppressive laws and to Catholic emancipation. A firm believer in non-violence, he came near to the repeal of the union but his final years were clouded by the Great Famine when nearly a million died and two million emigrated.

Parnell became leader of the Home Rule Party in 1877, and, with Gladstone's support, a home rule bill nearly succeeded. Other leaders followed: Arthur Griffith founded Sinn Féin as a non-violent movement and James Larkin and James Connolly became key people in the labour movement. In 1912 the Commons passed the home rule bill. Ireland was to have self-government after World War I.

There was no rejoicing among the Protestants in Ulster. They quickly armed themselves to fight to maintain the link with Britain. In Dublin a group of volunteers decided they could not wait for the end of the war, and began the Easter Rising of 1916. Although unsuccessful and condemned by most Irish people, the execution of its leaders changed public opinion. The Anglo-Irish war lasted from 1919 to 1921.

The treaty of 1921 gave independence to 26 of the 32 counties; six of the Ulster counties remained under British rule with a parliament in Belfast. A sector of the Republican movement opposed this compromise and a bitter civil war followed, culminating in the death of Michael Collins, the brilliant young Corkman who masterminded the war of independence. World War II imposed great strains on the Free State (economically stagnant for many years) which stayed neutral. Séan Lemass later adopted a more vigorous, expansionist economic policy which brought new prosperity and paved the way for Ireland's entry to the European Economic Community (EEC) in 1972.

Today the Republic of Ireland is a parliamentary democracy with a president as head of state. There are two houses of parliament, the Dáil and the Seanad, and three major political parties, Fianna Fáil, Fine Gael, and the smaller Labour Party. Northern Ireland has suffered some unrest since 1921. In 1968 the Civil Rights movement called for power sharing and equality in jobs and housing. Since then there has been an upsurge of extremist republican and loyalist paramilitary violence. However, despite its beleaguered image, it is quite safe to visit.

Geography

Ireland, an island in north-west Europe, has an area of 84,421 sq km (32,595 sq miles). At its

Provinces and Counties of Ireland

greatest it is 486 km (302 miles) long and 275 km (171 miles) wide and consists of a central lowland surrounded by a broken range of hills and small mountains.

The climate is mild on account of the Gulf Stream, without extremes of heat or cold. Average temperatures in January are 4-7°C and in July 14-16°C, rising occasionally as high as 25°C. May and June are often the sunniest months, and North American visitors in particular will notice that there are many more daylight hours in summer than in the US. Rainfall is heaviest in the mountainous west and lightest in the east but the weather is at all times very changeable. A day of prolonged and depressing drizzle can end with a clear sky, a spectacular sunset and the promise of a sunny day to follow. Even so it is wise to have a raincoat or umbrella to hand while touring.

There are 32 counties and four provinces: Connaught, Leinster, Munster and Ulster. Six of the 9 Ulster counties are part of the United Kingdom and the other 26 form the Republic of Ireland. The population of the Republic is 3,500,000 and of Northern Ireland 1,580,000. Dublin is the capital of the former, with an urban population of about one million. The principal cities and towns are Dublin, Belfast, Cork, Derry, Limerick, Waterford and Gal-

way. Of these only the first three have a population in excess of 100,000.

Food, drink, tobacco, engineering, textiles, chemicals and electronics are the chief manufacturing industries. The recession has caused many redundancies but exports show a steady increase in real terms. The Industrial Development Authority (IDA) conducts a vigorous campaign to attract foreign companies to the Republic with a package of financial incentives for foreign and Irish firms. Many firms from the USA, Britain, Germany, the Netherlands and France among others have located in Ireland. In the north the old reliance on linen and shipbuilding has been largely replaced now by light engineering and textiles, most of it from Britain and located in the east of the province.

Ireland does not have great mineral resources. There are some small coal deposits, cement is made at Limerick, Drogheda, Larne and Cookstown, and there is a large lead and zinc mine at Navan. Natural gas was discovered off the Cork coast and brought ashore in 1979. It now counts for 14 per cent of Ireland's primary energy. While oil exploration goes on there has not yet been a major find. Other minerals are dolomite, gypsum, barytes and salt.

Turf is one natural fuel found in abundance. Bord na Móna, a state company, produces over 4 million tonnes of peat and 1 million tonnes of moss peat annually. Production is highly mechanised and much of the peat is used for electricity generation as well as by the domestic and industrial consumer. Other sources of electricity are oil, natural gas, hydroelectric systems and coal.

Farming is a major industry, being mainly of a mixed pastoral nature. Irish beef, lamb and pork, along with dairy products such as cheese, butter, yoghurt and cream, are famous. Output and profitability have greatly increased in recent years, largely as a result of Ireland's entry into the EC.

The main types of sea fish landed are herring, cod, mackerel and plaice. Shellfish include lobsters, mussels, periwinkles and oysters. Much of this is exported to Europe, where pollution-free Irish seafood is greatly prized. Salmon and trout are taken in large numbers, particularly from inland waters, and are also highly valued.

About 5 per cent of Irish land is under forest and coniferous trees grow particularly well in Irish soil. Over 350 forests are open to the public, and many are laid out with car parks, picnic areas, nature trails and walks. Among the loveliest are Glenveagh (Co. Donegal), Lough Key (Co. Roscommon), Connemara, Lough Navar (Co. Fermanagh) and the John F. Kennedy park (New Ross, Co. Wexford).

Ireland, as everyone knows, is very green. This is caused by the mild, damp climate which encourages growth. Two areas of great botanical interest may be cited. Around Glengarriff, Co. Cork, which enjoys the full benefit of the Gulf Stream, there is a luxuriant growth of tropical flora such as arbutus, fuchsia and other delightful flowering plants. A trip to Garinish Island, just offshore from Glengarriff, with its beautiful plant collection is well worthwhile. By contrast the Burren is an area of Co. Clare which resembles a lunar-like landscape of bare, carboniferous limestone. It is 40 ha (100 sq miles) in size but in spring and early summer produces a host of exotic orchids, ferns and rare plants.

There are at least 380 wild birds to be seen in Ireland, for migration goes on all year. The most common species are blackbird, thrush, goldcrest, starling and curlew. Among the indigenous animal species are the Irish hare (once seen on the old three pence coin), the Irish stoat, fox and red deer. Wild deer roam the Kerry and Wicklow mountains and are also to be seen in the Phoenix Park, Dublin.

Irish horse breeding is world famous, being centred on counties Meath and Kildare. The national stud at Tully, Co. Kildare (near the Curragh) can be visited at certain times of the year. There are seven distinct breeds of Irish dog, the best known being the giant Irish wolfhound, the Irish setter and the Irish water spaniel. There is only one reptile, the common lizard, and, thanks to St Patrick, no snakes!

Ancient Monuments

All archaeological remains in Ireland are under state care and most can be easily visited, including those on private land. Please take care to close gates, not to disturb farm animals and to respect the landowner's property. A good detailed map, a pair of stout shoes or boots and occasionally a torch will be useful, especially for the more remote examples. Once you are in the area ask the locals for directions. They will tell you exactly where to find them – and a lot more besides.

There is a vast number of ancient monuments including dolmens, crannógs, forts, clocháns, tumuli, cairns, passage graves, stone circles, round towers and high crosses. Many of the finest examples have been photographed by Kenneth McNally for his book *Standing Stones and other monuments of early Ireland,* and it is well worth visiting at least some of these, as they reveal much about how people have lived in Ireland over the last 5,000 years.

Forts were ramparts built of clay (raths) and stone (cahers or cashels). They have given their name to many Irish towns, for example Rathdrum, Rathfriland, Cahirciveen and Cashel. Since there are said to be 40,000 forts it would be hard to miss them. This term was used for any strengthened structure including stockades and cattle enclosures. Staigue Fort in Kerry, Garranes in Cork, Grianan of Aileach in Donegal and Navan Fort near Armagh City are among the best. Tara, once the palace of the high kings of Ireland, has a number of raths.

Dolmens are tombs dating from about 2000 BC and consist of two or more unhewn stones supporting a flat capstone. There is a huge one at Kilternan, Co.Dublin. Others are at Proleek, Co. Louth, Knockeen, Co. Waterford and Legananny, Co. Down.

Stone Circle, Castletownbere, Co. Cork

Passage graves are set in a mound of earth or stone with a passage leading to the central chamber, and often have side chambers. Many are 4,500 years old and show a sophisticated knowledge of construction, design and astronomy. They are often decorated with geometrical motifs, spirals, concentric circles, triangles, zigzags, the human face and of course the sun. Their meaning has not yet been deciphered but presumably they are connected with the religion of the people who built them.

Passage graves often occur in groups and those found in the Boyne valley are superb: Newgrange, Knowth and Dowth. Newgrange is a vast earthen mound penetrated by a long narrow passage. The tumulus is surrounded by a ditch with a number of the original pillar stones in place. A kerb of 97 huge stones (many with spiral motifs) supports a dry wall. The threshold stone is carved with a triple spiral, circles and diamonds about whose meaning we can only speculate.

The passageway is narrow and low and the central chamber artificially lit. However, on one day of the year, the Winter Solstice (21 December), a shaft of light enters the passage at dawn and for a few minutes strikes the centre of the floor illuminating the chamber. It is by all accounts an extraordinary experience.

Stone circles (cromlechs) are quite rare but can be visited at Lough Gur, Co. Limerick, whose shores have a large number of ancient monuments including forts and tiny remains of stone age dwellings.

Pillar stones or gallans can often be seen in fields alongside the road. The most interesting are indicated by a signpost. Some have traces of carving and many have inscriptions in ogham writing. The letters consist of up to five lines cut above, below or across the stem line and may record a name or event in Irish. They date from about AD 300 and are the earliest form of writing known in Ireland. While it is easy enough to transliterate ogham

the meaning is often unclear because the Irish use is very obscure. Dunloe, Co. Kerry, has a number of ogham stones in good condition. One inscription reads 'Cunacena' – probably someone's name. There are many more in Kerry and Cork.

Crannógs are lake dwellings built on a small island, sometimes reached by a causeway. There are crannógs at Fair Head, Co. Antrim and a splendid reconstruction at Quin, near Shannon Airport in Co. Clare. There the Craggaunowen Project has recreated a number of ancient dwellings and ring forts which vividly show the lifestyle of people in Ireland 3,000 years ago.

Clocháns are the distinctive beehive huts built of stone which were used as monk's cells. Many are on offshore islands such as Bishop's Island, Co. Clare, High Island, Co. Galway, Inishmurray, Co. Sligo, and the breathtakingly beautiful Skellig Michael, Co. Kerry. There are many more accessible ones on the Dingle peninsula, including the delightful Gallarus Oratory.

Round towers are spread evenly across the country, with about 65 examples to be seen. Many are still intact with the distinctive conical cap. They were used as places of refuge and as belfries, usually with the entrance high off the ground. Once the occupants were inside the ladder was drawn up. It is worth climbing at least one round tower just for the view of the surrounding countryside. Among the best are those at Glendalough, Co. Wicklow, Ardmore, Co. Waterford, Devenish, Co. Fermanagh, Clonmacnois, Co. Offaly and that beside St Canice's Cathedral, Kilkenny.

High crosses vary from small inscribed stones to massive free-standing sculptures with beautifully detailed carvings and a celtic circle around the head of the cross. Good examples are Muiredach's Cross at Monasterboice, Co. Louth and Clonmacnois, where a number of inscribed crosses are individually displayed. Both sites have round towers and

extensive monastic remains. Another high cross and the stump of a round tower are located at Drumcliff, Co. Sligo, burial place of the poet William Butler Yeats.

Architecture

The Rock of Cashel, once the palace of the kings of Munster, dominates the surrounding plain and has a fine collection of early Irish buildings. The 13th-century cathedral, although a ruin, is a most impressive edifice. Nearby there is a round tower and the delightful 11th-century Cormac's Chapel built in Irish-Romanesque style. It is similar to Clonfert cathedral with its ornate yet delicate doorway.

Gothic architecture was brought to Ireland by the Normans and the expanding monastic orders. The ruined Mellifont Abbey which still has part of its cloister and octagonal lavabo is an early example. Boyle Abbey, also built around 1200, retains its solid arcade but St Patrick's Cathedral, Dublin , and St Canice's, Kilkenny, are perhaps the finest examples of gothic architecture intact today. Also worth a visit is Jerpoint Abbey which has a 15th century tower and an elaborately decorated cloister. Nearby is the cleanly restored Duiske Abbey at Grainguenamanagh with its outstanding processional doorway and delightful medieval tiles (ask to see them).

Castles or fortified houses are found in great numbers in Ireland. One of the largest is Trim Castle, whose extensive ruins cover several acres. It was built in 1170 by Hugh de Lacy. Reginald's Tower in Waterford dates from the same period and is a circular building with a conical roof and walls 3 m (10 ft) thick. Once used as a prison, it now houses a small museum. Blarney Castle is a large tower with a parapet 25 m (83 ft) from the ground and houses the famous Blarney Stone, which promises eloquence to all who kiss it. The 15th-century Bunratty Castle near Shannon Airport has been carefully restored and holds a good collection of old Irish furniture and tapestries. In the grounds is the Folk Park, where typical thatched farmhouses, fishermen's and labourers' cottages have been reconstructed.

Kilkenny city has a number of first rate buildings. The medieval castle of the Dukes of Ormonde stands on a commanding site above the River Nore. Rothe House dates from the 16th-century and is built around a cobbled courtyard. Other noteworthy buildings are the Black Abbey, the Tholsel and St Canice's Cathedral.

Among other superb castles worth visiting are Carrickfergus, Cahir, Malahide, Dunguaire, Thoor Ballylee (once home of W.B. Yeats) and Dublin Castle. An outstanding unfortified 16th-century house is that of the Ormondes at Carrick-on-Suir. Town walls have survived in part at Limerick, Dublin, Clonmel, Fethard (near Clonmel), Youghal, Wexford and Kilmallock. The walls of Derry are complete and give an excellent view over the whole city.

Dating from the late 17th-century is one of

Cahir Castle, Co. Tipperary

Ireland's prize buildings, the Royal Hospital, Kilmainham. Originally an old soldiers' home, it is in the form of an arcaded quadrangle with dormer windows on its two stories. It also has a spacious hall and a beautiful clock tower. The Irish Museum of Modern Art has been added.

Classical architecture came to Ireland in the early 18th century when Castletown House was built for William Connolly, speaker of the Irish House of Commons. Many of the finest buildings, including Trinity College, the Bank of Ireland (old Parliament House), Leinster House, the Rotunda, the Custom House, Powerscourt House, the Four Courts, the Marino Casino, Carton House, the King's Inns and the City Hall were built in the Palladian style. They are the supreme jewels of Irish architecture. This was also the period when the gracious Georgian squares of Dublin were laid out - Merrion Square, Fitzwilliam Square, Parnell Square, Mountjoy Square and St Stephen's Green. The interior of many of these buildings are equally beautiful. Visit Russborough House, Castletown, Powerscourt Town House, 85-86 St Stephen's Green, and you will appreciate the exquisite plasterwork, carving and decor of these magnificent houses. Outside Dublin several towns were built along classical lines, for example Tyrellspass, Hillsborough, Birr, Armagh, Portarlington and Westport.

The 19th century saw an upsurge in church building. Noted examples are Killarney and Enniscorthy cathedrals – both by Pugin the gothic revivalist – St Finbarre's, Cork and St Saviour's, Dublin. The railway companies have also left a valuable heritage in the large number of elegant stations. In Dublin the terminals of Heuston, Connolly, the Broadstone and Harcourt Street are gracious buildings. When travelling by train it is also worth noting the many excellent country stations, especially en route to Galway/Sligo and Kilkenny. Their structure has, for the most part, scarcely altered since the day they opened. From the same period are the sturdy coastal forts known as Martello towers, built to counter the threat of a French invasion. The best known is probably James Joyce's tower at Sandycove, south of Dublin.

Not all interesting buildings were designed for the wealthy. All over Ireland the traditional thatched cottage may be seen, especially in the west and in Adare. There are also elaborate, brightly painted shop fronts in every town along with neat little churches and simple public houses that have escaped 'modernisation'. The local Protestant church is usually older and of more interest than its Catholic counterpart.

Twentieth-century architecture is the subject of some controversy. Most towns have undergone ribbon housing development, and modern rural bungalows sometimes show a depressing sameness with unimaginative sitting. The population of inner cities has fallen as people move to the suburbs, and a number of architectural horrors have been inflicted on Dublin – notably O'Connell Bridge House and the ESB headquarters in Lower Fitzwilliam Street. However, some new buildings blend happily into their background, such as the Irish Life Centre in Abbey Street and the corporation housing schemes in Ringsend, the Coombe and along the south quays of the Liffey. A great addition to the Smithfield area is the attractive Irish Distillers' building, while the Central Bank, the Arts Block in Trinity College and the Abbey Theatre deserve favourable mention.

Literature and Theatre

From the 6th to the 17th century most literature was composed in Irish. Some has been lost but a good deal is still available in the original and in translation. The early monks produced a large body of poetry, much of it religious, but they also recorded a great deal of pre-Christian material. Perhaps the best known of these is the *Tain Bo Cuailnge* (the

Grand Opera House, Belfast

Cattle Raid of Cooley). This is the epic account of the raid by the men of Connaught led by Queen Maeve to capture the marvellous bull owned by the men of Ulster. It has been beautifully translated by Thomas Kinsella, among others. The *Navigatio Brendani* (Voyage of St Brendan) is another example of this type of writing.

Later classics include the *Book of the Dun Cow* and the *Book of Leinster* which date from the 12th century and feature the adventures of Cuchulain, Fionn McCool, Oisin, the Fianna and other legendary heroes who succumbed to Patrick's crozier. These works provided great inspiration for writers such as Yeats and James Stephens.

Also dating from this period are the *Annals of the Four Masters,* a magnificent historical record of events in Ireland from the earliest times. Much of our knowledge of Irish history comes from the work of these Donegal scholars. In the 18th century a schoolmaster from

Clare, Brian Merriman, composed *The Midnight Court* (Cúirt an Mheán Oíche), a witty satire on the reluctance of Irish men to marry. Writing later in the same century Jonathan Swift was the first Irish author to win fame for work in English. He lampooned social and political mores at the time and the English attitude to Ireland in *A Tale of a Tub, A Modest Proposal* and *Gulliver's Travels.* Contemporary with him was George Berkeley, the noted philosopher and author of *Principles of Human Knowledge.*

Other outstanding figures of this period are Edmund Burke, the philosopher and orator whose statue stands outside Trinity College and Oliver Goldsmith, the gentle author of *The Vicar of Wakefield, The Deserted Village* and *She Stoops to Conquer.* Richard Brinsley Sheridan is remembered for his dramatic works including *The Rivals* and *The School for Scandal* while Thomas Moore gained a reputation as a poet, author and musician. The brilliant wit and bohemian lifestyle of

Oscar Wilde coupled with his novel *The Picture of Dorian Gray* and comedies such as Lady Windermere's Fan and *The Importance of Being Earnest* have made his name immortal.

George Bernard Shaw had no doubt of his ability and compared his best works, *Arms and the Man, Saint Joan and Candida,* to those of Shakespeare; his *Pygmalion* was the basis for *My Fair Lady.* In 1925 he won the Nobel Prize for literature. William Butler Yeats is probably Ireland's best known poet and has had an immense influence on Irish letters. He won the Nobel Prize in 1923. Collections of his poetry and plays are now available in many languages. In celebration of life on the western seaboard John Millington Synge wrote his *Riders to the Sea* and *The Playboy of the Western World.*

The Blasket Islands off the Kerry coast were Irish-speaking and have produced three great writers: Peig Sayers (*An Old Woman's Reflections*), Tomás Ó Criomhtáin (*An t-Oileanach*) and Muiris Ó Súilleabháin (*Fiche*

Blian ag Fas). They lyrically portrayed the hard but contented life of the islanders at the turn of the century. *Irish Fairy Tales* and the exquisitely written *The Crock of Gold* are the fanciful work of James Stephens while Sean O'Casey is remembered for his tragicomedies *The Shadow of a Gunman, Juno and the Paycock* and *The Plough and the Stars.* James Joyce, the author of *Ulysses* and *Dubliners,* now has a worldwide following. Samuel Beckett (another Nobel Prize winner), was a magnificent novelist as well as playwright, who first achieved fame with his play *Waiting for Godot.*

Among the leading contemporary poets are Patrick Kavanagh, Louis MacNeice, Thomas Kinsella, Seamus Heaney, John Montague, Richard Murphy and Derek Mahon. Prominent prose writers include masters of the short story such as Sean O'Faolain, Frank O'Connor, Liam O'Flaherty, Bryan McMahon, Benedict Kiely, Mary Lavin and James Plunkett. Brian Moore, Francis Stuart, Flann O'Brien and Edna O'Brien have also been widely praised. Of the major living Irish playwrights mention must be made of Brian Friel, Tom Murphy, M.J. Molloy and Hugh Leonard.

The founding of the Abbey Theatre in 1904 by Lady Gregory, Edward Martyn and W.B. Yeats marks a turning point for Irish drama. The early years of the Abbey were marked by great controversy. One of the first productions was *The Playboy of the Western World* and it caused a small riot when members of the audience disrupted the performance, saying it was an attack on rural life. This was one of the occasions when Yeats delivered his famous rebuttal of the audience's narrow-mindedness. Such protests occurred from time to time when any works considered remotely salacious or critical of the old Gaelic-Catholic way of life were performed. Indeed at one point such a disrupted performance became the guarantee of a work's success.

These events marked the growing pains of the literary movements as Irish writers fought to free themselves from the suffocating constraints of a narrow nationalist philosophy. It was a time when any foreign work of art was considered suspect and led to the vicious and absurd censorship laws which plagued Irish writing for half a century, driving many of the finest authors into exile.

Happily times have changed and there is now a diverse richness in the literary and theatrical diet which is unsurpassed. Modern farce, Shakespeare, classical pieces and modern Irish plays can now be seen happily co-existing. Every large town has its own amateur drama group which puts on at least one production a year. Ask at the tourist office for details of amateur dramatics in your area.

As the National Theatre, the Abbey is today dedicated to producing the best works of Irish and international playwrights. Michael MacLiammoir and Hilton Edwards set up the Gate Theatre in 1928 to produce a broad range of plays while the Project Arts Centre is an experimental theatre. In addition there are a large number of repertory groups, amateur enthusiasts, lunchtime plays and pub theatres offering a rich programme of drama throughout Ireland. Among them is Siamsa

Tire, the National Folk Theatre established in Tralee, which presents authentic folk productions in the Kerry area. Garter Lane arts centre, Waterford, has a resident theatre company.

Folklore

Ireland has a vast heritage of folklore going back to pre- Christian times. The sagas, epics, legends, stories, poems, proverbs, riddles, sayings, curses and prayers are all part of that tradition. Much of it comes by way of the seanachie, the storyteller who sat beside the fire and enchanted his audience with tales of times past. Often he was a nomad and moved from house to house earning his bed and board by storytelling. The characters featured in the main tales are identified by Ronan Coghlan in his *Pocket Dictionary of Irish Myths and Legend,* a useful handbook which will introduce you to the best known legendary persons and events. The Department of Irish Folklore at University College, Dublin, has recorded and preserved a great part of the country's heritage, and there are many fascinating books on various aspects of the topic, such as Patrick Logan's guide to Ireland's 'unofficial' medicine, *Irish Country Cures.*

Almost every sizeable town in Ireland has a small museum where the life and history of the local community is documented in antiquities and relics of the past. A good place to start is the National Museum in Dublin which has a large collection dating from pre-history to the recent past. Also in Dublin are the Civic Museum for items relating to the capital, the Heraldic Museum where you can trace your ancestors, the Guinness Museum, dedicated to Dublin's famous brew, and the Royal Hospital, Kilmainham, which has a superb array of folklore items gathered over many years. Other recommended museums are the Ulster Museum in Belfast, the Ulster Folk and Transport Museum, Co. Down, Rothe House in Kilkenny, the James Joyce Museum at Sandycove, Enniscorthy Museum, Co. Wexford, Limerick and Galway Museums, and Kinsale Museum, in Co. Cork, which displays mementoes of the ill-fated Lusitania sunk off Kinsale in 1915. A number of towns have developed heritage centres and folk parks where the richness of local life is displayed in a less formal setting. Fine examples are located at Damer House, Roscrea (Co. Tipperary), Glencolumbkille (Co. Donegal), Bunratty (Co. Clare), Cultra (Co. Down) and the Ulster-American Folk Park near Omagh (Co. Tyrone).

A delightful way to see a collection of old furniture, farming implements and kitchenware is to visit one of the many pubs displaying such items and imbibe a pint and some culture at the same time. Among them are the Seanachie (Dungarvan, Co. Waterford), Durty Nelly's (Bunratty, Co. Clare), the Asgard (Westport, Co. Mayo) and the Hideout (Kilcullen, Co. Kildare).

Craftworkers now produce a wide range of first class products such as pottery, ceramics, leatherwork, wood carving, jewellery, weaving, basketry, linen, lace, crystal, tweed, pewter and other quality souvenirs. Almost everywhere you will find a shop selling the products of local craftworkers, many of whom employ techniques handed from one generation to the next. Craft centres where these skills can be seen in practice will be found at Marlay Grange and Powerscourt Town House in Dublin and at Muckross House, Killarney (see also 'Shopping').

Fleadh Ceoil, Ballycastle, Co. Antrim

Festivals

Wherever you go in Ireland you can't avoid coming across a festival.

Some of the best known are the Rose of Tralee Festival, a week-long Irish beauty contest which draws the comely daughters of exiles from as far afield as Australia and the USA. The Galway Oyster Festival offers the chance of sampling delicious Irish shellfish in the pleasant city of Galway, washed down with Guinness, of course, while the Yeats Summer School in Sligo is a gathering of the followers of Ireland's foremost poet. The Wexford Opera Festival has international status and attracts

CALENDAR OF EVENTS

January
National Crafts Trade Fair, Royal Dublin Society (RDS), Ballsbridge, Dublin.
Aer Lingus Young Scientist Exhibition, RDS, Dublin.

February
Ulster Motor Show, King's Hall, Belfast.

March
St Patrick's Day, 17 March: national holiday with parades in Dublin and many other centres.
Arklow Music Festival, Arklow, Co. Wicklow
Traditional Irish Music Festival, Dublin.
Western Drama Festival, Tubbercurry, Co. Sligo.
West Cork Drama Festival, Clonakilty, Co. Cork.
Church Music International Choral Festival, Limerick.
Galway International Band Festival, Salthill, Co. Galway.
Limerick International Marching Band Parade, Limerick.

April
Spring Season of Opera, Dublin Grand Opera Society.
Killarney Easter Folk Festival.
Cork International Choral and Folk Dance Festival, City Hall, Cork.
Sligo Feis Ceoil, Sligo.
West of Ireland Golf Championships, Rosses Point, Co. Sligo.

May
All-Ireland amateur drama festival, Athlone, Co. Westmeath.
Dublin International Piano Competition.
Dundalk International Maytime and Drama Festival, Dundalk.
Birr Castle Exhibition, Birr, Co. Offaly.
Spring Show and Industries Fair, RDS, Dublin: superb display of Irish agriculture, horses, cattle and industry.
Belfast Civic Festival.
Dublin Grand Opera season, Dublin and Cork.
International 3-day event, Punchestown Racecourse.
Sligo School of Landscape Painting.
Royal Ulster Agricultural Show, Belfast.
Listowel Writers' Week.
Belfast City Marathon.

June
Kinsale Arts Week.
Ardara Weavers' Fair, Co. Donegal.
Kenmare walking Festival, Co. Kerry.
Dublin International Organ Festival.
Walter Raleigh potato festival, Youghal, Co. Cork.
Carroll's Irish open golf championship.
Music Festival in Great Irish Houses: recitals by world famous artists in lovely 18th-century mansions.
Glengariff Festival.
Spancilhill Horse Fair, Ennis.
Ballybunion Batchelor Festival.
Wexford Strawberry Fair, Enniscorthy.

July
Dun Laoghaire Summer Festival
Clones Agricultural Show, Co. Monaghan.
An Tostal, Drumshanbo.
West Cork Festival, Clonakilty.
Festival of the Erne, Co Cavan.
North of Ireland amateur golf championship, Portrush.
Willie Clancy Summer School, Miltown Malbay.
Drimoleague Festival.
Schull Festival.
Cobh International Folk Dance Festival.
Kerry Summer Painting School, Cahirsiveen.
Glens of Antrim Feis, Glenariff: music, dancing, sports.
Bandon Week.
Skibbereen Annual Show.
Orangeman's Day, 12 July: parades throughout Ulster.
Mary from Dungloe Festival, Dungloe.
Sham fight, Scarva, re-enacts Battle of the Boyne.
Ulster Steam Traction Rally, Shane's Castle, Antrim.

August
Ballyshannon International Folk Festival.
Gorey Arts Week.
O'Carolan Harp and Music Festival, Keadue.
Stradbally Steam Rally.
Claddagh Festival, Galway.
Sligo School of Landscape Painting.
Yeats International Summer School, Sligo.
Irish Antique Dealers' Fair, Dublin.
Dublin Horse Show, RDS, Dublin.
Granard Harp Festival.
Feile Rock Festival, Thurles
John Millington Synge Summer School, Co Wicklow

Puck Fair, Killorglin.
Percy French Festival, Newcastle, Co. Down.
Oul' Lammas Fair, Ballycastle: one of the oldest fairs in Ireland.
Connemara Pony Show, Clifden.
Ulster Grand Prix (motorcycling), Belfast.
Schull Regatta.
Carroll's Irish Open Golf Tournament
Birr Vintage Week.
Merriman Summer School, Lahinch.
Limerick Show.
Carlingford Oyster Festival.
Letterkenny International Folk Festival.
Fleadh Cheoil na hEireann: top festival for traditional music, song, dance; location changes each year.
Kilkenny Arts Week.
Galway Races: more than just horse racing.
Rose of Tralee Festival.
Wexford Mussel Festival.
All-Ireland Road Bowls Final, Armagh.

September
Autumn Fair, RDS, Dublin
Clifden Arts week, Co Galway.
Cork Folk Festival.
Waterford International Festival of Light Opera.
Listowel Harvest Festival and Races.
Lisdoonvarna Folk Festival.
All Ireland Hurling and Football Finals, Dublin.
Galway Oyster Festival.
Dublin Theatre Festival.

October
Kinsale Gourmet Festival.
Flower Festival, St Nicholas, Galway.
Ballinasloe October Horse Fair.
Cork film Festival.
Wexford Opera Festival.
Guinness Jazz Festival, Cork.
Queen of the Burren Autumn Festival, Lisdoonvarna.

November
Belfast Festival at Queen's.
Dublin Indoor International Showjumping, RDS, Dublin.

December
Grand Opera International Season, Dublin.
Irish Craft Fair, Arnotts, Dublin.

world stars but you need to book months in advance.

There are many more which take in dancing, traditional music, drama, steam traction, boating, agricultural shows and sports of all kinds. In fact there are very few you need to book beforehand so look through the list and plan your vacation to take in those that interest you most. Dates and venues may change so check with the tourist office on arrival.

Music

Like the seanachie, the music teacher of old once wandered the country, playing an instrument and teaching music and dance to his pupils. The best known is probably Turlough O'Carolan, the blind harpist and composer of the late 1600s. His beautiful lilting airs are now available on record. Two 19th century composers are particularly outstanding: John Field, the inventor of the nocturne, and Thomas Moore, whose famous *Irish Melodies* includes the 'Last Rose of Summer' and 'The Vale of Avoca'. There is a monument to Moore at the Meeting of the Waters near Avoca, in Co. Wicklow , where he is said to have composed this song; it is a magical spot. Notable among modern composers are A.J. Potter, Gerard Victory, Seoirse Bodley and Seán Ó Riada, who wrote the haunting *Mise Éire*.

It is easy to join in a traditional ballad session. Traditional music and dance is jealously guarded by Comhaltas Ceoltoíri Éireann

which organises music festivals all over the country and has regular sessions at its Monkstown headquarters in south Dublin. (For an interesting introduction to Irish traditional music, Ciaran Carson's book on the subject can be recommended.) Many pubs also hold impromptu ballad evenings. In Dublin they occur regularly at O'Donoghue's, the Abbey Tavern, the Chariot Inn, Slattery's, the Stag's Head, and the Old Shieling. Irish cabaret can be seen at Jury's, the Burlington and Clontarf Castle. There are nightly sessions also at the Granary in Limerick, McCann's and O'Connor's in Doolin, near Ennis, Co. Clare, Duchas in Tralee, Teach Beg in Cork and O'Flaherty's in Dingle, but every town has at least one pub with music. All you have to do is stroll around until you hear singing or the sound of an accordian, tin whistle or the wail of uileann pipes. You can even acquire your own personal tin whistle tutor in the form of a kit devised by Brian and Eithne Vallely. Their *Making Music: The Tin Whistle* consists of a tin whistle, a self-standing teach-yourself music book, additional sheet music and a cassette with tunes and tips.

The National Concert Hall in Dublin has become the centre for music in Ireland. There is a musical event there every day of the year ranging from classical to jazz, traditional, folk music, piano recitals and pop concerts. There are two principal orchestras, the National Symphony Orchestra in the Republic and the Ulster Orchestra in Northern Ireland. Both can be heard throughout the year at the National Concert Hall in Dublin and the Ulster Hall in Belfast respectively, with occasional

performances in other centres. The Dublin Grand Opera Society has one or two seasons in the Gaiety Theatre, Dublin, and at the Opera House, Cork. In Dublin, other concerts and recitals take place in the Royal Dublin Society, Ballsbridge, the National Stadium and the Examination Hall of Trinity College. In Belfast the recently refurbished Opera House provides an impressive venue for concerts, plays and musicals.

During the winter months musicals and light opera are performed in many provincial towns by amateur groups, culminating in the Waterford Festival of Light Opera. For those who like them, discos and night clubs will be found in the major cities, sometimes attached to hotels. In Dublin the area around Leeson Street and Baggot Street has a number of such places.

Sport

The traditional Irish games are known as gaelic games and include hurling (very old), football, handball and camogie. The Gaelic Athletic Association (GAA) organises hundreds of local clubs, and county teams compete in hurling and gaelic football at the All Ireland finals each year in Croke Park, Dublin. Hurling is a fast game played with wooden hurley sticks while gaelic football resembles Australian rules football.

There are over 200 golf courses in Ireland including several of championship standard. They are sited in some beautiful locations and

Hurling final, Croke Park, Dublin

welcome visitors; many more are being made. Horse racing is a national passion and race meetings go on most of the year. The Irish Grand National is run at Fairyhouse on Easter Monday and the Irish Sweeps Derby at the Curragh in June. Bloodstock sales are conducted at Kill, Co Kildare, and at Ballsbridge in Dublin. A list of stables which hire out horses can be had from the tourist boards (Bord Failte and the NITB).

Ireland's waters teem with fish and offer first-class sport. Anglers come from all over the world for the game and coarse fishing which can be enjoyed throughout the island. The major sea angling centres are Kinsale, Valentia, Kilmore, Rosslare, Achill and Westport. Yachting and windsurfing are popular in Cork, Dun Laoghaire, Howth and Bangor with a number of sailing schools in Dublin, Cork and Kerry.

Many other sports have a good following among participants and spectators including squash, rowing, tennis, swimming, scuba diving, greyhound racing, basketball, road bowling, cycling and flying, to name but a few. Soccer is widely played and rugby reaches its peak during the international season when Ireland plays against England, Scotland and Wales for the Triple Crown. Whatever sport you follow you will be able to enjoy it in Ireland.

Food and Eating Out

Four thousand years ago the Irish cooked enormous joints of meat by filling a ditch with water and dropping in heated stones to keep the water boiling. Recent duplicate experiments proved that this method works perfectly although it seems rather troublesome! In pre-Christian times the feasts at Tara and other royal palaces were known to go on for several weeks without a break. Since then the Irish have lost little of their enthusiasm for food although appetites are now more moderate.

A unique pleasure of a stay in Ireland is enjoying the unpretentious but delicious native cooking. Fresh ingredients simply prepared and served without fuss make eating in Ireland a real pleasure. The rich pastures produce meat of the highest quality so that beef, lamb and dairy products like cream, cheese and butter are second to none. Among the tempting dishes on offer are Limerick ham, Irish stew, bacon and cabbage, Galway oysters, sirloin steak and onions, game of all sorts, smoked salmon, Dublin Bay prawns, spring lamb, grilled trout, fresh farm eggs and delicious brown soda bread. Having sampled these, you'll want to recreate the dishes at home, and there are plenty of fine cookery books to choose from, such as John Murphy's *Traditional Irish Recipes* and Mary Kinsella's *An Irish Farmhouse Cookbook*.

In Irish cooking the basic ingredients are so good that elaborate sauces are unnecessary to bring out the flavour of the food. The humble potato is appreciated as nowhere else and a plate of steaming, floury 'spuds' with butter, salt and a glass of milk is a meal in itself.

Restaurant Na Mara, Dun Laoghaire, Co. Dublin

Indeed potatoes are the principal ingredients of several dishes which once formed the bulk of the countryman's diet. Colcannon is mashed potato with butter and onions. Boxty is grated potato fried in bacon fat. Potato cakes are often served with breakfast or high tea but are delicious anytime.

It is difficult to suggest food items to take home as dairy products and the like do not travel well. However no-one should leave Ireland without at least one side of smoked salmon which keeps fresh for up to ten days. Whiskey cake, brack and soda bread can also be carried easily.

An Irish breakfast is a substantial affair: fruit juice, cereals, bacon, egg, sausage and tomato, brown bread, toast, tea or coffee. Many pubs serve tasty lunches ranging from a simple sandwich to a full meal and this is a pleasant way to break up a day's sightseeing. Visit Bewley's in Grafton St or Westmoreland St, if in Dublin, for excellent tea, coffee and cakes, or one of the tea rooms attached to many of the stately homes. For dinner eat in your hotel or choose a restaurant to suit your taste and pocket from the list provided by the tourist board or from the booklet of the Irish Country Houses and Restaurants Association. Some people prefer to go out to a hotel to eat and this is quite acceptable. If you're still hungry after that you could visit a wine bar for a nightcap and a plate of smoked salmon. The next day you can start all over again!

International cooking is available in Ireland and includes Italian, French, Spanish, Indian, Chinese, Greek, Russian and Japanese. There is also a wide price range from a simple one-course meal to *haute cuisine*. It is worth looking for restaurants which have the Bord Failte award for excellence, an independent commendation of good and reasonable value. In addition to table d'hôte and à la carte menus many restaurants also participate in the special value tourist menu scheme. This involves offering a three-course meal at a fixed price and is usually excellent value. Look for the symbol or ask Bord Failte for a list of participating restaurants. In Northern Ireland the Tourist Board publishes a useful booklet called 'Let's eat out' which will help you decide where to go.

Recommending restaurants is a highly risky business and the tourist is advised to use the restaurant guides available which give information on price range, opening hours and specialities. The following Dublin restaurants have been highly praised. For a tasty lunch try the Kilkenny Shop (Nassau St), Mitchell's (Kildare St), the National Gallery (Merrion Square), the Municipal Gallery (Parnell Square), or any of the very pleasant Bewley's cafes in Grafton St, Westmoreland St and South Great George's St. You could

---

IRISH SODA BREAD

200 g (8 oz) wholemeal flour
1 teaspoon baking soda
2 teaspoons salt
300 ml (¹/₂ pint) buttermilk
200 g (8 oz) white flour
3 teaspoons baking powder
1 egg, beaten

Sift flour, soda baking powder, salt. Mix buttermilk, egg and stir in. Knead all ingredients until smooth. Shape into a flat cake on greased paper. Mark a deep cross on the top and bake in preheated oven 190°C, 375°F, gas mark 5 for 35-40 minutes.

---

also drop into one of the many pubs serving lunch such as the Stag's Head (Dame Court), Henry Grattan (Lr Baggot St), Kitty O'Shea's (Upr Grand Canal St), or Foley's (Merrion Row). For dinner try Restaurant Na Mara (Dun Laoghaire), King Sitric (Howth), Le Coquillage (Blackrock), Locks (Portobello), Nico's (Dame St), Trocadero (Andrews St) or Digby's (Dun Laoghaire). The Powerscourt

Town House Centre (South William St) also has several excellent restaurants and coffee bars. Outside Dublin the Cork/Kerry region is excellent for eating out, with Kinsale as the gourmet capital of Ireland.

Other recommended restaurants include Ballymaloe House (near Cork), the Arbutus Lodge (Cork City), Aherne's (Youghal), Doyle's Sea-food Bar (Dingle), the Park Hotel (Kenmare), Ballylickey House (Bantry), Renvyle House Hotel (Connemara), the Galley Floating Restaurant (New Ross), Durty Nelly's (Bunratty), Restaurant St John's (Fahan), and Dunraven Arms Hotel (Adare). In Northern Ireland try Balloo House (Killinchy, Co. Down), The Nutgrove (Downpatrick), Nick's (Killinchy), The Grange (Waringstown), The Ramore (Portrush), Portaferry Hotel (Portaferry) and The Barn (Saintfield). There are many, many more and part of the fun will be discovering your own eating place.

decor with features such as solid mahogany bar furniture, brass lamps, lovely old mirrors and stained glass. To experience a traditional Irish pub it is best to head for one of these and avoid brash, modern places. There are some 900 pubs in Dublin alone and many are excellent. The following is just a representative sample of the best but there are lots more worth exploring.

Doheny and Nesbitt's (Merrion Row) has kept the original interior and has a delightful little snug. This is a small enclosed room with a hatch opening directly on to the bar for discreet imbibing and is found in many pubs. Toner's (Baggot St) has lots of atmosphere and traditional music and so has O'Donoghue's nearby. Neary's (Chatham St) is a pleasant watering hole with an attractive old bar while the Stag's Head (Dame Court) is noted for its beautiful stained glass and highly ornate snug. There is a fine collection of cartoons, photographs and drawings

Thatch (Ballysodare), Crown Liquor Saloon and Robinson's (Belfast), The Spaniard (Kinsale), Durty Nelly's (Bunratty), The Abbey Tavern (Howth), Morrissey's (Abbeyleix), the Granary, South's and Hogan's (Limerick), and O'Flaherty's (Dingle).

When someone asks for a pint they usually mean Guinness, the dark stout with a white head which is synonymous with Ireland. There is hardly a pub in the country that does not stock Guinness on draught or in bottles. Try it on its own or with some oysters. Other top quality beers are Murphy, Macardle's, Smithwick's, Bass, Harp and Beamish. German and American beers are popular.

Visitors are welcome at the Guinness brewery in Dublin, Smithwick's in Kilkenny, Beamish in Cork and Harp and Macardle's in Dundalk and will be invited to taste the product. Guinness is the oldest brewery; Arthur Guinness (Uncle Arthur as he is affectionately known) began brewing at St James's Gate in 1759. Telephone in each case before you go.

Equally famous is Irish whiskey (spelt with an 'e'). The word comes from the Irish *uisce beatha* meaning water of life and there is an old saying 'There's more friendship in a glass of spirit than in a barrel of buttermilk!' The whiskey is matured for 7 to 12 years and has a mellow distinct flavour. It is made from malted and unmalted barley, yeast and pure spring water.

The oldest (legal) distillery is at Bushmill's near the Giant's Causeway, dating from 1609, and it welcomes visitors by appointment. Most Irish whiskey is now distilled at Midleton, Co. Cork. At Irish Distillers' head office in Smithfield, Dublin, there is an excellent display of models, kits and tools showing the history of whiskey and how it is made. Midleton has a fine new whiskey heritage centre, and a whiskey heritage centre has been opened at Kilbeggan, Co Westmeath. A comparatively recent development is the number of cream liqueurs which are made from a blend of whiskey and cream. These include Bailey's, Carolans and Waterford Cream.

Irish people often drink their whiskey diluted with water. So if you order 'a ball of malt'

Hugh McBride's, Dunseverick, Co. Antrim

Pubs and Drink

The Irish have always had a close relationship with drink. Public houses (as bars are called) began as illicit drink shops or shebeens where people met to exchange news and drink poitín, a raw fiery spirit whose history is traced in John McGuffin's book *In Praise of Poteen*. Pubs are still very much a social centre and a convivial meeting place where you can chat to local people in informal surroundings.

Opening hours are 11 a.m.-11 or 11.30 p.m. on weekdays and 12.30 – 2 p.m. and 4 – 10 p.m. on Sundays. In Northern Ireland most pubs are open between 11 a.m. and 11 p.m. on weekdays and between 12.30 and 2.30 p.m. and 7 and 10 p.m. on Sundays.

Many pubs have preserved their original

of noted customers in the Palace Bar (Fleet St) and Mulligan's (Poolbeg St) has a low beam inscribed 'John Mulligan estd. 1782'. Ryan's (Parkgate St) is perfectly preserved and has lovely old bar furniture.

Other traditional pubs worth visiting on a pub crawl are McDaid's, Bowe's, Davy Byrne's, the Long Hall, the Auld Dubliner, Kitty O'Shea's, Conway's, Keogh's, Mulligan's (Stoneybatter), the Brazen Head, O'Brien's and the International.

Outside the capital you will find every Irish town is well endowed with pubs. You should have no trouble finding a welcoming hearth, a blazing turf fire and a cheering glass. But just in case you're stuck head for one of the following: Kate O'Brien's (Fermoy), the Breffni Inn (Dromod), Dan Lowry's, Teach Beag or the Vineyard in Cork, the Seanachie, Dungarvan and Kate Kearney's (Killarney), Taylor's (Moyasta), O'Shea's (Borris), The

IRISH COFFEE

Heat the glass, add one or more spoonfuls of sugar and strong, hot coffee to a height of 3 cm (1.5 in) from the top. Stir well, add a generous measure of Irish whiskey and carefully pour on cream over a spoon so that it rests on the surface. Drink without stirring and then have another one.

you will usually get a jug of water with it. Try it on its own first. Some of the 12-year-old whiskeys are like nectar and are as good as a fine brandy.

Irish coffee is now world famous and often drunk at the end of a meal or on a cold day (see above for recipe). Another warming drink is a hot whiskey which is simply whiskey with hot water, sugar, lemon and cloves. Black Velvet is a delicious mixture of Guinness and champagne, although you can use cider.

Genealogy

Many people visiting Ireland would like to find out more about their family history. What makes ancestor research so fascinating is that it tells you about yourself, who you are and where you come from. You would expect to find Christian names recurring in a family but you might be surprised to see the same occupation held by members of the family over several generations or even spot similarities between your handwriting and theirs! You can engage a professional to do the research work or you can have a go yourself. There are many sources of information although some records have been lost in the various upheavals of Irish history.

It will make things much easier if you do some simple research before you leave home. Try to find out: the full name of your emigrant ancestor; where he came from in Ireland; dates of birth, marriage and death; occupation and background (rich, poor, farmer, tradesman, professional, etc.); religion; date of emigration from Ireland. The more details you have the greater the chance of success. Sources are old letters and diaries, family bibles, military service records, emigrant ship lists, newspapers, local church and state records. Ask the oldest member of your family about their earliest memories too.

Armed with as much information as you can muster you can then visit the following places in Ireland: The Registrar General in Joyce House, 8-11 Lombard Street East, Dublin 2 holds the general civil registration of births, marriages and deaths from 1864. Non-catholic marriages are listed from 1845. You can make the search yourself or have it done for you. A small fee is payable.

The Public Record Office (now The National Archive), Four Courts, Dublin 7, although badly damaged in 1922 has many valuable records including tithes dating from 1800 (the first valuation records), wills and abstracts of wills and marriage licences for some families. The returns for the extensive 1901 census may be seen here.

The Registry of Deeds, Henrietta Street, Dublin 2 has documents from 1708 relating to property such as leases, mortgages and settlements. You make the search yourself and a small fee is due.

The National Library, Kildare Street, Dublin 2 has an enormous collection of useful sources including historical journals, directories, topographical works, private papers and letters and local and national newspapers from the earliest times. It is necessary to contact the Library for a reader's ticket in advance. Catholic Parish Records can now be consulted in the National Library on microfilm. The staff are helpful and there is no charge.

The Genealogical Office, Kildare Street, Dublin 2 records official pedigrees, coats of arms and will abstracts of the more well-to-do families. Staff will conduct a search on your behalf for a fee.

The detailed full colour brochure published by Bord Failte, *Tracing Your Ancestors*, has

Some Irish Family Names

useful information on the subject, including a full listing of all 27 heritage centres now in operation throughout the Republic. Information on the 243 Irish clans researched to date from the Clans of Ireland Office, *c/o Genealogical Office, 2 Kildare Street, Dublin 2*, ☎ *(01)618811, extn. 410.*

Ida Grehan's *Pocket Guide to Irish Family Names* lists and describes the most common names and explains their origins and associations. For a reference guide to first names the *Pocket Guide to Irish First Names* by Ronan Coghlan explains the meanings of most popular names, whether derived from Irish words or based on the names of legendary Irish figures and saints.

The Public Record Office, Four Courts, Dublin 1 has the excellent and comprehensive *Griffith's Valuation*. This was a national survey of land ownership and leases made in the 1850s. There is an immense amount of detail in it. The Valuation Office, 6 Ely Place, Dublin 2 has records of subsequent alterations in land ownership.

If your ancestors came from Northern Ireland (6 counties) the Public Record Office of Northern Ireland at 66 Balmoral Avenue, Belfast BT9 6NY will help. It has tithe appointment books and other valuable sources. Linked to it is the Ulster Historical Foundation which will carry out a search for you.

The Presbyterian Historical Society at Church House, Fisherwick Place, Belfast 1 also has various records of its members. You

might also contact the Registrar General's Office, Oxford House, 49 Chichester Street, Belfast BT1 4HL.

If you know the parish where your ancestor came from start there. Every parish keeps records of the baptisms performed in it giving details of the child's parents and sometimes their date of birth and domicile. Many go back 150 years and some over 200 years. Some Church of Ireland registers go back to the 1700s. To see them apply to the parish priest or minister. Study the baptismal and marriage registers for five years before and after the date you have. Jot down each name that seems likely. Remember too that there is another useful source nearby – the graveyard. Note the details of each gravestone bearing your family name, rubbing away the moss and using a piece of chalk to bring up faint lettering.

Contact the local historical society. Their journal may well have interesting information and perhaps articles on the history of the parish. They will put you in touch with any genealogist specialising in the families of that district. If there is a parish newsletter ask the editor if he would insert an item on your search: 'Information sought about Sean Murphy, believed born in this parish about 18—, emigrated 18—. Please contact...' A similar letter should be sent to the local newspaper; every county has at least one. Lastly, before you leave the area ask to speak to the person who knows most about local history. Even if he or she can't shed light on your elu-

Grafton Street, Dublin

sive ancestor you will learn a great deal about the place where your family originated and that alone should make the trip worthwhile. If you are unsuccessful or don't want to do a search you can employ a professional to do it for you. Results cannot be guaranteed but for a modest sum they will complete an initial search and let you know the likelihood of success. Try one of the following: Irish Genealogical Office, Kildare Street, Dublin 2; Heraldic Artists, 3 Nassau Street, Dublin 2; Hibernian Research, Windsor Road, Dublin 6. For coats of arms, plaques, parchments and the full range of heraldic goods visit Mullins, 36 Upr O'Connell Street, Heraldic Artists (see above) or Historic Families, 8 Fleet Street, Dublin 2.

Shopping

Shopping in Ireland is leisurely and while the choice may not be as wide as London or New York you will discover lots which cannot be found elsewhere. Opening hours are usually 9 a.m.-5.30 p.m. Monday to Saturday. Most shops close on Sunday and in smaller towns for lunch and on one afternoon a week. Bank hours in the Republic are 10 a.m.-12.30 p.m. and 1.30-3.30 p.m. (Mon-Fri), late opening (until 5 p.m. on Thursdays). The larger shops will change currency and traveller's cheques but you will get a better rate in the bank. In Northern Ireland only British currency may be used. There is a value added tax (VAT) refund scheme for goods taken out of the Republic. You must have the invoice stamped by customs at the exit point before returning it to the shop for refund. Ask Bord Failte or the Tourist Information office for a leaflet explaining how the system works and the allowances.

Visitors to Ireland will want to take home some gifts or mementoes of their stay and there is a wide choice of quality Irish-made goods available. Avoid those displaying an excessive amount of shamrocks, leprechauns, etc. – they probably came from the Far East!

If it is not marked ask the assistant where the item is made and look for the 'Guaranteed Irish' symbol, an assurance that the product is quality Irish made. Many of the larger shops will pack, insure and mail goods home for you and don't forget to visit the enormous Duty Free Shop if passing through Shannon Airport where you can save a lot of money on the full price.

In Dublin the main shopping areas are all within easy walking distance: Grafton Street, Wicklow Street, O'Connell Street and Henry Street. The Powerscourt Town House in South William Street has a large assortment of shops, boutiques, restaurants and a craft centre all within a carefully restored 18th-century mansion. There are more shopping complexes in the ILAC Centre off Henry Street, Creation Arcade, Grafton Street, and the Irish Life Centre, Talbot Street. The principal department stores are Clery's (O'Connell St), Switzer's and Brown Thomas's (Grafton St), Arnott's, Dunne's and Roche's (Henry St). Not to be missed at any cost is the Kilkenny Shop in Nassau Street which displays and sells only the best designed Irish goods such as clothing, pottery, jewellery, glass and furniture. It is also a pleasant spot for lunch or afternoon tea. In Belfast the principal shops are located in Donegall Place/Royal Avenue and the streets nearby.

Cork, the Munster capital, is pleasantly sited on the River Lee and has Patrick Street and Grand Parade as the main shopping thoroughfare. In Galway the aptly named Shop Street has a good selection of stores, especially for clothes and crafts. In fact every town, no matter how small, has its main street and in addition many shops stay open late on Friday and Saturday. Watch out for the combined grocery shop and bar where you can order your rashers and have a pint under the same roof.

What to buy

Waterford is almost synonymous with crystal and the factory just outside the town welcomes visitors by appointment. There you can see the ancient skill of moulding, blowing and cutting glass. The factory does not sell direct to the public but the glass is available in outlets everywhere. Less well known but equally

beautiful crystal is made in Galway, Dublin, Cavan, Kilkenny, Cork, Sligo and Tyrone and many have shops attached where you can pick up first rate bargains.

Tweed is a strong woollen fabric used in making suits, skirts, curtains, jackets, ties, hats and carpets. It comes in many beautiful designs, much of it from Donegal and Connemara where the rugged landscape provides the colour and texture of this versatile cloth. You can buy tweed garments made up or choose a pattern and order a length to be made up at home. A tweed hat or cap is a useful precaution against unpredictable Irish weather.

Aran sweaters have been worn by west coast fishermen for generations. The patterns are so varied and intricate that it is said a drowned man could be recognised by his pullover alone. The bainín or undyed wool came originally from the Aran Islands and makes the garment warm and rain resistant. You can buy sweaters, cardigans, dresses, caps and mitts in Aran patterns. Ask for a card explaining the meaning of the pattern. A hand-knitted Aran sweater (more expensive than hand-loomed) will last for more than 15 years if looked after.

The north-east has a long tradition of weaving linen for tablecloths, glasscloths, sheets, handkerchiefs and blouses. Irish poplin is now woven in Cork. Locally made pottery is on sale in most towns although Kilkenny is now the mecca for potters (and most other crafts). The tiny village of Belleek in Fermanagh is the home of delicate, almost transparent porcelain. Other well-known potteries are Noritake (Arklow), Stephen Pearce (Shanagarry, Co. Cork), Royal Tara and Wedgewood (Galway). In these you can buy anything from an egg cup to a full dinner service.

Claddagh rings, celtic design plaques and jewellery in gold and silver are popular souvenirs and you can have a pendant engraved with your name in ogham (ancient Irish lettering). Every record shop stocks a selection of traditional Irish music. Among the well-known performers are the Chieftains, Clannad, the Dubliners, Paddy Reilly, the Furey Brothers and the Clancy Brothers. Irish publishers produce an enormous range of books on every aspect of Irish life and there are bookshops in every large town. In Dublin the main ones are Hanna's, Eason's, Hodges Figgis, Waterstone's and Greene's.

Public Transport

All train services in the Republic are operated by Iarnrod Eireann-Irish Rail. Provincial bus services are run by Bus Eireann, while Bus Atha Cliath-Dublin Bus operates services in the greater Dublin area. Fast trains operate from Dublin to the main centres of population, namely Cork, Belfast, Sligo, Westport, Ballina, Galway, Limerick, Tralee, Waterford and Wexford. There are two main line stations in Dublin: Connolly Station (Amiens St) runs services to Belfast, Sligo and Wexford/Rosslare. All other long distance trains depart from Heuston (Kingsbridge). The number 24 bus runs at regular intervals between the two stations.

Train frequency varies according to the route and time of year but there are at least three or four trains in each direction daily, and double that number to Cork and Belfast. The service is sparse on Sundays and public holidays. Travel information is available at any station or bus office, at 59 Upr O'Connell St, 35 Lr Abbey St, and the Central Bus Station (Busaras), Store St – all in central Dublin – and at Dublin Airport. Dublin city bus enquiries, ☎ (01)734222. Provincial bus enquiries, ☎ (01)366111. Train enquiries, ☎ (01)366222. Also, travel centre, Lr Abbey Street, Dublin 1.

The suburban rail lines in Dublin stretch from Drogheda to Greystones and westwards to Maynooth. The three city centre stations are Connolly, Tara Street and Pearse. The DART (Dublin Area Rapid Transit) electric service is a marvellous way to get about on the 32 km (20 mile) coastal line. Trains run from early morning to late at night at 5 minute intervals during peak hours and every 15 minutes at other times.

There are many kinds of tickets available for use on Dublin public transport. Weekly and monthly commuter tickets are valid on suburban rail and all city bus services. Ten-journey tickets can be bought for a specific journey and used without a time limit. Dublin buses cover the entire city. If possible avoid buses at peak times, as they are very crowded. Reduced fares at off-peak periods apply for journeys within the city centre.

Northern Ireland Railways (NIR) operate trains north of the border and run the Belfast-Dublin service jointly with CIE. From Central Station, Belfast, trains run to Derry, Portrush, Bangor and Dublin. York Road (connecting bus from Central) is the station for the ferryport of Larne. Local trains to Bangor, Portadown, Ballymena and Larne are frequent, with fare reductions for travel at certain times. For full information contact Central Station, ☎ (0232)230310. Citybus services in Belfast are one-man operated. On boarding you pay the driver and when alighting, ring the bell to stop the bus. For enquiries ☎ (0232)246485/6. In Cork there is one suburban rail line to Cobh, once a stop for transatlantic liners when it was known as Queenstown. There are a number of city bus services to the suburbs, most of which pass through Patrick Street, the main thoroughfare. Further information from Cork Station, ☎ (021)504422.

When travelling by train at peak times it may be worthwhile reserving a seat for a small charge. In addition, restaurant and buffet cars are provided on the main services where you can enjoy a drink, a snack or a full meal (served at your seat in first class). The food is in the main excellent and the service courteous. It is a very pleasant way to travel. Check that the train that you are aiming for has a restaurant car.

The provincial bus network in Ireland is extensive; there is hardly a village in the country that does not have a bus passing through at some time or another. Some operate in conjunction with trains so that on arrival at the station you can continue your journey without delay. For example, buses to Dingle and Clifden connect with the Tralee and Galway trains respectively. Full details are available in the bus and train timetables. Expressway buses run between the major towns and cities on a number of routes not served by the railways. These include crossborder routes and services to Britain. Many buses start from Busaras, the Central (Provincial) Bus Station in Store Street, Dublin. This is also the starting point for the airport coach and Bus Eireann coach tours which can be booked for a half day or up to two weeks with accommodation and guides included. Further details from Bus Eireann, ☎ (01)366111 and Dublin Bus, ☎ (01)734222.

Ulsterbus has a similar itinerary of provincial routes and express buses. These normally depart from two points in Belfast, Great Victoria Street (near the Europa Hotel) and Oxford Street. For enquiries ☎ (0232)320011. Tourist excursions run during the summer to the main beauty spots of Ulster. If you plan to use public transport a lot enquire about Rambler and Overlander tickets. These are valid for 8 or 15 days and give unlimited travel by rail or rail and bus. For a supplement you can include both Northern Ireland and the Republic in your itinerary. They are very good value in deed and cost no more than the price of two or three ordinary return tickets. Further information from Bus Eireann, NIR and the tourist boards.

While timetables are issued for all services in every case it is worth enquiring locally before setting out, especially in rural areas. Expressway buses and mainline trains are usually reliable but in remoter areas the local bus may not adhere so painstakingly to the schedule. Nevertheless you will enjoy a spin on such a vehicle. Notice how the driver will usually know all his passengers and take a personal interest in delivering their post, luggage, groceries and children safely to their destination.

Where to Stay

Before departure contact Bord Failte or the NITB in your own country for full information on the range of accommodation available in Ireland. You can stay in anything from a hostel to a luxurious castle. In tourist board approved premises the rates are fixed and if you wish you can make your booking through the tourist office (see Useful Addresses). During the summer it is advisable to book well in advance and remember that some places close for part of the winter. Tourist staff will help you choose accommodation and give advice on eating out, excursions, sightseeing, shopping, public transport, etc.

Each year Bord Failte and the NITB assess and grade hotels and guesthouses listed in their brochures, based on the overall standard of accommodation and service. Grading also establishes the maximum price which may be charged. A new grading system is being introduced in the Republic.

Some community groups organise rural holidays. Details in the Bord Failte, *Irish Country Holidays* brochure. This brochure also contains details of working farms that are open to visitors.

Hotels
A* The top grade awarded to hotels with a particularly high standard of comfort and service with excellent cuisine; suites available and most rooms have a private bathroom.
A Hotels with a high standard of comfort and service; many bedrooms with private bath.
B* Well furnished hotels with very comfortable accommodation and good cuisine; private bathrooms available.
B Well kept hotels with good accommodation and bathroom facilities; limited but good cuisine.
C Clean and comfortable hotels with satisfactory service; hot and cold running water with heating in all bedrooms.

Guesthouses
A Those offering a very high standard of comfort and personal service; private bathrooms available.

Dromoland Castle, Shannonside, Co. Clare

B Well furnished premises with very comfortable accommodation; limited food and service.

C Clean and comfortable guesthouses with hot and cold water in all bedrooms. Adequate bathroom facilities.

Bord Failte approved guesthouses ensure consumer protection.

Town and Country Homes

A large number of houses in urban and rural areas ranging from period style houses to modern bungalows; evening meals by appointment.

Farmhouses

Many farming families offer accommodation in a unique rural setting where fresh farm produce and tranquillity are guaranteed. Ideal for children; evening meals by arrangement.

Self-Catering

Houses, cottages and apartments can be rented at numerous locations across the country with sleeping accommodation for up to 10 people. These are very popular and should be booked well in advance. Contact the Regional Tourism Organisation in the area of your choice for a list of such places (see Useful Addresses).

Camping and Caravanning

With quiet country roads and approved sites this can be a perfect holiday for those who don't want to rush. Many sites have shops, laundry, cafes and play areas for children.

Boating

Ireland's waterways are beautiful, uncrowded and clean and you can hire a fully equipped 2-8 berth cruiser. Cruisers are fitted with a fridge, cooker, central heating, hot water, shower, charts, dinghy, bed linen, crockery, etc. They are easy to handle and the inexperienced sailor can receive instruction before casting off. The River Shannon is the most popular cruising waterway but equally attractive are the Grand Canal, the River Barrow and the River Erne. Hire companies are located at Carrick-on-Shannon, Co. Leitrim; Whitegate, Co. Clare; Portumna, Co. Galway; Tullamore, Co. Offaly; Athlone, Co Westmeath; Belturbet, Co. Cavan; Kesh, Enniskillen, Killadeas, Lisbellaw, Bellanaleck, Co. Fermanagh.

Rates

The current brochures from Bord Failte and the NITB contain the rates for all approved accommodation in Ireland. Check that these apply when booking. Reductions are usually available for children under 12 and those under 4 are free if they share their parents' bedroom. Special rates apply for full board and a stay for a week or longer; ask for details. Generally you will pay less and have greater choice outside the high season (June to August).

Please contact the tourist boards if you are particularly pleased with your accommoda-

tion. Any complaints should be taken up with the manager in the first instance. Failing satisfaction, contact the Regional Tourism Organisation who will investigate the matter and if appropriate refer it to Bord Failte or the NITB. Every effort will be made to satisfy the complainant.

Ireland in Season

Bord Failte now have special offers for the spring and autumn periods (1 October – 31 May). If you would like to visit Ireland during this period and take advantage of the reduced rates (20☎-30☎ discounts), contact your local travel agent or nearest Bord Failte office. In addition the 'Springtime in Ireland' Consumer Bonus Offer brochure lists a whole range of suggestions and special offers for the independent visitor.

Useful Addresses and Information

Tourist Information Offices

Bord Failte – Irish Tourist Board, PO Box 273, Dublin 8 (postal enquiries). The following offices are open all year round or for most of the year. Approximately 50 others open for the summer period only (details from Bord Failte).

Athlone, 17 Church Street, ☎ (0902)94630.
Belfast, 53 Castle Street, Belfast BT1 1GH, ☎ (0232) 327888, fax (0232) 240201
Cashel, Town Hall, ☎ (062) 61333.
Cork, Tourist House, Grand Parade, ☎ (021) 273251, fax (021) 273504.
Derry, Foyle Street, ☎ (0504) 369501.
Dublin City, 14 Upper O'Connell Street, Dublin 1, ☎ (01) 747733, fax (01) 786275.
Dublin Airport, ☎ (01) 376387, fax (01) 425886.
Dundalk, Market Sq., ☎ (042) 35484, fax (042) 38070.
Dun Laoghaire, St Michael's Wharf, ☎ (01) 280 6984, fax (01) 280 6459.
Ennis, Bank Place, ☎ (065) 28366.
Galway City, Aras Failte, Eyre Square, ☎ (091) 63081, fax (091) 65201.
Kilkenny, Rose Inn Street, ☎ (056) 21755, fax (056) 63955.
Killarney, Town Hall, ☎ (064) 31633, fax (064) 34506.
Letterkenny, Derry Road, ☎ (074) 21160, fax (074) 25180.
Limerick City, Arthur's Quay, ☎ (061) 317522, fax (061) 315634.
Mullingar, Dublin Road, ☎ (044) 48650, fax (044) 40413.
Nenagh, Kickham Street, ☎ (067) 31610.
Rosslare Harbour, ☎ (053) 33232.
Shannon Airport, ☎ (061) 61664.
Skibbereen, Town Hall, ☎ (028) 21766.
Sligo, Temple Street, ☎ (071) 61201, fax (071) 60360.
Tralee, Godfrey Place, ☎ (066) 21288.
Waterford, 41 The Quay, ☎ (051) 75788, fax (051) 77388.
Westport, The Mall, ☎ (098) 25711.
Wexford, Crescent Quay, ☎ (053) 23111.

Regional Tourism Organisations

Cork/Kerry, Tourist House, Grand Parade, Cork, ☎ (021) 273251, fax (021) 273504.
Donegal/Leitrim/Sligo, Tourist Centre, Temple Street, Sligo, ☎ (071) 61201, fax (071) 60360.
Dublin, 1 Clarinda Park North, Dun Laoghaire, ☎ (01) 280 8571, fax (01) 280 2641
Midland-East Tourism (Kildare, Louth, Wicklow, Meath, Cavan, Laois, Longford, Monaghan, Offaly, Roscommon, Westmeath), Dublin Road , Mullingar, ☎ (044) 48650, fax (044) 40413.
Shannon Free Airport Development Company (Clare, Limerick, North Tipperary, South-East Offaly), Shannon Airport, Co. Clare, ☎ (061) 361555, fax (061) 361903.
South-Eastern (Carlow, Kilkenny, South Tipperary, Waterford, Wexford), 41 The Quay, Waterford, ☎ (051) 75823, fax (051) 77388.
Western (Galway, Mayo), Aras Failte (Ireland West House), Galway, ☎ (091) 63081, fax (091) 65201.

N.I. Tourist Offices *(open all year)*

Armagh, 40 English Street, ☎ (0861) 527808.
Ballycastle, 7 Mary Street, Co. Antrim, BT54 6QH, ☎ (026 57) 62024.
Ballymena, 80 Galgorm Road, Co. Antrim, BT42 1AB, ☎ (0266) 44111.
Banbridge, Downshire Road, Co. Down, BT32 8JY, ☎ (082 06) 62799.
Bangor, 34 Quay Street, Co. Down, BT20 5ED, ☎ (0247) 270069.
Belfast Information Office, 59 North Street, Belfast BT1 1NB ☎ (0232) 246609, fax (0232) 240960.
Carnlough, Post Office, Harbour Road, Co. Antrim, BT44 0EU, ☎ (0574) 885210.
Cookstown, 12 Burn Road, ☎ (064 87) 62205.
Derry, Foyle Street, ☎ (0504) 267284.
Enniskillen, Lakeland Visitor Centre, Shore Road, Co. Fermanagh, ☎ (0365) 323110/325050.
Killymaddy, Amenity Centre, Dungannon (M1 Extension), Co. Tyrone, ☎ (086 87) 67259.
Larne, Council Offices, Victoria Road, Co. Antrim, BT40 1RU, ☎ (0574) 72313.
Larne Harbour, Terminal Building, Larne, Co. Antrim, ☎ (0574) 70517.
Limavady, 7 Connell Street, Co. Londonderry, BT49 0HA, ☎ (050 47) 22226.
Magherafelt, Council Offices, 43 Queen's Avenue, Co. Londonderry, BT45 6BX, ☎ (0648) 32151.
Newry, Arts Centre, Bank Parade, Co. Down, BT35 6HP, ☎ (0693) 66232.
Omagh, 1 Market Street, Co. Tyrone, BT78 1EE, ☎ (0662) 247831/2
A number of other offices open for the summer only; information from NITB.

Travel

Air
Belfast City Airport, ☎ (0232) 457745.
Belfast International Airport, ☎ (084 94) 22888.
Cork Airport, ☎ (021) 965974.
Dublin Airport, ☎ (01) 379900.
Shannon Airport, ☎ (061) 61333.
Horan International Airport, ☎ (094) 67222.

Aer Lingus:
41 Upr O'Connell St, Dublin.
42 Grafton St, Dublin.
12 Upr George's St, Dun Laoghaire.
Terminal, Dublin Airport.
for bookings from Dublin area ☎
377777 *(Ireland & U.K.),* 377747
(Europe & U.S.A.).
46/48 Castle St, Belfast, ☎ (0232)
245151.
38 Patrick St, Cork, ☎ (021) 24331.
136 O'Connell St, Limerick, ☎ (061)
45556.
British Airways:
60 Dawson Street, Dublin 2, ☎ (01)
610666.
9 Fountain Centre, College St,
Belfast, ☎ (0232) 240522
For details of other airlines contact local travel agents.

Sea
B & I Line (Dublin-Liverpool, Dublin-Holyhead, Dublin-Douglas), 16 Westmoreland St, Dublin 1, ☎ (01) 724711.
Brittany Ferries (Cork-Roscoff), 42 Grand Parade, Cork, ☎ (021) 507666.
Irish Ferries (Rosslare-Cherbourg, Rosslare-Le Havre, Cork-Le Havre), 2-4 Merrion Row, Dublin 2, ☎ (01) 610533.
Sealink (Dun Laoghaire-Holyhead, Larne-Stranraer, Rosslare-Fishguard), 15 Westmoreland St, Dublin 1, ☎ (01) 714455. 33 Castle Lane, Belfast, ☎ (0232) 227525.
P&O European Ferries (Larne-Cairnryan), Larne Harbour, ☎ (0574) 74321.

Rail
Connolly Station, Amiens St, Dublin ☎ (01) 363333.
Heuston Station, Dublin, ☎ (01) 363333.
Passenger enquiries (Dublin), ☎ (01) 787777.
Belfast Central Station, ☎ (0232) 235282
York Road Station, Belfast, ☎ (0232) 235282,
Passenger enquiries (Belfast), ☎ (0232) 230310.

Bus
Busaras Central Bus Station, Store St, Dublin, ☎ (01) 366111.
Oxford Street Bus Station, Belfast ☎ (0232) 232356.
Gt Victoria Street Bus Station, Belfast, ☎ (0232) 320574.
CIE Tours International 35 Lower Abbey Street, Dublin 1, ☎ (01) 771871.

Embassies
Australia, 6th Floor, Fitzwilton House, Wilton Terrace, Dublin 2, ☎ (01) 761517.
Belgium, 2 Shrewsbury Road, Dublin 4, ☎ (01) 692082/691588.
Canada, 65-68 St Stephen's Green, Dublin 2, ☎ (01) 781988.
France, 36 Ailesbury Road, Dublin 4, ☎ (01) 694777.
German Federal Republic, 31 Trimleston Avenue, Booterstown, Co. Dublin, ☎ (01) 693011.
Italy, 63/65 Northumberland Road, Dublin 4, ☎ (01) 601744.
Netherlands, 160 Merrion Road, Dublin 4, ☎ (01) 693444/693532.
Spain, 17a Merlyn Park, Dublin 4, ☎ (01) 691640/692597.

FURTHER READING

A wide range of Appletree Press books are available on the following subjects:

History
Belfast: The Making of the City, J. C. Beckett et al.
Faces of Ireland, Brian Walker, Art O'Broin, Sean McMahon.
Ireland's Inland Waterways, Ruth Delany.
One Hundred and Fifty Years of Irish Railways, Fergus Mulligan.
Standing Stones and other monuments of early Ireland, Kenneth McNally.
The People of Ireland, ed. Patrick Loughrey.

Social Studies
Caught in Crossfire: Children and the Northern Ireland Conflict, Ed Cairns.
Dressed to Kill: Cartoonists and the Northern Ireland Conflict, John Darby.
Northern Ireland: The Background to the Conflict, ed. John Darby.
Religion, Education and Employment: Aspects of Equal Opportunity in Northern Ireland, ed. R. J. Cormack and R. D. Osborne.
Ulster's Uncertain Defenders, Sarah Nelson.
Worlds Apart: Segregated Schools in Northern Ireland, Dominic Murray.

Travel and Guidebooks
Irish Place Names, P. W. Joyce.
The Cliffs of Moher, Tony Whilde.
A Dictionary of Irish Place Names, Adrian Room.
Pocket Irish Atlas.
Dublin: The Complete Guide, Hugh Oram.

Food and Drink
A Little Irish Cookbook, John Murphy.
An Irish Farmhouse Cookbook, Mary Kinsella.
In Praise of Poteen, John McGuffin.
Traditional Irish Recipes, John Murphy.

Books of General Interest
Haunted Ireland, John Dunne.
Irish Country Cures, Patrick Logan.
Dictionary of Irish Myth and Legend, Ronan Coghlan.
The Animals of Ireland, Gordon D'Arcy.
The Birds of Ireland, Gordon D'Arcy.
Irish Family Names, Ida Grehan.
Irish First Names, Ronan Coghlan.
Irish Phrase Book, Paul Dorris.
Real Ireland, Liam Blake and Brendan Kennelly.

Switzerland, 6 Ailesbury Road, Dublin 4, ☎ (01) 692515.
United Kingdom, 33 Merrion Road, Dublin 4, ☎ (01) 695211.
United States of America, 42 Elgin Road, Dublin 4, ☎ (01) 688777.

Cultural Institutes
Goethe Institute, 37 Merrion Square, Dublin 2, ☎ (01) 766451.
Alliance Francaise, 1 Kildare St, Dublin 2, ☎ (01) 761732.
Instituto Italiano di Cultura, 11 Fitzwilliam Square, Dublin 2, ☎ (01) 766662.

Instituto Cultural Español, 58 Northumberland Road, Dublin 4, ☎ (01) 682024.

Government Offices
Department of Foreign Affairs, 80 St Stephen's Green, Dublin 2, ☎ (01) 780822.
Government Information Services, Upr Merrion St, Dublin 2, ☎ (01) 607555.
European Commission Press & Information Office, 39 Molesworth St, Dublin 2, ☎ (01) 712244.
National Library, Kildare St, Dublin 2, ☎ (01) 765521.
National Museum, Kildare St, Dublin 2, ☎ (01) 765521.
Northern Ireland Information Office, Stormont Castle, Belfast BT4 3ST, ☎ (0232) 763255.

Public Holidays
In the Republic the following are public holidays: 1 January, 17 March (St Patrick's Day), Easter Monday, first Monday in June, first Monday in August, last Monday in October, 25 and 26 December. Northern Ireland: 1 January, 17 March, Easter Monday, first and last Mondays in May, 12 July, last Monday in August, 25 and 26 December.

Currency
Northern Ireland uses the pound sterling (£) while the Republic uses the punt (IR£). Until 1979 the punt had parity with sterling, but the two currencies are no longer interchangeable.

Banking hours in the Republic are Mon-Fri, 10 a.m.-12.30 p.m.; 1.30 p.m.-3 p.m. In most towns there is opening until 5 p.m. one day a week (Thur in Dublin). In Northern Ireland banks are open Mon-Fri 9.30 a.m.-12.30 p.m.; 1.30 p.m.-3.30 p.m. Some central Belfast banks now remain open over the lunchtime period.

Measurements
The following is a basic guide to the most common sizes in men's and women's shoes and clothing. Shoppers should, however, bear in mind that items can vary considerably in size depending on the make, and it is always wise to try on a garment before buying.

Women's clothing

Ireland	32	34	36	38	40	42
Europe	38	40	42	44	46	48
USA	32	34	36	38	40	42

Women's shoes

Ireland	3½	4		4½	5		5½	6		6½
Europe	36	36½	37		37½	38		38½	39	
USA		4½	5		5½	6		6½	7	7½

Men's Clothing

Ireland	36	38	40	42	44
Europe	38	42	44	46	48
USA	36	38	40	42	44

Men's Shoes

Ireland	8	8½	9	9½	10
Europe	42	43	44	45	46
USA	26	26½	27	27½	28

Electric Current
In Ireland the usual voltage is 220v, AC current. Visitors should note that 13 amp, square-pin plugs are commonly in use – adapters are readily available from shops if required.

Motoring in
IRELAND

If you plan a motoring holiday it is worth contacting your local automobile association and the tourist board beforehand. They will supply you with full details of the rules of the road, insurance, breakdown services, petrol, road signs, etc. Most of this information can be had in Ireland but it is better to find out before you arrive. Bring your driving licence and insurance certificate, and display a nationality plate if bringing your car into Ireland.

There are lots of sea routes to choose from. B&I Line operate car ferries from Holyhead-Dublin, Liverpool-Dublin, Pembroke-Rosslare; Sealink: Holyhead-Dun Laoghaire, Fishguard-Rosslare; Stranraer-Larne; Belfast Car Ferries: Liverpool-Belfast; Townsend Thoresen: Cairnryan-Larne; Irish Continental Line: Le Havre-Rosslare, Le Havre-Cork; Brittany Ferries: Roscoff-Cork; Swansea-Cork ferry. There are also regular summer sailings from the Isle of Man to Belfast and Dublin.

Cars can be hired from a number of companies in Ireland. Bord Failte and the NITB will supply you with a list of authorised car hire firms and you can pick up your chauffeured or self-drive car at the port or airport. If you plan to cross the border check with the hire company that your insurance is valid north and south. Rates vary according to the model, time of year and hire period. Weekend rates are good value especially in the off-season. Make sure you know whether the rate is for limited or unlimited mileage. You can also save money by transferring you own insurance to the hire car. In Ireland, petrol is bought in imperial gallons: one imperial gallon is approximately 4½ litres, while one U.S. gallon is about 3¾ litres.

Distances and Average Driving Times				
From	To	Km	Miles	Hours
Belfast	Derry	117	73	2¼
Belfast	Dublin	167	104	3
Cork	Dublin	257	160	4½
Cork	Limerick	105	65	2
Derry	Belfast	117	73	2¼
Dublin	Athlone	126	78	2¼
Dublin	Belfast	167	104	3
Dublin	Cork	257	160	4½
Dublin	Donegal	222	138	4
Dublin	Galway	219	136	4
Dublin	Killarney	309	192	5½
Dublin	Limerick	198	123	3½
Dublin	Rosslare H.	163	101	3
Dublin	Shannon	222	138	4¾
Dublin	Sligo	217	135	4
Dublin	Waterford	158	98	3
Dublin	Westport	261	162	4¾
Larne	Donegal	214	133	4¼
Rosslare H.	Dublin	163	101	3
Rosslare H.	Killarney	275	171	5¼
Shannon	Dublin	222	138	4¾

You can avail of numerous packages involving travel by sea or air and a self-drive car for the duration of your holiday. Hotel or farmhouse accommodation can be included. If you choose to stay in one area you can arrange your holiday through CIE, travelling by train to Galway or Killarney, for example, and picking up a car at the station. For full details of all these combinations and special offers contact your local tourist board, Aer Lingus, B&I or CIE (see Useful Addresses).

Ireland has the lowest population density in Europe so there is lots of room on the roads, which makes driving a pleasure. The speed limit is 96 kmph (60 mph) and 48 kmph (30 mph) in towns. On motorways and dual car-

Moll's Gap, Co. Kerry

riage-ways in Northern Ireland the speed limit is 112 kmph (70 mph); otherwise limits are as in the Republic. In the Republic roads are classed as motorway (M7), national primary (N5), secondary (N71) and regional (R691). In the north you will find motorways, class A and class B roads numbered M1, A5 and B52 respectively. However, when seeking directions it is more common to refer to 'the Longford road' than 'the N4'. The road network is very extensive and while the principal highways are good those in more remote areas will vary. In the country watch out for cows, sheep and other animals being herded along the road.

You will find most routes well signposted although there may not be much advance warning. It's hard to get really lost and in any case it is a pleasure to wander along a country road admiring the countryside. Ask someone along the road or stop at a country pub or shop and you'll get all the directions you need and a great deal more besides. Placenames are written in Irish and English in the Republic and many signposts have been converted to kilometres. Look for 'km' after the figures. (To convert kilometres to miles divide by 5 and multiply by 3 as a rough guide.) Motorists should take care when reading roadsigns since at present some distances are given in miles and some in kilometres.

In Ireland drive on the left and yield to traffic from the right. All drivers and front-seat passengers must wear a seat belt at all times; the gardaí (police) are likely to stop you for not wearing one. Children under twelve are not

SOME COMMON TRAFFIC SIGNS

Direction Sign
indicating distance
in kilometres

Direction Sign
indicating distance
in miles and route
number

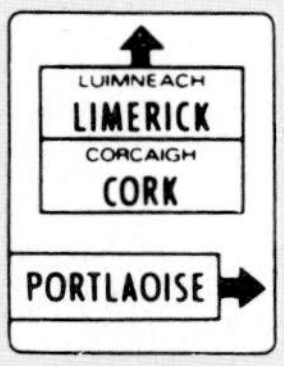

▲ Direction Sign ▼

Left junction

Dangerous bend

Slippery surface

Children crossing

Parking prohibited

No entry

Speed limit of
48 k.p.h. (30 m.p.h.)

Priority road ahead,
give way to traffic

Follow direction of arrow

Stop

allowed on front seats. While in Dublin you would be advised to park your car in an attended car park, place all valuables in the boot and lock the car securely. Parking is unrestricted in country towns and there are many lay-bys, picnic sites and beauty spots where you can pull in to take a break from driving. You must not park in town centres in Northern Ireland. For security reasons these are classed as control zones and unattended cars will be removed. Watch out also for ramps and be prepared to stop for security checks.

Roadsigns of various kinds are in operation. Hazards are indicated by black and yellow symbols on a diamond shaped board. Speed limits and parking restrictions are shown by black spots which are clearly marked. These often indicate dangerous junctions or very sharp bends and can be deceptive, especially at night. An unbroken white line in the centre of the road indicates that overtaking is forbidden.

Parking meters are common in cities although you can park at one after 6 p.m. without charge. The meter works by clocking up one or two hours according to the number of coins inserted. A single yellow line next to the kerb allows parking for a short period only. A double yellow line forbids par king at any time. In Cork you must display a parking disc inside the car indicating the time of day. These may be bought from newsagents and tobacconists. Bus lanes operate in cities and are reserved for buses and cyclists at certain times of the day. Watch out for the signs. Although some leniency is extended to visitors it is worthwhile observing the traffic regulations otherwise you may be fined or have your car towed away!

Ten Touring Ideas

These ten scenic tours are designed to help you get the most from your motoring holiday in Ireland – to show you the most beautiful scenery, and to introduce you to Ireland's many interesting cities and towns. As all ten tours are circular you can commence at any point of the given routes. The daily distance covered is shown with each tour, in miles and kilometres. Included are maps of the ten tours, with alternative routes indicated by broken lines.

TOUR OF IRELAND

A ten-day tour over 1,600 kilometres (1,000 miles), suggested starting point – Dublin.

Day 1: Dublin-Tramore 190 km (118 miles)

Having seen Dublin's historic buildings and Georgian squares and having sampled its lively cosmopolitan atmosphere, you're on your way to Enniskerry, a pretty hillside village just twelve miles south of the city. Nearby you can visit the splendid Powerscourt Estate, with its gardens, deer herd and waterfall. Continue on through Roundwood to Glendalough and see the ruins of an early-Christian settlement in a beautiful wild setting of mountains and lakes. Your next stop, via Rathdrum, is Avoca, made famous by Thomas Moore's song 'The Meeting of the Waters'. Southwards is the prominent holi-

day resort of Arklow, overlooking the sea. Onwards to Enniscorthy, with its old-world charm – just 53 km (33 miles) from the car ferry port of Rosslare Harbour – and then by New Ross, with its twisting lanes and Dutch-type houses, to Waterford. Or visit Wexford and on to Waterford by the Ballyhack/Passage East car ferry. Spend your first night at Tramore, a family resort with 4 km (3 miles) of sandy beaches.

Day 2: Tramore-Cork. 117 km (73 miles)

After lunch leave for Cork, via Dungarvan and Youghal, a popular holiday resort. Continue through the market town of Midleton to Cork. Enjoy the friendly atmosphere of Cork, built on the banks of the River Lee. Visit St Mary's Shandon, where the famous Shandon Bells are played on request, and admire the many fine public buildings.

Day 3: Cork-Killarney. 151 km (94 miles)

Leaving Cork on the third day your first stop is Blarney Castle with its famous stone, said to impart the gift of eloquence to all who kiss it! Continue through Macroom, Ballingeary, Pass of Keimaneigh - 3 km (2 miles) from Gougane Barra Forest Park - Ballylickey, and into the beautiful holiday resort of Glengarriff. Then in a northerly direction you drive through Kenmare into Killarney, enjoying one of the finest scenic drives on the way. You'll find plenty to do in Killarney – pony riding, boating and visiting islands and ancient abbeys. Drive around the 'Ring of Kerry', a brilliant 174 km (109 mile) scenic drive bringing you to Killorglin, Cahirciveen, Waterville, Sneem, Parknasilla, Kenmare and back to Killarney.

Day 4: Killarney

It's worth spending a day in Killarney, setting out the next day for Galway.

Day 5: Killarney-Galway. 251 km (156 miles)

On the fifth day your drive takes you through Abbeyfeale, Newcastle West, the lovely village of Adare, and into Limerick, 25 km (16 miles) from Shannon Airport on the River Shannon, a graceful and historic city, featuring King John's Castle, the Treaty Stone and St Mary's Cathedral. Traditional mediaeval banquets can be enjoyed at Bunratty Castle (13 km (8 miles) from Limerick) and Knappogue Castle (13 km (8 miles) from Ennis). Continuing on you reach Ennis with its old abbey and the seaside resort of Lahinch, featuring excellent golf courses. You should make your next stop by the breathtaking Cliffs of Moher, before driving to Lisdoonvarna, Ireland's premier spa. Drive through the bare limestone hills of the Burren to Ballyvaughan, to Kinvara (mediaeval banquets at Dunguaire Castle), Clarinbridge and into Galway. Galway is the capital of the 'Western World' with its famous Spanish Arch and Church of St Nicholas, where, tradition holds, Columbus prayed before sailing to America.

Day 6: Galway-Westport. 138 km (86 miles)

The next day your route through Connemara takes you to Moycullen, Oughterard, Recess, Clifden (capital of Connemara), Leenane and Westport – on Clew Bay, with over 100 islands.

Tour of Ireland

Kilometres

Miles

Bloody Foreland, Co. Donegal

Day 7: Westport-Bundoran. 154 km (96 miles)

Head north next day to Castlebar, Pontoon, Ballina and the family resort of Inniscrone. Enjoy a swim before driving on to Sligo, where you can look around the thirteenth-century Franciscan Friary and the museum, situated in the county library. Head on to Drumcliff (burial place of W.B. Yeats) to complete your day's driving at Bundoran.

Day 8: Bundoran-Dunfanaghy. 193 km (120 miles)

On the following day head further up the Atlantic Coast through Ballyshannon to Donegal town, visiting the Franciscan Friary and castle. Drive through Dunkineely, Ardara, Glenties, Maas and Kinscasslagh – noted for their cottage industries and Donegal tweed. Then by Annagry, Crolly, Bunbeg, Bloody Foreland, Gortahork into Dunfanaghy, nestling in the cosy inlet of Sheephaven Bay.

Day 9: Dunfanaghy-Carrick-On-Shannon. 177 km (110 miles)

Next day your tour takes you south via Portnablagh to Letterkenny-Donegal's chief town. This is an excellent point from which to extend your drive, by taking the 'Inishowen 100' – an extremely scenic trip around the Inishowen Peninsula, to Buncrana, Malin Head and Moville. Return to Letterkenny by

Manorcunningham. Total mileage for the trip is 193 km (120 miles). Continue south through the picturesque Finn Valley to the twin towns of Stranorlar and Ballybofey, completing your round trip of County Donegal in Donegal town. The next stage takes you to Ballyshannon and Bundoran in a southerly direction to Manorhamilton. Overlooking the town you'll see the picturesque ruin of Sir Frederick Hamilton's castle – built in 1638. Continue south through Drumkeeran along the beautiful shores of Lough Allen into Drumshanbo. Drive on through Leitrim into Carrick-on-Shannon, an important cruising and angling centre.

Day 10: Carrick-on-Shannon-Dublin. 240 km (150 miles)

On the final day head for Cavan, travelling by Mohill, Carrigallen, Killeshandra and Crossdoney, enjoying the lake scenery on the way. Continue to Bailieborough - 14 km (9 miles) - from the important angling centre of Virginia) and into the attractive town of Carrickmacross. The last stage of your trip takes you to Drogheda – a historic town in County Louth. From Drogheda visit the prehistoric tombs at Newgrange, Knowth and Dowth. Drive on by Slane into Navan. Ten km (6 miles) from here see the Hill of Tara, a former residence of Irish High Kings. Complete your tour of the Boyne Valley in Trim, rich in historical associations

and ancient monuments, before returning to Dublin, via Black Bull, Clonlee, Blanchardstown and the Phoenix Park.

The following alternative two-day route from Dunfanaghy to Dublin takes in the Antrim Coast and the Mourne Mountains.

Day 9: Dunfanaghy-Belfast. 240 km (150 miles)

Take the road from Dunfanaghy to Letterkenny, travelling north-east from here to Londonderry (you will cross the border into Northern Ireland at Bridgend). Stop to explore this historic city on the banks of the River Foyle, whose walls (the only remaining unbroken fortifications in either Britain or Ireland) afford superb views of the surrounding countryside and of the city itself. Continue north-east to Limavady, Downhill, Castlerock and Coleraine and on to the bracing seaside resort of Portrush. Then follow the coastal road eastwards to see the famous Giant's Causeway, the beautiful beaches at White Park Bay and the Carrick-a-Rede Rope Bridge (not for the faint-hearted!). The steep, winding road around Torr Head and down to picturesque Cushendun is worth the slight detour – views are breathtaking. From Cushendun head for Larne, departure point for ferries to Scotland. The final stage of your journey takes you to Belfast via Carrickfergus, where you can visit the country's best-preserved Norman castle.

Day 10: Belfast-Dublin. 192 km (120 miles)

The last day of your tour takes you south out of Belfast through the heart of County Down towards the spectacular Mourne Mountains. Stop at Downpatrick en route to see Down Cathedral, in whose churchyard you will find St Patrick's grave marked by a crude slab.

Giant's Causeway, Co. Antrim

Continue towards Newcastle, County Down's most popular holiday resort, where, in the words of the song, 'The Mountains of Mourne

Carrick-a-Rede, Co. Antrim

sweep down to the sea'. Stroll along the beach at Dundrum or, if you're feeling energetic, make an assault on Slieve Donard (the Mournes' highest peak), which can be reached either through Donard Park or from Bloody Bridge (just outside Newcastle). Follow the road from Newcastle via Kilkeel and Warrenpoint to Newry, cross the border into the Republic, then continue to Dundalk (Cuchulainn's country), whose surrounding hills and forests are full of history and charm. Then make your way south to Drogheda (stop-

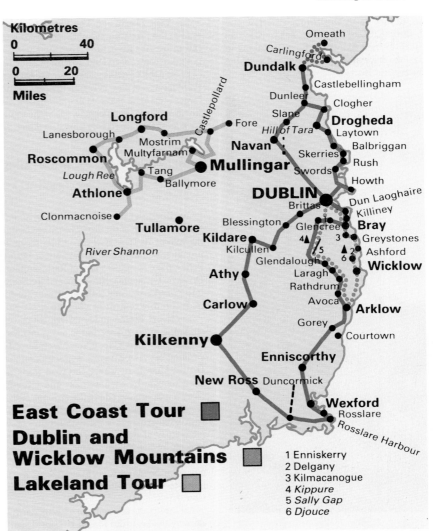

East Coast Tour ■
Dublin and Wicklow Mountains ■
Lakeland Tour ■

1 Enniskerry
2 Delgany
3 Kilmacanogue
4 *Kippure*
5 *Sally Gap*
6 *Djouce*

ping at Monasterboice on the way to admire one of the most magnificent High Crosses in the country). From Drogheda, the mysterious passage tomb of Newgrange is easily accessible and well worth a visit. The last stretch of road takes you south into Dublin city.

EAST COAST TOUR

Two circular tours – one north, the other south of Dublin.

Day 1: Northern tour. 306 km (190 miles)
Take the Navan road out of Dublin for Tara – site of a former royal acropolis, situated in an area rich in ancient monuments and historical associations. Continue north to Navan, Donaghmore and Slane. Visit the Bronze Age cemeteries at Brugh na Boinne, King William's Glen, Mellifont Abbey and Monasterboice, before heading for Dunleer, Castlebellingham and Dundalk – an ideal base for exploring the surrounding countryside. If you wish you can travel further north to see the delightfully rugged little Carlingford Peninsula, taking you through Ballymascanlon, Carlingford, Omeath and back into Dundalk.

Heading south you reach Castlebellingham, Clogher, Termonfeckin, Baltray, with its fine beach and golf course and on into Drogheda, on the River Boyne. In Bettystown, further south, there's a long sandy beach linking up with Laytown, while further on is Julians-

town. Following the coast enjoy a pleasant drive through Balbriggan, Skerries, Rush, Lusk, Swords and Howth, stopping to admire the magnificent views from the rocky Hill of Howth. Return to Dublin via Sutton.

Day 2: Southern Tour. 467 km (290 miles)
Next day the southern tour takes you through Dun Laoghaire, Dalkey and Killiney – with its magnificent view over the bay from the Vico Road – into Bray, one of Ireland's premier seaside resorts. Continuing you reach Enniskerry, a pretty village beneath the Sugarloaf Mountain and near the beautiful Powerscourt Estate. The scenic mountain drive takes you to Glendalough, with its ancient ruins and picturesque lakes, passing through Glencree, Glenmacnass and Laragh. If you wish you can return to Dublin by Blessington, making a short but enjoyable trip – or keep south to Rathdrum, Avoca and Woodenbridge into Arklow, where you can enjoy a swim or go sea fishing. Driving on through County Wexford takes you to Gorey, Courtown Harbour (seaside resort), Ferns, Enniscorthy and Wexford, which is within easy reach of Rosslare Harbour. These charming old towns are well worth a visit. Follow the coast through Rosslare, Duncormick, Arthurstown and into New Ross. From here take the road to Kilkenny, a cheerful city steeped in history. Visit the Kilkenny Design Workshops, Rothe House and Kilkenny Cas-

tle. Return to Dublin through Carlow and County Kildare towns of Athy, Kildare, Kilcullen, and Ballymore Eustace, taking in the lake drive near Blessington and reaching the city via Brittas.

Glendalough, Co. Wicklow

LAKELAND TOUR

This is a two-day circular drive of about 240 km (150 miles). This tour of Ireland's quiet heart offers a charm of a different kind from the coastal tours.

Day 1: Athlone-Mullingar. 135 km (84 miles)

The starting point is Athlone – 'Capital' of the midlands. From here drive to Roscommon visiting Hodson Bay and Rinndown Castle en route. Have a look around Roscommon Abbey. North-east of Roscommon is Lanesborough, a popular angling centre at the head of Lough Ree. Then visit the busy market town of Longford with its nineteenth-century cathedral. Move on to Edgeworthstown, which gets its name from the remarkable literary family. Continue to Castlepollard, a good angling centre near Lough Derravaragh - featured in a tragic legendary romance – 'Children of Lir'. See nearby Tullynally Castle. Drive to Fore, with its ancient crosses and Benedictine Abbey, returning to Castlepollard and south via Multyfarnham to Mullingar – an important town and noted angling centre. Spend the night there.

Day 2: Mullingar-Athlone. 105 km (65 miles)

Next day a westward drive takes you to Ballymore and to the Goldsmith country via Tang. Visit Lissoy and The Pigeons on the road to the pretty village of Glasson, passing the tower-like structure marking the geographical centre of Ireland. Return to Athlone.

From Athlone make an excursion to Coosan Point for a good view of Lough Ree, one of the largest Shannon lakes. Going downriver it's worth a visit to Clonmacnois, one of the country's most celebrated holy places, completing your tour in Athlone.

DUBLIN AND WICKLOW MOUNTAINS

This is a one-day scenic tour of about 177 km (110 miles).

Leave Dublin by the suburb of Rathfarnham, four miles south of the city. The ruined building known as 'The Hell Fire Club' forms a prominent landmark to the summit of Mount Pelier, 6 km (4 miles) south of Rathfarnham. Drive via Glencullen, Kilternan and the Scalp into Enniskerry – one of the prettiest villages in Ireland. From here you can visit the Powerscourt Estate and Gardens, which include the highest waterfall in these islands. Continue to Sally Gap, a notable crossroads situated between Kippure Mountain and the Djouce Mountain, where the road leads to Glendalough, by Glenmacnass and Laragh. Have a look around Glendalough – one of the most picturesque glens of County Wicklow with extensive ruins of the sixth-century Irish monastery of St. Kevin. Drive on through Laragh by the Military Road to Rathdrum. Head south by the Vale of Avoca into Arklow, a popular holiday centre. From Arklow drive north to Wicklow where you can admire the view over the bay.

Ashford is the next village on your route – close by the beautiful Mount Usher Gardens with countless varieties of trees, plants and shrubs. These gardens are open from March to September. Move on through the rugged Devil's Glen to Newtownmountkennedy, Delgany and into the attractive resort of Greystones, which retains the atmosphere of the former quiet fishing village. Head back through Delgany to the Glen of the Downs, Kilmacanogue (from where you can climb the great Sugar Loaf) into Bray. From this fine resort at the base of Bray Head take the route to Killiney and the Vico Road to Dalkey, enjoying the superb views of Killiney Bay. Follow the coast road to Dun Laoghaire into Dublin.

SOUTH-WEST TOUR

This is a two-day circular tour of about 700 km (440 miles) on main route.

Day 1: Cork-Killarney. 359 km (223 miles)

The suggested starting point is Cork – a charming city on the River Lee, excellent for shopping and offering first-class pubs and restaurants with entertainment for every member of the family. Blarney Castle, with its famous Stone of Eloquence is 8 km (5 miles) away. Visit there to kiss the stone, before continuing to the old-world town of Kinsale. Drive on to Timoleague – where you'll see the remains of the once largest friary in Ireland – to Clonakilty, Rosscarbery, Glandore, Union Hall and Skibbereen. Continue this exceptionally beautiful drive through Ballydehob, Schull,

Toormore, Durrus and Bantry into Glengarriff – visiting the Forest Park and Garinish Island, with its ornate gardens. Afterwards take the 'Tunnel Road' to Kenmare or head west over the Healy Pass.

Some of the finest sea and mountain scenery in Ireland can be enjoyed on the next stage of the tour, around the 'Ring of Kerry' – through Sneem, Castlegrove, Derrynane, Waterville, Cahirciveen, Glenbeigh and Killorglin into Killarney. There are some lovely quiet beaches in this region – for example Rossbeigh near Glenbeigh. Spend the night in Killarney.

Day 2: Killarney-Cork. 352 km (220 miles)

From Killarney drive direct to Tralee or alternatively explore the Dingle Peninsula, the heart of *Ryan's Daughter* country. Places along the route are: Inch, Annascaul, Dingle, Ventry, Slea Head, Dunquin, Ballyferriter, Murreagh, back to Dingle and on through Stradbally and Camp to Tralee. An unforgettable drive of breathtaking beauty. Follow the coast from Tralee to Ardfert, Ballyheigue, Causeway, Ballyduff, Lisselton Cross Roads, Ballylongford, and Tarbert, where a car ferry operates to Killimer, County Clare. Drive through Foynes along the Shannon Estuary via Askeaton to Limerick – an old and historic city, not far from Bunratty Castle, with its mediaeval-style banquets.

Having spent some time looking around Limerick head back to Cork through Tipperary and Cashel, visiting the magnificent ruins of the Rock of Cashel – including a cathedral, castle, chapel and round tower. Enjoy the mountain views on the way to historic Cahir town and into Cork by Clogheen, Lismore and Fermoy, providing a splendid trip through the Knockmealdown Mountains.

CORK AND 'RING OF KERRY'

A one-day tour about 354 km (220 miles) Travel west from Cork via Ovens to Macroom. Turn off for Toon Bridge and Inchigeelagh through the wild mountain scenery of the Pass of Keimaneigh into Ballylickey. Along the way you could visit Gougane Barra Forest Park which is just north of your route.

From Ballylickey enjoy the superb views of Bantry Bay en route to Glengarriff, from where you can visit the beautiful Italian gardens of Garinish Island. Head north to Kenmare through rugged mountains. Here your trip around the 'Ring of Kerry' begins – encircling the Iveragh Peninsula, which features Ireland's highest mountains, the Macgillycuddy's Reeks. Excellent views are provided over Dingle Bay to the north and the estuary of the Kenmare River to the south. Travel south-west through Parknasilla and Sneem, into Caherdaniel, where you'll find excellent swimming and diving along the fine beach. Go north to the well-known resort of Waterville, continuing your tour by Cahirciveen, Glenbeigh and Killorglin, completing this exceptionally scenic trip to Killarney.

Your route back to Cork takes your through the Derrynasaggart Mountains to Macroom, turning off the main road for Dripsey and Blarney Castle, where you can stop to kiss the famous Blarney Stone.

Blarney Castle, Co. Cork

WEST COAST TOUR

This is a four-day circular tour of about 842 km (523 miles)

Day 1: Athlone-Limerick. 151 km (94 miles)

Atholone is the suggested starting point for a tour of this richly varied region. From this impressive town south of Lough Ree you pass the early-Christian site of Clonmacnois to the south and on to Birr, where the gardens of Birr Castle are open to visitors. Driving in a southerly direction you come to Nenagh with its fine castle, built about 1200. Continue via Portroe with fine views over Lough Derg into Killaloe, a popular water-skiing centre. From here drive to O'Brien's Bridge, Ardnacrusha and on to Limerick for the night.

Day 2: Limerick-Galway. 232 km (144 miles)

Having seen the sights of Limerick head for Bunratty Castle where mediaeval banquets are held, and visit the Bunratty Folk Park. Drive south-west from Ennis to the resorts of Kilrush and Kilkee, going north to Lahinch and around Liscannor Bay to the magnificent ruggedness of the Cliffs of Moher, reaching up to 213 m (700 ft). Move on to Ireland's premier spa, Lisdoonvarna, enjoying the remarkable 'Burren Country', consisting of a desert of bare limestone hills which are a botanist's paradise in the spring. Take the road from Lisdoonvarna through Black Head, Ballyvaughan, Kinvara and Clarinbridge into Galway. Discover Galway for yourself – its Church of St Nicholas, the Spanish Arch and the gathering of salmon (in season) under the Salmon Weir Bridge. Salthill, Galway's fashionable seaside suburb offers you top-class restaurants and hotels, pubs, discos and many other forms of entertainment, including the amenities of the Leisureland complex.

Day 3: Galway-Westport. 196 km (122 miles)

Next day start your tour of Connemara by Spiddal, Costelloe, Screeb, Gortmore, Carna, Toombeola, Ballynahinch and Glendalough.

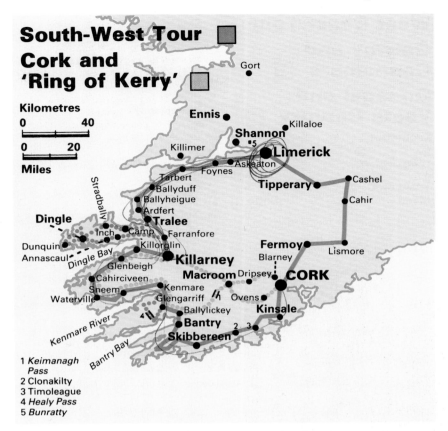

From Clifden you head northwards to Tullycross and on to Leenane, on the corner of picturesque Killary Harbour. Drive northwards through the mountains to Louisburgh, in the shadow of Croagh Patrick. Stop in Westport, an important sea angling centre. Alternatively you can get from Leenane to Westport through Joyce Country, talking you to Maam, Cong, Ballinrobe, Partry Mountains, Ballintubber with its famous abbey and into Westport.

Day 4: Westport-Athlone. 262 km (163 miles)

The following day explore the beauties of Achill Island, taking the road to Newport, Mulrany, through Curraun Peninsula, Achill Sound and on to Keel and Dooagh. Return via Newport to Castlebar, visiting Clonalis House. Then on to Claremorris, Ballyhaunis, Castlerea, Roscommon and back to Athlone.

GALWAY AND CONNEMARA

This is a one-day tour of about 257 km (160 miles)

Travel north-west of Galway to the pretty village of Oughterard, with views of Lough Corrib along the way. Continue through the rugged countryside of Connemara, dominated by the craggy peaks of the Twelve Bens, via Maam Cross and Recess into Clifden – the capital of Connemara.

From Clifden drive to Letterfrack and on to Leenane, at the head of picturesque Killary Harbour. Along the way you'll see the magnificent Kylemore Abbey. Having left Leenane turn off the main road for Louisburgh and Westport, passing Doo Lough and the lofty Croagh Patrick. The town of Westport was designed by James Wyatt – an architect of the Georgian period. Castlebar, principal

Macgillicuddy's Reeks, near Killarney, Co. Kerry

town of County Mayo, is the next on your route – offering you a charming old-world atmosphere. Of particular note is the pleasant tree-lined Mall. Return to Galway by Ballintubber, with its impressive abbey, Ballinrobe and Headford.

West Coast Tour ■

Galway and Connemara ■

Donegal and Yeats Country ■

Kilometres

0   40

0   20

Miles

1 Letterfrack
2 Recess
3 Oughterard
4 Kilrush
5 Killimer
6 *Rosguill Peninsula*
7 *L. Glencar*
8 *L. Mask*
9 *Croagh Patrick*
10 *Bunratty*

[Map showing West Coast Tour route through counties including Donegal, Sligo, Galway and Limerick, with towns such as Carndonagh, Buncrana, Moville, Letterkenny, Ballybofey, Donegal, Ballyshannon, Sligo, Ballina, Boyle, Carrick-on-Shannon, Westport, Roscommon, Athlone, GALWAY, Ennis, Nenagh, Limerick marked.]

Kylemore Lough, Co. Galway

Horn Head Peninsula, Co. Donegal

DONEGAL AND YEATS COUNTRY

This is a two-day circular tour over 515 km (320 miles) on main route.

Day 1: Carrick-on-Shannon-Carrigart. 322 km (200 miles)

The popular centre of Carrick-on-Shannon – well known for cruising and coarse fishing – is the starting point for this tour. The first town on this route is Boyle – 3 km (2 miles) from Lough Key Forest Park, with its numerous facilities, from boating to nature trails. Your drive will continue to Collooney, entering the magical country of Yeats. Share his experiences as you drive through Ballisodare, Kilmacowen and Strandhill on your way to Sligo, a beautifully situated town, surrounded by mountains. Pay a visit to Sligo Abbey and the museum, situated in the county library. Follow the road through Drumcliff (Yeats' burial place) to Grange and Cliffoney into Bundoran – a re-

sort where you'll find enjoyment for all the family.

Begin your tour of Donegal from Ballyshannon, heading north to Donegal town and on to Killybegs by way of Mountcharles, Inver and Dunkineely. Following the coast to Glencolumbkille, a popular holiday centre, you are now in a part of Ireland's 'Gaeltacht' or Irish speaking region. This area of Donegal is noted for its excellent crafts and the production of handmade Donegal tweed. From Glencolumbkille head east to Ardara, Maas and Dungloe – a remarkable tract of rocky lakeland. Drive north from Crolly to the lovely fishing village of Bunbeg, along the coast to Gortahork and Dunfanaghy , with its lovely beaches and superb cliff scenery. Turn off at Creeslough for Carrigart – beautifully situated on Mulroy Bay. Spend the night here.

Day 2: Carrigart-Carrick-on-Shannon. 193 km (120 miles)

From Carrigart there is a charming twelve-mile trip around the little Rosguill Peninsula, taking in Tranarossan Bay and Rosapenna. Continue south to Letterkenny via Milford. Before driving south for Donegal town again you could take a trip around the Inishowen Peninsula, an extra 192 km (129 miles) in all, giving unrivalled views, a top class resort at Buncrana and some very interesting antiquities, such as the cross of Carndonagh. Complete your tour from Donegal by Ballyshannon, Bundoran, Kinlough, Manorhamilton, Killarga, Drumkeeran and along the shores of Lough Allen by Drumshanbo into Carrick-on-Shannon.

NORTH-EAST TOUR

Two circular tours – one north, the other south of Belfast.

Day 1: North Coast Tour. 288 km (180 miles)

Travel north out of Belfast through Carrickfergus to the car ferry port of Larne. Continue along the scenic route to Cushendall and Ballycastle, enjoying the gently scooped-out contours of the Antrim Glens to your left. (You can turn inland to visit Glenariff Forest Park, where wooded paths lead to superb viewpoints.) Continue to the popular town of Ballycastle – famous for its Ould Lammas Fair – before following the road to Portrush via the Giant's Causeway. (Bushmills, home of the world's oldest distillery, is only 5 km (3 miles) away, and can be visited.) Pass through Portrush and Coleraine towards Downhill and Limavady, taking in the view from the Binevenagh plateau on the way. Then head for Derry, whose historic features deserve to be explored. When you are ready to leave, turn south-east towards Dungiven and cross the Glenshane Pass into Castledawson. From here you can go on to Antrim town and back to Belfast.

Day 2: Mourne Country 166 km (104 miles)

Leave Belfast on the south side and drive via Lisburn to Hillsborough, a remarkably pretty small town with adjacent fort, park and lake – ideal for a quiet stroll. Continue through Dromore and Banbridge to Newry, where you can turn eastwards along the shores of Carlingford Lough to the picturesque fishing port of Kilkeel. Take a walk down by the har-

Glenariff Glen, Co. Antrim

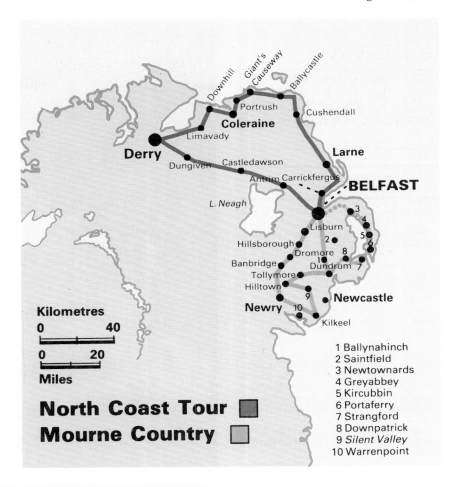

Kilometres
0   40

0   20
Miles

North Coast Tour ▪

Mourne Country ▫

1 Ballynahinch
2 Saintfield
3 Newtownards
4 Greyabbey
5 Kircubbin
6 Portaferry
7 Strangford
8 Downpatrick
9 *Silent Valley*
10 Warrenpoint

bour to admire the fleet – and perhaps buy some freshly-landed fish – before heading north and inland towards the Silent Valley, in the heart of the beautiful Mourne Mountains (follow Hilltown directions). It is worth stopping the car for a breath of the clear mountain air and the chance to enjoy the wonderful views. Then proceed via Tollymore (with its forest park) to Dundrum, whose long, unspoilt beach is always inviting. From here you can head straight back to Belfast through Ballynahinch, or travel to Downpatrick and Strangford, visiting Castleward before taking the ferry across

Greyabbey, Co. Down

Strangford Lough to Portaferry. Drive up the Ards Peninsula via Kircubbin and Greyabbey (interesting ruins) to Newtownards, overlooked by Scrabo Tower. From here it's only a short drive back to your Belfast base.

The EAST

Dublin

Pop. 1 million,166 km (103 miles) S of Belfast, 262 km (160 miles) NE of Cork and 198 km (122 miles) NNE of Limerick. Train enquiries: Iarnrod Eireann ☎ *(01)366222, Mon- Sat, 9 a.m.- 9 p.m. Sun: 10 a.m.-6 p.m. Dublin City bus enquiries:* ☎*(01)734222, Mon-Sat, 9 a.m.-7 p.m. Coach tours and rail breaks,* ☎*(01)731100. Enquiries Mon-Fri, 9 a.m.-5.15 p.m. Sat, 9 a.m.- 1.15 p.m.*

Taxis: Aston Quay ☎ *(01)778053; Angle Rane-lagh* ☎ *(01)972735; Crescent, Malahide Road* ☎ *(01)336507; Eden Quay* ☎ *(01)777054: Lansdowne Road, by Jurys hotel* ☎ *(01)617222; Upper O'Connell Street, opposite Gresham hotel* ☎ *(01)744599; Lower O'Connell Street, opposite Easons* ☎ *(01)786 150; Upper Rathmines Road* ☎ *(01)973276. Taxis may be hired fairly easily at most times of day. Youth Hostel: 61 Mountjoy Street,* ☎ *(01)301766 open 24 hours. TIO: Upper O'Connell Street,* ☎ *(01)747733.*

Nearly 2,000 years old, in turn, a Viking, a Norman and an English city, and since 1922 the capital of an independent state.

During the early 1900's, the city enjoyed a revival of Irish culture, including literature. Today, however, it is falling to a new 'invader'—a brash Anglo-American 'pop' culture. Some parts of the city are being devastated by developers, but despite the ravages of the last 20 years, many areas of Dublin such as the Liberties, retain much of their individual character. Not far S of the traffic-clogged central streets, the mountains form a breath-taking backdrop, and a reminder that rural Ireland is not far away.

Major festivals: St Patrick's Week festivities *(Mar)*; Feis Ceoil-Irish Music Festival *(Mar)*; Dublin Grand Opera Society spring season *(Apr)*, RDS Festival *(May)*, Dublin Liberties' Festival *(May)*; Dublin Horse Show *(Aug)*; Irish Antique Dealers' Fair *(Aug)* ; Dublin Grand Opera Society winter season *(Dec)*; Festival of Music in Great Irish Houses: feast of classical music in Dublin area Georgian mansions *(June)*. ☎ *TIO (01)747733.*

CATHEDRALS & CHURCHES

Christ Church Cathedral (CI), *Christchurch Place.* Founded 1038, rebuilt by the Normans following their invasion in 1169. Magnificent stonework on nave and aisles. Have a look at alleged tomb of Strongbow. Crypt dates from Norman times.⅋ *St Patrick's Cathedral* (CI) *Patrick's Close.* Founded 1190, restored about 1860. Jonathan Swift was Dean from 1713 to 1745, tomb in South aisle, 'where savage indignation can no longer rend his heart'. Also see monument to Turlough O'Carolan, last of the Irish bards. ⅋ *St Mary's Pro Cathedral* (C), *Marlboro Street, behind O'Connell Street, Dublin 1:* built in early 19th c. Its famous Palestrina choir sings Mass in Latin on Sun. *St Michan's Church* (CI), *Church Street, near Four Courts.* 17th c church famous for the bodies in its vaults, where the dry atmosphere has prevented decomposition. Handel is said to have played the organ. *Tours of church and vaults Mon-Fri. St Audoen's Church* (C), *High Street.* Oldest parish church in the city, dating from late 12th c. Although partially ruined, a portion is still used.

O'Connell Street, Dublin, at night

NOTABLE BUILDINGS

Custom House, Custom House Quay: not open to visitors, but the fine façade may be admired while strolling along by the river. *Dublin Castle, Dame Street:* once seat of British administration in Ireland. See State Apartments, including vast St. Patrick's Hall with lofty panel led ceiling; once residence of English Viceroys, today, used for

St Patrick's Cathedral, Dublin

State occasions. Church of the Most Holy Trinity: formerly Chapel Royal. Magnificent interior decorations. Exchange Court: where three men were put to death in 1920, during War of Independence. Medieval undercroft has heritage centre, shop and coffee shop. *Mon-Fri, 10 a.m.-12.15 p.m.; 2 p.m.-5 p.m. Sat, Sun, BH, 2 p.m.-5 p.m.* ☎*(01)777129. Trinity College, College Green:* Ireland's oldest university. Behind the magnificent 18th c façade is Library Square and the extraordinary library, which has over a million volumes. Its most distinguished possession, the Book of Kells, is on display with other early Christian masterpieces, in the new Colonnades gallery. *Mon-Sat, 9.30 a.m.-5 p.m.; Sun, noon-5 p.m. The Dublin Experience* is a multi-media presentation on Dublin and guide to main events of Irish history. *May-Oct, daily, 10 a.m.-5 p.m. Bank of Ireland, College Green:* conducted tours of 18th c Parliament House during banking hours. *The Bank of Ireland Arts Centre, Foster Place,* is a new exhibition venue. ☎ *(01)711671. Leinster House, Kildare Street:* seat of Dáil (Chamber of Deputies) and Seanad. Members of public only admitted to Dáil visitors' gallery with introduction from a T.D.* ☎ *(01)789911. City Hall, Dame Street:* see Dublin Copporation Assembly Rolls, mace and sword of City of Dublin and 102 royal charters. ☎ *(01)679 6111.* **General Post Office**, *O'Connell Street:* The 1916 Easter Rising started here. The present building is a reconstruction. See statue of the Dying Cuchulainn, a figure from Celtic mythology. *Mon-Sat, 8 a.m.- 8p.m.; Sun, BH, 10 a.m.-6.30 p.m.* ⅋

MUSEUMS

National Museum. Many fascinating exhibits dating from prehistoric times. Kildare Street: vast and diverse collection of antiquities including Bronze Age gold ornaments, Tara Brooch, Ardagh Chalice, Cross of Cong, 6th c ecclesiastical bells and

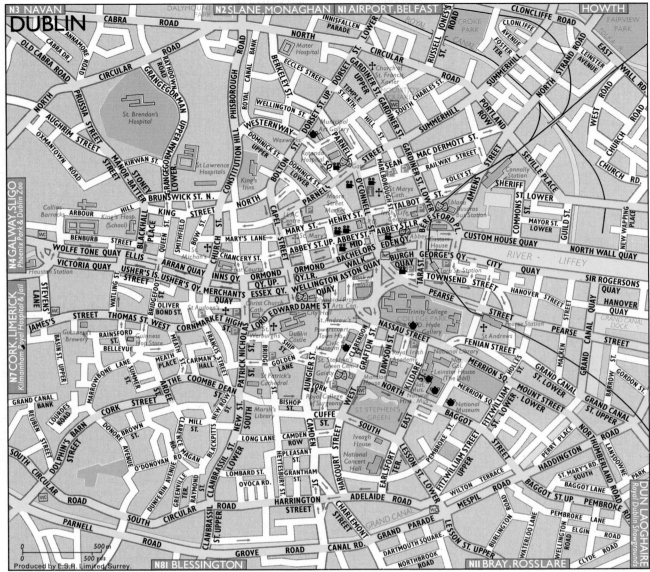

12th c church door, a good overview of prehistoric, early-Christian and medieval Ireland, plus range of 18th and 19th c dress, silverware, coins and porcelain. Another room is devoted to the 1916 Easter Rising and the War of Independence, while there is an interesting new music section. Many of the rooms are closed intermittently, due to staff shortages, but the Treasury Collection, with many of the museum's finest pieces is open permanently. The modern annexe in Merrion Row is used for exhibitions, while the natural history section, near the National Gallery, has been refurbished and contains many examples of Irish and worldwide mammals and birds. Some extinct species can be seen, like deer that roamed prehistoric Ireland. *Tues-Sat, 10 a.m.-5 p.m. Sun, 2 p.m.-5 p.m. Closed Mon.* ☎ *(01)618811.* **Irish Whiskey Museum,** *Bow Street, daily tours, Mon-Fri, 3.30 p.m.,* ☎ *(01)725566.* **St Patrick's Hospital,** *off James's Street, near the Guinness brewery.* Built with a legacy from Dean Swift in the 18th c. The boardroom is veritable treasure trove of Swiftiana, including the desk at which he is reputed to have written *Gulliver's Travels. To view,* ☎ *(01)775423.* **Pearse Museum,** *St Enda's Park, Rathfarnham.* Patrick Pearse, leader of the Easter Rising was headmaster at St Enda's school in this 18th c house. Audio visual show, exhibitions, tea room. Extensive park includes beautifully situated lake and nature trail. *Nov-Jan, daily, 10 a.m.-1 p.m.; 2 p.m.-4 p.m. Feb-Apr, Sept, Oct, daily, 10 a.m.-1 p.m.; 2 p.m.-5 p.m. May-Aug, 10 a.m.-1 p.m.; 2 p.m.-5.30 p.m.* ☎*(01)934208.*

Museum of Childhood, *20 Palmerston Park.* Wonderful collection of dolls dating from early 18th c. Also toys, prams, rocking horses and miniature furniture, *July-Aug, Wed, Sun 2 p.m.-5.30 p.m., Sept-June, Sun 2 p.m.-5.30 p.m.,* ☎ *(01)973223.* **Irish Railway Records Society,** *Heuston Station.* Relive bygone days of the Irish railways. *Tues, 8 p.m.-10 p.m.* **Irish Jewish Museum,** *3 and 4 Walworth Road, Portobello, Dublin 8.* Memorabilia of Ireland's Jewish community; restored synagogue. *May-Sept, Tues, Thurs, Sun, 11 a.m.-3 p.m.; Oct-Apr, Sun, 10.30 a.m.-2.30 p.m.* ☎*(01)974252.* **Garda Síochána Museum,** *Garda depot, Phoenix Park.* Fine collection of material: uniforms, photographs and medals depicting Irish police history. *By app.* ☎ *(01)771156.* **Dublin Civic Museum,** *South William Street (behind Grafton Street):* fascinating collection of items relating to social history of the city. Stone Age flint axes, coins from Dublin's Viking mint, old maps and prints, and Nelson's head, from the pillar blown up in 1966. Regular exhibitions on particular themes. *Tues-Sat, 10 a.m.-6 p.m., Sun, 11 a.m.-2 p.m.,* ☎ *(01)679 4260* **Classical Museum,** *University College, Belfield.* Archaeological items from ancient Greece and Rome. *By app.,* ☎ *(01)693244.* **Bewley's Museum,** *on the first floor of the Grafton Street cafe:* an absorbing collection of material related to the firm, which was founded by the Quaker Bewley family in 1840. *Daily, 10 a.m.-6 p.m.,* ☎ *(01)776761.* **Freemason's Hall,** *Molesworth Street.* This large 18th c building with fine portico is headquarters of the Masonic Order in Ireland; the building

and historical contents may be seen by app., ☎ *(01)679799/6795465.* **Heraldic Museum,** *2 Kildare Street.* Founded in 1911, it has an impressive collection of family coats of arms, essential fodder for genealogists. *Mon-Fri, 10 a.m.-4.30 p.m.* ☎ *(01)614877.* **National Wax Museum,** *Granby Row (off Parnell Square):* features many Irish and international personalities modelled in wax, from the Pope to Paisley. It has some spooky side-shows for children. *Mon-Sat, 10 a.m.-5.30 p.m., Sun, 1 p.m.-5.30 p.m.* ☎ *(01)726340.* **Guinness Museum,** *Crane Street (off Thomas Street).* A 19th c hop store has been converted very skilfully into a museum and exhibition centre. The audio-visual presentation details the brewery's history since it was set up in 1759, much early machinery is preserved. In the ground floor bar, visitors can sample the product free of charge. *Mon-Fri, 10 a.m.-3.30 p.m.* ☎ *(01)536700.* **Dublin Writers' Museum.** Dublin has innumerable literary connections; Beckett and Joyce were natives of the city. This new museum has many permanent displays and temporary exhibitions on Dublin's noted writers. Gallery of Writers, with busts and portraits, in the salon. Bookshop, restaurant. *Oct-Apr, Fri, Sat, 10 a.m.-5 p.m., Apr-Oct, Mon-Sat, 10 a.m.-5 p.m; Sun, BH, 2 p.m.-6 p.m. 18/19 Parnell Square North, Dublin 1.* ☎*(01)722077.* **Irish Museum of Modern Art** is an imaginative new extension to the Royal Hospital, Kilmainham, and features Irish and international 20th c art. *Tues-Sat, 10 a.m.-5.30 p.m.; Sun, 12 noon-5.30 p.m.* ☎*(01)718666.* **Newman House,** *85-86 St Stephen's*

AROUND DUBLIN

Green, Dublin 2. Splendid restoration of two 18th c Georgian houses, where University College, Dublin began in 19th c, is almost complete. Video details history. Range of interiors includes the Bishops' Room. June-Sept, Tues-Fri, 10 a.m.-4 p.m.; Sat, 2 p.m.-4.30 p.m.; Sun, 11 a.m.-2 p.m. ☎(01)757255/751752. **Iveagh Gardens**, to rear, delightful city centre park, with fountains, water cascades and statue-lined walks. **Number 29 Lower Fitzwilliam Street**, Dublin 2. The Electricity Supply Board has done a thorough restoration of this 18th c Georgian house, complete with period furniture, artefacts and works of art. Tues-Sat, 10 a.m.-5 p.m.; Sun, 2 p.m.-5 p.m. ☎(01)765831. **Dublinia**: Synod Hall, Christchurch, Dublin 8: high tech portrayal of medieval Dublin life, due to open 1993. ☎ (01)758137. **Shaw House**, 33 Synge Street, Dublin 8. House being restored to 19th c condition, with artefacts and Shaw memorabilia. ☎ (01)280 8571. **Ashton Castle**, Phoenix Park: interpretative centre now open, including audio-visual presentation on history of the park. Tearoom. Wed-Fri, 10 a.m.-5 p.m.; Thurs, 10 a.m.-4 p.m. (last admission 45 mins before closing). Details: OPW, ☎ (01) 613111. **Rathfarnham Castle**: medieval castle with fine plasterwork and other decorative features, in course of restoration. Details: OPW, ☎ (01) 613111.

LIBRARIES

National Library, Kildare Street. Repository of information about Ireland, very useful if you're ancestor tracing. Vast collection of Irish newspapers and magazines — virtually every issue of every title ever published. More recent newspapers are on microfilm, not the easiest to read . Mon, 10 a.m.-9 p.m., Tues, Wed, 2 p.m.-9 p.m., Thurs, Fri, 10 a.m.-5 p.m., Sat, 10 a.m.-1 p.m. Closed Sun and Bank Holidays, ☎ (01)618811. **Marsh's Library**, St Patrick's Close (behind St Patrick's Cathedral). 1701 library with some 25,000 volumes. Interior, where readers are locked into wired alcoves with rare books, has great atmosphere. Librarian Mrs Muriel McCarthy is mine of information. Extensively but tastefully renovated. Mon, Wed, Thurs,

Fri, 10 a.m.-12.45 p.m.; 2 p.m.-5 p.m. Sat, 10.30 a.m.-12.45 p.m. Closed Tues. ☎ (01)534511. **Royal Irish Academy**, Dawson Street: one of the largest collections of ancient Irish manuscripts in the country. Mon-Fri, 9.30 a.m.-5.30 p.m. Closed most of August, ☎ (01)764222. **Chester Beatty Library and Gallery of Oriental Art**, 20 Shrewsbury Road. Outstanding collection of books, paintings, papyri, clay tablets, bindings, wall hangings, costumes, carvings and drawings illustrate the history of mankind from 2700 BC (Babylonian clay tablets) to present day. Vast array of Japanese prints, outstanding collection of Islamic material. Tues-Fri, 10 a.m.-5 p.m. Sat, 2 p.m.-5 p.m. Closed BH. Conducted tours Sat, Wed, 2.30 p.m., ☎ (01)692386. **Central Catholic Library**, 74 Merrion Square: 80,000 volumes of religious and general interest. Large Irish section. Lending, reference department open to non-members on payment of small fee. Reading Room, Mon, 12 noon-7 p.m., Sat, 12 noon-6 p.m. **Pearse Street Library**. Impressive collection of Irish interest material including items to do with local printing and book binding, ☎ (01)777662. **Goethe-Institute Library**, 37 Merrion Square: Mon-Tues and Thurs, 4 p.m.-8 p.m., Wed and Fri. 10 a.m.-6 p.m., Sat, 10 a.m.-1 p.m., ☎(01) 611155. **ILAC Centre Library**, off Henry Street. Impressive high tech commercial reference library and music library; many audio visual facilities, Mon, Tues, Wed, Thurs, 10 a.m.-8 p.m., Fri, Sat, 10 a.m.-5 p.m. ☎(01)734333. **Dublin Diocesan Library**, Clonliffe Road: extensive reference facilities. Details, ☎ (01)741680. Mon-Fri, 10.30 a.m.-9.30 p.m., Sat, 10.30 a.m.-1 p.m. ☎ Trace your ancestors at **Genealogical Office**, Kildare Street, ☎ (01)618811.

GALLERIES

National Gallery, Merrion Square West: some 2,000 paintings from all major European schools, exhibits include world-famous Poussins, Goyas and Gainsboroughs. In Irish rooms, outstanding works by Jack and John B. Yeats, Hone, Osborne, Lavery and Orpen. Bar and restaurant. The building has been extensively renovated since 1990. Frequent visiting exhibitions. Mon-Sat, 10 a.m.-6 p.m. Sun,

2 p.m.-5 p.m. Late opening, Thurs, 9 p.m. Art reference library, by app. ☎ (01)615133. ☎ **Municipal Gallery**, Parnell Square: Impressive collection of works by 19th and 20th c Irish and European artists. Also Lane collection of paintings, stained glass by Harry Clarke and Evie Hone and sculptures. Restaurant. Tues-Fri, 9.30 a.m.-6 p.m.; Sat, 9.30 a.m.-5 p.m. ☎ (01)741903. **Solomon Gallery**, Powerscourt Centre; impressive array of contemporary art in equally impressive surroundings, Mon-Sat, 10 a.m.-5.30 p.m. ☎ (01)679 42. ☎ **Douglas Hyde Gallery**, Trinity College: about 12 exhibitions a year of Irish and international fine and applied art. Mon-Sat, 11 a.m.-6 p.m., ☎ (01)772941, ext 1116. ☎ **Wellesley Ashe Gallery**, 25 South Frederick Street: Irish paintings, including watercolours, from 18th to 20th c, also bronzes. Mon-Fri, 10 a.m.-6 p.m., ☎ (01)6796439. **European Fine Arts Gallery**, 5 Clare Street: Dutch and Flemish old masters, also Irish and English paintings and prints from 18th and 19th c. Mon, Wed, Fri, 10.30 a.m.-12.30. ☎ (01)765371. **Davis Gallery**, 11 Capel Street, Dublin 1, ☎(01)726969. **Oriel Gallery**, 17 Clare Street: regular exhibitions of mainly 20th c Irish paintings in attractive two level gallery, Mon-Fri 10 a.m.-5.30 p.m., Sat, 10 a.m.-1 p.m., ☎ (01)763410. **Óisín Arts Gallery**, 10 Marino Mart, Dublin 3. Oils, prints and watercolours by Irish and European artists. Mon-Fri, 9 a.m.-6 p.m.; Sat, 10 a.m.-6 p.m. ☎ (01)333456. **Taylor Galleries**, 35 Kildare Street: mainly contemporary works, including paintings, lithographs. Mon-Fri, 10.30 a.m.-5.30 p.m. Sat, 2 p.m.-1 p.m., ☎ (01)766055. **Temple Bar Gallery**, Temple Bar Studios, 4-8 Temple Bar, Dublin 2. Contemporary painting exhibitions. Mon-Fri, 11 a.m.-5.30 p.m., Sat, 12 noon-4 p.m. ☎ (01)710073. **Oliver Dowling Gallery**. 19 Kildare Street: mainly paintings by contemporary Irish artists. Mon-Fri, 10 a.m.-5.30 p.m., Sat, a.m., ☎ (01)766573. **Tom Caldwell Gallery**, 31 Upper Fitzwilliam Street. Figurative and abstract works by contemporary artists, mostly Irish. Tues-Fri, 11 a.m.-5 p.m., Sat, 11 a.m.-1 p.m., ☎ (01)688 629. ☎ **Alliance Française**, 1 Kildare Street: regular exhibitions on French themes, ☎ (01)761732. **Gallery of Photography**, 37/39 Wellington Quay: exhibitions of photographic prints, Mon- Sat, 11 a.m.-6 p.m. Sun, 12 noon-6 p.m., ☎ (01)714654. ☎ **Guinness Hop Store** , Crane Street, off Thomas Street. Frequent exhibitions in finely restored building. Also Guinness museum, shop. Bar has best draught Guinness in Dublin— free. Mon-Fri, 10 a.m.-3 p.m., ☎ (01)536700. **United Arts Club**, 3 Upper Fitzwilliam Street. Regular exhibitions of members' work, Mon-Sat, 12.30 p.m.-11 p.m., Sun, 8 p.m.-11 p.m. ☎ (01)611411. **Kerlin Gallery**, 38 Dawson Street. Contemporary paintings displayed in stylish modern gallery. Mon-Fri, 10 a.m.-6 p.m., Sat, 11 a.m.-5.30 p.m., Sun, 2.30 p.m.-5 p.m. ☎ (01)779179. **Malton Gallery**, 23 St Stephen's Green. Dublin drawings and paintings. Mon-Sat, 9.30 a.m.-5.30 p.m., ☎ (01)766333. **Project Arts Centre**, East Essex Street, Avant garde, contemporary work. Mon-Sat, 12 noon-6.30 p.m., ☎ (01)712321. **Riverrun Gallery**, Dame Street (corner of Parliament Street). Contemporary work. Restaurant. Mon-Sat, 10 a.m.-5.30 p.m., ☎ (01)679 8606. **RHA Gallery**, Ely Place. Large scale modern venue for exhibitions. Mon-Sat, 10 a.m.-5 p.m., Thurs until 9 p.m., Sun, 2 p.m.-5 p.m., ☎ (01)610762.

THEATRES

Abbey and Peacock theatres, Lower Abbey Street: regular performances of Irish and international plays at Abbey; Peacock stages Irish language and experimental work. Occ. art exhibitions in Abbey foyer, which has been extended and refurbished. Bookings Mon-Sat 1-.30 a.m.-7 p.m. ☎ (01)787222. ☎ **Focus Theatre**, Pembroke Place, Pembroke Street. Irish and international drama, ☎ (01)763071. **Gate Theatre**, Cavendish Row, Parnell Square: Irish and international plays by its own and visiting companies, ☎ (01)744045.

Powerscourt Town House, Dublin

Olympia Theatre, *Dame Street:* drama, pantomime, revue and variety, also worth seeing for ornate 19th c interior. ☎ *(01)778962.* **Gaiety Theatre,** *South King Street:* 19th c theatre with fabulous plush interior. ☎ *(01)771717.* **Projects Arts Centre,** *39 East Essex Street;* Avant garde drama. ☎ *(01)712321.* **Players' Theatre,** *No.3 Trinity College: excellent performances of student drama.* ☎ *(01)774673.* **Andrew's Lane Theatre,** *Andrew's Lane.* Contemporary sometimes experimental work in intimate modern theatre. ☎ *(01) 679 5720.* **Tivoli Theatre,** *Francis Street, Dublin 8.* Contemporary productions, including good comedies. ☎ *(01) 535998, 54472.* **Point Theatre,** ☎ *(01) 363633.*

ROUND & ABOUT

Royal Dublin Society, *Ballsbridge.* Regular trade and art exhibitions, concerts and lectures, ☎ *(01)680645.* **National Concert Hall,** *Earlsfort Terrace:* stimulating variety of musical events. Lunch, pre-show suppers. *Bookings: Mon-Sat, 11 a.m.-7 p.m. Credit card bookings,* ☎ *(01)711533,* ☎ *(01)711888.* ♿ **Powerscourt House,** *South William Street (off Grafton Street):* 1774 Georgian town house with outstanding plasterwork and wood carvings, meticulously restored. Covered market in courtyard, restaurants. *Mon-Sun, 9.30 a.m.-5.30 p.m.* **Casino,** *Malahide Road. Dublin 3* One of Ireland's finest 18th c classical buildings. *Guided tours, June-Sept, daily, 9.30 a.m.-6.30 p.m.* ☎ *(01)331618.*

Wood Quay, *by Christ Church Cathedral:* most of this Viking site has been covered by two enormous tower blocks housing Dublin Corporation offices. On opp. side of river, see impressive façade of **Four Courts. Clondalkin Round Tower** (NM). Only remaining relic of a 7th c monastery. **Kilmainham Jail,** *Inchicore.* Received its first political prisoners in 1796. The last was Éamon de Valera in 1924. 1916 Rising leaders executed here. Fascinating museum, recently extended with absorbing audio-visual show. *June -Sept, daily, 11 a.m.-6 p.m.; Oct-May, Wed, Sun, 2 p.m.-6 p.m.*

☎ *(01)535984.* **Royal Hospital,** Kilmainham. Restored 17th c French Chateau-style building. Frequent exhibitions, café. *Daily,* ☎ *(01)718666.* **Pleasure flights:** Iona National Airways, *Dublin Airport,* ☎ *(01)8424400.* Horse drawn cabs: touristy perhaps, but an ideal way to tour city. **Bewley's** Dublin city centre restaurants: the city's most famous eating places, where you can see and be seen. Frequented by most Dublin celebrities. *South Great George's Street* cafés worth seeing for genuine late Victorian/Edwardian decor. *Grafton Street* for Harry Clarke stained glass windows. This branch also has a small but fascinating museum about the company and its founding Quaker family, the Bewley's. *Open daily.* ♿ **Stock Exchange,** *28 Anglesea Street:* small public gallery, open for 45 mins at 9.30 a.m. and 2.15 p.m., *Mon-Fri , by arr.* ☎ *(01)778808.* **Antiquarian Bookcrafts,** *Marlay Park Craft Centre, Dublin 16.* Leather bookbinding. *Mon-Fri, by arr.* ☎ *(01)942834.* **Drimnagh Castle,** *Long Mile Road, Dublin 12.* Medieval castle, an incongruity in an industrialised area, has been well restored, including Great Hall, undercroft, gardens and yard. *Apr-Oct, Wed, 10 a.m.-4 p.m.; Sun, 2 p.m.-5 p.m. Nov-April, Sun, BH only, 2 p.m.-5 p.m.* ☎ *(01)502530.* **St Mary's Abbey,** *Meetinghouse Lane, off Capel Street, Dublin 1:* medieval monastery, founded 1139. *June-Sept, Weds, 10 a.m.-5 p.m., Nov-Apr, Sun, BH, 2 p.m.-5 p.m.,* ☎ *(01)721490.* **Number 12 Merrion Square,** *Dublin 2:* built 1764, once home of Sir John Arnott, one-time owner of The Irish Times. *May-Sept, Sat, Sun, 12 noon-4 p.m.* **James Joyce Cultural Centre,** *35 North Great Georges Street, Dublin 2:* due to be completed 1993. Lectures, exhibitions. **Grand Canal interpretative centre,** *Ringsend:* history of the canal, due to open 1993. *Details: OPW,* ☎ *(01)613111.* **Temple Bar district:** district being upgraded, with pubs, restaurants and many cultural projects, including the **Irish Film Centre,** which opened recently.
Walks: College Park: entrance at Lincoln Place, through Trinity College grounds to College Green. Dodder river bank: upstream from Clonskeagh bridge, taking in Rathfarnham linear park. Georgian area: Merrion Square, Upper Mount Street, Fitzwilliam Street and Fitzwilliam Square. Ideal time—Sun, no traffic. Grand Canal towpaths and

canalside footpaths: start at Lower Mount Street and go as far as Portobello. Best stretch from Baggot Street bridge to Leeson Street bridge. See seats by canalside, Baggot Street bridge, in memory of poet Patrick Kavanagh and artist/songwriter, Percy French. Ringsend: walk past ESB station along breakwater as far as Poolbeg lighthouse. Sandymount Strand: can be walked safely if tide out. However, it sweeps in again at great speed. North Bull Island. Fine outdoor recreational area connected to Clontarf Road by causeway. Interpretative Centre details birdlife, ☎ *(01)338341.* Guided tours daily. Good walk along adjacent Bull Wall. **Iveagh Market,** *Francis Street:* old clothes and furniture. *Tues-Fri a.m.-6 p.m., Sat, 9 a.m.-5.30 p.m.,* ☎ *(01)751343.* Daily market at back of *Mother Redcap's Tavern* has many interesting stalls. **Liberty Market,** *Meath Street:* clothes, drapery and household goods. *Fri and Sat, all day.* **Moore Street Market,** *off Henry Street:* fruit, vegetables and classic Dublin wit. *Mon-Sat, 9 a.m.-6 p.m.* **Vegetable Market,** *St Michan's Street:* fruit, vegetables, fish and flowers. *Mon-Thurs, 8 a.m.-5 p.m. Tues, Fri, closes at 4 p.m. Sat, 8 a.m.-11 a.m.,* ☎ *(01)730155.*
Ryans, *Parkgate Street (near Heuston railway station):* superb traditional bar, complete with snugs and old-fashioned lamps. Remodelled in 1896 and little changed since. **Brazen Head,** *Bridge Street:* dates from 1688. **Stag's Head,** *Dame Court, off Dame Street;* one of the city's oldest pubs, founded in 1770, largely remodelled in 1895. Plenty of atmosphere. **Palace Bar,** *Fleet Street:* genuine, old-time Dublin pub. Tiled floor, dark panelling, mirrors and leaded glass in entrance doors. Upstairs lounge has character. **Bowes Pub,** *Fleet Street:* favoured by Irish Times' journalists. **Mulligan's** dark, authentic pub, *Poolbeg Street,* is another favourite spot for writers and journalists. **Long Hall,** *51 South Great George's Street:* Dublin's most ornate traditional pub. Richly carved interior wood work, chandeliers and ceilinghigh mirrors date back to 19th c. The Grafton Street area has several well-known pubs. **McDaid's,** *Harry Street,* has noted literary connections. **The Bailey,** *Duke Street,* extensively renovated, has literary and political connections going back many years. Also door of No. 7

Eccles Street, immortalised by Joyce as home of Leopold Bloom. **Davy Byrne's,** *Creation Arcade;* famous meeting place. Merrion Row/ Lower Baggot Street area: **O'Donoghue's,** *Merrion Row,* **Toner's** *Lower Baggot Street,* both noted for folk music. Also see **Doheny and Nesbitt's,** *Lower Baggot Street:* dark wood and dark Guinness.

PARKS

Phoenix Park. Largest park in Europe, 709 ha (1752 acres). Numerous tree-lined roads, several lakes, herds of deer. Furry Glen nature trail in NW of park has many trees and plants. From the Fifteen Acres, you will see many of Dublin's landmarks. **Herbert Park,** Ballsbridge, oasis near city centre. **Dublin Zoo,** *Phoenix Park:* one of finest in Europe, with many species of animals and reptiles to be seen in modern houses and outdoor enclosures. Cafe and restaurant. *Mon-Sat, 9.30 a.m.-6 p.m., Sun, 10.30 a.m.-6 p.m.* ☎ *(01)771425.* ♿ **National Botanic Gardens,** *Botanic Road, Glasnevin.* Extensive selection of trees, flowering shrubs and tropical plants. In large

Grand Canal, Dublin

conservatories, often glorious displays of rare and exotic species. Fine walks in gardens and along adjacent bank of River Tolka. *Summer, Mon-Sat, 9 a.m.-6 p.m. Sun, 11 a.m.-6 p.m. Otherwise, Mon-Sat, 10 a.m.-4.30 p.m. Sun, 11 a.m.- 4.30 p.m. Suns: greenhouses open 2 p.m.,* ☎ *(01)374388.* **St Stephen's Green:** an oasis of lawns and lakes in heart of Dublin. Ideal for walking, relaxing or observing the antics of one's fellow creatures. Summer, concerts. *Mon-Sat, all year, from 8 a.m. to dusk. Sun from 10 a.m.,* ☎ *(01)747733.* ♿ **St Catherine's Park,** *off Thomas Street.* Fine new inner city oasis created from old graveyard. **St Anne's Park Rose Garden,** *Mount Prospect Avenue, Clontarf.* Magnificent collection of roses. *Daily, all year.* **Marley Park,** *Rathfarnham.* Extensive park with woodlands and large pond. Nature trail. Start of Wicklow Way walk. Model steam railway. Fine house, rebuilt in 19th c, restored. Stable courtyard has remarkable collection of craft workshops. *daily, 9 a.m.-5 p.m.,* ☎ *(01)942083.*

SPORT

Croke Park, main Dublin venue for Gaelic Athletic Association games, ☎ *(01)363222.* **Lansdowne Road:** international rugby stadium, ☎ *(01)684601.* **Dalymount Park:** the national football arena, ☎ *(01)300994.*
  Gala Leisure Centre, Ballyfermot (snooker), *daily,* ☎ *(01)264648.* Crumlin Super Bowl, ☎ (01)501438. Swimming pools: indoor, heated. Ballyfermot. *Le Fanu Park;* Ballymun, *Seven Towers Shopping Centre;* Coolock, *Northside Shopping Centre;* Crumlin, *Windmill Road;* Finglas, *Millowes Road;* Iveagh Baths, *Bride St;* Rathmines, *Williams Park;* Seán McDermott Street, *city centre.* Open air: Clontarf. *Details, all pools:* ☎ *(01)727666, extn. 283.* **Dundrum Bowl,** *Ballinteer Road, Dublin 14.* ☎ *(01)980209/980400/980532.*
  Riding: Ashtown Equestrian Centre, *Castleknock,* ☎ *(01)387611/384698;Callaighstown Riding Centre, Callaighstown, Rathcoole,* ☎ *(01)589236;* Riding Centre, *Castleknock,* ☎ *(01)201104.* Bicycles: Joe Daly, *Lower Main Street, Dundrum,* ☎ *(01)981485;* Ray's bike shop, *Milltown,* ☎ *(01)283 0355.*

  Golf Clubs: Royal Dublin, *Dollymount, 18 holes,* ☎ *(01)336346;* Newlands, *Clondalkin, 18 holes,* ☎ *(01)592903;* Grange, *Rathfarnham, 18 holes,* ☎ *(01)932832;* Edmondstown, *Rathfarnham, 18 holes,* ☎ *(01)904207;* Castle, *Rathfarnham, 18 holes,* ☎ *(01)904207;* Clontarf, *18 holes,* ☎ *(01)331877;* (Setting for Carrolls Irish Open Championship, Aug, ☎ *(01)956777).* Elm Park, *Donnybrook, 18 holes,* ☎ *(01)693438.*

North of Dublin

Balbriggan, *32 km (20 miles) N of Dublin on N1 Dublin-Belfast road.* Pleasant seaside town, with enjoyable walk from main street to beach and harbour. **Ardgillan castle and demesne,** *Tues-Sat, 2.30 p.m.-4.30 p.m.* Demesne *open daily, 10 a.m.- dusk,* ☎ *(01)849 2212.*

Baldongan Castle, *5 km (3 miles) S of Skerries:* 13th c fortress now in ruins, but fine views from top of tower.

Donabate, *between Dublin and Balbriggan,* small town with a profusion of golf clubs. Dublin and County Golf Club, *Corballis, 18 holes,* ☎ *(01)843 6228;* Donabate Golf Club, *18 holes,* ☎ *(01)843 6059;* Island Golf Club, *18 holes,* ☎ *(01)843 6104.*

Dunsink Observatory, *between Finglas and Blanchardstown.* Founded in 1783, one of oldest in world. *Occ. shows, telephone in advance for details.* ☎ *(01)387 9591.*

Dunsoghly Castle, *6 km (4 miles) NW of Finglas, E of N2 Dublin, Ashbourne road:* from parapets of 15th c castle, fine views of N Co. Dublin, including airport. *Key from nearby cottage. All reasonable times.*

Fairyhouse Races, *22 km (14 miles) NW of Dublin, E of N3 Dublin-Navan road:* main meeting: three day Easter event. ☎ *(01)256167.*

Howth: Pleasant residential district and popular summertime seaside resort. **Howth Castle,** rhododendron gardens. *Daily all year, 8 a.m.-sunset. Flowering season Apr. May. June. Castle closed,* ☎ *(01)322624.* **Irish Transport Museum,** *Castle grounds.* Many old commercial vehicles, including the No 9 Howth tram, fully restored. *All year, Sat, Sun, BH, 2 p.m.-5 p.m.* ☎ *(01) 847 5623.* **Abbey Tavern:** traditional music, ☎ *(01)322006.* Howth harbour's two piers provide good walks. Howth Head: take cliff walk from Howth village. Path dangerous in places, fine views. Howth Head to Sutton: in case of weariness, bus runs from Howth station, via the summit to Sutton Cross and the city centre. Boat trips from Howth pier to Ireland's Eye, *May-Sept, daily, departure as required.* ☎ *F. Doyle (01)314200.* Howth Golf Club, *18 holes,* ☎ *(01)323055.*

Kilsallaghan Church (C), *5 km (3 miles) NW of Finglas:* see 1917 Michael Healy window depicting Christ the King. ♿

Malahide, *14 km (9 miles) N of Dublin.* Small coastal town being turned into heritage town, complete with heritage centre. Big marina development under way. **Malahide Castle:** many features worth seeing, including Great Hall, Front Hall, Oak Room, Library and Drawing Room. Fine furniture, panelling and National Portrait Collection. Concerts; craft, antique shop; guided tours. Fry Railway Museum. Extensive parkland, with sporting facilities, picnic areas, nature trails, Botanic Gardens, Castle and restaurant, *Jan-Dec, Mon-Fri, 10 a.m.-5 p.m.; Nov-Mar, Sat, Sun, BH, 2 p.m.-5 p.m. Apr-Oct, Sat, 11 a.m.-6 p.m.; Sun, BH, 2 p.m.-6 p.m.* ☎ *(01) 845 2528.*

Newbridge House, *Portrane Road, off main Dublin-Belfast Road 0.5 km (¹/₂ mile) N of Swords.* This impressive 18th c mansion has been meticulously restored, along with the kitchens. In the courtyard, craft workings are on show; there is also a traditional farm. Surrounding estate, picnic area. *Apr-Oct, Tues-Fri, 10 a.m.-1 p.m.; 2 p.m.-5 p.m.; Sat, 11 a.m.-6 p.m.; Sun, BH, 2 p.m.- 6 p.m. Nov-March, Sat, Sun, BH, 2 p.m.-5 p.m.* ☎ *(01)843 6534.*

Portmarnock. Good beach and coastal walks. 18 hole golf course, ☎ *(01)324674.* Portmarnock Raceway: regular trotting races, ☎ *(01)846 2834.*

Rush/Lusk, *29 km (18 miles) N of Dublin.* Twin villages: Rush is fine fishing village with two sandy beaches. In Lusk, see round tower and nearby parish church. For round tower key, ☎ *(01)843 7276.* **Lusk Heritage Centre:** local history museum in old church, adjoining round tower. *Mid June-Sept, daily, 9.30 a.m.-6.30 p.m.* ☎ *(01) 843 7683.*

Skerries, *30 km (19 miles) N of Dublin.* Pleasant holiday resort and fishing town, good walks along the front, taking in pier. Shenick's Island, offshore, can be reached on foot at low tide. Golf Club, *18 holes,* ☎ *(01)849 1204.*

St Doulagh's Church, Ballygriffen, *3 km (2 miles) W of Portmarnock:* parts date back to 12th c, also subterranean chamber called St Catherine's Well. The church and surrounding graveyard have been renovated. *Open daily in summer, for key,* ☎ *(01)846 0636.*

Swords: CI church, square tower in grounds, dating from 6th c monastery founded by St Colmcille. *By arr,* ☎ *(01)840 4056.* **Swords Castle,** *Main Street:* built in 1200. Most of the structure is in good condition. The entire courtyard has been cleared, giving access at all times.

Velvet Strand, *Portmarnock.* Fine expanse of beach.

Drogheda

Pop. 25,000, 48 km (30 miles) N of Dublin. EC. Thurs, TIO: ☎ *(041)37070 June-Aug. Bus enquiries:* ☎ *(041)38747. Train enquiries: Iarnrod Eireann, MacBride Station,* ☎ *(041)38583. Taxis: Laurence Street, near Tholsel; railway station.*

Hilly town, over 2,000 years old, will be heritage town, complete with heritage centre. The Danes settled here in 911 and later, under Anglo-Norman rule, two separate towns developed, one on each side of the Boyne river. In 1649, after a bitter siege, Cromwell took Drogheda and killed most of its inhabitants. Today, though a busy industrial town, the wharfsides and the historic back lanes are extremely atmospheric.

St Peter's Church (C), *West Street:* Drogheda's parish church houses shrine of St Oliver Plunkett, Primate of All-Ireland martyred at Tyburn, London, in 1681. The jewelled casket containing his head is a centre of pilgrimage ♿ *St Mary's* (CI), *top of Peter Street:* commanding views from churchyard, where Henry Ussher, Archbishop of Armagh, is buried. Church built in 1807; earlier building damaged during Cromwellian siege. ♿ *Augustinian abbey,* *Abbey Lane, behind West Street Shopping Centre:* only the fine 13th c tower remains. If you are lucky, a stroll along the lane will evoke the 'feel' of old Drogheda. *Siena Convent* (C), *Chord Road:* built in 1796, peaceful private chapel, *open daily.* ♿ *Millmount Museum* has been renovated. The museum has been relocated in much bigger premises; it has many relics of domestic and industrial life in Drogheda. *Summer, daily, 10 a.m.-1 p.m.; 2 p.m.-5 p.m. Winter, Wed, Sat, Sun, 3 p.m.-5 p.m.* ☎ *(01)36391.* The surrounding craft shops, which include a weaver's, are open *Mon-Sat, 9.30 a.m.-6 p.m.* The picture windows in the Buttergate restaurant give good views of the town, by day and by night. *Courthouse, Fair Street:* houses sword and mace presented to Drogheda Corporation by William III after Battle of the Boyne, 17th c charters and assorted municipal regalia. *By arr., Town Clerk's Office, Mon-Fri. Library, Fair Street: extensive selection of local material and information. Tues-Sat,* ☎ *(041)36649. Railway Arms, Dublin Road:* opens at 7.30 a.m., one of few early licences granted, for workers on nearby quays. *St. Laurence Gate,* top of Laurence Street: only survivor of ten 13th c town gates, interesting walk from here down to riverside, taking in 19th c warehouses. Riverside walk: upstream for 5 km (3 miles) on S bank, beyond second road bridge. Bicycles: P.J. Carolan, 77 Trinity Street, ☎ (041)38242.

AROUND DROGHEDA

Baltray, *8 km (5 miles) E of Drogheda.* Small village with fine golf links on N shore of Boyne estuary. Beyond links one of E Ireland's finest beaches. Baltray Golf Club, *18 holes,* ☎ *(041)22329.*

Bellewstown, *6 km (4 miles) S of Drogheda:* races, *June, July,* ☎ *TIO, Drogheda, June-Aug,* ☎ *(041)37070.*

Bettystown. *8 km (5 miles) E of Drogheda.* Also train from Drogheda to 'twin' village of

Newgrange, Co. Meath

Laytown. Popular holiday resort on S side of Boyne estuary. One of longest strands in Ireland— 9 km (6 miles) —ideal for walking at all states of tide. Horse racing along the strand for one day in August. ☎ Joseph Collins, *27 Fair Street, Drogheda.* Bettystown Amusement Park. **Sonairte,** *Laytown.* National ecology centre includes vegetable garden and orchard. *Easter-Oct, Mon-Fri, 10 a.m.-5 p.m. Sat, Sun, 12 noon-5 p.m.* ☎ *(041) 27572.* Laytown and Bettystown Golf Club, *18 holes,* ☎ *(041)27534.*

Brugh na Boinne (Palace of the Boyne), *11 km (7 miles) W of Drogheda, immediately S of N51 to Slane. TIO: Newgrange,* ☎ *(041)24274. Apr-Oct.* Within this 5 km (3 miles) by 3 km (2 miles) area there are at least 15 passage graves, Newgrange, Knowth and Dowth being the most striking. **Newgrange,** probably dating from 2,500 BC, is one of finest and most sophisticated passage graves in W Europe, construction required an estimated 250,000 tonnes of stone, which was originally finished with a dazzling coat of pebbles. On the day of the winter solstice, the sun shines straight down the entrance passageway; Newgrange is believed to have been a prehistoric astronomic site. This sun effect is artificially recreated for visitors. Frequent guided tours. *Nov-mid Mar, Tues-Sun, 10 a.m.-1 p.m.; 2 p.m.-4 p.m.-4.30 p.m. Mid Mar-May, daily, 10 a.m.-1 p.m.,; 2 p.m.-5 p.m. June-mid Sept, daily, 10 a.m.-7 p.m. Mid Sept-Oct, daily 10 a.m.-1 p.m.; 2 p.m.-5 p.m.* ☎ *(041) 24488.* Interpretative centre planned. The megalithic tombs of Dowth and Knowth are being excavated and are closed to the public. At nearby King William's Glen, the site of the Battle of the Boyne (1690) is marked. Newgrange farm, farm animals, vintage farm machinery adjacent to Newgrange site. Guided tours. ☎ *(041) 24119.*

Clogher, *14 km (9 miles) NE of Drogheda.* Walk from village to nearby fishing harbour of Port Oriel, about 1.6 km (1 mile). From headland above harbour, excellent views of entire Co. Louth coast and Mountains of Mourne.

Dunleer, *8 km (5 miles) NW of Drogheda on N1:* **White River Mills.** Restored water-powered flour mill; waterwheel dates back to 1691. This living museum produces stoneground wholemeal flour. *Mon-Fri, 10 a.m.-5 p.m.* ☎*(041)51141. Pref by arr.*♿

Monasterboice, *8 km (5 miles) W of Drogheda, just off N1* remains of ancient monastic settlement. Main interest today is High Cross, 5.4 metres (17'8"), one of best-preserved in Ireland; surface almost entirely ornamented. Nearby, explore ruins of 33 m (110 ft) high round tower. Key held by Patrick Crilly, house at gate. Mellifont Youth Hostel, ☎ *(041)26127.*

Mornington, *6.5 km (4 miles) E of Drogheda on L125 road to Bettystown.* Maiden Tower can be climbed, but it's dangerous. Visit Moran's pub, one of finest traditional pubs in Ireland, complete with snugs and mahogany shelves for groceries. Bicycles: Christy Reynolds, ☎ *(041)27088.*

Mosney Holiday Centre, *Mosney, 8 km (5 miles) S of Drogheda.* Facilities include indoor and outdoor swimming, amusement park, horse-riding. Audio-visual presentation of ancient Boyne Valley themes. ☎*(041)29200. Open to day visitors, SO May-Sept.* ♿

Slane, *14 km (9 miles) W of Drogheda.* Climb Slane Hill, where St. Patrick lit his Paschal fire in AD 433, proclaiming Christianity in Ireland, also remains of 16th c church and monastic school. From the top of the hill, see whole of Boyne valley from Trim to Drogheda. The *Francis Ledwidge Museum,* a modest stone cottage, was once home for the early 20th c poet, who was just beginning to win recognition for his work when he was killed in World War I. *Mar-Oct, Mon, Tues, Wed, 10 a.m.-6 p.m., closed 1 p.m.-2 p.m.* ☎ *(041)24285.*

Termonfeckin, *near Baltray:* **Muriel Gahan Museum.** Details country life. *By arr,* ☎ *(041)22119.* **Termonfeckin castle and high cross.** 15th/16th c three storey tower house. Key from house across road.

Townley Hall, *6.5 km (4 miles) W of Drogheda on N51 to Slane:* forest walks, nature trail, picnic area

High Cross, Monasterboice, Co. Louth

and car park. One of points on nature trail overlooks the site of the Battle of the Boyne, fought on July 12, 1690. Towards the end of the trail, good views of the Obelisk bridge across the river Boyne. Worth taking the detour off the trail to explore King William's Glen.

Dundalk

Pop. 31,000, 84 km (52 miles) N of Dublin and the same distance S of Belfast on main N1 road, E.C. Thurs. TIO: Market Square, Dundalk, ☎ (042)35484. All year. Bus enquiries: Bus Eireann, ☎ (041)34075. Train enquiries: Iarnrod Eireann Dundalk station. ☎ (042)35521. Taxis: Market Square.

Closely associated with the legendary early-Christian hero Cuchulainn, in 1177, though fortified, the town fell to the Anglo-Normans, and for the next 300 years was repeatedly attacked as a frontier town of the English Pale. Most of its fortifications were removed during the 18th c and little of Dundalk's historic past is to be seen today, nevertheless parts of the town are interesting, particularly the area around the Courthouse. Maytime Festival: wide variety of entertainment, social and sporting events, *late May,* ☎ *(042)32276.* Parts of **St Nicholas Church** (CI) in Clanbrassil Street date from the 15th c; it was rebuilt in the early 18th c. In the graveyard is the tomb of Agnes Galt, sister of Robert Burns, the 18th c Scottish poet. **St Patrick's Cathedral** (C), nearby, was built in the mid 19th c, with King's College Cambridge as its inspiration. Dundalk's new museum and interpretative centre details local history, including industrial. *Details: TIO.*

Seatown Castle, *junction of Castle Road and Mill Street:* see tower of 13th c Franciscan monastery. Library: *Tues-Sat, 10 a.m.-1 p.m.; 2 p.m.-5 p.m. Tues and Thurs, 6 p.m.-8 p.m.,* ☎ *(042)35457.* Theatre: amateur and professional performances at the Town Hall. Occasional visits by touring companies, ☎ *(042)32276.* Factory visits: Carroll's cigarette factory, *3 km (2 miles) S of Dundalk on Dublin road. 2 hour tours by arr. all year,* ☎ *(042)36501.* Harp lager brewery, *near railway station: tours by arr. all year,* ☎ *(042)34793*

Leisure Activities: Racecourse: regular meetings. ☎ *(042)34419.* Greyhound racing: *Mon, Fri, eve, all year. Occasional extra meetings for charity,* ☎ *(042)341183.* Riding: Ballymascanlon House Ho-

tel, *near Dundalk,* ☎ *(042)71124.* Dundalk golf club, 18 holes, ☎ *(042) 21731.* Bicycles: The Bike Shop, *11 Earl Street,* ☎ *(042) 33399.*

AROUND DUNDALK

Annagassan, *near Castlebellingham.* Founded by the Danes. Good walk along seashore to nearby small bathing resort of Salterstown.

Ardee, *20 km (13 miles) SW of Dundalk.* See St Mary's (CI), Main Street. Incorporates part of 13th c Carmelite church. Ardee Golf Club, *Townparks, 9 holes,* ☎ *(041)53227.*

Ballymascanlon, *7 km (4 miles) NE of Dundalk on Carlingford road:* Proleek Dolmen, with huge capstone resting on two 1 m (3ft) support stones. Pathway from nearby Ballymascanlon Hotel.

Bellurgan, *8 km (5 miles) N of Dundalk, turn N of Ballymackellett off Ravensdale-Carlingford road:* forest walks, picnic sites, car parks, scenic views of Dundalk Bay.

Blackrock, *6 km (4 miles) SE of Dundalk. Violet private bus from Dundalk.* Popular seaside resort. Good walk along promenade, *June-Sept, daily.* Golf Club, *18 holes,* ☎ *(042)35379.*

Carlingford, *20 km (13 miles) NE of Dundalk:* **King John's Castle,** built in the 13th c, dominates the town. It is open at all times. Also worth seeing are the exteriors of the 15th c **Mint Tower** and **Taaffe's Castle,** a fortified town house built in the 16th c. As part of its new heritage town status, Carlingford now has a heritage and cultural centre. A new Darcy Magee museum commemorates a local 19th c patriot and poet, who emigrated and became a leading Canadian statesman. *Details: Dundalk TIO.* Carlingford Oyster Festival, *Aug. Details: Dundalk TIO.*

Castlebellingham, *13 km (8 miles) S of Dundalk.* Attractive village that once had thriving brewery.

Castletown, *3 km (2 miles) W of town:* ancient Dun Dealgan, mound over 18 m (60 ft) high and said to have been birthplace of Cuchulainn. On summit is ruin of 1780 house. Nearby, well-preserved ruin of mediaeval Castletown Castle.

Castle Roche, *8 km (5 miles) NW of Dundalk:* fine views from this early 13th c castle (NM).

Cooley Peninsula. If you drive round the peninsula, starting in Dundalk, going via Gyles Quay (small fishing village, good bathing and sailing facilities), through Greenore, Carlingford and Omeath back to Dundalk, you will be rewarded with some spectacular views. To S, views of Dundalk Bay and Co. Louth coast. To N, magnificent backdrop of Mountains of Mourne, just across Carlingford Lough.

Faughart, *6 km (4 miles) N of Dundalk:* reputed to be birthplace of St Brigid, patroness of Ireland. From Faughart cemetery, burial place of Robert the Bruce's brother, tremendous views of area. Adjacent car park.

Greenore, Golf Club, *18 holes,* ☎ *(042)73212.*

Inniskeen, *14 km (9 miles) W of Dundalk.* The poet Patrick Kavanagh, born in the village, is commemorated at the folk museum here. There are also relics of the old Great Northern Railway and other artefacts of the local social order. *By arr,* ☎ *(042)78102.*

Kildemock, *3 km (2 miles) SE of Ardee:* Jumping Church, the gable, only remaining wall, stands 1 m (3 ft) inside its foundations. Tradition says that the wall 'jumped' inwards to exclude grave of excommunicated person. This explanation's main rival is almost as improbable: during a severe storm in 1715 the wall is held to have been lifted and deposited where it now stands.

Louth, *8 km (5 miles) SW of Dundalk.* Fine views from this hilltop village. **St Mochta's House,** a

10th c religious edifice, is in good condition. St Patrick was said to have made his first church in Ireland here in the 5th c.

Mellifont Abbey, *Collon:* Cistercian monastery founded 1142 includes lavabo and 14th c chapter house in idyllic setting. *May-mid June, Tues-Sat, 9.30 a.m.-1 p.m.; 2 p.m.-5.30 p.m., Sun, 2 p.m.-5 p.m. Mid June-mid Sept, daily, 9.30 a.m.-6.30 p.m.* ☎ *(041) 26459.*

Omeath, *30 km (19 miles) NE of Dundalk.* Popular seaside resort. Jaunting cars from strand to Calvary Shrine in Summer only. Daily ferry trips to Warrenpoint on N shore of Carlingford Lough, *All year.* Youth Hostel, ☎ *(042)75142.*

Ravensdale, *6 km (4 miles) N of Dundalk, turn E off N1:* car park, forest walks, nature trail, standing stones.

Slieve Foye, *3 km (2 miles) NW of Carlingford on T62 towards Omeath:* scenic drive to car park overlooking Carlingford Lough. Nature trail gives good climb through woods. Midway viewing point has excellent views of Rostrevor Forest, Co. Down.

Dun Laoghaire

Pop. 55,000, 11 km (7 miles) S of Dublin, TIO: ☎ *(01)280 6984. All year. Train enquiries,* ☎ *(01)366222. Bus enquiries,* ☎ *(01)734222. Taxis: Marine Road, opp. Post Office.* ☎ *(01)280 5263. Coach tours: SO. Details TIO.*

Many people's first glimpse of Ireland. Until early 19th c, this major ferry port was small fishing village, but after the opening of the railway from Dublin in 1834, the expansion of Kingstown, as it was then known, was rapid. Today, the town is a pleasant holiday and shopping centre, with several gourmet restaurants. Dun Laoghaire summer festival: concerts, cultural activities and exhibitions, *June. Details: Festival Office,* ☎ *(01)284 1888.* **St Michael's** (C), *corner Marine Road and George's Street:* original 19th c church burned down in 1965. Striking modern building effectively grafted onto the surviving bell tower. **National Maritime Museum,** *Haigh Terrace, SE corner of Moran Park:* highlight is great working optic from Baily lighthouse at Howth. Many models of ships, including Great Eastern, also 11 m (36 ft) French longboat captured at Bantry Bay in 1796, reckoned to be oldest surviving ship's boat in world. *May-Sept, Tues, Sun, 2.30 p.m.-5.30 p.m. Apr, Oct, Nov, Sat, Sun, 2.30 p.m.-5.30 p.m.* ☎ *(01)280 0969.* **The piers:** east pier, nearly 1 m (2 km) long, and seemingly never-ending, is the more popular for walks. *July, Aug, Sun aft,* concerts on band stand. If you prefer solitude, try during week or early Sat or Sun. West pier can be walked, but the going is much rougher. Also Marine Parade: as far as tiny beach at Sandycove and James Joyce Tower. Return by main Sandycove Road. Squares: elegant walking N of George's Street, particularly those at Clarinda Park and Royal Terrace E and W. People's Park; concerts, *July, Aug, Sun aft.*

Leisure Activities: Lambert Puppet Theatre, Monkstown, ☎ *(01) 286 7128* and seafront. *June, July and Aug, Mon-Sun,* ☎ *(01)280 6967.* Bicycles: Mike's Bikes, Unit 6, George's Mall, Dun Laoghaire shopping centre, ☎ *(01) 280 0417.* Dun Laoghaire Golf Club, *18 holes,* ☎ *(01)280 1055.*

AROUND DUN LAOGHAIRE

Ballinascorney, *Lower and Upper: 13 km (8 miles) from Rathfarnham on L199, keep right at first junction beyond Ballinascorney Gap:* layby, picnic places, forest walks, access to Seechon Mountain.

Barnaslingan, *on Barnaslingan Lane E off T43 near Kilternan.* Car park, picnic place, forest walks, scenic view overlooking the Scalp Mountain.

Blackrock, *Dublin Crystal Glass, Carysfort Avenue,* ☎ *(01)288 7932/288 8627/8. Mon-Fri,* see glass being hand cut.

Bray: *seaside town 12 km (8 miles) S of Dun Laoghaire. TIO: Heritage Centre, Town Hall. June-Aug,* ☎ *(01)286 7128. Train enquiries: Bray Station,* ☎ *(01)286 2007. Coach tours: SO, details: TIO.* Splendid esplanade ideal for strolling, both in summer and equally during the dramatic winter storms. Aquarium, nearby amusement arcades. SO. Laneways and attractive terraced streets between Main Street and seafront. Also walks alongside Dargle river in harbour area. **Harbour Bar,** has good collection of antique signs. There is a fine cliff walk from S end of esplanade to Greystones, about 8 km (5 miles). Sometimes path blocked by rock falls, check with Bray TIO. **Bray Heritage Centre,** in new Main Street location, has great potpourri of local history and artefacts. *Details: TIO.* Swimming pool: indoor, heated. Presentation College, *Putland Road. Daily by arr,* ☎ *(01)286 7517/286 2189.* Woodbrook Golf Club, *18 holes,* ☎ *(01)282 2532.* Bicycles: E.R. Harris & Son, *Greenpark Road & Main Street,* ☎ *(01)286 3357/286 7995.* Carrickmines Equestrian Centre, *Carrickmines,* ☎ *(01)955990.* Horse riding instruction.

Cruagh, *8 km (5 miles) S of Rathfarnham, E off L94 or W off L201.* Car park, picnic place, forest walks, nature trail, wilderness trek via Featherbed Mountain to Military Road car park.

Dalkey, *near Dun Laoghaire.* Popular resort town, recently immortalised by Flann O'Brien and Hugh Leonard: a prominent port during the Middle Ages. **Archibold's Castle,** *Castle Street,* is one of few reminders of mediaeval walled town. Dalkey has been designated as a heritage town, so a new heritage centre should detail local history. Magnificent coastal walk from Dalkey village up Coliemore Road to Vico Road. Continue into Killiney, with its fine beach. There is also a fine walk around Bullock Harbour and up Harbour Road to Dalkey village.

Dalkey Island, ideal place for picnic, even if long grass makes walking hard. See ruins of military barracks and church, also Martello Tower in good condition. Boat trips from Coliemore harbour (next to Dalkey Island Hotel) on summer weekends.

Enniskerry, Glencree Youth Hostel: ☎ *(01)286 7290.* Knockree Youth Hostel, ☎ *(01)286 7196.* **Powerscourt,** ruins of 18th c mansion destroyed by fire in 1974. A restoration is planned. 13,759 ha (34,000 acre) estate has Italian and Japanese gardens, dramatically backed by the Wicklow mountains. On the south of the estate, the waterfall is said to be the highest in Ireland or Britain. Shop, café. Gardens, *Mar-Oct, Mon-Sat, 9 a.m.-5.30 p.m., Sun, 10.30 a.m.-5.30 p.m.* Waterfall, *all year, Mon-Sun, 10.30 a.m.-7.30 p.m.* ☎ *(01)286 7876.*

Glencree, *8 km (5 miles) W of Enniskerry:* cemetery where German servicemen who died in and around Ireland in World War II are buried.

Glencullen, *Co. Dublin.* Frauchan (type of berry) festival, good excuse for all kinds of merriment, *early July.*

Great Sugar Loaf mountain, *6 km (4 miles) SW of Bray:* fine views from summit. Track to near mountain top.

Greystones, *Co. Wicklow. Train enquiries: Greystones Station,* ☎ *(01)287 4160.* Excellent walk around harbour and along seafront. You can follow the track between railway line and beach for about 5 km (3 miles) S. Greystones Golf Club, *18 holes,* ☎ *(01)287 4136.*

Hell Fire Club, *6 km (4 miles) S of Rathfarnham on L201:* car park, picnic place, forest walks, access to ruins of 18th c Hell Fire Club, panoramic views.

James Joyce Tower, *Sandycove:* good collection of Joyceana. *May-Sept, Mon-Sat, 10 a.m.-1 p.m.; 2 p.m.-5 p.m. Sun, BH, 2 p.m.-6 p.m. Otherwise, by arr.* ☎ *(01)280 8571/280 9265.*

Killakee, *Dublin mountains.* Take L94 road from Rathfarnham to Killakee, good views of city, hill

Fields near Glencree, Co. Wicklow

walking to Glendhu, Pine Forest and Glenasmole beauty spots.

Killiney Hill. Public park, thickly wooded in places, rising above coast road between Dalkey and Killiney. Fine views from summit.

Kilmashogue, *on cul-de-sac off L93 Rockbrook-Sandyford road, 2 km (1 mile) E of Rockbrook,* car park, picnic place, forest walk to Three Rock Mountain, Bronze Age tomb.

Kilruddery House and Gardens, *Bray:* attractively set at foot of Little Sugar Loaf mountain, only 17th c garden in Ireland. *Open most afternoons. Check in advance,* ☎ *(01)286 3405.*

Leopardstown, frequent horse racing, ☎ *(01)289 3607.* Squash: *Leopardstown Racecourse. Details of this and other Dublin area squash facilities, Anglesea House, Church Road, Dalkey,* ☎ *(01)280 8426.*

Monkstown, *Co. Dublin.* Comhaltas Ceoltoiri Eireann, *32 Belgrave Square,* cultural Institute and Irish music museum. Basement converted into traditional Irish country kitchen, with open fire and flagstone floor. Irish music concerts, great fun. ☎ *(01)280 0295.* ♿

Sandycove, *Co. Dublin.* Forty foot near James Joyce Tower is used for male-only bathing—in spite of Women's Lib protests. **Tudor Galleries,** *30 Sandycove Road,* ☎ *(01)280 3427.*

Sandyford. *Co. Dublin:* Fernhill Gardens, on slopes of Three Rock Mountain, specimen trees, rhododendrons, rock and water gardens. *Mar-Nov Tues-Sat, BH, 11 a.m.-5 p.m., Sun, 2 p.m.-6 p.m. Nursery, all year, Tues-Sat, 11 a.m.-5 p.m., Sun 2 p.m.-6 p.m.* ☎ *(01)956000.*

Source of the Liffey, just past Lough Bray, near E of *Liffey Head bridge on L94,* see where the river rises.

Stepaside, *turn right off main Dublin-Enniskerry road:* mountain road towards Pine Forest and Glencullen for about 6 km (4 miles). Excellent views over Dublin and Killiney bays.

Stillorgan Bowl: Tenpin bowling, seven days a week, ☎ *(01)288 1566.*

Three Rock Mountain, car, picnic place, panoramic views, access to summits of Three Rock and Two Rock Mountains and Kilmashogue car park.

Tibradden, *8 km (5 miles) S of Rathfarnham on L201:* car park, picnic place, forest walks, nature trail.

Wicklow Way, fully marked trail that starts at Marley Park, Rathfarnham and runs for some 48 km (30 miles) S, across the Dublin mountains, past Loughs Dan and Tay, through Glendalough to Glenmalure.

Wicklow

Pop. 5,500, 126 km (16 miles) N of Arklow, 32 m (51 km) S of Dublin, 96 km (60 miles) N of Wexford. EC: Thur. TIO: Fitzwilliam Square, ☎ (0404)69117. All year.

A seaside resort and county town, with a pleasant harbour area. In centuries past, Wicklow was repeatedly attacked in squabbles between O'Byrnes, O'Tooles and the English. Today, though much modernised, the old town retains a certain historical flavour.

Fitzwilliam Square, see granite obelisk commemorating Wicklow-born captain of Brunel's 'Great Eastern', which laid the first cable across the Atlantic. Memorial, *Market Square:* commemorates Wicklow men who fought in 1798. The 18th c St Lavinius church (CI), with its green onion-shaped cupola is worth seeing for its elaborate interior and memorials, including one to Captain Halpin. The old town jail is being turned into a heritage and genealogical centre, due to open in 1993. *Details: TIO.* **Black Castle,** *on rocky promontory at E end of town;* begun by Maurice Fitzgerald in 1176 and frequently attacked over the following five centuries, now in ruins. Also remains of 13th c Franciscan friary in grounds of presbytery; Norman doorway in S porch of C of I. The

Murrough: take a turn round the harbour area, then N towards this fine stretch of sward, now public promenade. Viewing point on heights above town gives excellent views of coastline.

Leisure Activities: Blainroe Golf Club, *18 holes,* ☎ *(0404)68168;* Wicklow Golf Club, *9 holes,* ☎ *(0404)67379.*

AROUND WICKLOW

Annamoe Trout Farm, *between Glendalough and Laragh,* ☎ *(0404)45145, daily.*

Arklow, *14 km (9 miles) S of Wicklow, bus, train, from Wicklow.* Bustling resort town with access to two excellent beaches. **Maritime Museum,** *St Mary's Road:* about 1,000 items relating to the town's nautical history. *All year, Mon-Sat, 10 a.m.-1 p.m.; 2 p.m.-5 p.m.* **Tyrrell's,** *South Dock:* fine tradition of ship and yacht building, ☎ *(0402)32403.* **Pottery:** *guided tours, mid-June-Aug 31, at 9.30 a.m., 12 noon, 1.30 p.m., 3.45 p.m. Closed last week July, first two Aug,* ☎ *(0402)32134.* **Arklow Rock,** *along S Strand, past golf course, about 3 km (2 miles) from town:* 126 m (415 ft), fine view of coast; Our Lady's Well is on the Rock. 9 km (6 miles) walk along minor coast road NE to ruined tower on Mizen Head. Amusement centre: pitch and putt, games room, outdoor swimming pool, *daily, 10 a.m.-7 p.m.* Golf Club, *18 holes,* ☎ *(0402)32492.* Bicycles: J.J. Owen & Son, *Main Street,* ☎ *(0402)32638.*

Ashford, *8 km (5 miles) NW of Wicklow.* **Mount Usher Gardens.** These attractive gardens cover more than 20 acres by the Dargle River. More than 5,000 species are represented, from azaleas to rhododendrons. Craft shops, café. *Mar 17-Oct 31, Mon-Sat, 10.30 a.m.-6 p.m., Sun, 11 a.m.-6 p.m.* ☎ *(0404)40205.* **Devil's Glen,** *3 km (2 miles) NW village:* here the Vartry River falls nearly 30 m (100 ft) into the Devil's Punchbowl, a deep basin in the rock. Walks, nature trail, vantage points with good views of coastline to E. **Tiglin Adventure Centre,** sports such as orienteering, caving and hang

Wicklow Mountains near Glendalough, Co. Wicklow

gliding, ☎ *(0404)40169.* Bel-Air Riding School, ☎ *(0404)40109;* Broom Lodge Riding Centre, ☎ *(0404)40404.* Tiglin Youth Hostel, ☎ *(0404)40259.*

Aughavannagh, *by Aughavannagh bridge, on Rathdangan-Glenmalure road:* fine forest walk to foot of Lugnaquilla mountain, 926 m (3,039 ft).

Aughrim, *14 km (9 miles) NW of Arklow on L19:* forest walks, viewing point at Mucklagh, on Aughrim-Greenane road; forest walks on both sides of Aughrim-Aughavannagh road. Aughavannagh Youth Hostel: ☎ *(0402)36102.*

Avoca, *26 km (16 miles) S of Wicklow.* Beautifully set village. See Tom Moore's tree, near Meeting of the Waters; where the poet is said to have spent many hours in contemplation. Avoca Handweavers, craft weaving, shop restaurant, ☎ *(0402) 35105.* Also at Kilmacanogue, *near Bray,* ☎ *(01) 286 7466.*

Avondale Estate, *2.5 km (1.5 miles) S of Rathdrum:* Charles Stewart Parnell, great 19th c Irish leader, lived in 1779 house, now finely restored, with rooms open to the public. The vast estate has car parks, many planned walks and nature trail. House and estate, *all year, daily, except Christmas Day, 11 a.m.-6 p.m.*

Ballymoyle Hill, *6 km (4 miles) N of Arklow.* Take L29 to 3 km (2 miles) S of Jack White's Cross, turn right at Scratenagh crossroads, continue for 1.5 km (1 mile) NW: forest walks, scenic views, picnic area, car park.

Brittas Bay, *13 km (8 miles) S of Wicklow Head:* popular 5 km (3 mile) stretch of sandy beach backed by dunes. Ideal for bathing, picnicking, large car park.

Glendalough, *24 km (15 miles) E of Wicklow, T7 via Rathdrum:* One of Ireland's most attractive monastic sites. The principal ruins, just E of Lower Lake, are the cathedral, consisting of 11th c nave, chancel and St Kevin's Church, commonly called St Kevin's Kitchen, a fine example of early

Irish barrel-vaulted oratory, with a 1,000 year old, almost perfect round tower. Less accessible, on the S shore of Upper Lake, are Teampall na Skellig (Church of the Rock) and St Kevin's Bed, cut into the cliff face. **Glendalough Visitors Centre:** audio-visual presentation, fully equipped theatre; guided tour of monastic settlement, incorporating seven churches. *Nov-mid Mar, Tues-Sun, 10 a.m.-4.30 p.m.; mid Mar-mid May, daily, 10 a.m.-5 p.m.; mid May-mid June, daily 9.30 a.m.-6 p.m.; mid June-mid Sept, daily, 9.30 a.m.-7 p.m. mid Sept-Sept 30, daily, 9.30 a.m.-5 p.m. Oct, 10 a.m.-5 p.m.* ☎ *(0404)45325.* **Craft centre:** weaving and jewellery, with details from local churches; gallery and tearooms. *Mon-Fri, 10 a.m.-6 p.m., by app.* Shop *Mon-Sun, 10 a.m.-6 p.m.,* ☎ *(0404)45156.* Glendalough Woods, *1.5 km (1 mile) W of Laragh on L107:* 1.5 km (1 mile) nature trail, forest walks, picnic area, car park. Riding Stables, *Laragh,* ☎ *(0404)45282.* Youth Hostel: ☎ *(0404)45143.*

Greenane, *3 km (2 miles) SW of Rathdrum:* Glenmalure Youth Hostel.

Jack's Hole, *9 km (6 miles) S of Wicklow Head:* secluded stretch of sand.

Laragh Trout Farm, *Rathdrum road, Laragh,* equipment supplied free, pay for your catch. *June-mid-Sept, Mon-Sat, 9 a.m.-6 p.m. Sun, 2 p.m.-7 p.m. Also Easter,* ☎ *(0404)45282* **Laragh Trekking Centre:** pony trekking over local forest trails and mountains. ☎ *(0404)45282.*

Loughs Tay and **Dan:** *3 km (2 miles) W of Roundwood:* adjacent countryside most desolate in E Ireland. Interpretative centre at Luggala, due to open in 1993. Large portions of Co Wicklow have been designated as a national park.

Motte Stone, *3 km (2 miles) W of Avoca:* glacial stone perched on hill overlooking village, extensive views.

Rathdrum, *116 km (10 miles) SW of Wicklow.* Attractive small town set high on W side of Avonmore valley, Vale of Clara to N and Vale of Avoca to S. Forest walks at Croneybyrne, Ballinastraw, plus picnic area, car park at Ballygannon. A Parnell memorial park, complete with statue of the great fallen political leader, opened in 1991, the centenary of Parnell's death. **Clara-Lara Funpark and Trout Farm,** *Vale of Clara, Rathdrum.* Fishing, boating, adventure playground, picnic areas, café, daily, ☎ *(0404)46161.*

Rathnew, *3 km (2 miles) N of Wicklow Town:* Hunter's Hotel has riverside gardens and interesting historical photographs, including the first car in Ireland. Tinakilly House hotel has many mementoes of captain Robert Halpin, who built this late 19 c mansion as his home.

Roundwood, *19 km (12 miles) SW of Bray,* ☎ *281 8119.* Highest village in Ireland, 238 m (780 ft) above sea level. A walk along Main Street takes in almost the entire village. **Ballinastoe Studio Pottery and Gallery,** Daily, ☎ *(01)821 8151.*

Shelton Abbey, *3 km (2 miles) NW of Arklow:* fine rhododendrons in demesne of state forestry school.

Shillelagh, *8 km (5 miles) Picturesque village S of Tinahely:* good hill walks. Picturesque village.

Silver Strand, *immediately S of Wicklow Head:* popular sandy beach backed by cliffs.

Tinahely, *13 km (8 miles) SW of Aughrim:* Horse Fair and Agricultural Show, *early Aug.* A heritage centre is planned for the old courthouse.

Woodenbridge, *8 km (5 miles) NW of Arklow.* One of the most beautifully situated villages in Ireland, where Avoca, Arklow and Aughrim valleys meet. **Glenart** *just E of Wooden-bridge on N11:* forest walks, rhododendrons, picnic area, car park. Trout Farm, catch your own fish, equipment supplied free, pay for the fish you land. *Summer daily, 10 a.m.-5 p.m. Visitors welcome in and out of season.*

The SOUTH

Bantry

Pop. 3,000, 45 km (28 miles) S of Kenmare, (92 km 57 miles) W of Cork, 350 km (218 miles) SW of Dublin. EC. Wed. TIO, ☎ *(027)50229, July-Sept.*

A delightfully situated town nestling beneath hills at the head of Bantry Bay. Despite the proximity of the Whiddy Island oil terminal, change has been so slight you can almost imagine this century has passed Bantry by. Some good hotels for exploring the largely natural wonders of W Cork and adjacent SW Kerry.

Bantry House, Georgian mansion filled with treasures, many from Lord Bantry's tours abroad in the early 19th c. Chippendale, Sheraton furniture, Waterford chandeliers, Aubusson tapestries, Pompeii mosaics, Italian gardens terraces with superb views across the bay to the Caha Mountains in Co Kerry. The new **French Armada Centre** details the attempted French landings in Bantry Bay, 1796. *Daily, except Christmas Day, 9 a.m.-6 p.m. Open till 8 p.m. May-Sept.* Tea room, craft shop, ☎ *(027)50047.* **Kilnaurane Inscribed Stone,** *Rope Walk Road, near West Lodge Hotel:* early 7th c carving unique in Co Cork. Bantry Bay Horse and Pony Mountain Trekking Centre, *Rooska,* ☎ *(027)50221.*

AROUND BANTRY

Abbeystrewery, *2 km (1 mile) W of Skibbereen:* abbey set on the banks of the River Ilen, dates from 14th c, mass famine graves. Famine memorial planned.

Adrigole, *road N to Lauragh taking in Healy Pass.* Started during the famine, but only completed in 1931. Crucifixion Shrine at top. Difficult drive but tremendous views. Riding: Mrs T. O'Sullivan, Bayview House, Faha, ☎ *(027)60026.*

Ahakista, *18 km (12 miles) SW of Bantry.* Just before the tiny, windswept village is the impressive memorial to the 329 victims of the Air India jumbo jet that crashed into the Atlantic Ocean in 1985. The narrow, winding road continues for a further 16 km (10 miles) to the tip of the Sheep's Head peninsula.

Allihies, *9 km (6 miles) W of Castletownbere:* 19th c copper workings, explore with care. The village has a fine strand. **Black Bull Tower,** *near Lickbarran,* 18th c structure, impressive views of coast and mountains. Ballydonegan Strand, bathing, surfing, Youth Hostel.

Ballingeary, *29 km (18 miles) NE of Bantry on T64.* Stronghold of the Irish language, good views of nearby Lough Allua. Scenic drive through hills to N, via Reananerree village, to N22, back through Macroom and Inchigeelagh. About 48 km (30 miles).

Ballycrovane ogham stone, *just N of Eyeries, near Ballycrovane harbour:* tallest ogham stone in Ireland, 6 m (18 ft).

Ballydehob, *16 km (10 miles) S of Bantry on N71.* Quaint harbour, a veritable warren of craft workshops. The tramway viaduct offers panoramic views of Roaring Water Bay, Carbery's hundred isles, Mount Gabriel. **Cush Strand,** *3 km (2 miles) W of village:* bathing. Yachts (daily, weekly, monthly): Andrew Scott, *Rossbrin Cove,* ☎ *(028)37165.*

Ballylickey, *5 km (3 miles) N of Bantry:* beautiful stretches of coastal scenery at the head of Bantry

Bay. Waterfalls, wooded glens just off N71 to Glengarriff. The nearby road to Priest's Leap climbs nearly 600 m (2,000 ft).

Ballynacarriga Castle, *6 km (4 miles) SE of Dunmanway:* 16th c ruins overlooking lake, scenic views.

Baltimore, *13 km (8 miles) SW of Skibbereen.* Centuries old fishing village, full of atmosphere. The tall, whitewashed 'Beacon' offers fine views of the harbour and Sherkin Island across the bay. There is a regular daily ferry crossing to Sherkin Island; in good weather, the trip takes 15 mins. Regular passenger sailings to Clear Island, *details: Comhar Chuman Chléire Teo,* ☎ *(028)39119.* Baltimore Boat Hire, *The Pier,* ☎ *(028)20141.* Also boats to Hare Island and Long Island, also in Roaring Water Bay.

Bantry-Durrus Road, *5 km (3 miles) S of Bantry.* A great anchor, that once belonged to a ship in the French invasion fleet that tried to land near Bantry in 1796, stands by the roadside.

Barley Cove, magnificent sandy beach. Barley Cove Beach Hotel swimming pool: indoor, heated. Weekly, monthly tickets, ☎ *(028)35234.*

Beara Peninsula, *Milleens, nr Eyeries:* wonderful to see cheese being made in a traditional way on a full-time commercial basis. *Preferably by arr.*

Bawntemple Pillar Stone, *4 km (3 miles) NW of Ballingeary:* nearly 6 m (20 ft) high, permission from farm.

Bere Island, *ferry from Castletownbere. Summer: Four services daily. Winter less frequent, details,* ☎ *(027)75004.* The journey takes about 30 mins in fine weather; tourist accommodation is limited, with one registered guesthouse. The ruins of the former Royal Navy base, evacuated in 1938, are worth exploring. Glenans Sailing Centre, ☎ *(027)75012; weekly, fortnightly sailing courses; Sean Harrington, West End,* ☎ *(027)75009;* Brendan Murphy, *the Village,* ☎ *(027)70004.*

Cahermore Strand, *W tip of Beara Peninsula:* good bathing.

Castletownbere, sheltered by Slieve Miskish mountains on SW side of Beara peninsula. Once an anchorage for the British Atlantic fleet, now a major deep sea angling centre, with beaches on both sides of the town. Nightly fish auction on quayside, 9 p.m. The large town square is surrounded by interesting pubs and shops. 2.5 km (1.5 miles) S of the town, the ruins of the vast 19th c mansion once owned by the Puxleys, owners of the Allihies mine, are substantial. Prehistoric stone circles at Harbour View and the Rock, West End. Boats: Jack Downey, ☎ *(027)70037;* Pearse Lyon, *Main Street,* ☎ *(027)70084;* Dan O'Driscoll, *East End,* ☎ *(027)70077;* Mrs Greeff, *Waterfall,* ☎ *(027)70021,* dinghies. Surf sailing: Craigie's Cametringane House Hotel, ☎ *(027)70379.* Riding: Craigie's Cametringane House Hotel, ☎ *(027)70379.* Bicycles: Dermot Murphy, Bridge House, ☎ *(027)70020.* Youth Hostel, *Glanmore Lake.*

Castletownshend, *8 km (5 miles) SE of Skibbereen:* very beautiful single street village on W shore of Castlehaven. The two trees that stood half-way down the very steep main street have been felled. At the foot of the street is a tiny harbour. Edith Somerville and Violet Martin, co-authors of *The Irish RM and his Experiences,* lived in the village and are buried in the graveyard of St Barrahane's CI church, reached by steep steps just off the foot of the main street.

Clear Island, *Frequent Ferry Service, all year, Mon-Sat,* ☎ *(028)39119.* Access to the island has been improved with the new pier. The island has just one minute village, Cummer. Iarsmalaan Chléire (Clear Island Museum), near a church at the centre of the island. Old photographs, newspaper cuttings about area, farm implements. *Aug, daily, aft.* Bird observatory, SO, book in advance, *details:* Colin Rhind. **Dunamore Castle,** ruins on

Bantry House Co. Cork

NW of island. The old lighthouse, nearby, was built in 1848 and closed only six years later. From South Harbour, see the famous **Fastnet Lighthouse**, *6 km (4 miles) out to sea* on Fastnet Rock, Ireland's most southerly point. Youth Hostel on Clear Island.

Creagh Gardens, *6 km (4 miles) SW of Skibbereen on R595 to Baltimore:* privately owned gardens covering some 12 ha (5 acres) with variety of trees and shrubs. Walks by the shores of River Ilen estuary. *Easter-Sept 30, daily, 10 a.m.-6 p.m.,* ☎ *(028)21267.*

Crookhaven: the Pilchard Palace, to the W of the charming harbour, originally used for storing fish until destroyed in 1641. During the Great Famine, there was a meal house on the site. Boats: Tom O'Driscoll, Billy O'Sullivan, ☎ *(028)35319;* James E. Pyburn, ☎ *(028)28338.*

Cullenagh, *10 km (7 miles) NE of Drimoleague:* four standing stones, fifth nearby.

Derreen Woodland Garden, *1 km (1 mile) from Lauragh on Castletownbere Road:* established over 100 years ago on the S shores of Kenmare River. Internationally known for splendid setting and many specimen trees and shrubs. *Apr 1-Sept 30, Sun, Tues, Thurs, 2 p.m.-6 p.m.,* ☎ *(064)83103.*

Diarmuid and Grainne's Bed, *W of Cullenagh Lake, near Drimoleague:* prehistoric chamber tomb.

Dinish Island, *in Castletownbere inner harbour:* connected to mainland by bridge.

Dunmanway, St Mary's Cemetery, grave of Sam Maguire after whom the All Ireland senior football championship cup is named. Swimming pool: indoor, heated, *Tues-Sun,* ☎ *(023)43328.*

Durrus, *11 km (7 miles) SW of Bantry:* ruins of early 17th c Durrus Court at start of Sheep's Head peninsula.

Dursey Sound, *cable car to Dursey Island: all year, Mon- Sat, 9 a.m.-11 a.m.; 2.30 p.m.-5 p.m. July, Aug, also 7 p.m.-8 p.m., details, inc. Sun times: James Sheehan, Ballagh Bay, Garinish,* ☎ *(027)73018.* On the island, there are few facilities and very limited accommodation. It has one tiny village, Kilmichael; the main attraction is walking the island's only road and going to see the old and new Bull Rock lighthouse at the W end.

Eyeries, *on L62 from Castletownbere:* from here on to Ardgroom and Lauragh, fine views of the Kenmare River estuary. The small village is quite desolate looking, but full of rugged character.

Falls of Donemarc, *3 km (2 miles) N of Bantry on N71 to Glengarriff:* path through woods runs very close to cascade on River Mealagh.

Garinish Island, *just offshore from Glengarriff:* marvellous Italian island gardens, with rare subtropical plants. Also shrubberies, miniature Japanese and rock gardens. From Grecian temple and old Martello Tower, splendid views. Boats to Garinish Island from The Pier, Blue Pool and Ellen's Rock on Castletownbere road. *Mar, Oct, Mon-Sat, 10 a.m.-4 p.m., Sun, 1 p.m.-5 p.m. Apr, May, June, Sept, Mon-Sat, 10 a.m.-6 p.m., Sun, 1 p.m.-7 p.m. Frequent boat connections from mainland; last landing 30 mins before closing time.* ☎*(027) 63040.*

Garnish Strand, *W tip of Beara peninsula:* good bathing.

Barley Cove, Co. Cork

5 km (3 miles) from village on Bantry road, ☎ *(027)63069. June- Sept.*

Gougane Barra lake, *24 km (15 miles) NE of Bantry off R584:* surrounded on three sides by mountains, source of the River Lee. Forest park in nearby valley (turn off T64 at Pass Keimaneigh). Walks, nature trail, St Finbarr's Oratory on island reached by causeway. Monument at Gougane Barra crossroads to poetess Máire Bhuí Ní Laoghaire, and grave of Tailor and Ansty (from Eric Cross's famous book, *The Tailor and the Ansty*) at Gougane Barra shore cemetery.

Healy Pass, best reached from Adrigole on the Beara peninsula. The road climbs for 11 km (7 miles) in a series of spiralling corkscrew turns, until the summit, from where there are incredible views on a clear day.

Hungry Hill, *5 km (3 miles) W of Adrigole:* waterfall on hill tumbles 230 m (770 ft). From mountain top, extensive view over most of Beara peninsula.

Inchigeelagh, *at E of Lough Allua:* good walks alongside River Lee and over adjoining hills. Riding: T. McCarthy, *Tír na Spideoga.* The R584 to Macroom has fine views of the Shehy Mountains.

Inchiquin Lough, *13 km (8 miles) SW of Kenmare, turn S off R571.* Forest walks amid striking scenery, good views of surrounding lakes and waterfall, car park, picnic area. *Inchiquin Waterfall, near Inchiquin Lough:* worth seeing, particularly in full flood. Best approached by minor road that leads off R571 near Cloonee Loughs.

Keamcorravoly, *3 km (2 miles) N of Ballingeary:* megalithic tomb off Ballyvourney Road. Permission: Michael Creed, farmer.

Kilmakillogue Harbour, *near Lauragh:* boats for hire from local publican for use in an almost totally enclosed harbour.

Kilmichael, *13 km (8 miles) NE of Dunmanway on R587:* memorial to War of Independence ambush. On Nov 28, 1920, Tom Barry and his West Cork Flying Column of 36 riflemen ambushed British Auxiliaries, killing 18; smaller stones mark main ambush positions.

Knockdrum Hill, *2 km (1 mile) NW of Castletownshend:* fine views over Castlehaven. Nearby ring fort.

Lough Hyne, *6 km (4 miles) S of Skibbereen, turn S beyond golf course on Skibbereen-Baltimore R593.* This enclosed lake, with a narrow outlet to the sea, is a marine nature reserve, with many rare species. Because of the sea urchins, bathing is not rec-ommended. A forest track near the N side of the lake leads to a fine vantage point.

Mizen Head, *reached by minor road off R591 at Goleen:* fine walk across headland summit, striking cliffscapes. **Brow Head,** *3 km (2 miles) SW of Crookhaven:* ruins of the radio station from which Marconi sent early transmissions to America.

Mount Gabriel, *3 km (2 miles) N of Schull:* good climb to top, passing futuristic satellite tracking station near summit. Wonderful views over Roaring Water and Dunmanus Bays. Bronze Age copper workings (NM).

Schull, *6 km (4 miles) SW of Ballydehob on R592.* Delightfully set around an almost totally enclosed harbour. *Planetarium,* only one in S of Ireland, has frequent shows. *Check times,* ☎ *(028)28552.* Popular sea angling venue. Bookshops, restaurants. Bicycles: The Black Sheep Inn, *Main Street,* ☎ *(028)28203.* Passenger ferry to Cape Clear Island. *June-Aug, daily, 2.30 p.m., returning 5.30 p.m. 10 km (6 mile) trip takes about an hour. Details:* Kieran Molloy, *Pier Road, Schull,* ☎ *(028)28138.* Also boats to Hare Island and Long Island, also in Roaring Water Bay. *O'Mahony's White Castle, 2 km (1 mile) from village off Ballydehob road:* 14th c ruins. Disused water mills. There is an interesting drive SW to Goleen and Crookhaven. From Goleen, with its secluded sandy beach, a choice of two routes to Mizen Head, through Crookhaven or directly across mountains.

Sheep's Head Peninsula, *extends for some 24 km (15 miles) SW of Bantry.* Minor road goes to Sheep's Head heights at end of peninsula. Beaches, near Kilcrohane and Ahakista villages on SE side. Walks: Goat's Path along NW coast.

Sherkin Island: *regular passenger boat from Baltimore at 12 noon, 2 p.m., 4 p.m., 6 p.m., 8 p.m. daily, June 1-Sept 30. Otherwise, 12 noon, 3 p.m. daily. Boat returns shortly after arrival. Details, Sherkin Marine Station,* ☎ *(028)20187.* O'Driscoll castle ruins, near landing place, and the ruins of 15th c Franciscan friary. Outdoor Pursuits Centre: wide variety of outdoor sports, ☎ *(028)20187.* Bathing: beyond church, *Silver Strand, Tragowenmore.*

Skibbereen, *34 km (21 miles) SW of Bantry, TIO:* ☎ *(028)21766, all year.* Pro-Cathedral dates from 1826. West Cork Arts Centre: Frequent Exhibitions. Bicycles: Roycroft's Stores, Ilen Street, ☎ *(028)21235 (21810 after hours).* Lissard Riding and Driving Club, ☎ *(028)21109.*

Union Hall: *Ceim Folk Museum.* Therese O'Mahony's one-woman, fascinating collection of historic artefacts. *Daily, by arr.* ☎ *(028)36280.*

Glengarriff, *18 km (11 miles) NW of Bantry on N71. TIO:* ☎ *(027)63084, July-Aug.* Small village delightfully set in a glen. Harbour is an inlet at NW head of Bantry Bay. In the early 19th c Eccles Hotel, George Bernard Shaw wrote part of his play, *St Joan.* The ground floor of the hotel has interesting historical photographs. Glengarriff and Garnish Boat Service, The Pier, ☎ *(027)63116.*

Glengarriff Woods, *just N of village:* nature trail. After completing this walk, cross the Carnarooska River by stepping stones of footbridge to continue along the far bank. For Carrigour Hill, take the second road branching E of Glengarriff, turn L again at dolmen, to emerge on Kenmare road. Cromwell's Bridge: short walk from village on Castletownbere road, attractive stroll among trees overhanging Glengarriff River. Lady Bantry's Lookout: 3 km (2 miles) from village on Castletownbere road, return by magnificent Shrone Hill viewpoint. Alternatively, walk beyond lookout to Eagle's Nest and return to seashore by Biddy's Cove, good bathing spot. Leary's Point by Bantry Road, about 8 km (5 miles). Poulgorm, take pathway to W of Post Office, a two minute walk giving very good views. O'Donoghue's Riding Stables,

Garinish Island, Co. Cork

Cork

Pop. 136,000, 87 km (54 miles) SE of Killarney, 207 km (129 miles) W of Rosslare, 259 km (161 miles) SW of Dublin. TIO, Grand Parade, ☎ (021)273251, all year. Bus timetable enquiries, ☎ (021)508188, Bus Travel Centre, ☎ (021)506066. Train timetable enquiries, ☎ (021)506766, Train Travel Centre, Patrick Street, ☎ (021)504888. Taxis: Patrick Street railway station, City tours, coach tours, details TIO. Youth Hostel: Western Road, ☎ (021)543289. Cork Tourist Hostel, Wellington Road, ☎ (021)505562.

The second city of the Republic is notoriously aware of its individuality, indeed few of the locals doubt that it is in fact Ireland's leading town. After a varied and chaotic history Cork emerged in the 19th c as a centre of the Fenian Movement, earning the title 'Rebel Cork', and suffering badly in the War of Independence, when two Lord Mayors died and a large portion of the centre was burned down. Today, it is a lively city with a keen sense of its own cultural identity. There is much of interest to see around the city centre and in the adjoining hilly districts. Cork Film Festival: *usually Oct,* ☎ *(021)271711, Fran Berginor TIO.* Jazz Festival: *Oct,* ☎ *(021)545782/ 294783.* Choral and Folk Dance Festival: *May,* ☎ *(021)502221.*

St Finbarre's Cathedral *(CI), near South Mall:* built in early French Gothic style just over 100 years ago. Fine carvings, mosaics. In S transept, see cannon ball fired in 1690 siege, found embedded in tower of site's previous church. **Christ Church,** *(now an archives centre) South Main Street:* built 1 702. Some of foundations date from Norman church, built about 1270 and badly mangled in 1690 seige. **Church of Christ the King** *(C), Turner's Cross, NW Cork:* one of most striking modern churches in Ireland. Stunning view of city from front. **Red Abbey,** *between George's Quay and Douglas Street:* only square tower left of mediae-

val abbey, the oldest piece of architecture in Cork. **St. Annes:** where would-be Quasimodos can peal the merry Shandon bells, *daily, all year.* **Honan Chapel,** *University College.* Built in 1915/16, with superb Harry Clarke and Sarah Purser stained glass windows. *Usually closed during vacations.*

Public Museum, *Fitzgerald's Park.* Natural history, old photographs, notably of 1916-1922 period, old documents, silver, small reference library. **Ogham Stone Collection,** *tours available, summer. All year, Mon-Fri, 11 a.m.-1 p.m.; 2.15 p.m.-5 p.m. Sun, 3 p.m.-5 p.m. June-Sept, Mon-Fri until 6 p.m. Closed BH weekends, inc Sun, all public holidays. University College. By app,* ☎ *(021)276871*

Triskel Arts Centre, *Tobin Street, off South Main Street, opp. TIO.* Exhibition area for paintings and sculptures, book shop, auditorium, restaurant, wine bar, ☎ *(021)272022.* Adjacent public park. **Crawford Municipal School of Art,** *Emmet Place:* many local scenes in oils and watercolours, sculptures, collection of classical casts from Vatican galleries, *Mon-Fri, 10 a.m.-5 p.m; Sat, 10 a.m.-1 p.m.* Restaurant. **Cork Arts Society Gallery,** *16 Lavitts Quay: Tues-Sat, 11 a.m.-6 p.m. Closed 2 p.m.-3 p.m.,* ☎ *(021)277749.* **Opera House,** *Emmet Place:* regular theatrical performances, ☎ *(021)270022.*

Granary Theatre, *University College:* regular term-time performances, ☎ *(021)276871.* **Everyman Palace Theatre,** *MacCurtain St.* This 19th c music hall theatre has been revived, ☎ *(021)501673.* **Cork School of Music,** *Union Quay:* regular evening concerts, *Wed, Fri, eve.,* ☎ *(021)270076/ 965583.*

Daly's Suspension Bridge, *Sunday's Well:* dates from early part of century, good river views. **South Gate Bridge,** *South Main Street:* atmospheric views of old quays. **Elizabeth Fort,** near Beamish & Crawford brewery. Built in early 17th c, with many changes of use since, the fort gives excellent views over the city. **Cork City Women's Gaol,** *Sunday's Well,* is being turned into a heritage centre, likely to include restored gallows. **Tanto Footbridge,**

adjoining Church of Annunciation, Blackpool: rebuilt 1946, origins of name obscure. Good views. **Carey's Lane,** *off Patrick Street.* Once the heart of Cork's Huguenot settlement, this pedestrianised street has many interesting craft and other shops, including Collins' bookshop. **An Sraidbhaile,** Grand Parade Hotel, *Grand Parade,* recreates Irish village life of 100 years ago. **Christ Church Lane,** *off Grand Parade:* one of oldest passageways in Cork, dating back 1,000 years. Heart of the medieval city. John Manley, 20 Greater William O'Brien Street, ☎ *(021) 508394:* traditional saddle making and repairing. **Shandon Craft Centre,** *opp. St Anne's Church.* St Patrick's Hill, *Patrick Street, far side of River Lee:* a steep climb rewarded by superb city views. **Kent Station:** 1848 steam engine built for Great Southern Railway. Withdrawn in 1874 after nearly half a million miles' service. **English Market,** *Prince's Street* in the city centre are well worth seeing, also **Coal Quay open air market,** *Cornmarket Street.* **Le Chateau,** *Patrick Street:* founded in 1793, often used by performers from nearby Opera House and journalists from the adjacent Cork Examiner. **An Bodhran,** *Oliver Plunkett Street:* atmospheric inn noted for its traditional Irish music. **Dan Lowrey's,** *MacCurtain Street:* old world atmosphere. Stained glass, period furniture. **The Vineyard,** *Market Lane, near Patrick Street:* unofficial home of Cork rugby. Other interesting Cork pubs: **Long Valley,** *Winthrop Street,* **O'Flynn's,** *Hanover Place* (both traditional style pubs); also try **Oyster Restaurant,** *Market Lane*—lots of old-fashioned atmosphere. **Lee Walk Fields:** riverside walk opp. County Hall. Quayside walks: good strolls upstream from city centre. University College: charming riverside walks in the lower grounds, access from Western Road. Marina Park: pleasant riverside walks on way to Blackrock, 3 km (2 miles) from city centre. **Fitzgerald Park,** two marvellous sculptures by Cork artist Seamus Murphy: Madonna of the Twilight and Michael Collins. **The Lough,** *off Lough Road, SW Cork,* fishing, wildlife habitat.

Leisure Activities: Swimming pools: indoor, heated: Gus Healy Pool, *Douglas,* ☎ *(021)293073, all year;*

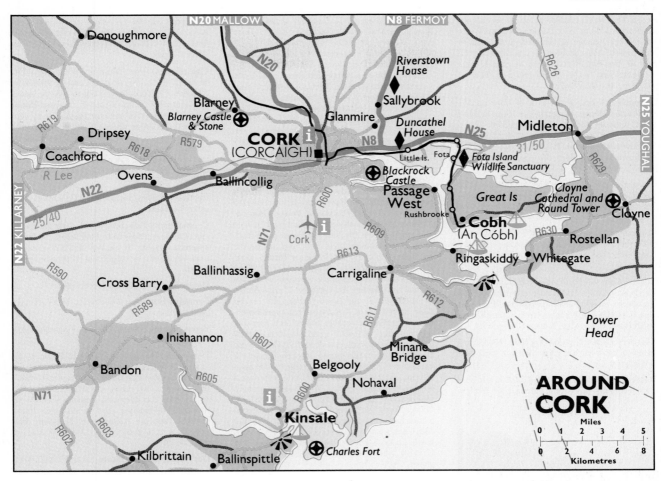

Matt Talbot Pool, *Churchfield, 2 bus from Patrick Street,* ☎ *(021)303931, all year; Mayfield Sports Complex, Old Youghal Road,* ☎ *(021)505284.* For details of all city sports facilities, contact Cork Corporation (environment section), ☎ *(021)966222, extn. 323/333.* Bicycles: Cycle Repair Centre, *6/7 Kyle Street,* ☎*(021)276255,* Cycle Scene, *Blarney Street,* ☎*(021)301183,* AA Bike Shop, *68 Shandon Street,* ☎ *(021)304154,* Carroll Cycles, *Dillon's Cross,* ☎ *(021)508923.* Skevanish Riding Centre, *Innishannon,* ☎ *(021)775476* Ballymaloe Riding Stables, ☎ *(021)652531.* Lee Rowing Club, ☎ *(021)966093.* Cork Boat Club, ☎ *(021)291258.* Douglas Golf Club, *18 holes,* ☎ *(021)291086.* Monkstown Golf Club, *18 holes,* ☎ *(021)841225.* Cork Golf Club, *18 holes,* ☎ *(021)821263.* Mahon Municipal Golf Club, ☎ *(021)362480.*

AROUND CORK

Ahenesk Castle, *5 km (3 miles) SW of Midleton;* medieval ruins overlooking Cork Harbour inlet.

Ballincollig, good 3 km (2 mile) walk from Powder Mills, along banks of River Lee, past weir to Inishcarra Castle. White Horse Inn: tudor style pub, with wooden beam ceilings, open fires. Ballincollig has a new riverside theme park, centred around the old gunpowder mills.

Ballymakeera/Ballyvourney, *13 km (8 km) NW of Macroom on N22:* Irish language and culture continues to flourish in the area of the twin villages.

Barryscourt Castle, *0.8 km (0.5 miles) S of Carrigtwohill on N25:* strategically sited within Cork Harbour, extensive late medieval ruins. Craft shop and tearooms, ☎ *(021)883864.*

Blarney Castle and Stone, *8 km (5 miles) NW of Cork on L69.* Climb 120 steps to battlements to kiss the stone and win the gift of the gab. If you're the strong, silent type, admire views of lush countryside. Good walks in castle grounds, including Rock

Close, grove of ancient trees said to have been centre of Druid worship. *All year, daily, from 9 a.m. Closing time varies; June, July, Aug, 7.30 p.m.* ☎ *(021) 385252.* Riverside walks and waterfall. Blarney castle is a fully restored 19th c house designed in the Scottish baronial style, with fully refurbished interior. *Gardens open all year, daily, from 9 a.m. Summer closing is at 8.30 p.m.; in winter, closing is at sundown. The castle is open June-Sept, Mon-Sat, 12 noon-6 p.m* ☎ *(021)385252.* **Blarney Woollen Mills,** *across the village green,* is an impressive shop converted from a 19th c factory.

Carrigaline, *10 km (6 miles) S of Cork:* **Carrigdhoun Pottery,** *tours by arr.* ☎ *(021)372305.*

Carrigrohane Castle, *3 km (2 miles) E of Ballincollig:* 14th/16th c ruins.

Cloyne, *29 km (18 miles) SE of Cork:* once an ancient royal seat, now a sleepy village nestling amid E Cork hills. *Cloyne Cathedral* (CI): restored 14th c building has monument to one time bishop of Cloyne and famous philosopher, George Berkeley. *Cloyne Round Tower, opp. cathedral:* built around 900, still in good condition. Key from house in corner of cathedral grounds. Small charge.

Coachford, *22 km (14 miles) W of Cork on R618:* fine view of River Lee valley.

Cobh, *8 km (5 miles) E of Cork on Great Island, Trains from Cork:* St Colman's Cathedral (C). Impressive 19th c Gothic revival style. Regular carillon recitals in summer, fine views over harbour from entrance. *Cobh Museum:* housed in former Presbyterian 'Scots' church. Many items relating to district: maritime relics. *All year, Sun, 3 p.m.-6 p.m. Also May-Sept, Wed, 3 p.m.-6 p.m.* ☎ *(021)811562.* *Queenstown Experience,* due to open in 1993, will be a vast heritage centre based around the railway station, highlighting Cobh's past emigrant links. Annie Moore's statue at Deepwater Quay depicts the first emigrants to leave Queenstown a century ago. *Lusitania Memorial, quayside.* Hundreds of

'Lusitania' victims are buried in Cobh's Old Church cemetery. Cork Harbour trips: Marine Transport, *Cobh,* ☎ *(021)811485.* Ballywilliam Riding Centre, ☎ *(021)811908/811932.* Swimming pool: indoor, heated, *Carrignafoy, daily,* ☎ *(021)811786.* **Cobh Folk Festival,** *July.*

Coolea, *near Ballymakeera:* Seán Ó Riada, composer and musician, d. 1971, lived here the last few years of his life.

Crosshaven, *27 km (17 miles) SE of Cork.* Delightful seaside village, a favourite with Cork visitors. The narrow main street has interesting pubs and shops. From here, walk up the hill behind the village to St Brigid's C church, for views over the harbour. Royal Cork yacht club, dating back to 1720, is the world's oldest. Bicycle Hire, Barry Twomey, *"Whispering Pines",* ☎ *(021)831843.*

Currabinny, *across Owenboy River from Crosshaven, entrance 6 km (4 miles) E of Carrigaline, turn L off L66 at Carrigaline Catholic church:* nature trail, scenic views, Giant's Grave Bronze Age burial cairn, car park, picnic area.

Dún Ui Mheachair, fort, built 1798 on headland overlooking vast sweep of Cork Harbour. Bathing: Church Bay, Grall Bay, Myrtleville Bay, Robert's Cove (sandy beach near Carrigaline), Weaver's Point.

Fort Camden, *3 km (2 miles) NE of Crosshaven:* great fortifications built at end of 18th c on S side of Ram's Head. Fine harbour views. Not open to the public, but a military museum is planned.

Fota Island, *10 km (6 miles) E of Cork.* The wildlife park has many species, like antelope and giraffes. A tour train runs daily in the summer season. The arboretum is one of the finest in Ireland, with many trees and shrubs from all over the world. *Fota House* was built in the Regency style in the 1820s and its interiors have been richly recreated, with many examples of 18th and 19th c Irish furniture. The Irish landscape paintings on view are dated from 1750 to 1870. Despite the plans for extensive development of Fota island, the wildlife park and the house will remain unspoiled. *Mar17-Sept 10, Mon-Sat, 10 a.m.-5.15 p.m. Sun, 11 a.m.-5.15 p.m. Sept 11-Oct 30, Sat and Sun, 11 a.m.-5.15 p.m. ☎ (021)812678.*

Glanmire, *6 km (4 miles) E of Cork on N8.* **Dunkathel House,** attractive late 18th c building full of antiques and paintings. *May-Sept, Thurs-Sat, 2 p.m.-6 p.m., or by arr. ☎ (021)821014.* **Riverstown House,** built 1602, rebuilt 1745, fine plasterwork, art gallery, *May-Sept, Wed-Sun, 2 p.m.-6 p.m. or by arr., ☎ (021)821014.*

Glenday, *9 km (6 miles) N of Macroom on R582,* then 2 m (3 km) W of Carriganimmy on unclassified road: extensive forest walks amid impressive scenery.

Inniscarra, *11 km (7 miles) W of Cork on T29:* Sean O'Riordain, one of Ireland's greatest modern poets, commemorated by plaque on family house at Garravagh.

Kilcrea Abbey, *8 km (5 miles) SW of Ballincollig:* with grave of Noble Art O'Leary, murdered in 1773 because he wouldn't sell his mare for £5. At that time, Catholics were prevented from owning a horse worth more. *Opp. abbey,* Kilcrea Castle ruins.

Kilmurry, *27 km (17 miles) W of Cork.* MacSwiney memorial museum has many items of local folklore interest. *By arr.*

Macroom, *37 km (24 miles) W of Cork.* Lively mid-Cork town once property of Admiral Sir William

Fitzgerald Park, Cork

Penn, whose son founded the American state of Pennsylvania. Penn Castle mostly demolished, entrance stands at one side of town square.

Midleton, *22 km (14 miles) E of Cork:* **Irish Distillers** has turned the old distillery building, used for whiskey making between 1825 and 1975, into a fine industrial heritage centre. *May-Oct, daily, 10 a.m.-4 p.m., or by arr. ☎ (021)631821.*

Mullaghanish Mountain, *N of Ballyvourney:* from top, near RTE transmitting mast, superb views of surrounding countryside. Easily accessible by road.

Rostellan, *5 km (3 miles) W of Cloyne at E edge of Cork Harbour:* old stone bridge with three ancient milestones telling distance to almost every place in Ireland. **Rostellan Forest,** *turn W off Midleton-Whitegate road at Farsid:* forest, seashore walks, car park, picnic area.

Trabolgan Holiday Centre, *Midleton, Co. Cork, ☎ (021)661579.*

Tracton, *6 km (3 miles) S of Carrigaline on R611:* enter by 'Overdraft' pub for extensive forest walks.

Killarney

Pop. 9,000, 32 km (20 miles) SE of Tralee, 87 km (54 miles) NW of Cork, 109 km (68 miles) SW of

Limerick, *305 km (190 miles)) SW of Dublin. EC Mon. In summer, most shops ignore it. TIO: Town Hall, all year, ☎ (064)31633. Bus enquiries: ☎ (064)34777, train enquiries: ☎(064)31067. Taxis: College Square. Coach tours: SO, daily.*

At first glance a rather undistinguished town, very touristy in summer, Killarney is nevertheless a busy and likeable place, with plenty happening at most levels of cultural interest. It owes its fame almost entirely to its situation in the heart of Ireland's beautiful lake district, for which it's the perfect touring centre. *Killarney regatta: July.* Kerry Boating Carnival: *Sept.*

Cathedral of St Mary of the Assumption (C), *New Street:* designed by Pugin, great 19th c architect and recently renovated. & **St Mary's parish church** (CI), *Main Street:* richly decorated Victorian interior. **Prince of Peace Church,** *Fossa:* modern church designed and built by men and women from the four provinces of Ireland. Main door has delightful dove and ark motifs by Helen Moloney. **Franciscan friary,** *Fair Hill, College Street:* dates from 1860. Fine Harry Clarke stained glass window over main entrance. **Killarney Art Gallery,** *47 High Street, ☎ (064)34628.* **Frank Lewis Gallery,** *6 Bridewell Lane, ☎ (064)31570.* **Killarney Transport Treasures,** collection of vintage and veteran cars and memorabilia. *All year, daily, 10.30 a.m.-6.30 p.m.(winter), 8 p.m.(summer). ☎ (064)32638.* **Ross Castle,** on peninsula jutting into Lough Leane, 3 km (2 miles) SW of town, off N71: remains of magnificent 15th c keep. From Ross Castle, waterbuses leave at regular intervals during the summer for a tour of Lough Leane. *☎ (064)32638.* **Speir Bhan,** *College Street:* the foot of Seamus Murphy's statue is inscribed with the names of the great 17th and 18th c Kerry poets. Old Market Lane, Barry's Lane, Green Lane, Bóithrin Caol (Narrow Lane), and Brewery Lane (off Kenmare Place), are very atmospheric. The Knockreer Estate, off Cathedral Place, has pleasant walks, excellent views of Lough Leane. Bridle and cycle paths. *Open at all times.*

Leisure Activities: Jaunting car: time-honoured way of seeing the area's sights. *Check prices at TIO.* Fair Green fun fair, amusement park: *nightly, July, Aug.* Kerry Glass, *Fair Hill:* glass blowing and moulding. *Mon-Fri, 8 a.m.-1 p.m.; 2 p.m.-4 p.m.* Adjacent shop, *☎ (064)32587.* Kerry Woollen Mills, *Beaufort: Mon-Fri, 8.30 a.m.-1 p.m.; 2 p.m.-5 p.m. Sat by app., ☎ (064)44122.* Racecourse, *Ross Road. May, July, Oct, ☎ (064)31860/31125.* Boat hire: Ross Castle, *details: H. Clifton, ☎ (064)32252.* Swimming pool: indoor, heated, for non-residents at Gleneagle Hotel, *☎ (064)31870,* Great Southern Hotel, *☎ (064)31262,* Killarney Park Hotel, *☎ (064)35555,* Killarney Riding School, *Ballydowney, ☎ (064)31686:* The Arch Farm, *Tralee Road, ☎ (064)33149.* Rocklands Riding School, *Tralee Road, ☎ (064) 32592.* Bicycles: O'Callaghans, *College Street, ☎ (064)31465.* Killarney Golf Club, *Mahony's Point, 18 holes, ☎ (064)31034.* Youth Hostel: *☎ (064)31240.*

AROUND KILLARNEY

Abbey Island, *Derrynane Bay:* remains of early Christian monastery. A short walk across at low tide.

Aghadoe Hill, *5 km (3 miles) N of Killarney:* ruins of 7th c church and castle, superb views of Killarney lakes and mountains.

Ballinskelligs, *facing Waterville across Ballinskelligs Bay.* Irish-speaking resort. Miles of golden beaches, ideal for surfing.

Baslicon Dolmen, *3 km (2 miles) S of Waterville, off N70:* nearby, fine standing stone.

Beenbane Fort, *W shore of Lough Currane:* horseshoe-shaped prehistoric structure. Before you reach fort, beehive huts with 2 m (7 ft) thick walls.

Black Valley, *6 km (4 miles) SW of Lough Leane:* Youth Hostel.

Caherdaniel, *16 km (10 miles) SE of Cahirciveen,* attractively set village. Walk: NW of Eagle Hill as far as Lamb's Head for excellent views of Kenmare River estuary.

Cahirciveen, *40 km (25 miles) E of Killarney, TIO: ☎ (0667) 2141, July-Aug.* **O'Connell Memorial Church** (C), *Main Street,* built in 1888 to honour the memory of Daniel O'Connell. **Carhan House,** *1.5 km (1 miles) NE of Cahirciveen, just off main N70:* ruins of house where O'Connell, 'The Liberator', was born in 1775. The old RIC barracks, beside the river, has been turned into a heritage centre, which tells the story of the Valentia Weather Observatory and Daniel O'Connell. Local history, arts and crafts.

Castlecove, *5 km (3 miles) NE of Caherdaniel:* fine sandy beaches.

Coomanaspig Pass, *5 km (3 miles) S of Portmagee:* one of highest places in Ireland accessible by car, spectacular views. If you continue SW, a narrow road winds down to magnificent S facing St Finan's Beach.

Coomshane, *near Kells:* forest walks.

Cromane Strand, *8 km (5 miles) W of Killorglin:* good bathing.

Cross Strand, *6 km (4 miles) W of Kenmare:* good bathing.

Derrynane House and National Park, *1.5 km (1 mile) W of Caherdaniel on N70:* home of Daniel O'Connell restored as museum, with period furnishings and personal relics. Audio visual show, tearoom. Park has exceptional coastal scenery, nature trail, sea bathing. *Park open all year. House, Oct-Apr, Tues-Sun, 1 p.m.-5 p.m.; May-Sept, Mon-Sat, 10 a.m.-6 p.m.; Sun, 11 a.m.-7 a.m., ☎ (0667)5113.*

Derrynane Ogham Stone, *1.5 km (1 mile) SW of Caherdaniel on Derrynane road:* transferred here from below the waterline, this does not mean, however, that the country is capsizing! Walk, along 'Smuggler's Path' from Derrynane to Bunavalla pier.

Dromore, *10 km (6 miles) W of Kenmare on N70:* forest walks overlooking Kenmare Bay, seashore walk, car park, picnic area.

Druid's Circle, *1.5 km (1 mile) SW of Kenmare, off Market Street:* 15 prehistoric standing stones.

Dunloe Castle, *10 km (6 miles) W of Killarney off T67,13th c ruins in hotel grounds, nearby ogham stones.*

Farranfore, *16 km (10 miles) N of Killarney:* Kerry Airport, flying, parachuting lessons. Charter a plane for unusual views of Kerry, *☎ (066)64350.*

Foileye Bay, *near Kells:* good bathing.

Gap of Dunloe, *start at Kate Kearney's cottage, 1.5 (1 miles) S of Dunloe Castle Hotel.* Magnificent 11 km (7 mile) trip by pony or pony and trap. The passage is bordered by a string of dark tarns, with something interesting at almost every turn of the track. Bar at Kate Kearney's cottage. Nearby café. Pony trekking, *☎ (064)44116/44146.*

If you can afford to take it in style, hire a jaunting car at Killarney, as far as Kate Kearney's cottage. Then go through the Gap of Dunloe by pony or trap and pony, by the Logan Stone, as far as the Upper Lake. From here, the Gap boats take you through the Long Range of the Meeting of the Waters, where you shoot the rapids and go across Lough Leane to Ross Castle. From the castle, a jaunting car will take you back to Killarney. About 40 km (25 miles).

Glenbeigh, *8 km (5 miles) SE of Killorglin:* small fishing village. Flapper (horse) races, *last week July.* The bar of the Towers Hotel has historic photographs of the village taken at the turn of the century, including the railway that ran from Tralee to Cahirciveen. **Kerry Bog Museum** has traditional 19th c houses, turf cutting, blacksmith's forge.

Ladies' View, Co. Kerry

Daily. Good bathing on the strand. Forest walks off nearby Rossbeigh road. Hill climbing paths on Seefin Mountain to SE. Panoramic views of Dingle Bay and peninsula. Good climbs on near by Curra Mountain. Enjoyable walk following glen of River Beigh to tarn that is source of river. Splendid views of 'Glenbeigh Horseshoe' amphitheatre of mountains. Coomacarea, 774 m (2,541 ft) is an excellent viewpoint. Bicycles: John O'Sullivan, the Garage, ☎ *(066)68207.* Dooks Golf Club, *18 holes,* ☎ *(066)68205.*

Gortboy, Corran Tuathail Youth Hostel, ☎ *(064)44187.*

Inishfallen Island, *1.5 km (1 mile) from Ross Castle:* near landing stage are ruins of abbey, dating from about 600. Annals of Innisfallen, chronicle of Irish and world history, written in Irish and Latin here between 950 and 1320. Now in Bodleian Library, Oxford.

Kells, *midway between Glenbeigh and Cahirciveen, off N70.* Panoramic views of Dingle Bay, Blasket Islands, Kells Bay. Abandoned railway tunnels at Drung Hill and Gleensk Viaduct, relics of old GSR railway that ran from Cahirciveen to Farranfore Junction. Kells Bay: good bathing.

Kenmare, *34 km (21 miles) S of Killarney on N71. EC Thurs. TIO:* ☎ *(064)41233.* Delightfully set where River Roughty opens into Kenmare River estuary. The three main streets of the town form a triangle; there is also an agreeable green. Kenmare is backed by fearsome mountains. Designated as a heritage town, Kenmare's heritage centre, detailing local history, should be ready in 1993. Bathing from pier, also off Glengarriff road on outskirts of town. Surfing equipment at pier. Bicycles: John P. Finnegan, *Henry Street,* ☎ *(064)41083;* Kenmare Golf Club, 9 holes, ☎ *(064)41291.*

Killarney National Park, *5 km (3 miles) S of Killarney on N71:* wonderful walks. Keep a lookout for deer and a fine herd of pedigree Kerry cattle. *Open at all times.*

Killeenagh Strand, *8 km (5 miles) W of Kenmare:* good bathing.

Killorglin, *21 km (13 miles) W of Killarney on T67. EC Wed.* Hilly town overlooking River Laune. Rather desolate looking, but full of warm, quixotic Kerry character. Puck Fair: three days and nights of drink and revelry as tens of thousands of people crowd in to see a mountain goat crowned 'King' of the fair and enjoy the free flow of Guinness, *Aug.* Nearby Caragh Lake area has forest walks, viewing points. Bicycles: J. O'Shea, *Bridge Street,* ☎ *(066)61180. Conway castle:* 12th c ruins. Also see ogham stones, caves and forts in vicinity.

Kilreilrig, *near Ballinskelligs, far W of Iveragh peninsula:* village abandoned some 20 years ago, cottages built with their backs to the westerly winds, without doors or windows on that side, to keep out ocean spray. Local barracks once used by Royal Irish Constabulary; design is Moorish. A craft village and crafts centre is being built. Kilreilrig stone fort: *on road from Ballinskelligs to Bolus Head.*

Kimego, *6 km (3 miles) N of Cahirciveen via Castlequin village:* forest walks, sea views, ruins of 18th c turf drying plant.

Ladies' View, *19 km (12 miles) SW of Killarney on N71.* Over a century ago, Queen Victoria and her ladies-in-waiting were enchanted by the view, hence the name. Nearby tearoom.

Leacanabuaile Fort, *5 km (3 miles) NW of Cahirciveen, access by minor road to Cooncrome Harbour:* massive fort of uncertain date, excellent interior. Fine coastal views from ramparts.

Lickeen Forest, *S end of Lough Caragh on lakeside road to Killorglin to Ballaghbeama:* scenic walks, lay-by, picnic area.

Loo Bridge, *6 km (4 miles) SE of Lough Guitane,* Youth Hostel, ☎ *(064)53002.*

Lough Caragh, *near Glenbeigh:* 10 km (6 mile) walk round W and N shores and lake.

Lough Currane, near S shore, by road to Tooreens, (cul-de-sac), you can see part of intriguing submerged castle. If walking, you can continue from Tooreens over mountain path to Sneem, *11 km (7 miles).*

Macgillicuddy's Reeks, excellent climbing, including Carrantuohill, Ireland's highest mountain. *Details,* Sean O'Sullivan, Killarney Mountaineering Club, *Langford Street, Killorglin,* ☎ *(066)61127.*

Mangerton, *8 km (5 miles) S of Killarney on N71, turn L at Muckross Hotel:* mountain walks, panoramic lake views, car park, picnic area.

Meeting of the Waters, *10 km (6 miles) SW of Killarney on Kenmare road:* picturesque spot, where luxuriant plants and shrubs flourish in the particularly mild Kerry climate.

Milltown, *6 km (4 miles) NE of Killorglin:* ruins of 13th c Kilcoman Abbey. Also large prehistoric circular fort.

Muckross House and folk museum, *7 km (4 miles) S of Killarney, off N71:* built in Elizabethan style in 1843. Many of its rooms retain Victorian furnishings. Museum of Kerry folklife has locally carved period furniture, maps, tools of trades and crafts (some now extinct), old printing presses, coins and natural history section. In basement craft centre, you can see weaver, blacksmith and potter at work. A pub in the basement is re-created in the 19th c style and there is also an old-fashioned printer's workshop, with old presses and hand-set type.

Gap of Dunloe, Co. Kerry

Country Life Experience brings to life Kerry rural life in early 20th c, with buildings, farming and craft practices. Magnificent gardens, with nature trails and exquisite rock garden. Excellent views of surrounding lakes, mountains and woodlands. Allow at least half day to tour house and gardens . *Nov-Mar, daily, 9 a.m.-5.30 p.m. Mid Mar-June, daily, 9 a.m.-6 p.m. July, Aug, daily, 9 a.m.-7 p.m. Sept, Oct, daily, 9 a.m.-6 p.m.,* ☎ *(064)31440.*

Muckross Abbey, *just N of park off N71:* mid-15th c ruins in good repair. Old Kenmare Road, *starts near House:* good walk across mountains to Kenmare just E of present road. Mangerton Track: *starts near House,* climbs for about 5 km (3 miles) to near Devil's Punch Bowl.

Our Lady's Holy Well, *off Killarney road, 1.5 km (1 mile) N of Kenmare:* waters reputed to have healing powers.

Parknasilla, *3 km (2 miles) S of Sneem, entrance 1.5 km (1 mile) E of Great Southern Hotel, off N70:* pleasant walks through woods, good views of surrounding bay, safe bathing in nearby coves, picnic area. Parknasilla Golf Club, *9 holes.*

Pass of Coomakista, *between Caherdaniel and Waterville:* fine views of Ballinskelligs Bay and Skelligs rocks.

Peter and Paul's Holy Well, *3 km (2 miles) N of Kilgarvan on Mangerton road.* On June 29, local people circle well, reciting prayers.

Rossdohan Island, *5 km (3 miles) SE of Sneem, S of N70:* delightful gardens, wonderful trees, including cypresses. Many botanical wonders. *By arr.,* ☎ *(064)45114.*

Sheen Falls, *3 km (2 miles) from Kenmare on Glengarriff road:* 'must' for visitors to area. Sheen Falls luxury hotel worth a detour for afternoon tea or longer stay.

The Skelligs, *two rock islets 13 km (8 miles) out to sea, off Bolus Head. Make arrangements with a boatman in either Ballinskelligs, Cahirciveen, Knightstown Harbour on Valentia Island or Waterville.* Little Skellig is uninhabited: landing is rarely possible. Landing on Great Skellig is very difficult and only possible in calm weather. Be careful if taking a boat - insurance cover can be a problem. Cliff pathways rise to a 7th c monastic settlement: church, two oratories, six beehive cells. If you are an experienced climber, you can go as far as cross carved in the 'summit', a hazardous ascent indeed. A visit to Great Skellig is probably the most memorable experience to be had in Co. Kerry. *The Skellig Experience* is a worthwhile substitute.

Sneem, *17 km (11 miles) E of Kenmare:* charmingly situated where estuary of Ardsheelaun River flows into Kenmare River, noted angling centre. Safe sandy beaches. The short pier is ideal for a short stroll. In the two impressive squares, Chaim Herzog, the Dublin-born president of Israel and Ceabhaill Ó Dalaigh, a former president of Ireland. Sneem has a small village museum. *St Michael's* (C) has grave of Fr Michael Walsh, the Father O'Flynn of the famous song. *Church of the Transfiguration* (CI), dates from Elizabethan times. The interior has fine photographs of the former 'big houses' in the vicinity. Bicycles: Michael Burns, *North Square,* ☎ *(064)45140.*

Staigue Fort, *3 km (2 miles) NE of Castlecove:* probably finest Iron Age fort in Ireland, N side in perfect condition; stairways run inside the walls. The entire fort is in almost perfect condition; stairways run inside the walls. Accessible at all times.

Torc Waterfall, *8 km (5 miles) S of Killarney, just S of main Killarney-Kenmare road:* one of finest in Ireland. Climb up footpath that wends upwards alongside waterfall. Magnificent lake views. Signposted.

Valentia Island, *11 km (7 miles) long, 3 km (2 miles) wide: connected to mainland by bridge at Portmagee. Car or bike essential, no public transport. Skellig Experience.* The visitor centre on Valentia Island uses modern audio-visual techniques to tell the story of the Skellig islands; visitors then take a 1½ hour trip round the islands on a purpose-built boat. *Easter-Sept, daily, 9.30 a.m.- 7 p.m. Three cruises daily. Details,* ☎ *(066)76306.* Magnificent cliffs and seascapes and profusion of sub-tropical flowers and shrubs. Valentia Regatta: highlight is traditional seine (fishing) boat race, *Aug. Knightstown,* the island's main settlement, has an attractive harbour, and lots of atmosphere. Site of now-disused Western Union Cable Station where the first trans-Atlantic cable was joined in 1866. Knightstown slate quarry, now disused, with its magnificent grotto, has fine views of harbour and Dingle peninsula. *Bray Head,* SW tip of island, 241 m (792 ft), excellent views. *Geokaun Mountain, on N,* 268 m (880 ft) excellent vantage point. Beginish Island, off Valentia and half covered by sand is good for bathing. Adjacent Church Island has ruins of early monastic settlement. Youth Hostel, ☎ *(0667)6154.* Bicycles from hostel.

Waterville, *W edge of Iveragh peninsula:* popular resort town, and noted angling centre. The Butler Arms Hotel has fascinating photographs in its entrance showing Charlie Chaplin, the American film comedian, who was a regular visitor to Waterville for the fishing. Fine sandy beaches. Inland from the village, the lakeside drive beside Lough Currane leads into wild countryside, before petering out in the mountains. Fine sandy beaches. Salmon and trout festival and regatta, *late July, early Aug.* Boat hire: ☎ *(0667)7101.* Vincent O'Sullivan, 'Southview'; P. Donnelly, *Lake Road:* Jim Quinlan, ☎ *(0667)4232.* Car tours: G. Cronin, ☎ *(0667)4294;* A. McGillycuddy, ☎ *(0667)4252.* Bicycles: Jim Quinlan, *the village,* ☎ *(0667)4232,* Waterville Golf Club, *18 holes,* ☎ *(0667)4261.*

White Strand, *5 km 93 miles) SW of Cahirciveen:* good bathing and surfing.

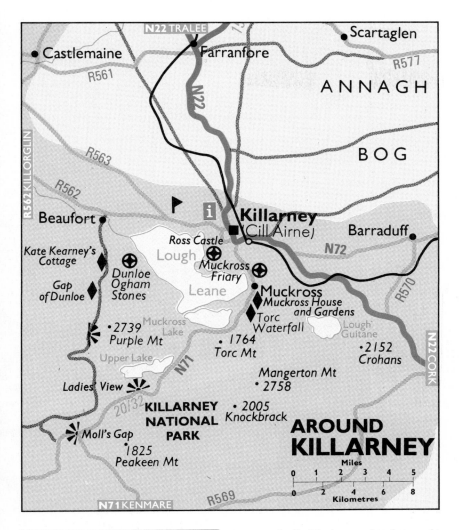

AROUND KILLARNEY

Kinsale

Pop. 1,700, 29 km (18 miles) S of Cork, 35 km (22 miles) NE of Clonakilty, 288 km (179 miles) SW of Dublin. EC Thurs. TIO, ☎ (021)772234. June-Sept. Bus enquiries: Bus Eireann, Cork, ☎ (021)508188.

Extravagantly beautiful town overlooking the Bandon estuary, a consistent winner in Tidy Town competitions. Kinsale has a strong Spanish flavour. Its narrow, winding streets have been compared to those of Toledo; in 1601-2 a Spanish force took the town and held it against English armies.

Recaptured, and anglicised, Kinsale became one of the chief ports of the British navy. In recent years it has happily enjoyed a more peaceful prosperity, it now boasts a number of gourmet restaurants and is one of Ireland's major sea angling centres. Autumn Gourmet Festival: feast of good eating and drinking in Kinsale's many bistros and restaurants, *Oct, ☎ (021)772443.*

St Multose Church (CI): built 1190, subsequently enlarged. In fine interior, see old town stocks and flags carried at Battle of Waterloo. Three victims of the 'Lusitania', torpedoed off Old Head of Kinsale in May, 1915, are buried in graveyard. *Daily, ☎(021)772220. St John the Baptist Church* (C), *Friar's Street:* ornate, T-shaped 19th c church with interesting slate memorials. *Carmelite Friary, Carmel Avenue:* excellent views from front of friary. *Kinsale Museum, Old Town Hall:* among exhibits in 17th c building, model of HMS Kinsale, local lace and silver, photographs, maps and several of the famous all-enveloping Kinsale cloaks. Also charters granted to the town by Elizabeth I in 1590 and James I in 1610. The 'giant' Patrick Cotter O'Brien (1760-1806), who found fame and for-

tune on the English stage, was born here: see his slippers, outsize boots, gigantic knife and fork. *All year, Mon-Sat, 11 a.m.-5 p.m.; Sun, 3 p.m.-5 p.m. Or by arr, ☎ (021)772044. Desmond Castle:* 16th c tower house, known as the 'French Prison', recently restored. *Bowling Green:* small, treelined public park on flat ground half-way up the hill overlooking the harbour.

Walks: Compass Hill: start on S heights of Kinsale above the Trident Hotel. The road follows semi-circular route for about 3 km (2 miles), giving excellent views of harbour and estuary before bringing you back to the town. Scilly: walk along harbour, past new marina, for about 1.5 km (1 mile) to tiny 'suburb' of Scilly. Stop off at old-world 'Spaniard' pub, with attractive interior decor, including súgán (Irish-style rope) chairs, wooden beam ceilings and mahogany fittings.

Leisure Activities: Kinsale Angling Centre, *Lower O'Connell Street:* fishing tackle, boats, ☎ *(021)72611, or 75241 after hours.* For small boats for use in harbour only: (021)72242/72301. Bicycles: Mylie Murphy, *Pearse Street, ☎ (021)772703;* Coolcorrow Equestrian Centre, ☎ *(021)71353.* Golf Club, *9 holes, ☎ (021)72197.*

AROUND KINSALE

Ballinascarthy, *8 km (5 miles) N of Clonakilty on N71:* birthplace of Henry Ford, founder of American motor industry.

Ballycatteen ring fort, *4 m (6 km) SW of Kinsale:* remains of circular prehistoric fort. From top, good views of nearby Ballinspittle village.

Bandon, *21 km (13 miles) NW of Kinsale, EC Thurs. Bus enquiries:* ☎*(021)508188.* Good salmon and sea trout angling centre. Agricultural Show,

late May. **Kilbrigan Church** (CI), built 1610, has old town stocks. *Heritage Centre,* in former Christchurch (CI) has historical exhibitions on locality. *June-Sept, Mon-Sat, 10 a.m.-6 p.m.; Sun, 2 p.m.-6 p.m. ☎ (023)44193.* R. & J. Forrester craft shop and gallery, *83 North Main Street:* pottery made in workshop. *All year, Mon-Sat, 10 a.m.-6 p.m., ☎ (023)41360.* Bicycle hire: Jerry O'Donovan, *4 South Main Street, ☎ (023)41227.*

Béal-na-mBláth, *3 km (2 miles) SW of Crookstown on L41:* memorial to General Michael Collins, killed here in 1922.

Charles Fort, *near Summer Cove on E shore of Kinsale harbour:* magnificent ruin of 1677 sea fort, occupied until British left in 1922. Dungeons, armouries, arches and buildings, most atmospheric. *Mid Apr-mid June, Tues-Sat, 9 a.m.-4.30 p.m., Sun, 11 a.m.-5.30 p.m. Mid June-mid Sept, daily, 9 a.m.-6 p.m. Mid Sept-early Oct, Mon-Sat, 9 a.m.-5 p.m., Sun, 10 a.m.-5 p.m. Guided tours. ☎ (021)772263.*

Clonakilty, *35 km (22 miles) SW of Kinsale. EC Wed. TIO: ☎ (023)33226.* Good sea angling centre at head of Clonakilty Bay. The town with its winding streets, has many shop fronts with their names in Irish. *The Wheel of Fortune* is an extravagant cast iron concoction, dating from the start of the town's water supply, about 1840. The old railway station can be seen, once part of the West Cork Railway System. *Lisnagun Fort:* site of early Christian ring fort. Visitor centre being developed to show the locality in those times. *Model village:* many facets of local life will be shown in model form, including the old West Cork railway and the town's industrial heritage as it stood in the 1940's. *Details: ☎ (023)33380.* West Cork Festival, *end June, beginning July. Details: TIO ☎ 023-33226, July/ Aug.* 100 year old pure Gothic Catholic church, stained glass and statuary worth seeing. *June-early Sept.* **West Cork Regional Museum,** *Western Road, opposite Vocational School:* archaeological relics, industrial mementoes, especially from the post office and the old West Cork railway that once ran through the town, records of social life and much material on Michael Collins. *June-Sept. Mon-Sat, 10.30 a.m.-12.30 p.m.; 3 p.m.-5 p.m. Closed Sun.* Georgian houses, *Emmet Square.* Nearby Kennedy Gardens, a mass of flowers. Riding: West Cork Travel Agency, *Rossa Street, ☎ (023)43220.* Bicycles: MTM Cycles, *33 Ashe Street, ☎ (023)33584.*

Coppinger's Court, *3 km (2 miles) SW of Rosscarbery:* ruin of 1610 mansion burned down 30 years later. According to legend, it had a chimney for every month, a door for every week and a window for every day of the year.

Courtmacsherry, *just W of Courtmacsherry Bay:* attractive seaside village backed by woods. Hotel has interesting historical provenance. Sea angling centre.

Drombeg Stone Circle, *3 km (2 miles) E of Glandore:* one of finest West Cork circles, dating from 150 BC. Layout, information signs on site.

Garretstown, good beaches on shores of Courtmacsherry Bay. *1.5 km (1 mile) W of O'Neill's Hotel on unclassified road to Kilbrittain:* woodland walks, picnic place, car park. See remains of 'Big House', including orangery.

Glandore, *6 km (4 miles) W of Rosscarbery.* Beautifully set village looking over Glandore harbour. The higher part of the village, with its broad street, gives fine views of the harbour.

Inchadoney Island, *3 km (2 miles) S of Clonakilty.* Despite its name, part of mainland. Noted for long, golden sands, ideal for bathing and surfing. Strand divided by grass-topped hill called Virgin Mary's Bank.

Innishannon, *13 km (8 miles) NW of Kinsale on R6083.* Ruined Dundaniel Castle, built in 1476 on banks of river Bandon, amid luxuriant foliage and woodlands.

Kinsale, Co. Cork

James's Fort, *opp. Charles Fort, first bridge over Bandon River from Kinsale, turn E for 3 km (2 miles)* built about 1601/2, ruins include well-preserved remains of blockhouse at water level, explore with care.

Kilbrittain, *11 km (7 miles) NW of Clonakilty:* pleasantly situated village, forest walks.

Kinneigh, *6 km (4 miles) N of Enniskean:* round tower built in 1015, 21 m (68 ft) high, next to St Bartholomew's church.

Old Head of Kinsale, *13 km (8 miles) S of Kinsale:* good walks and seascapes. Ruins of 15th c de Courcey castle. Fair walk from Kinsale if you haven't car or bicycle, but you could well be offered a lift.

Owenchincha, *7 km (11 miles) SW of Clonakilty:* sandy beach, some 3 km (2 miles) long. Trotting races, St Patrick's Day, *Mar 17.*

Palace Anne, *on R586 3 km (2 miles) E of Enniskean:* ruins of 17th c house.

Rosscarbery, *head of Rosscarbery Bay.* Set around a square of enormous proportions, Rosscarbery has a striking 17th c CI cathedral and the nearby remains of the monastery, founded in the 6th c by St Fachtna. From Rosscarbery, cross the main road and follow the narrow lane seawards to the small pier at the entrance to the estuary. Safe, sandy beaches in the vicinity.

Sam's Crossroads, *8 km (5 miles) SW of Clonakilty:* Seamus Murphy memorial to Michael Collins, born at nearby Woodfield. The ruins of the house where Michael Collins was born can still be seen, preserved as part of the Collins memorial centre. The outhouse where the family lived after the house was burned by the Black and Tans during the War of Independence; it has been partially restored.

Shippool, *3 km (2 miles) S of Inishannon on L41 from Kinsale:* forest walks to river Bandon, viewing points, picnic place, lay-by. Ruins of Shippool Castle, built 1543.

Summer Cove, *3 km (2 miles) SE of Kinsale:* from Rincurran churchyard the view S over Kinsale harbour is breathtaking. Just before the steep descent into the village, turn left for about 90 m (300 yds). Bulman pub faces harbour: pine panelled walls lined with fascinating photographs of old fishing and hurling triumphs. Youth Hostel, ☎ *(021)772309.*

Timoleague, *16 km (10 miles) SW of Kinsale.* Small village on estuary of Argideen River. *Timoleague Abbey:* one of 13 best-preserved Franciscan friaries of pre-Reformation Ireland, built around 1240, much of present building dates from early 16th c, sacked in 1642 by British forces under Lord Forbes. At entrance commemorative plaque by Oisin Kelly, Dublin sculptor. The village's early 20th c Catholic church has one of last stained glass windows produced by Harry Clarke. CI church has Italian mosaic work. *Castle Gardens,* laid out and maintained by Travers family for past 150 years. Palm trees thrive in mild W Cork climate. Car park, picnic sites, childrens' playground. *Easter weekend and mid-May-mid Sept, Mon-Sun, 12 noon-6 p.m. Otherwise by arr.* ☎ *(023)46116.*

Mallow

Pop. 8,000, 35 km (22 miles) NW of Cork 67 km (42 miles) E of Killarney, 240 km (149 miles) SW of Dublin. EC Wed. TIO: Mallow, ☎(022)42222. Bus and train enquiries, ☎ (022)21120.

Now a quiet, prosperous market town noted for its fishing, Mallow was once a much livelier proposition: up to a century ago, the now-defunct Spa drew thousands of visitors who would sup the water and conversely indulge in riotous living, if the song 'The Rakes of Mallow' is anything to go by. Today the area has interesting historical remains, good walking and sport, all very sedate. Fishing controlled by local hotels.

The Clock Tower with art gallery, *at the E end of the main street,* is a half-timbered edifice built in the mock Tudor style. *Mallow Castle* is not open, but visitors may visit the extensive park and see the deer. At the entrance to the estate is the impressive ruin of a four storey 17th c fortified house. In the grounds of St James CI church are the ruins of St Anne's church, dating from the 13th c, where Thomas Davis, the 19th c patriot writer, born in Mallow, was baptised.

Race meetings: occasional, ☎ *(022)21338.* Swimming pool: indoor heated, daily, ☎ *(022)21863.*

AROUND MALLOW

Annes Grove Gardens, *1.5 km (1 mile) SE of Castletownroche on N72.* Famous gardens sloping down to River Awbeg, a Black-water tributary. Formal walled garden, woodland garden, water garden, exotic plants, delightful riverside walks. A must for every true gardener: *Easter-Sept 30, Mon-Fri, 10 a.m.-6 p.m., Sat, Sun, 1 p.m.-6 p.m.* ☎ *(022)26145.*

Ballintlea/Glenanaar, *16 km (10 miles) NE of Mallow on N73:* forest walks in Canon Sheehan country. Car park, picnic place.

Ballyporeen, *13 km (8 miles) E of Mitchelstown on R665.* Reagan homestead ruins. Great grandfather of Ronald Reagan, a former US president, lived here 150 years ago. Also Ronald Reagan pub, parish church with Reagan family records and heritage centre standing at the crossroads, with material relating to the Reagan family and the visit to the village by Ronald and Nancy Reagan in 1984.

Burncourt House, *13 km (8 miles) NE of Mitchelstown:* 17th c building, said to have been burned to prevent occupation by Cromwell. Shell has 26 gables, several tall chimneys. Ask at nearby farm for permission.

Buttevant, *ruins just S on Mallow road.* Ruins of 13th c Augustinian abbey, dovecot in near perfect condition.

Castletownroche: *Bridgetown Abbey, 2.5 km (1.5 miles) from the village* is an extensive ruin, in a dangerous condition, of a 14th c Franciscan foundation.

Castlyons, *6 km (4 miles) SE of Fermoy:* Barrymore Castle ruins, just S of village, once home of noted 16th, 17th c landowners.

Cooper's Wood, *off N8 at Skeheenarinky between Cahir and Mitchelstown:* riverside forest walk, car park, picnic place.

Annes Grove Gardens, near Castletownroche

Corrin Hill, *2 km (1 mile) S of Fermoy on N8, turning R to golf course:* forest walks, access to Carntiarna, an Iron Age fort.

Doneraile, *10 km (6 miles) NE of Mallow.* Canon Sheehan memorial: the author was parish priest here from 1895-1913. *Doneraile Court Forest Park,* includes forest walks, deer herds.

Fermoy, *30 km (19 miles) E of Mallow. All day closing: Wed.* Delightfully set on banks of River Blackwater, a noted fishing spot. Old, stately trees line both riverbanks—ideal for scenic walks. Swimming pool: *Tues-Sun,* ☎ *(025)31949.* Bicycles: Cavanagh's, *McCurtain Street, SO,* ☎ *(025)31339.* Fermoy Golf Club, *18 holes,* ☎ *(025)31472.*

Galtee Castle, *8 km (5 miles) NE of Mitchelstown on N8:* forest walk, car park, picnic area. *Galtee Mountains:* S slopes provided many easy routes to peaks, most notably Galtymore Mountain 920 m (3,018 ft), from which there are fine views.

Glengarra Wood, *13 km (8 miles) NE of Mitchelstown in N8:* well laid out nature trail near Burncourt River. Many exotic trees of Indian origin along main avenue. Car park.

Island Wood, *2 km (1 mile) S of Newmarket on by-road:* forest, riverside walks, viewing point, car park, picnic area.

Kanturk, *16 km (10 miles) NW of Mallow.* Attractive market town set on the rivers Allua and Dallua, and spanned by three bridges. The main bridge has interesting late 18th c poetic inscriptions carved on its parapets. Kanturk Castle is 1.5 km (1 mile) S of the town. The local chief, MacDonagh MacCarthy, was ordered to stop its construction about 1609, because the English privy council considered it too grand for an Irish subject. The castle was never finished, but its substantial ruins are intact and can be explored. Riding: Assolas Country House, ☎ *(029)76015;* Collins Riding School, *Meelehera,* ☎ *(029)50152.* Bicycles: F. J. Jones, *Strand Street,* ☎ *(029)76118;* Nolan's, *Main Street.* Kanturk Golf Club, 9 holes.

Kilcoman Bog, bird observatory, various species, including Greenland white-fronted goose. *Details: Kilcoman Wildfowl refuge, Buttevant,* ☎ *(022)24200.*

Kilcoman Castle, *5 km (3 miles) NW of Doneraile:* ruins of building where English poet Edmund Spenser once lived for eight years; he may have written the *Faerie Queen* here.

Kildorrey, *13 km (8 miles) W of Mitchelstown on N73.* Site of Bowen's Court, where distinguished novelist Elizabeth Bowen once lived. House had to be sold as financial embarrassment in 1959, then pulled down. She said: 'It was a clean end. Bowen's Court never lived to be a ruin.'

Killavullen, *10 km (6 miles) E of Mallow.* 250 year old house of ancestor of Hennessy, original distillers of brandy. Picturesque setting on cliff overhanging River Blackwater. Ballymacroy House now a bed and breakfast establishment. The adjoining caves have been opened to visitors.

Longueville House, *5 km (3 miles) W of Mallow off the N72* is a fascinating early 18th c house, now converted into a hotel, complete with its own vineyard. In the restaurant, there are portraits of all the presidents of Ireland. ☎ *(022) 47156.*

Michelstown, *34 km (21 miles) NE of Mallow.* Centre of great butter and cheese producing area. *New Square:* monument to John Manderville, and three local men shot by police at Land League meeting here in 1887. On pavement at S end of square, three crosses mark where they fell. *St. Fanahan's Holy Well.* The saint died over 1,500 years ago. Waters said to have curative powers. Feast day: Nov 25. Swimming pool, *turn R at Dublin end of town, SO, Mon-Sun.* Bicycles: O'Sullivans, *Main Street,* ☎ *(025)24316.*

Mitchelstown Caves, *16 km (10 miles) NE of Mitchelstown off N8.* Two groups of caves, signposted. Old or Desmond cave must be entered by rope or ladder. New cave easier access. Local guide will take you through 3 km (2 miles) of passages and chambers at any reasonable time. *All year, daily, 10 a.m.-6 p.m.* Contact: John English, ☎ *(052)67246.*

Mount Hillary, *3 km (2 miles) SE of Banteer, off R579:* forest walks, good views of Blackwater valley from top after energetic climb.

Nano Nagle Heritage Centre, *12 km (7 miles) E of Mallow on N72.* The centre commemorates this remarkable 18th c educational pioneer, who founded the Presentation Sisters in Cork.

Newmarket graveyard, *32 km (20 miles) NW of Mallow:* Sarah Curran, Robert Emmet's beloved, buried here.

Waterford

Pop. 41,000, 63 km (39 miles) W of Wexford, 166 km (103 miles) SW of Dublin. EC Thurs. TIO: 41 The Quay, ☎ *(051)75788, all year. Bus and train enquiries:* ☎ *(051)73401.*

Busy port set on the S bank of the broad River Suir, riddled with interesting little laneways and graced by some notable Georgian buildings. In recent years, city centre has been much improved. Waterford Light Opera Festival: the hills come alive with the sound of song, *every Sept, details: TIO.*

French Church, *Greyfriars Street:* built 1240 as Franciscan foundation. Once housed Huguenot refugees, now in ruins. Key: Mrs N. White, *5 Greyfriars Street, opp.* Any reasonable time. **Holy Trinity Church,** (CI) *Barronstrand Street:* fine edifice, completed 1796. **Blackfriars Dominican Priory,** *Arundel Square:* founded 1226 and used as court until end of 18th c; square tower only major remnant. Key: City Hall, *The Mall.* **Library.** *Lady Lane, Mon-Sat.* **Colbeck Street:** Birthplace of composer William Vincent Wallace. **Municipal Theatre,** *Theatre Royal, The Mall,* two lovely old buildings, used mainly for variety shows, amateur dramatics. **Reginald's Tower,** *corner Parade Quay, The Mall:* mighty stone fortress built in 1003 by the Vikings. Houses Civic Museum, with fine collection of Corporation archive material and regalia; **Maritime Museum.** *May-Sept, Mon-Fri, 10 a.m.-3 p.m., or by arr,* ☎ *(051)73501.* **Waterford Heritage Centre** has many Viking relics and early

Norman settlement of Waterford, discovered during extensive excavations. *May-Sept, Mon-Fri, 10 a.m.-3 p.m.* ☎ *(051)71227.* **Genealogical Research Centre,** *Jenkins Lane, off George's Street. All year, Mon-Thurs, 9 a.m.-1 p.m.; 2 p.m.-5 p.m. Fri, 9 a.m.-2 p.m.* ☎ *(051)73711.* **Chamber of Commerce,** *George's Street:* Georgian house, built 1795 with beautiful staircase and fine carvings. *All year, Mon-Fri, 9.30 a.m.-5 p.m.* Traces of the Danish walls can be seen near railway station, Mayor's Walk, Castle Street. Try Downes' Pub, *Thomas St, People's Park. Downes' No 9 whiskey,* unique to the area. **Walsh's pub,** Ballybricken Hill, is good for local 'characters'. **Garter Lane Arts Centre,** *O'Connell Street:* regular cultural exhibitions, theatre performances. *Details,* ☎ *(051)55038/77153.* **Waterford Glass,** *Cork Road:* factory tour takes in all stages of production, from blowing molten glass to polishing. No children under 12, no photographs. *Tours all year, Mon-Fri, six times daily. Closed most of Aug.* ☎ *TIO or (0 51)73311.* Waterford Craft Centre, *28 Michael Street:* demonstrations, *Mon-Sat, 9 a.m.-5.30 p.m.*

Leisure Activities: River cruises: depart from quayside: *May-Sept, daily departures,* Waterford Viking Cruises, *4 Gladstone Street,* ☎ *(051)72800.* Greyhound racing: *Kilcohan Park,* ☎ *(051)74531.* Riding: Joan O'Mahoney, Killotteran Equestrian Centre, ☎ *(051)84158.* Bicycles: Wright's Cycle Depot, *Henrietta Street,* ☎ *(051)74411.* Golf Club, *18 holes,* ☎ *(051)76748.* Waterford Castle Golf course, *18 holes,* ☎ *(051)78203,* Faithe Legge Golf Course, *18 holes,* ☎ *(051)82241,* Waterford Golf Course, *18 holes,* ☎ *(051)74182.*

AROUND WATERFORD

Annestown, *20 km (12 miles) W of Tramore:* small resort with good sandy beach. Nearby secluded beach at Kilfarrasy.

Arthurstown, *E bank of Waterford Harbour:* bicycles, King's Bay Inn, ☎ *(051)89173.* Youth Hostel. Car and passenger ferry.

Ballyhack, *E side of Waterford Harbour.* Ferry to Passage East, Waterford side, *all year, daily,* ☎ *(051)82488.* Picturesque fishing village with ru-

ined castle. Further down the road is the attractive fishing village of Arthurstown.

Ballymacarberry, *10 km (6 miles) S of Clonmel:* pony trekking, Melody's, ☎ *(052)36147;* Slievenamon Centre.

Bannow, *on S Wexford coast opp. Fethard-on-Sea:* first town in Ireland founded by the Normans, it disappeared under sand during the 17th c. Only the ruins of St Mary's church remain. Miles of beach below low cliffs.

Brownstown Head, *E of Tramore:* fine walks,

Bunmahon, *18 km (11 miles) W of Tramore.* Tiny fishing village with fine sandy beaches, surrounded by cliffs. Bracing 6 km (4 mile) cliff walk to Stradbally.

Carrick-on-Suir, *27 km (17 miles) NW of Waterford. EC Thurs.* One of Munster's most picturesque towns, scenically set on banks of River Suir. **Ormond Castle** is a 15th c castle fronted by a 16th c Elizabethan manor house, which has the finest Tudor plasterwork in Ireland. The castle and house, set in a magnificent parkland, have been thoroughly restored. *Mid June-Sept, daily, 9.30 a.m.-6.30 p.m.* ☎ *(051)40787. Heritage centre,* in former CI church, has historical and genealogical information, exhibitions. ☎ *(051)40200.* Whitechurch Riding Centre, ☎ *(051)40289.*

Cheekpoint, *13 km (8 miles) E of Waterford:* Suirway Inn has lots of atmosphere, many curios. Cheekpoint Hill, excellent views of Waterford city and harbour.

Clonea, *5 km (3 miles) E of Dungarvan:* fine, sandy beach.

Clonmel, *48 km (30 miles) NW of Waterford. EC Thurs. TIO:* ☎ *(052)22960. July, Aug. Otherwise Waterford TIO.* Tipperary's main town, most attractively set in River Suir valley, includes a number of interesting old buildings. Excellent base for exploring Comeragh and Knockmealdown Mountains. **Franciscan church,** *Abbey Street:* 19th c restoration on site of 13th c foundation. *St Mary's* (C), near Franciscan church: also dates from 19th c, magnificent ceiling, elaborate high altar, interesting

A crystal jug in the making at the Waterford Glass factory. For many years Ireland has been one of the world's foremost producers of high-quality, hand-blown glass.

Passage East, Co. Waterford

graveyard. **Museum and Art Gallery**, *Parnell Street*: Impressively renovated, large collection of local material, paintings and photographs. *All year, Tues-Sat, 10 a.m.-1 p.m., 2 p.m.-5 p.m.* ☎ *(052)21399.* Town Hall, Corporation regalia. *By arr,* ☎ *(052)22100.* **Old Town Wall**, best-preserved section partly encloses historic St Mary's CI, *Mary Street.* Clonmel's most interesting building, the 17th c Main Guard, which faces the West Gate at the other end of O'Connell Street, the main shopping thoroughfare, is due to be restored. **Hearn's Hotel**, *Parnell Street*: This newly refurbished hotel was starting point for Bianconi's horsedrawn car service in 1815. Gladstone Street offers superb views across river to mountains: attractive old shopfronts, **Mitchel Street**, *off Gladstone Street*: narrow, shop-lined, interesting. Pleasant quayside walks by the fast-flowing River Suir and in the park on the S side of the river.

Leisure Activities: Racing, regular meetings at Powerstown, ☎ *(052)22852 / 22971.* Greyhound racing: twice weekly races at Davis Road track, ☎ *(052)21118.* Swimming pool: indoor, heated, *Emmet Street, daily,* ☎ *(052)21972.* Powers 'o' the Pot, pony trekking centre, Harneys Cross. Bicycles: Hackett, *West Gate,* ☎ *(052)21869;* Michael McDermott, *Foodmarket, Irishtown,* ☎ *(052)22272;* Bill Purcell, *The Mall,* ☎ *(052)21831.* Clonmel Golf Club, 18 holes, ☎ *(052)21138.*

Clonmines, *head of Bannow Bay*: medieval town fell into decay: all you can see today are parts of four castles and three churches, overlooking a pleasant estuary.

Coolfin, *just beyond Portlaw C church*: forest walks, rhododendrons.

Curraghmore House, *Portlaw 16 km (10 miles) W of Waterford*: gardens in beautiful setting, fine bronze statues, only shell of house remains; *Apr 1-Sept 30, Thurs and BH, 2 p.m.-5 p.m.* NE of demesne, Mother Brown's Hill, ☎ *(051)87101 / 87102.*

Dunbrody Abbey, *near Campile*: great roofless church dating from 12th c. Fine views to confluence of Nore and Suir rivers.

Dunmore East, *14 km (9 miles) SE of Waterford*: Breton-style fishing village, neat, thatched cottages. Tiers of houses rise steeply from harbour. Sea angling centre. Walks around harbour area and to nearby Creadon Head and Black Knob promontory. Coves also worth exploring.

Geneva Barracks, *3 km (2 miles) S of Passage East*: settlement founded in 1785 by gold and silversmiths from Geneva. Later used as military barracks and prison, now ruins, in process of restoration.

Hook Peninsula, *32 km (20 miles) SE of Waterford*: craggy 'finger' of land pointing into the Atlantic. Fethard-on-Sea is the main town in the Hook area. Its 'shell' garage has its facade covered in shells from the seashore. The small village of Slade on the E side of the peninsula, near the lighthouse, has ruins of 14th c castle and 18th c salt houses. Whatever the wind direction, one side of the Hook is always calm. **Lighthouse**, one of the oldest in the world. Tower over 700 years old, but a light has been burning here for over twice as long. The peninsula has many undisturbed beaches and coves. Dollar Bay, on W side reputedly hides an 18th c Spanish treasure. Also on the W side of the peninsula is Loftus Hall, built in the 18th c. The Devil is said to have left the house in a hurry, leaving a large crack in the ceiling that could never be repaired. At Baginbun Bay on the S side of the peninsula, the Normans made their first landing in Ireland in 1169. The entire Hook peninsula drive is well signposted.

John F. Kennedy Park, *8 km (5 miles) S of New Ross*: 165 ha (410 acre) park, opened 1968, over looks Kennedy ancestral home at Dunganstown, 1.5 km (1 mile). 109 ha (270 acres) devoted to arboretum, with world-wide selection of trees and shrubs. Forest garden, tremendous views from the car park at the top of nearby Slieve Coillte hill. Many varied walks in vicinity. Picnic area, visitor centre, café, shelters. *May-Aug, daily, 10 a.m.-8 p.m. Apr, Sept, daily, 10 a.m.-6.30 p.m. Oct-Mar, daily, 10 a.m.-5 p.m.* ☎ *(051)88171.* At nearby Dunganstown, one room **Kennedy homestead** has memorabilia on the John F. Kennedy visit to New Ross area, part of his 1963 Irish tour. *Ask at adjoining farmhouse.*

Kilcash, *6 km (4 miles) N of Kilsheelan, between Carrick-on-Suir and Waterford*: forest walks, viewing points. **Kilcash Castle**: ruins, overshadowed by Slievenamon Mountain, well worth the climb.

Kilclooney, *on Carrick-on-Suir-Dungarvan T56*: forest walks, access to Crotty's Rock and Comeragh Mountain lakes. Car park, picnic area.

Kilsheelan, *near Clonmel*: forest, riverside walks, scenic walks, 1.5 km (1 mile) N of village and bordering old Clonmel-Kilsheelan road W of River Suir.

Knockeen Dolmen, *5 km (3 miles) N of Tramore*: excellently preserved.

Lady's Abbey, *2 km (1.5 miles) S of Ardfinnan*: ruins of ancient Carmelite foundation.

Lyreanearla, *8 km (5 miles) S of Clonmel on Nire valley road*: walks with extensive views, car park, picnic area.

Mount Congreve Demesne, *8 km (5 miles) W of Waterford, just N of N25*: attractive gardens, woodlands.

New Ross, *34 km (21 miles) NE of Waterford: TIO,* ☎ *(051)21857, June-Aug.* one of Co. Wexford's oldest towns, on banks of the River Barrow. Narrow streets have medieval air. Very fetching tall, Dutch-style houses on quays. The town rises steeply from the quayside; on the hilltop above the town, there are substantial remains of the medieval fortifications. **St Mary's (NM)** *Church Lane*: ruins of early 13th c parish church. *Tholsel,* civic insignia and documents, including James II Charter, ☎ *(051)21284.* River cruises along Barrow and Nore rivers, *Tues-Sat, dep. 7 p.m.* Three hour cruise, dinner served aboard, ☎ *(051)21723.* Kennedy Memorial pool; indoor, heated, *daily,* ☎ *(051)21169.* Golf Club, 9 holes, ☎ *(051)21433.* Bicycles: Donovan Cycles, *Robert St,* ☎ *(051)21937.* Ballylane Farm Tours: tour of large mixed farm near New Ross and surrounding rural areas. *May-Sept, daily tours,* ☎ *(051)21315.*

Nire Valley, *6 km (4 miles) E of Ballymacarbery on T27*: walks, car park, picnic area.

Oaklands, *1.5 km (1 mile) S of New Ross on Campile road*: forest walks, picnic place, lay-by.

Old Ross, *8 km (5 miles) E of New Ross* was the original town, but all that remains today is a hillock in a field, covering the Anglo-Norman motte built by the first settlers.

Passage East, *11 km (7 miles) E of Waterford*: charming, old world riverside village with good views from hill behind village. Ferry to Ballyhack. Regular daily service, *details,* ☎ *(051)82488.* Also forest walks to N.

River Suir, two roads, one each side, run E from Clonmel. Many fine views of river and Comeragh Mountains.

St Patrick's Well, *1.5 km (1 mile) W of Clonmel*: still a place of pilgrimage. One of Tipperary's most attractive glens.

Stradbally, *10 km (6 miles) NE of Dungarvan*: small, attractive village that is a mass of flowers in summer, interesting coves, fine cliff walks.

Tintern Abbey, *6 km (3.5 miles) N of Fethard*: Cistercian, built about 1200, ruins hidden among trees. Approached by long drive, signpost at gate.

Tipperary Crystal, *5 km (3 miles) E of Carrick-on-Suir on N24 road*. This new crystal glass making company, staffed by former craftsmen from Waterford Glass has already established a fine reputation. Visitors are welcome. *Mon-Sat, 8 a.m.-7 p.m. Sun, BH, 11 a.m.-6 p.m.* ☎ *(051)41188.*

Tory Hill, *13 km (8 miles) N of Waterford, off N9*: superb views of surrounding plain, Waterford city and harbour.

Tramore, *13 km (8 miles) S of Waterford. TIO:* ☎ *(051)81572.* Top holiday resort, with 5 km (3 miles) of sandy beach. *Celtworld:* impressive new centre depicts ancient Celtic mythology using modern audio-visual and computer techniques. Interactive area, theme shop. *All year, daily,* continuous shows. *Details,* ☎ *(051)81330.* Waterworld, a large water-based leisure centre, is due to open in 1993. Attractions include an amusement park covering more than 20 ha (50 acres), miniature railway, marina. Tramore races: *Feb, June, Aug (four day event), Sept, Nov.*

Walks: SW, along the Doneraile cliffs—tremendous natural views, plus three white pillars, 18th c navigational aids topped by 'The Metal Man'. Also along the promenade to a range of sandhills known as The Burrows. Garrarus Strand and Kilfarrasy Strand, W of town. Bicycles: Pickardstown Service Station, ☎ *(051)81094.* Tramore Golf Club, 18 holes, ☎ *(051)81247.*

Woodstown Strand, *5 km (3 miles) S of Passage East*: pleasant, secluded beach. Ballyglan Riding Centre, ☎ *(051)82133.*

Wexford

Pop. 15,000, 26 km (16 miles) NW of Rosslare, 144 km (90 miles) S of Dublin. EC Thur. TIO: The Quays, ☎ *(053)23111, all year. Bus and train enquiries:* ☎ *(053)22522.* Taxis: Redmond Road.

An ancient town with a tangy sea air and a refreshing, individual character. The narrow main streets and innumerable little laneways are full of atmosphere, and during the summer, choked with cars and people.

Wexford Opera Festival: attracts the cosmopolitan black-tie crowd to the tiny and charming Theatre Royal. Many fringe events, such as art exhibitions. *Late Oct,* ☎ *(053)22144 / 22240.* **Wexford Mussel Festival**: mussel-tasting contests, seafood banquets, surf-gliding, lectures and exhibitions. *Early Sept. Details: TIO.*

Westgate Tower: restored early 13th c gate tower, part of Wexford's Viking/Norman town wall. Visitor centre uses audio-visual techniques to portray town history; Wexford has been designated a Heritage Town. *May-Sept, Mon-Sat, 10 a.m.-9 p.m. Oct-Apr, Mon-Sat, 10 a.m.-6 p.m.* ☎ *(053)42611.*

Selskar Abbey, *Westgate*: 12th c ruins, Henry II spent entire season of Lent here in 1172 as penance for murder of Thomas à Beckett. Key: P. Murphy, 9 Abbey Street. **St Francis** (C), *School Street*: L-shaped Franciscan friary church founded 1230, plundered in Cromwell's time. Remodelled 1784. ♿ **Twin Sisters**: Church of Immaculate Conception (C), *Rowe Street*, Church of Assumption (C), *Bride Street*, 19th c, of almost identical appearance. ♿ **Arts Centre**, *Cornmarket*: something for everyone all year, concerts, dance, drama, art and historical exhibitions. Coffee bar in basement. *All year, Mon-Fri, 10 a.m.-6 p.m. Also some eves,* ☎ *(053)23764.* Summer theatre: Talbot and White's Hotels, *details: TIO.* Main Street: narrow, shopfronts and shops worth exploring. Also atmospheric narrow alleyways running to quays. Walking tours: conducted by members of Old Wexford Society, starting Talbot and White's Hotels, *every summer eve.* **White's Hotel**, where the opera festival was founded, has many interesting historical photographs in its lobby area, while the town library, next door, also has much material on Wexford.

Leisure Activities: Wildfowl Reserve, *N shore of Wexford harbour, 5 km (3 miles) from town*: observation tower, lecture hall, laboratory, library, car park, picnic area. *All year, daily.* & Racing: Bettyville, ☎ *(053)22307. Swimming pool: indoor, heated. Ferrybank, all year, daily,* ☎ *(053)2327.* Bicycles: The Bike Shop, *9 Selskar Street,* ☎ *(053)22514,* Hayes Cycle Shop, *108 South Main Street,* ☎ *(053)22462.* Golf Club, *18 holes,* ☎ *(053)22238.*

AROUND WEXFORD

Bunclody, *21 km (14 miles) N of Enniscorthy.* Large square, divided in two by a fast-flowing stream. Ideal base for climbing the Blackstairs Mountains.

Carley's Bridge Pottery, *near Enniscorthy:* the oldest in Ireland, founded over 300 years ago. Still makes gardenware. Open to visitors all year, *Mon-Fri, 8.30 a.m.-5.30 p.m.* ☎ *(054)33512.* Just up the road is *Paddy Murphy's Hillview Pottery:* also making pots in the traditional way. ☎ *(054)35443.* *The Kiltrea Bridge Pottery, 3.5 m (6 km) W of Enniscorthy,* is very modern and does mostly glazed ware to a high level of Finnish-inspired design. Also weaving workshop. Open daily. ☎ *(054)35107.*

Carne, *E side of Carnsore Point:* attractive fishing village, safe, sandy beach.

Courtown, *6 km (3.5 miles) SE of Gorey.* Popular seaside resort, beach. Harbour: 19th c bar, front bar little changed over 160 years. Gorey Little Theatre group play Tara Hall twice weekly, *July, Aug.* Smuggler's Cove adventure park includes golf, 10 pin bowling. ☎ *(055)25280.* Walks: Boro Road, small harbour area and immediate environs. Forest walks W of village on L31, car park, picnic area. Golf Club, *18 holes,* ☎ *(055)25166.*

Enniscorthy, *24 km (15 miles) N of Wexford. TIO:* ☎ *(054)34699. June, Sept. Bus and train enquiries: (054)32488.* Delightful town set on steeply sloping ground on banks of River Slaney. Lots of historical atmosphere and interest. Worth exploring quaysides and narrow streets.

Strawberry Fair, plenty of outdoor amusements and an abundance of locally-grown strawberries, *late June, early July.* Wexford Agricultural Show, *July.*

St Aidan's Cathedral (C), fine Gothic building designed by Pugin in 1840s. & *Castle,* rebuilt around 1586, perfectly preserved, houses county museum with interesting folk section. Relics of 1798 and of the town's industrial history *June-Sept, Mon-Fri, 10 a.m.-6 p.m. Sat, Sun, 2 p.m.-6 p.m. Oct-May, Mon-Fri, 2 p.m.-5.30 p.m. Sat, Sun, 2 p.m.-5 p.m. Antique Tavern, Slaney Street:* full of interesting curios. Customers are advised not to carry muskets inside! Slaneyside Park, *due S of town:* pleasant walks.

Greyhound racing, *Show Grounds,* regular meetings, ☎ *(054)32174.* Slaney View Riding School, *Brownswood,* ☎ *(054)33102.* Bicycles: P.J. Kenny, *Slaney Street,* ☎ *(054)33255.* Golf Club, *9 holes,* ☎ *(054)32191.*

Ferns, *34 km (21 miles) N of Wexford.* Once capital of Leinster. Imposing ruins, include 13th c castle, 12th c Augustinian abbey, cathedral. On high ground just outside town, ruins of 16th c St Peter's Church.

Forth Mountain, *6 km (4 miles) SW of Wexford:* forest walks, magnificent panoramas of Wexford coast from Kilmore Quay to Hook Head.

Gorey, *TIO: Gorey,* ☎ *(055)21248.* St. Michael's (C), 19th c. designed by Pugin, has massive square tower. The Church of Ardamine (CI) was designed by George Edmund Street, who restored Dublin's Christ Church Cathedral. & *Funge Arts Centre, Rafter Street:* hosts major arts festival with many internationally known names, *July, Aug,* ☎ *(055)21470.* &

Irish National Heritage Park, *5 km (3 miles) N of Wexford:* full-scale replicas of the types of homesteads, burial modes, places of worship etc used in prehistoric Ireland. Goes up to Viking and Norman times. Lectures, guided tours. *Mar-Nov, Mon-Sun, 10 a.m.-7 p.m. Last admittance to Heritage Park 5 p.m.* ☎ *(053)41733.*

Johnstown Castle, *near Murntown, 6 km (4 miles) S of Wexford:* fine landscaped grounds of agricultural research centre. The ornamental ground have over 200 species of trees and shrubs. There is the ruin of a medieval tower house, three ornamental lakes with wildfowl and a picnic area in the sunken garden. On working days, visitors can see the walled gardens and hothouses. *The Irish agricultural museum* has extensive displays of rural transport and farming and a section on dairying. Large scale replica workshops depict the crafts of the basket maker, the blacksmith, the cooper and the harness maker. The excellently presented museum also has a fine collection of Irish country furniture. *Nov-Mar, Mon-Fri, 9 a.m.-12.30 p.m.; 1.30 p.m.-5 p.m., Apr, May, Sept, Mon-Fri, 9 a.m.-12.30 p.m.; 1.30 p.m.-5 p.m., Sat-Sun, 2 p.m.-5 p.m. Jun-Aug, Mon-Fri, 9 a.m.-5 p.m., Sat, Sun, 2 p.m.-5 p.m. Castle gardens, all year, daily, 9 a.m.-5.30 p.m.* ☎ *(053)42888.*

Kilmore Quay, *16 km (10 miles) S of Wexford.* The long, straggling Main Street, lined with over a dozen thatched cottages, runs down to the harbour. The old lightship in the harbour is now a *maritime museum. June-Sept, daily, 2 p.m.-8 p.m.* Beach extends 10 km (6 miles) NW; development is under way of a coastal walk along the entire Co Wexford coastline.

Lady's Island, *just W of Carnsore Point:* place of pilgrimage in sea inlet. Interesting ruins, including tower of Norman castle that leans at greater angle than Pisa. Causeway joins island to mainland. Annual pilgrimage, *Aug 15.*

Mayglass, *11 km (7 miles) S of Wexford on L29:* ruins of church built in 1798. Plaque on N wall marks grave of Bagenal Harvey, leader of 1798 rising.

Mount Leinster, *10 km (6 miles) SW of Bunclody:* best views in the whole SE. Road runs to summit.

Rosslare Harbour, *26 km (16 miles) SE of Wexford. TIO: Rosslare harbour,* ☎ *(053)33622. All year.* Terminal of car ferries from Wales and N France.

Rosslare, *18 km (11 miles) SE of Wexford,* fine arc of beach, stretching for some 10 km (6 miles). St Helen's Pony Trekking Centre. Golf Club, *18 holes. Details, TIO at Kilrane,* ☎ *(053)33232.*

Saltee Islands, *5 km (3 miles) S of Kilmore Quay.* Boats from quay in suitable weather. ☎ Bill Bates, (053)29644. Two main islands, each about 0.8 km (0.5 miles) long, form Ireland's largest bird sanctuary. A leader of the 1798 Rising, Bagenal Harvey, was captured here after fleeing from the Battle of Vinegar Hill near Enniscorthy.

Tacumshin Windmill, *just W of Lady's Island:* 19th c, was totally restored 40 years ago. The sails are in perfect condition, as is the interior. Key at adjoining house.

Tara Hill, *5 km (3 miles) N of Courtown:* 254 m (833 ft), forest walks, viewing points.

Vinegar Hill, *just E of Enniscorthy:* scene of the decisive battle of the 1798 Rising, when Wexford men were defeated by General Lake. Fine views from summit over River Slaney and surrounding countryside, car park.

Youghal

Pop. 6,000, 48 km (30 miles) E of Cork, 74 km (46 miles) SW of Waterford and 240 km (149 miles) SW of Dublin. TIO: ☎ *(024)92390. June-Sept. Bus enquiries: (021)508188.*

An historic seaport and market town set most attractively between steep hillsides and the broad expanse of the Blackwater River. Founded by the Anglo-Normans in 13th c, and an important base during the succeeding centuries, the town acquired magnificent walls which, in their prime had 13 towers.

North and South Main Street, running for 1.5 km (1 mile) is a perfect historic entity, with many sights in a town little changed since the 1950s. Now

Johnstown Castle, Co. Wexford

that Youghal has been designated a Heritage Town, the Old Market House is being turned into an interpretative centre. *The Devonshire Arms Hotel, at Pearse Square, at the S end of Main Street,* has many photographs of the old Youghal schooners. The four storey clock tower, straddling Main Street, was built in 1777. During the state of insurrection in the 1790s, rebels were often hung from the windows as a warning to the rest of the populace. *The Red House* is an excellent example of early 18th c Dutch domestic architecture. *Tynte's Castle, just opposite,* was built in the 15th c on the waterfront. All that is left of the town's 14th c Benedictine abbey are relics in a passageway off Main Street. *St Mary's Collegiate Church,* originally built in the 11th c and one of Ireland's finest churches, has a very impressive interior. The churchyard lies in the shadow of the town walls. The adjacent *Myrtle Grove House,* where Sir Walter Raleigh once lived, is open. Visitors can see the four yew trees outside, under which Sir Walter Raleigh is said to have smoked his pipe and dreamed of El Dorado; nearby, he planted the first potatoes grown in Ireland. *May-Sept, Tues, Thurs, Sat, guided tours at 2.30 p.m. and 4 p.m.* ☎ *(024)92274.* On the heights above the town, the walls are the most extensive in Ireland, apart from those in Derry. Just off the quaysides, the *Moby Dick* pub has many photographs showing the filming of Moby Dick in Youghal in 1954.

Walks: Green's Dock, Market Dock, Mall Dock and Market Square; also S of town, as far as old lighthouse on Cork road. 8 km (5 miles) of sandy beaches in vicinity. River Blackwater scenic drive: start Youghal, continue along minor roads to W to Lismore, Cappoquin.

Leisure activities: Perks Indoor Amusements. *Dodgems, ghost trains, etc. All year.* Bicycles: Fergus McLean, ☎ *(024)92733,* Bob Troy, ☎ *(024)92509.* Golf Club, *18 holes,* ☎ *(024)92787.*

AROUND YOUGHAL

Ardmore, *13 km (8 miles) E of Youghal.* Pleasant seaside resort, long, sandy beach. Cliff walks above the village. *St Declan's:* 7th c monastic settlement, includes round tower, oratory and cathedral. Ardmore amusement park: dodgems, amusement arcade, *Easter-Sept 30.* St Declan's Stone: glacial boulder on beach.

Ballycotton, *32 km (20 miles) SW of Youghal.* Fishing village on hill overlooking bay. In season, harbour crammed with fishing boats. Sandy beaches. Cliff walk, good views.

Ballynagaul, *1.5 km (1 mile) E of Ring:* old-world village with small harbour.

Bohernagore, *on L34 at Vee hairpin bend:* Knockmealdown mountains viewing point, forest walks, picnic area.

Cappoquin, *30 km (19 miles) N of Youghal.* Noted coarse fishing spot at head of tidal section of River Blackwater, near slopes of Knockmealdown Mountain walks: excellent exercise and nice, best route along T27, N through Ballymacarberry to Clonmel.

Castlemartyr, *1.5 km (1 mile) W of village, off N25:* lakeside walks, car park, picnic area.

Clogheen, *19 km (12 miles) E of Mitchelstown:* splendid views, road zig-zags up to Knockmealdown Gap, thence to Lismore and Cappoquin.

Coolatoor, *10 km (6 miles) W of Dungarvan:* forest walks, viewing points over Drum hills.

Cunnigar Peninsula, *near Dungarvan:* safe, sandy beaches.

Dromana, *between Villierstown and Cappoquin, 16 km (10 miles) N of Youghal:* forest walks, strolls along banks of River Blackwater, Hindu-Gothic arch, lay-by, picnic area.

Dungarvan, *30 km (19 miles) NE of Youghal. EC Thur. TIO.* ☎ *(058)41741, June-Sept.* Attractive town set on lovely stretch of coast where River Colligan broadens into Dungarvan Harbour.

Good beach NE of town. **Town museum**, in library, has many relics of Dungarvan's maritime history, daily. Long promenade faces the sea. St Augustine's Church, has an attractive setting on the edge of the sea. **Augustinian Priory**, *Abbeyside:* square tower of 13th c building used as belfry by church next door. *Dungarvan Castle*, built 1185, huge circular keep surrounded by fortified walls, remains of barracks. **Abbeyside Castle**: only W wall of 12th/13th c building remains. **Seanachie Inn**, *Cork Road:* fine traditional atmosphere, rebuilt interior, old furniture, kitchen tools. **Shell Cottage**, *Abbeyside:* walls covered by thousands of shells. *Walks* round docks, harbour area full of character. Seawater swimming pool: *esplanade, by park.* Bicycles: F. Murphy, *Main Street,* ☎ *(058)41376;* Colum's Shop, *O'Connell Street,* ☎ *(058)41278.*

Garryvoe Strand, *6 km (4 miles) N of Ballycotton:* good bathing beach.

Glenbower, *13 km (8 miles) W of Youghal, entrance at Thatch Inn, Killeagh village, on N25;* forest, lakeside walks, nature trail, car park, picnic area.

Glenshelane, *3 km (2 miles) N of Cappoquin, turn right at Grotto on Mount Melleray road:* forest walks, strolls by Glenshelane River, car park, picnic area.

Grubb's Grave, *3 km (2 miles) SE of Clogheen on Vee Road, on N slope of Sugar Loaf hill:* where Quaker Samuel Grubb was buried in a large cairn overlooking his estates.

Helvick Head, tremendous ocean views from promontory.

Kilmore Rath, *5 km (3 miles) S of Aglish on T27:* great kidney-shaped prehistoric earthwork.

Achill Island, Co. Mayo

Lismore, *6 km (4 miles) W of Cappoquin.* Beautifully set village on banks of River Blackwater. Streets with Tudor style houses and interesting laneways. **Lismore Experience:** new heritage centre in the old courthouse uses multi-media presentation to tell the story of the town since St Carthage's arrival in 636. Historical display room. *June-Aug, Mon-Fri, 10 a.m.-8 p.m. Sat, 10 a.m.-6 p.m., Sun, 2 p.m.-6 p.m. Sept, Oct, Mon-Sat-10 a.m.-5.30 p.m., Sun, 2 p.m.-5 p.m.* ☎ *(058) 54975.* **St Carthach's Cathedral,** (CI): one of the country's most striking medieval churches, with Gothic vaulting and elegant memorials, in total contrast to modern Italianate C cathedral nearby. **Lismore Castle gardens:** magnificent setting overlooking river, many rare shrubs. *Mid-May-mid-Sept, daily except Sat, 1.45 p.m.-4.45 p.m.,* ☎ *(058)54424. Castle closed.* St Carthach's Holy Well, in private grounds near castle, open on Pattern Day, *May 14.* Forest walks beside Vee Road to Clogheen. Ballyrafter Indoor Riding School. *Apr-Sept,* ☎ *(058)54002.* Golf Club, *9 holes,* ☎ *(058)54026.* Youth Hostel.

Macallop Glen, *3 km (2 miles) W of Ballyduff on N72 to Fermoy:* delightful rhododendron paths, excellent in early summer, lay-by.

Master McGrath monument, *junction of Clonmel-Cappoquin road, 3 km (2 miles) NW of Dungarvan:* commemorates the late 19th c dog that was only beaten once in 37 races.

Mine Head, *10 km (6 miles) S of Helvick Head:* good vantage point.

Monatrea, *just across Blackwater from Youghal:* picturesque bathing spot.

Mount Mellerary Abbey, *on slopes of Knockmealdown Mountains above Cappoquin:* peaceful Cistercian Foundation, monks undertake various crafts, including baking. Tel first: ☎ *(058)54404.*

Rhincrew Abbey, *3 km (2 miles) N of Youghal, on hill overlooking Rhincrew Bridge:* founded by Knights Templar in 1183, now ruined.

Ring, *Waterford Gaeltacht.* Good, small beaches in Irish-speaking area. Fine coastal drive to Ring from Dungarvan along L177.

Shanagarry, *3 km (2 miles) NW of Ballycotton:* ruins of home of 17th c Quaker William Penn who founded American state of Pennsylvania. The castle is being restored by Stephen Pearce, whose nearby pottery is open daily.

Strancally, *16 km (10 miles) E of Tallow:* forest walks on W bank of River Blackwater, viewing points.

Tagoat, *15 km (9 miles) SE of Wexford:* **Yola farmstead and genealogy centre:** the Norman settlers who came to Co Wexford from the 12th c onwards used the Yola dialect, which survived until the 19th c. New centre has restored farmhouse, the genealogy centre for Co Wexford, and stages traditional Irish nights. Also farmyard buildings, with animals. *Daily,* ☎ *(053) 31177.*

Tallow Hill, *19 km (12 miles) N of Youghal:* fine views of Bride and Blackwater valleys.

Youghal Bay, sandy beaches.

The WEST

Achill Island

46 km (28 miles) NW of Westport. TIO: ☎ *(098)45384 July-Aug.* Joined to mainland by a swivel-bridge at Achill Sound, this is the largest island off the Irish coast, 19 x 24 km (12 x 15 miles) at widest point. The scenery on this largely heather-covered island is truly superb, with great mountains on the N side and magnificent cliffs and strands, it is a popular get-away-from-it-all spot.

Achill Sound: all island roads radiate from here. Good fishing, boat hire centre. Atlantic Drive: Achill Sound, round coast to Dooega, superb views. Bicycles: Achill Sound Hotel, ☎ *(098)45245.*

Bullsmouth, *NE Achill:* near Dooniver strand; Achill Island Crafts Centre: candles, pottery, craft shop. *Mon-Fri, 10 a.m.-7.30 p.m. Shop, Mon-Sun, 10 a.m.-9 p.m.*

Corrymore House, *near Dooagh village:* once home of Captain Boycott, whose ostracism during the 19th c Land League campaign gave the English language a new word.

Croghaun Mountain, *near Keem:* 668 m (2,192 ft), magnificent views. On seaward side, cliff falls nearly 600 m (2,000 ft) to ocean. Don't go too near the edge, as cliff face curves inwards at some points.

Dugort, *at the foot of Slievemore:* popular resort, with good bathing strand at Poulavaddy. Dugort boatman will take you on fascinating trip to Seal Caves, which extend far into the cliffs under Slievemore, 3 km (2 miles) NW of Dugort.

Giant's Grave, *3 km (2 miles) SW of Dugort:* ruined cairn, also chamber tomb, the Cromlech Tumulus, and the Keel West Giant's Grave.

Downpatrick Head, Co. Mayo

Keel, *15 km (9 miles) NW of Achill Sound:* charming village set in curving, S facing bay, with a great stretch of sandy beach. Sheltered to N by Slievemore. Walk a short distance up the road going due N from Keel towards Slievemore; stupendous views. Achill Island Pottery, coffee-shop, *Apr-Sept, Mon-Sun, 10 a.m.-6 p.m.,* ☎ *(098)45245.* Bicycles: O'Malley's Island Sports, *Keel Post Office,* ☎ *(098)43125.*

Keem Strand, *2 km (1.5 miles) past Corrymore:* popular bathing spot enlivened by the occasional basking shark.

Kildavnet Castle, *near S tip of Achill Island:* fine structure, once a stronghold of Gráinne Ui Mhaille (Grace O'Malley), a 16th c warrior queen. Nearby 12th c Kildavnet Church.

Minaun Heights, *N of Dooega:* one of the best hang gliding areas in Ireland.

Saddle Head, *N of Croghaun:* old signal tower, from here, coastline turns E towards Slievemore.

Slievemore village, *2.5 km (1.5 miles) N of Keel:* once a thriving village, populace driven out by 1840s Famine. Deserted ever since.

Trawmore Strand, *near Keel:* 5 km (3 miles) of Ireland's finest golden sand. SE are the striking Minaun Cliffs. From Holy Well, during low tide, see Cathedral Rocks.

Valley, *between Lough Doa and Lough Sruhill:* tiny village with two beaches to W. Local boatman will arrange trip to Inishbiggle and Annagh islands, between Achill and mainland.

Aran Islands

30 km (18 miles) off Galway. Regular sailings to the islands, and Aer Arann flights from Inverin. For transport details, Galway TIO, ☎ *(091)63081, all year. Aran Islands TIO,* ☎ *(099)61263, May-Sept.*

The three islands, where Irish is the everyday language, are renowned for a way of life that has changed little for generations. The cultural tradi-

tion is oral and the islanders have a rich fund of stories and legends. Many spin and weave their own clothes, such as the *bainín* (white coat), the *crios* (coloured woollen belt) and make *pampooties* (hide shoes without a heel). *Árainn* (Inishmore) is by far the largest island. The smaller islands are **Inish Meáin** (Inishmaan) and **Inish Oírr** (Inisheer), with its magnificent beaches and each has a wide variety of accommodation. A visit can be an unforgettable experience.

ÁRAINN [Inishmore]

Cill Éinne, long, sandy beach. *Teampall Bheanain, immediately S of village:* primitive church measuring 2.1 x 3.3 m (7 x 11 ft) reckoned to be one of smallest in world.

Cill Mhuirbhigh, two cottages by pier built by Robert Flaherty when making his film *Man of Aran.* He and his family stayed in adjacent large house. Film processing was done in old fishcuring shed by pier. Boats: Bairtle Óhlarnáin, *in village:* Stiophán ÓConghaile , *Sruthán.* Long, sandy beach.

Cill Rónáin, village 'capital' of the islands. Between lifeboat, slip and pier, a monument to Ridgeway and Blythe, who rowed Atlantic in 1966. Harbour boasts 140 m (150 yd) pier. Small beaches to E and S. Folk museum: shows history of Aran Islands, including photographs, old clothes and utensils. Kitchen and bedroom furnished in old style. Reading room features letters from Pearse, Casement. *All year, daily, 10 a.m.-7 p.m.,* ☎ *(099)61115.* **New Aran Interpretative centre.** *Church of Ss. Brigid and Oliver Plunkett,* recently restored, fine Stations of the Cross. ♿ Teampall Breachain, the 9th c Church of St Brecan, also Teampall an Cheathrair Ólainn (Church of the Heavenly Four). Dún Eoghanacht, fort on a ridge overlooking Teampall Breachain. Aran Bicycle Hire, or Liam ÓCoistealbha, *by quay.*

Creig an Chéirin, *near W of island:* remains of 19th c still-house where illegal poitín was surreptitiously distilled. The 'Eire' identification sign, used by aircraft during World War II, is also on the extreme W. Halla Rónáin, céilís, film shows.

Dún Aonghus, fort covering 4 ha (11 acres) on the edge of a cliff. Half the site, consisting of three 'con-

centric' enclosures, defended by vast walls of dry masonry, has fallen into the sea, nonetheless it is one of Europe's finest prehistoric sites. Superb views of mainland coast.

Dún Óghil, *near Eochail and Dubhchathair, on S cliffs, 3 km (2 miles) W of Cill Éinne,* may be oldest fort on island.

Teampall Chiaran (St Ciaran's Monastery) *halfway between Eochail and Cill Rónáin.*

INIS MEÁIN [Inishmann]

Baile an Dúna, Synge's cottage. The writer stayed here every summer from 1898 to 1902, visitors included Eoin MacNeill and Patrick Pearse. *Inis Meáin Museum:* a must for Synge devotees, housing his typewriter, camera, photographs, manuscripts. *Usually June-Sept, Mon-Fri, 11.30 a.m.-12.30 p.m., 2 p.m-4 p.m.* 1.5 km (1 mile) away, on cliff edge, see seat where Synge sat.

Cill Ceann Fhionnaigh (Church of the Fair-Headed One), *near slip, mid E coast:* once-splendid primitive church now in ruins.

Dún Chonchuir, *near village of Baile an Dúna:* magnificent fort, though the three outer rings have gone (but for remnants of the inner curtain) the massive fortress wall is almost intact. Most impressive.

INIS ÓIRR [Inisheer]

Folk Museum, near the main pier, has interesting artefacts of the island and old photographs. Daily in season. *O'Brien's Castle, S of landing point:* 15th c, set on rocky hill, one of the island's most striking features.

Teampall Chaomhain, *between airstrip and Baile an Chaisleáin:* church ruins now largely buried in sand, pilgrimage to it on June 14.

Trá Caorach, *E of island:* twenty years ago, a freighter was wrecked offshore, successive storms have left her beached upright.

Ballina

Pop.12,000, 65 km (41 miles) NE of Westport, 59 km (37 miles) SW of Sligo, 246 km (153 miles) NW of Dublin. EC Thur. TIO: ☎ *(096)70848, June-Aug. Train enquiries,* ☎ *(096)21011. Bus enquiries,* ☎ *(096) 21657.*

Ballina may not be the most architecturally impressive town in Ireland, with a dour, straggling main street, but it's one of the best angling centres in the country, noted for high quality salmon fishing. At the foot of the main street, the broad vistas of the River Moy's banks make up for the cramped town centre. Summer, fishing, sporting events, *details, TIO.*

Dolmen of the Four Maols, SW of town, across level crossing at railway station, up narrow road for 2 km (1 mile) Signposted. Walks, downstream, on both banks of River Moy, from bridge. Boat hire: John Walkin, *Tone Street,* ☎ *(096)22442.* Bicycles: Gerry's Cycle Centre, *Crossmolina Road,* ☎ *(096)70455*

AROUND BALLINA

Abbeytown, *2 km (1 mile) N of Crossmolina:* 10th c abbey.

Ardnaree Hill, *E bank of River Moy overlooking Ballina on L133:* ruins of 14th c Augustinian church.

Ballycastle, *26 km (16 miles) NW of Ballina on L133, 261 bus from Ballina.* Interesting prehistoric remains. Attractive N Mayo coast scenery. Bicycles: Barrett's Stores, ☎ *(096)43005.*

Barony of Erris, *S of Belderg, L133 crosses it to Glenamoy.* One of most desolate areas of Ireland.

Bartragh Island, large island at mouth of River Moy, ideal for secluded picnics. Boats, Ballina.

Bellacorick, *17 km (11 miles) W of Crossmolina on N59 to Belmullet.* Musical Bridge—play a tune by rubbing stone along N parapet. Local legend says that the bridge will never be completed; beware, a sudden end awaits anyone who tries.

Belmullet, *63 km (39 miles) W of Ballina.* Entrance to Mullet Peninsula, nine sandy beaches within easy driving distance. Belmullet Golf Club, *9 holes.*

Benwee Head, *16 km (10 miles) W of Belderg:* outstanding cliffscapes. Off-shore Stages of Broadhaven rocks rise dramatically out of the sea.

The Twelve Bens, Co. Galway

Castle Firbis, *5 km (3 miles) NE of Enniscrone:* ruined 12th c stronghold of MacFirbis clan, noted Gaelic poets.

Ceide Fields, *near Ballycastle:* the largest Stone Age monument in the world, including dwelling areas and megalithic tombs, stretching over 1,011 ha (2,500 acres). It is being developed with an interpretative centre, giving all-weather viewing. Nearby *Cliffs of Ceide* are awe-inspiring.

Crossmolina, *13 km (8 miles) W of Ballina on N59.* Beautifully set on River Deel under shadows of Nephin Mountains, less than 2 km (1 mile) from Lough Conn, in heart of fabulous salmon and brown trout fishing country. *North Mayo family history research and heritage centre.* New project has impressive genealogical records and collection of old farm implements and household artefacts. *Daily,* ☎ *(096)31809.* Deel Riding Centre, *Moylaw,* ☎ *(096)31197.*

Danish Cellar, *8 km (5 miles) N of Belmullet:* beautiful bay fringed with cliffs. **Doonamo Point,** *7 km (5 miles) NW of Belmullet.* Ruined prehistoric fort on cliff edge. Tremendous views of offshore Eagle Island with lighthouse. Elly Bay, on E side, has magnificent strand. *Fallmore, S end of peninsula:* remains of St Derival's Church. Also ruins of St Derival's Vat, a holy well believed to have great restorative powers.

Doonbristy, *Downpatrick Head:* striking ancient fort on isolated cliff.

Easkey, *26 km (16 miles) NE of Ballina.* Pleasant little seaside village guarded at either end by a Martello Tower. Nearby, dolmen held up by four pillars. Rare fossils at back of pier. *Split Rock,* Ice Age boulder: *3 km (2 miles) on Ballina side of village.* Children's playground. *Mar 17-June 1, weekends. June 2-Oct 31, daily.* Crazy golf, good surfing, golf, pitch and putt, tennis. Indoor amusements, Improvement Society Pavilion, *June 1-Sept 1.* Youth Hostel. The Atlantic Drive skirts O'Donnell Castle, pier, natural swimming pool.

Enniscrone, *14 km (9 miles) NE of Ballina on E side of Killala Bay.* 5 km (3 mile) beach. Medicinal baths. Many pleasant walks. Bicycles: G. Helley, ☎ *(096)36291.* Enniscrone Golf Club, *18 holes,* ☎ *(096)36392.*

Errew Abbey, *10 km (6 miles) S of Crossmolina,* on peninsula jutting into Conn, ruins of Augustinian foundation.

Foxford, *16 km (10 miles) S of Ballina.* **Foxford Woollen Mills'** visitor centre details the 100 year old history of the mills, renowned for their tweeds. 19th c style school room. Shop, restaurant. *All year, Mon-Sat, 10 a.m.-6 p.m., Sun, 2 p.m.-6 p.m.* ☎ *(094)56756.* Foxford has marked the birthplace, in the town, of Admiral Brown, who founded the Argentinian Navy in early 19th c.

Giant Rocking Stone, *Pontoon Bridge, just W of Pontoon Bridge Hotel:* huge chunk of granite that looks as if you can set it rocking with a gentle push. Trying is a great anticlimax.

Kilcummin Strand, *6 km (4 miles) N of Killala:* well signposted beach where French forces under General Humbert landed in August, 1798 to aid the '98 Rising. Nearby, St Cummin's monastery ruins.

Killala, *11 km (7 miles) NW of Ballina on W shores of Killala Bay.* CI cathedral, fine paintings, many historical records. In churchyard, elaborate souterrain. Nearby round tower. ♿ The quayside and its buildings are worth exploring.

Kilmoremoy, *3 km (2 miles) NW of Ballina on L133 to Killala.* Ancient church with rampart, founded by disciple of St Patrick. Beside church, cross-inscribed rock said to have been blessed by St Patrick.

Lough Cullin, *3 km (2 miles) W of Foxford on L22:* car park, picnic area, fishing, forest walks. Excellent views over lough and nearby Lough Conn.

Moista Sound, *W of Belderg:* narrow chasm enclosed by vertical cliffs.

Moyne Friary, *3 km (2 miles) SE of Killala:* stream runs through ruins. Most attractive. Etchings of 16th c ships on nave wall plaster. From top of nearby friary tower, magnificent views of Bartragh Island, Killala Bay.

Mullet Peninsula, Blind Harbour, *6 km (4 miles) NW of Belmullet,* remarkable silted inlet. **Cliffs of Erris,** *on W of Peninsula.* These run N from Bingham Lodge for 22 km (14 miles), wonderful views.

Pollatomish, *8 km (5 miles) NW of Glenamoy:* Youth Hostel.

Porturlin, *6 km (4 miles) E of Benwee Head:* excellent 5 km (3 miles) clifftop walk to tiny Portacloy harbour. Fine cliff scenery.

Poulnachantinny Puffing Holes, *Downpatrick Head:* magnificent natural display as caverns fill with sea.

Rosserk Friary, *5 km (3 miles) N of Ballina:* founded in 15th c, one of finest Franciscan friaries in Ireland. Well-preserved. Access at all times.

Clifden

Pop. 1,400, 79 km (49 miles) W of Galway, 296 km (184 miles) W of Dublin. EC Thurs. TIO, ☎ *(095)21155, May-Sept.*

'Capital' of Connemara, this wild, desolate-looking town with splendidly wide main street is the ideal base for exploring the great natural beauties of the West. The two hour bus journey from Galway provides a truly memorable approach. Situated between the Atlantic and the peaks of the Twelve Bens, Clifden has an almost Alpine air, most refreshing. Connemara Pony Show: *Aug.*

Two buildings dominate the town: the Protestant church built in 1820, just eight years after Clifden was founded has a silver copy of the Cross of Cong. The Catholic church, built 1830, stands on site of ancient 'clochán' or beehive-shaped monastic stone hut from which Clifden takes its name. Also see old railway station; the line to Galway closed over 50 years ago.

Clifden Castle, 2 km (1 mile) W of town: ruined mansion of John D'Arcy of Killtulla, who founded Clifden in early 19th c. Continue walk up sky road

Roundstone, Co. Galway

for exhilarating views of coastline, as far as Eyrephort beaches. **Owenglin Cascade,** *just below town:* where the Owenglin River falls steeply over boulders, most attractive. Walk: start at Quay Road, continue past beach and tiny harbour through castle grounds, returning by Cloghavard. **Connemara Pottery:** *all year except Dec, Mon-Sat, Sky Road.* This narrow road, running on high ground to the W of Clifden gives marvellous views over the town and Clifden Bay. ☎ *(095)21254.* See tweed being woven at Millars, *Main St.,* ☎ *(095)21038.* Errislannan Riding Centre, ☎ *(095)21134.* Connemara Golf Club, *18 holes,* ☎ *(095)23502.* Bicycles: John Mannion, *Railway View,* ☎ *(095)21160, (095)2115 after 8 p.m.*

AROUND CLIFDEN

Ballynahinch Lake, *on N59 from Clifden to Recess:* route skirts Twelve Bens and runs along N shore of lake, most attractive.

Carna/Killieran, sandy beaches at Callowfeanish, Mweenish, Moyrus, Ardmore.

Cashel, *22 km (14 miles) SE of Clifden:* angling, shooting centre at head of Cashel Bay. Takes its name from circular stone fort, remains of which lie on mountain slope NE of village.

Cleggan: Six safe, sandy beaches nearby, two within walking distance.

Cnoc Athy, *near Clifden:* spectacular views of lake, moor, sea from 120 m (400 ft) hill.

Connemara National Park, *near Letterfrack,* 200 ha (3,800 acres) with short distance walks, paddocks with pedigree Connemara ponies, nature trails, picnic areas, audio-visual centre, multi-media presentation, permanent exhibition, tearoom, visitors' lounge and restroom. *May-Sept, daily, 10 a.m.-6.30 p.m.* ☎ *(095)41054/41006.* ♿

Coral Strand, *6 km (4 miles) SW of Clifden:* one of many fine bathing strands in Mannin Bay.

Derreen, *6 km (4 miles) SE of Leenane on L100 to Maam:* interesting forest walks.

Derryclare Lough, breathtaking drive from Ballynahinch Lake, E of Twelve Bens, continue past Lough Inagh and Kylemore Lough, on both sides of valley, mountains rise over 609 m (2,000 ft). Good fishing country.

Derrygimlagh Bog, *6 km (4 miles) S of Clifden, 3 km (2 miles) NE of Ballyconneely:* foundations and some masts of Marconi company's first transatlantic wireless station, destroyed during Civil War. Nearby is spot where Alcock and Brown landed after first non-stop transatlantic flight in June, 1919. Cairn, on higher ground, 3 km (2 miles) away, 4 m (14 ft) stone monument in shape of plane.

Diamond Hill, *just E of Letterfrack:* 445 m (1,460 ft), marvellous views of N Connemara coast.

Dog's Bay/Gurteen Bay, *3 km (2 miles) SW of Roundstone off L102:* fine, sandy beaches. Nearby strands include Murvey, Dolin, Aillebrack and Dunloughan.

Doon Hill, *3 km (2 miles) SW of Ballyconneely on L102 to Clifden:* derelict coast watching post built during World War II. Hill 65 m (215 ft) an easy climb, fine beach at nearby Bunowen Bay.

Errisbeg Mountain, *W of Roundstone;* 300 m (987 ft). Worth easy climb for fine views of lake-dotted countryside to N and NW and seascapes to S and W.

Errislannan, walk: leave Clifden by Ardbear road. Cross Weir Bridge (salmon congregate beneath it during spawning season), keep R at Errislannan and Boat Harbour beaches, returning by N shores of Mannin Bay to Derrygimlagh. See Lough Fadda, wild bird haunt. Alcock and Brown memorial nearby.

High Island, *NW of Omey Island. 3 km (2 miles) W of Aughrus Point:* site of ruins of monastery of St Feichin, fine views of Connemara coast. No harbour; landing difficult even in fine weather.

Inishbofin Island, *19 km (12 miles) NW of Clifden. Mailboat sailings, Cleggan to Inishbofin: sailings all year, depending on weather. In summer, up to nine a day. Details,* ☎ *(095)45806.* Not a lot to do, but many tremendous seascapes and safe beaches. Two hotel, no shortage of creature comforts. One restaurant. Ideal for water-based sports and walking. Many varieties of wild flowers. Unspoilt Bofin Harbour is especially attractive. Bicycles, Days Hotel, ☎ *(095)45803.*

Killary Harbour, *24 km (15 miles) NE of Clifden.* 16 km (10 mile) inlet more like Norwegian fjord. Road skirting S side, through fishing village of Leenane, offers tremendous views. Youth Hostel.

Kylemore Lough*:* mountains rise almost vertically from its shores. Magnificent 19th c castle on lower slopes now Benedictine convent; in great hall, flag captured by Irish Brigade after battle of Fontenoy. Gothic chapel in grounds. Gift and craft centre, pottery, restaurant. Grounds and abbey *open Mar 17-Dec, daily, 10 a.m.-6 p.m.* ☎ *(095)41146.* Gift and craft centre, ☎ *(095)41113—Shops.* Tearoom, craft shop.

Leenane. This village, near the head of Killary harbour and W end of Party mountains, is ideal for exploring an area of outstanding scenery. *5 km (3 miles) W* is the Aasleagh waterfall on the Erriff River. Leenane cultural centre details history of wool and sheep. *Details.* ☎ *(095)42231.*

Letterfrack, *13 km (8 miles) NE of Clifden on N59.* Founded by 19th c Quakers as mission settlement. Impressive craft centre, *daily during season.* Excellent bathing strands at nearby Barnaderg Bay.

Maamturk Mountains, *take L100 from Leenane SE to Maam.* **Maam Valley Pottery,** *Maam: all year, Mon-Sat 10 a.m.-6 p.m.* Adjoining shop, ☎ *(091) 71109.* In Maam Cross: Peacocke's complex includes craft shop and restaurant, as well as rep-

lica of 'The Quiet Man' cottage, museum containing over 70 items of rural life. ☎ *(091)82306/82374.*

Mac Dara's Island, *13 km (8 miles) SW of Kilkieran:* ruins of church, grave of St Mac Dara.

Mweenish Island, *near Kilkieran:* sandy beaches. Holy well on S tip. Connected to mainland by bridge.

Omey Island, *9 km (6 miles) SW of Cleggan:* can be reached on foot at low tide. Fine strands, pony races in Aug. In sandhills on N side of island, ruins of Temple Feheen, small 7th c church and college.

Recess, *16 km (10 miles) E of Clifden,* ☎ *(095)34636.* Connemara Green Marble Shop: large general store with extensive craft shop and very good range of Irish books as well as café, pub and petrol station.

Renvyle Peninsula, *NW of Letterfrack:* Renvyle House Hotel. Run for many years by Oliver St John Gogarty, writer and contemporary of James Joyce. Sports facilities open to visitors: sailing, water skiing, riding, pony trekking, ☎ *(095)43511.* Ruins of 14th c O'Flaherty castle *2 km (1 mile) W of hotel.* Excellent nearby beaches. Renvyle Hill: fine views. *Little Killary Adventure Centre, Salruck.* Outdoor sports, ☎ *(095)43411.* Bicycles: Renvyle Stores, *Tully,* ☎ *(095)43485.*

Roundstone, *22 km (14 miles) SE of Clifden on L102.* Quiet village founded in early 19th c by Alexander Nimmo, a Scottish engineer. Almost landlocked harbour. Beach. Riding. Gurteen Beach Trekking Centre, *Errisbeg.* Bicycles: M.J. Ferron, ☎ *(095)35838.*

St Patrick's Bed and Well, *6 km (4 miles) SW of Maam:* take footpath up mountain from Maumeen. Well water believed to have medicinal properties. Pilgrimage last Sun in July.

Salrock, *at head of Little Killary:* tiny, beautiful village, fine view across the Killaries, surrounding mountains magnificent.

Toombeola Bridge, *5 km (3 miles) NW of Cashel:* Dominican abbey ruins. Founded 1427 by an O'Flaherty. Riding: The Angler's Return, ☎ *(095)31091.*

Gallarus Oratory, near Ballyferriter, Co. Kerry

Dingle

Pop 1,400, 50 km (35 miles) W of Tralee, 68 km (42 miles) NW of Killarney, 350 km (218 miles) SW of Dublin. EC Thurs. TIO, ☎ (066)51188. May-Oct. Bus enquiries: ☎ (066)21211.

The main town on the Dingle peninsula, set on an almost landlocked harbour, and a perfect centre for exploring the area's many ancient sites and

O'Flaherty's pub, Dingle, Co. Kerry

natural wonders. This fishing town's friendly atmosphere is enhanced by a number of good craft shops, some fine gourmet restaurants and many more modestly priced establishments, and a plentiful selection of pubs. A very popular resort during the season, especially with Germans. Dingle Regatta: currach races held amid carnival atmosphere, *mid-Aug.* Dingle Races: biggest 'flapper' race for untried horses in Ireland. Complete with fun fair. Great fun *early Aug.* The pier is ideal for a stroll and view of the bay, apart from times when fishing boats are being unloaded. **St Mary's Church,** *next to the library,* was built in the 1860s and substantially renovated in the 1960s and 1970s. Presentation Convent chapel, at back of the church, has fine Harry Clarke paintings. The Holy Stone in Upper Main Street may have prehistoric origins. **Library,** *Green Street:* collection of material relating to prominent local patriot Thomas Ashe. *Tues-Sat.* **Craft Village,** *on Dunquin Road.* O'Flaherty's, very popular old-fashioned pub, stone floor, traditional music during season. *Marina.* Dingle walking route extends for 152 km (95 miles) to Tralee, taking in the peninsula's best coastal scenery. Beaches: close to town at Doonsean and Slaidin. Eddie 'Hutch' Hutchinson builds currachs at Feothanach near Dingle. *By app.* Bicycles: J. Moriarty, *Main Street,* ☎ (066)51316; Michael O'Sullivan, *Waterside,* ☎ (066)51476. Riding: Thompson's, *Drumquin* ☎ (066)56144, Ballintaggart Hostel, *Dingle,* ☎(066)51454.

AROUND DINGLE

Anascaul, *16 km (10 miles) E of Dingle on T68.* From the small, attractive village of Anascaul, the road leads for 5 km (3 miles) to the car park beside Anascaul Lake, set high in the mountains, far from any sign of human habitation.

Ballinskelligs, Youth Hostel, ☎ (0667)9109.

Ballydavid, *NE corner of Smerwick Harbour:* see traditional currachs (canvas-covered boats) being built.

Ballyferriter, the heritage centre on Main Street has many artefacts and illustrations of the 19th c

way of life on the Dingle peninsula. Daily, in summer. *Details: Dingle TIO.* Since the village is in the heart of the Dingle Gaeltacht (Irish-speaking area), all the signs in the **Séipéal N. Uinseann** *(St Vincent's Church), on the opposite side of the street,* are in Irish. *Details: Dingle TIO.* Potadoireacht na Caolóige pottery, *Clogher.* Run by Louis Mulcahy, this pottery produces fine work that can be purchased in the extensive showrooms. *May-Sept, Mon-Sun, 9.30 a.m.-7 p.m. by app.* Shop *same hours,* ☎ (066)56229.

Blasket Islands, *W of Slea Head:* only one of the seven islands, the Great Blasket, was ever continuously inhabited and it was abandoned in 1953 after a spate of bad fishing seasons. One of smaller islands, Inishvickillane, is summer home of retired political leader Charles Haughey. During fine weather, the other islands can be visited from Dunquin. Most of the islands are being turned into a national park and the plans include restoration of some of the buildings on Great Blasket island. *Details: Dingle TIO.*

Brandon Mountain, *W from Ballybrack following rough track called Saint's Road:* 900 m (3,000 ft), well worth climbing, St Brendan's Oratory is near top.

Caherconree, *5 km (3 mile) climb from Camp, up mountain road to Beheenagh, climb W spur.* On triangular plateau, explore the old fort, seat of Curaoi Mac Daire, a king of ancient Ireland. Extensive views.

Castlegregory, Cathair na Máirtíneach and Cathair Murphy, two ancient circular stone forts, good beach.

Cloghane, *SW corner of Brandon Bay:* fine beach.

Conor Pass, *runs NE from Dingle for some 10 km (6 miles):* rises to a height of 450 m (1,500 ft). Road very narrow and in places only a small stone wall protects you from vast drop to valley below. In fine weather, view over surrounding mountains and rock-strewn valley is incredible. When clouds block the view, it's like being airborne.

Dingle-Dunquin road, spectacular sea views. The road skirts Ventry Harbour; there, you have a choice of routes, the minor road S of Mount Eagle, skirting Slea Head, is the more spectacular. Archaeological remains in this area include over 400 clocáns or beehive huts.

Dun an Oir, *S of Smerwick village on W shore of harbour:* ruins of fort built in 1580. Nearby memorial commemorates massacre of Geraldine and Spanish troops in fort not long after.

Dunbeg Fort, *3 km (2 miles) E of Slea Head:* ancient headland fort, rather too spectacularly situated, the outer edges have fallen into the sea. Signposted across fields from coast road.

Dunquin: Entrepreneur, raconteur and traveller, Kruger Kavanagh was a character to end all characters. At his bar, in Dunquin, perched above the sea at the W end of Europe, he was host to personalities from all over the world. Great atmosphere, adjoining guest house. Cottage birthplace of storyteller and folklorist Peig Sayers. New interpretative centre.

Ferriter's Castle, *3 km (2 miles) NW of Ballyferriter:* birthplace of Pierce Ferriter, one of the last Irish chiefs to hold out against Cromwell.

Gallarus Oratory, *3 km (2 miles) NE of Ballyferriter:* best preserved early Christian church in Ireland, believed to date from 8th c. Built in shape of upturned boat and still in almost perfect condition. Accessible at all times.

Inch, *S Dingle peninsula.* Magnificent 6 km (4 mile) golden strand at entrance to Castlemaine Bay, one of best bathing beaches in the region.

St Brendan's Oratory, *just S of Ballyferriter:* also ruined Chancellor's House, holy well.

Seven Hogs, or Magharee Islands: ask a boatman at Fahamore to take you across.

Smerwick Harbour, *NW Dingle Peninsula:* good walks along both sides of harbour. To E, land rises up to Ballydavid Head. At low tide, this great natural harbour becomes largely sandbanks. Slea Head drive, from Ventry with its deserted harbour, to Dunquin, offers spectacular seascape views.

Tralee Bay, *N of Camp village:* great sandy beach.

Ennis

Pop. 7,000, 26 km (16 miles) NW of Shannon airport, 68 km (42 miles) S of Galway, 233 km (145 miles) SW of Dublin. EC Thurs. TIO. Clare Road, Ennis, ☎ *(065)28366. All year. Bus enquiries: (065)24177.*

An interesting town set on the banks of the River Fergus, with narrow, winding streets and a rich historical atmosphere. In addition to having been the unlikely birthplace of the wife of Hector Berlioz, Ennis has been the scene of some notable political 'firsts', such as the election of Daniel O'Connell in 1828 and that of De Valera in 1917. Good centre for touring the Co. Clare coast, including the famous Cliffs of Moher and the remarkable Burren country for the N. Fleadh Nua: great festival of traditional Irish music, *late May. Details: TIO.* County Clare Show: varied programme, including horse cattle competitions. *Mid-Aug. Details TIO.*

Clare Abbey, *3 km (2 miles) SE of Ennis, just off N18:* ruins, including tower of Augustinian abbey founded in 1195. **Killone Abbey,** *5 km (3 miles) S of Ennis on W shores of Killone Lough:* founded in 12th c by Donal O'Brien, last king of Munster. St John's Holy Well is near the Abbey; track from abbey still called the 'Pilgrim's Road' after bygone pilgrimages. *Ennis Friary:* 13th c Franciscan foundation was in use until early 17th c. Many parts remain, including chancel, nave and tower. Interesting monuments. *Mid June-mid Sept, daily, 9.30 a.m.-6.30 p.m.* ☎(065)29100. **De Valera Library and Museum,** *Harmony Row:* includes museums with many mementoes of famous people with local connections, including de Valera, library, exhibition gallery, study centre. *All year, Mon, Wed, Thurs, 11 a.m.-5.30 p.m. Tues, Fri, 11 a.m.-8 p.m.,* ☎ *(065)21616.* **O'Connell Monument,** *town centre:* site of great 1828 meeting at which Daniel O'Connell was nominated to stand for election in Clare. Also see new De Valera statue. Laneways in the vicinity, some dating back to the 18th c, provide interesting strolls. *Railway station:* old steam engine from the famous now unfortunately extinct West Clare Railway, immortalised by Percy French in his song, 'Are you right there, Michael, are you right?' **Lenthall's,** *Abbey Street:* delightfully old-fashioned inn, with antique bars and nooks. **The Usual Place,** *in the market and* **May Kearney's,** *in Lifford Road,* are two traditional style pubs. Denis Maurer, *26 O'Connell Street:* makes gold and silver jewellery. *Mon-Sat, 9 a.m.-6 p.m.,* ☎ *(065)28974.* Attractive riverside stroll along Harvey's Quay to Wood Quay, returning to Parnell Street. Further upstream, you can take Newbridge Road alongside the river. Swimming pool: indoor, heated, Sandfield Park, *Gort Road, Tues-Sun. July-Aug, daily,* ☎ *(065)21604.* Bicycles: Michael Tierney, *17 Abbey Street,* ☎ *(065)29433.* Also from Co. Clare Rent-a-Cottage at Ballyvaughan, Broadford, Carrigaholt, Corofin, Feakle. Golf Club, Drumbiggle, *18 holes,* ☎ *(065)24074.*

AROUND ENNIS

Aillwee Cave, *3 km (2 miles) SE of Ballyvaughan, just off Ennis Road:* formed two million years ago. Quite safe for over 925 m (1,000 yds), the strange subterranean landscape includes stalagmites and stalactites, all dazzlingly lit. Aillwee Cave Centre, at entrance, is shaped like Stone Age cairn, restaurant, craft shop. *Mid-Mar-early Nov. Summer, daily, 10 a.m.-7 p.m. Spring, autumn, 10 a.m.-6 p.m.* ☎ *(065)77036.*

Ballyvaughan, *16 km (10 miles) NE of Lisdoon-varna:* pleasant seaside village with pier, facing Galway Bay. Fine drive to Black Head, Lisdoon-varna and Corkscrew Hill back to Ballyvaughan. Good views N over Galway Bay—especially when the sun's going down.

Bridges of Ross, *5 km (3 miles) `NE of Kilbaha, signposted track from Ross-Moneen-Loop Head road:* pair of arches formed by action of sea on N side of Loop Head peninsula.

Burren, *N of Corofin, E of Lisdoonvarna:* impressive area of limestone outcrops that looks like the moon's surface. Remarkable flora and fauna make it well worth exploring in depth. Now a National Park.

Cappagh Pier, *take Shannonside road E for about 35 km (22 miles):* good views of offshore Scattery and Hog islands and across to N Kerry coast.

Carrigaholt Castle, *set on headland on S side of Loop Head peninsula:* 14th c, overlooks attractive Carrigaholt harbour.

Cliffs of Moher, *10 km (6 miles) NW of Lahinch, TIO:* ☎ *(065)81171, May-Sept.* Little introduction needed. Extending for 8 km (5 miles), these thoroughly majestic cliffs are among the West's most striking features. Best seen from O'Brien's Tower, *May-Oct, daily, 10 a.m.-6 p.m.* The information centre at the car park has full details on the history of the area, a craft shop and a restaurant. *Open all year, daily, 10 a.m.-6 p.m.,* ☎ *(065)81171.* The drive N to Black Head, then E to Kinvara along L54/N67, is one of finest coastal routes in Ireland.

Corcomroe Abbey, *10 km (6 miles) E of Bally-vaughan at foot of Abbey Hill:* founded in 1182 by King Donal O'Brien. Church still in good condition. Yeats set *The Dreaming of the Bones* here.

Corofin, *15 km (9 miles) N of Ennis on L53:* Clare Heritage Centre in converted 18th c Protestant church. Displays in the fascinating museum section depict Co Clare life in the 19th c. The centre has extensive genealogical records for the county. *Open Nov-Mar, Sat, Sun, 9 a.m.-5 p.m.; Apr-Oct, daily, 10 a.m.-6 p.m.,* ☎ *(065)27955.* **Dysert O'Dea Castle,** and archaeology centre, just outside Corofin, includes an audio-visual show, photographic displays, local history exhibition, museum, trail guide details for 25 local archaeological and historical sites. *May-Sept, daily, 10 a.m.-7 p.m.* ☎ *(065)27722.* *12th c White Cross of Tola,* round tower.

Diarmuid and Gráinne's Rock, *N side of Loop Head:* separated from mainland by deep canyon. Tradition says that Cuchulainn jumped this chasm to avoid attentions of witch called Mal. She tried to follow but didn't quite make it.

Doolin, *8 km (5 miles) SW of Lisdoonvarna:* small fishing village on sandy bay, famous for its folk music. Doolin crafts gallery: workshops, shop, coffee shop, garden. *Daily.* Trips to Aran Islands in fine weather. *Details: Cliffs of Moher TIO.* Bicycles: Mrs Josephine Moloney, *The Horse Show,* ☎ *(065)74006.*

Ennistymon, *just inland from Lahinch.* Delightfully set in wooded valley beside River Cullenagh cascade. The main street has interesting, old-style shops, some with their names in Irish. Good brown trout fishing, boat trips on river. The Falls Hotel generates its own electricity in ingenious fashion. Willie Daly Riding Centre, *Ballinagaddy* .

Fanore, *S of Black Head:* good bathing.

Kilbaha, from its tiny harbour, road climbs W for 5 km (3 miles) to Loop Head lighthouse. Superb views.

Kilfenora, *11 km (7 miles) SE of Lisdoonvarna on L53:* Burren Display Centre is best possible introduction to the neighbouring Burren. Flora impressively recreated in silk and wax. Models of birds, butterflies, landscapes, moths. Library has good collection of reference material. Staff will suggest scenic routes for cyclists, drivers, walkers. Minibus tours of the Burren are also available. The cen-tre has a craft shop. *Mar, Apr, 10 a.m.-5.30 p.m.; June-Aug, 10 a.m.-7 p.m.; Sept, Oct, 10 a.m.-5.30 p.m.* ☎ *(065)88030.* **St Fachnan's Cathedral** (CI): nave used as church, remainder roofless. Doorty Cross and High Cross just W of cathedral.

Kilkee, *65 km (35 miles) SW of Ennis. EC Wed. TIO:* ☎ *(065)56112. May-Sept.* Popular seaside resort with exceptionally safe 1.5 km (1 mile) long strand, ideal for bathing. Deep sea and shore angling centre. See Old West Clare railway station. *Heritage centre:* household implements and old photographs of area. *July-Aug, Mon-Fri, 11 a.m.-1 p.m.; 2 p.m.-5 p.m.* ☎ *(065) 56169.* Children's amusement park. *SO.* Boat trips from pier to see caves and cliffs. Kilkee subaqua centre: full skin diving facilities, ☎ *(065)56211.* Boats: Manuel di Lucia, ☎ *(065)5612.* Bicycles: Williams, *Circular Road,* ☎ *(065)56041/56141.* **Edmund Point,** attractive walk SW of Duggerna Rocks, which protect town from Atlantic, going on to the Amphitheatre. With its tiers of rocklike seats, it is often used for outdoor concerts. Excellent views from nearby Lookout Hill. From this point, you can return to Kilkee by road or continue past Bishop's Island to Castle Point, from where you can see the coast as far as Loop Head. From East End, fine 8 km (5 mile) walk by Blackrock, Chimney Bay to Farrihy Bay and Corbally village, returning by road to Kilkee.

Killimer, *10 km (6 miles) E of Kilrush:* Ellen Hanly, the 'Colleen Bawn' is buried in the old graveyard. Her tragic death inspired Gerald Griffin's novel, *The Collegians* on which in turn were based Boucicault's drama, *The Colleen Bawn* and Benedict's opera, *The Lily of Killarney.* Regular daily ferry sailings to Tarbert, Co. Kerry. Details listed under Tarbert in 'Tralee' section. *TIO,* ☎ *(065)51577. June- Aug.*

Kilrush, *43 km (27 miles) SW of Ennis, EC. Thurs. TIO,* ☎ *(065)51577. June-Aug.* Kilrush is a striking market town, enlivened by weekly horse fairs, *usually Sat.* The banter of farmers selling their

The Burren, Co. Clare

horses is fascinating. Kilrush Creek Marina, Ireland's first fully integrated marina development, ☎ *(065)52072.* The heritage centre depicts the monastic settlements on Scattery Island and local history in the Kilrush area. *June-Aug, Mon-Sat, 10 a.m.-6 p.m.* ☎ *(065)51596.* Exhibition "Kilrush in Landlord Times", located at Kilrush Town Hall, ☎ *(065)51596, Mon-Sat, 11 a.m.-6 p.m., Sun, 2 p.m.-6 p.m.* Bicycles: Korner Shop, *Henry Street,* ☎ *(065)51037.* Kilrush Golf and Sports Club, *Ballykett,* 9 holes, ☎ *(065)51138.*

Knappogue Castle, *Quin, 10 km (6 miles) SE of Ennis on L31:* built 1467, seat of MacNamara fam-ily until 1815. In recent years, restored to medieval splendour, with craft shop and workshops, forge and replanted gardens and orchards. *May-Oct, Mon-Sun, 9.30 a.m.-5.30 p.m.* Medieval banquets, *5.45 p.m., 8.45 p.m., nightly.* ☎ *(061) 71103.*

Lahinch, *EC. Wed. TIO,* ☎ *(065)81474. May-Sept.* Popular resort with 1.5 km (1 mile) long sandy beach at NE corner of Liscannor Bay. Promenade, sea water swimming pool. Cumann Merriman, annual cultural orgy held late Aug in honour of author of *The Midnight Court,* a bawdy 18th c Irish language epic. *Details: TIO.* Resort Theatre, *July, Aug.* Entertainment centre: café, cinema, dance hall, pool, traditional music, well situated near beach, *all year, daily.* New entertainment centre planned. Bicycles: Lahinch camping and caravan park, *Seapark,* ☎ *(065)81424.* Championship Golf course, *18 holes,* ☎ *(065)81003.*

Leamaneh Castle (NM), *7 km (4 miles) E of Kilfenora on L53:* amalgam of 1480 residential

Church door, Kilfenora, Co. Clare

tower and early 17th c fortified house. The ruins are remarkably well preserved, and are freely accessible.

Liscannor, *just along bay from Lahinch:* small fishing village. John P. Holland, inventor of submarine, born here in Castle Street in 1831. **St Macreehy's,** 12th c church 1.5 km (1 mile) E of village on Lahinch road. *Joe McHugh's pub,* mecca for greyhound aficionados, with its collection of trophies. **Clahane shore,** *just W of village,* has safe bathing. Legend says that submerged reef at mouth of Liscannor Bay is site of lost city of Kilstephen. Boats: John Lysaght, ☎ *(065)81346.* Martin McMahon, ☎ *(065)81101.*

Lisdoonvarna, *37 km (23 miles) NW of Ennis on L53. EC Wed.* Ireland's leading spa. Spa Wells Health Centre is principal sulphurous spring, with pump house and baths, an ideal way of removing late night impurities from the system. *June-Oct,* ☎ *(065)74023.* Lisdoonvarna Fair: inc. the mating game, when Ireland's shy bachelors seek spouses, *Sept.* Three day folk festival, with many top international names, *July, details:* Jim Shannon, *Doolin, Co. Clare.* There is an interesting 3 km (2 mile) circular walk along the 'Bog' road via the Spectacle Bridge to SW. The bridge, a single span over River Aille, has a round hole in the masonry, same width as the arch. 10 km (6 mile) walk NW of town to 15th c ruins of Ballynalacken Castle. The area's cave system is dangerous and should only be explored with help of experienced local guide, *details: TIO.* Bicycles: Burke's Garage, *The Square,* ☎ *(065)74022/74321.*

Cliffs of Moher, Co. Clare

Loop Head peninsula, *SW of Kilkee:* good sea views and walks.

Miltown Malbay, Scoil Éigse Willie Clancy, in tribute to Clare's greatest piper, *July, details: Kilkee TIO.* **Silver Strand,** *3 km (2 miles) N of Miltown Malbay:* safe bathing, *Slieve Callan, 10 km (6 miles) E of Miltown Malbay:* the highest point in W Clare. It can be climbed from the Miltown Malbay-Inagh L55, *10 km (6 miles) E of Miltown Malbay.* Fine views of surrounding countryside. Bicycles: Byrne and Sons, *Ennis Road,* ☎ *(065)84079.*

Newtown Castle, *3 km (2 miles) S of Ballyvaughan:* five storey 16th c tower is round on square base.

Quilty, *6 km (4 miles) SW of Miltown Malbay on N67 coast road:* take a currach to Mutton Island, *3 km (2 miles) offshore.*

Quin Abbey, *10 km (6 miles) E of Ennis:* well-preserved ruins of Franciscan friary founded 1402. Remains of a Norman castle were used to build friary; three of the castle's towers still stand at angles of friary building. You should be able to climb spiral stairs to top of one tower for fine views.

St Brigid's Well, *3 km (2 miles) NW of Liscannor:* waters of roadside well said to have curative properties. Pilgrimages *July, Aug.*

Scattery Island, *3 km (2 miles) offshore from Cappagh Pier, near Kilrush:* 6th c monastic settlement remains include five churches, one round tower. Information point. *Guided tours, summer boat service, daily,* ☎ *(065)51272/51275/51276.*

Galway

Pop. 51, 000, 217 km (135 miles) W of Dublin, 320 km (199 miles) SW of Belfast. EC. Thurs. TIO: Áras Fáilte, near railway station, ☎ *(091)63081. All year. Bus and train enquiries: Ceannt station,* ☎ *(091)63555 or 61444. Coach tours, boat trips on Lough Corrib, SO. Details: TIO. Taxis: Eyre Square.*

The West's major town, set at the mouth of the River Corrib, on the edge of what is now the western Gaeltacht (Irish-speaking area), Galway was originally a fishing community, which grew prosperous on continental trade. It then supported an affluent merchant class which commissioned many fine buildings, and the visitor with a sense for the past will find much of interest here. The city has long since recovered the vigour it lost during the Famine, and today it is prosperous but not brash with plenty of pubs and restaurants. Its cultural tradition is vigorous. Oyster Festival: world oyster opening championships. Much socialising, *Sept, details, TIO.*

Cathedral, *University Road,* near salmon weir bridge; opened 1965, controversial modern design. ⌧ **Collegiate Church of St Nicholas,** *entrance just off Shop Street:* built by Anglo-Normans in 1320, later enlarged. Tradition has it that Columbus worshipped here before setting out on his voyage of discovery. Many fine carvings and relics from Middle Ages. 'Son et Lumière' performances tell story of Galway and church in enthralling blend of sound and light. *July, Aug only. Tues, Thurs, 9 p.m. De-*

tails: TIO. ⌧ **Reference library,** *Hynes Building, St Augustine Street:* much local interest material. *Mon-Sat,* ☎ *(091)62471; 61666.* **University College art gallery:** occasional exhibitions, ☎ *(091)24411.* **Kenny's Bookshop & Art Gallery,** *High Street:* huge selection of Irish-interest books, antiquarian books, prints and maps. Bookbindery specialises in handcrafted bindings using designs by Irish artists. *Mon-Sat, 9 a.m.-6 p.m.,* ☎*(091)62739/61014/61021.* **Sheela-na-Gig bookshop,** *Middle Street.* **Druid Theatre,** *Chapel Lane:* lunch-time, evening performances. Specialises in work by Anglo-Irish writers. *Summer,* ☎ *(091)68617.* **Taibhdhearc na Gaillimhe,** *Middle Street:* regular Irish language productions all year. *Fáilte,* popular summer presentation of traditional song, music, dance, drama, ☎ *(091)62024 after 2 p.m.* **Jesuit Hall,** *Sea Road:* Regular plays and entertainment in English. Beside **St Nicholas'** church, the traditional Galway Saturday market is held every week. In season, shoals of salmon can be seen moving through the weir on the river to the Lough Corrib spawning grounds. In the centre of Galway, doorways and windows from the 17th and 18th c merchant houses can be seen at Abbeygate Street, Middle Street, Shop Street and St Augustine Street.

Spanish Arch, built 1594 to protect quay where Spanish ships unloaded wares. Spanish Parade continues as Long Walk. Good views of estuary and entrance to docks. ⌧ Just past Spanish Arch, the city museum has many local history relics, including photographs of the old tramway system that ran from Galway to Salthill. *April-Oct, Mon-Fri, 10 a.m.-5 p.m.* ☎ *(091)68151.*

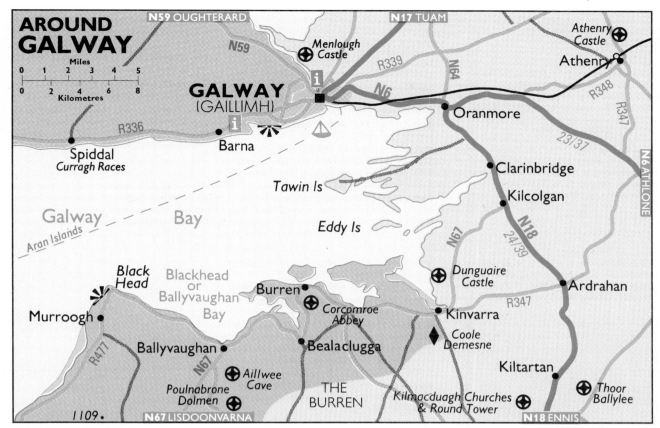

AROUND GALWAY

Lynch's Castle, corner of Shop Street, Abbeygate Street: incorporated in Allied Irish Bank, late 15th c, one of Ireland's finest surviving town castles. Photographs and texts explain history, *Mon-Fri, 10 a.m.-12.30 p.m ; 1.30 p.m.-3 p.m. Thurs, until 5 p.m.* ☒ *John F. Kennedy Park, Eyre Square:* plaque marks where President Kennedy addressed people of Galway in 1963, on receiving freedom of the city. Albert Power's celebrated statue of Pádraig O Conaire, pioneer of literary revival earlier this century, also great iron cannon presented to Connaught Rangers at end of Crimean War. ☒ *19 Eyre Square, (Bank of Ireland):* silver sword and Great Mace, Sword 19th c, 1710 Mace an exceptionally fine piece of Irish silverwork. *Mon-Fri, 10 a.m.-12.30 p.m., 1.30 p.m.-3 p.m. Thurs, until 5 p.m.* **Nun's Island Arts Centre** has regular exhibitions and other arts events. ☎ *(091)65886.*

Newtownsmith, pleasant riverside walk to salmon weir bridge. In season, salmon can be seen making their way to Lough Corrib. River Corrib, fine riverside strolls. University Road canal bridge, along tree-lined Upper Canal Road to Lower Canal Road, via Dominick Street to Claddagh Quay. *Claddagh* was once an individual, Irish-speaking fishing village on W bank of Corrib estuary and home of the Claddagh ring. The city centre lanes, including Buttermilk Lane (off Shop Street), O'Gorman's Lane (behind St Nicholas Collegiate Church) and Kirwan's Lane (off Cross Street) make for interesting rambling. Royal Tara China, **Tara Hall**: fine bone, china made, decorated, gilded. Visits by app, *Mon-Fri, 9 a.m.-1 p.m., 2 p.m.-5 p.m. Works closed first two weeks Aug.* Galway Crystal, *Merlin Park: crystal shop open 7 days.* Nora Barnacle's house, *at* **8 Bowling Green Lane**, has many artefacts commemorating Joyce's wife. *May-Sept, Mon-Sat, 10 a.m.-5 p.m. Or by arr,* ☎*(091)64743*

Leisure Activities: Greyhound racing, *New Sports Ground: Feb-Dec, Tues, Fri, 8.30 p.m.* During Galway Race Week at end of July, beginning of Aug, *Mon-Fri:* ☎ *(091)62273.* Galway Airport, *4 m (6 km) NE of Galway:* serving Dublin and Britain on daily basis. Aer Arann from Inverin airport, Connemara, to Aran Islands.

AROUND GALWAY

Annaghdown, *13 km (8 miles) N of Galway on E shores of Lough Corrib:* ruins of castle and ancient church on monastery site where St Brendan the Navigator said to have died. Nave and chancel can still be seen.

An Spidéal. Races, town's major attraction, *June.* ☎ *Galway TIO, (091)63081.* Church (C): completed in 1904 in Celtic Romanesque style renowned for architectural excellence. The Spiddal craft centre features locally-made handcrafts.

Ardamullivan Castle (NM), *8 km (5 miles) S of Gort:* ruins of 16th c O'Shaughnessy stronghold.

Athenry, *24 km (15 miles) E of Galway on T4.* Its Norman walls are best preserved in Ireland. Five out of six original wall towers survive; only imperious North Gate remains of five medieval entrances. *Athenry Castle,* 13th c. Adjacent public park, children's playground. Ruins of Dominican Priory of Ss, Peter and Paul, built in 1241, destroyed by Cromwellians in 1652.

Aughanure Castle, *5 km (3 miles) E of Oughterard:* built by O'Flahertys in 16th c. Four storey tower stands on island, protected by fast-flowing stream. Expertly restored. *June-Sept, Mon-Sun, 10 a.m.-6 p.m.* ☎ *(091)82214.*

Aughrim, *3 km (2 miles) SE of Kilconnell.* Small village takes name from battle fought on nearby ridge in 1691. Protestant Williamite forces defeated mainly Catholic Irish and French forces, determining future course of Irish history. *Aughrim interpretative centre* details the Battle of Aughrim. *Summer, daily, 10 a.m.-6 p.m., or by arr,* ☎ *(0905)73939.*

Ballinasloe, *64 km (40 miles) E of Galway on T4.* Bus and train enquiries: ☎ *(0905)42105.* TIO, ☎ *(0905)42131. July-Aug.* Best known for its great October Horse Fair, an eight day carnival. *St Michael's Church* (C), *S of town,* 19th c, stained glass by Harry Clarke. ☒ *Ballinasloe Castle,* ruins of 14th c structure that commanded strategic bridge over River Suck. Swimming pool: indoor, heated, *Station Road, Wed-Sat,* ☎ *(0905)42293,* Millbrook Riding Centre, ☎ *(0905)42372.* Bicycles:

P. Clarke, *Dunloe Street,* ☎ *(0905)42417.* Ballinasloe Golf Club, *9 holes,* ☎ *(0905)42126.*

Ballinderry Castle, *3 km (2 miles) SE of Tuam,* one of last castles built in Ireland. Good state of repair.

Ballybrit Racecourse, *3 km (2 miles) E of Galway:* main races held over five giddy days, *end July, beginning Aug.* Galway Race Week a remarkable social event. *Other races, Sept, Oct,* ☎ *(091)62870.*

Bermingham House, *3 km (2 miles) NE of Tuam off road to Levally Lough:* headquarters of Bermingham and North Galway Hunt. Georgian, magnificent plasterwork and furniture, *weekday aft.*

Carraroe, *W of L100:* many fine beaches, including unique Coral Strand.

Claregalway, *10 km (6 miles) NE of Galway on N17 to Tuam.* Ruins of Franciscan friary built in 1252, suppressed by Henry VIII. By bridge over River Clare, large 15th c de Burgo castle in good repair.

Clarinbridge, *13 km (8 miles) SE of Galway on N18:* Burke's Oyster Inn renowned for its oysters. Part of Galway Oyster Festival takes place here, *Sept,* ☎ *(091)86107.* Clarinbridge Crystal, made in the village, has a showroom.

Clonbur, Petersburg House, largely ruins, once home of Lynch family, one of whose members, John, was a signatory of American Declaration of Independence. Forest walks by S shores of Lough Mask. Take L101 through Cornamona to Leenane on Killary Harbour for one of Connemara's most scenic routes. About 40 km (25 miles).

Clonfert Cathedral, *24 km (15 miles) NE of Portumna:* original monastery founded by St Brendan the Navigator in 563. Destroyed six times before becoming Augustinian priory in 12th c. Late 12th c doorway is finest example in Ireland of Romanesque style.

Cloondooan Castle, *8 km (5 miles) SW of Gort on L55:* once one of strongest in Thomond, now ruined, destroyed after 1586 siege. Nearby is Lough Bunny.

Cong, *S Mayo, between Lough Corrib and Lough Mask.* 12th c abbey. Rory O'Connor, last High King of Ireland, buried here, Cross of Cong in National Museum, Dublin. **Ashford Castle**, 18th c, restored by Sir Benjamin Guinness, of a certain brewing family, now a luxury hotel. On payment of small fee, you can wander round beautiful demesne, see castellated towers and attractive bridge. ☎ *(092)46003. Boat trips on Lough Corrib, leaving from hotel landing stage.* The legendary *Quiet Man* film was made on location in this area, 40 years ago. Local mementoes. **The Crusheens**, *just outside village:* small heaps of crosses. Funeral corteges halt here, a prayer is said and more crosses added. *Cong Caves,* over 40 underground caves in and around village, once places of refuge for highwaymen and patriots. Some can be explored. Cong Salmon Hatchery: *by app,* ☎ *(092)46049.* **Cong Wood**, forest walks, viewing tower. Enter from Cong village, through abbey grounds, across the river.

Coole Demesne, *3 km (2 miles) N of Gort, due W of N18.* Once home of Lady Gregory, now national forest and wildlife park. Sadly, only ruined walls and stables remain of once fine house where she held literary court with such notables as Sean O'Casey, W.B. Yeats, G.B. Shaw, J.M. Synge, Frank O'Connor. Famous tree, where they carved their

Dunguaire Castle, Kinvarra, Co. Galway

initials while taking after dinner air, can be seen. Picnic areas, forest walks, nature trails. Leaflet detailing trails is available, and nearby Coole Lake still has swans. New **visitor centre** with audiovisual shows. *June-Sept, daily, 9.30 a.m.-6.30 p.m.* ☎*(091)31804.*

Corrib View, *3 km (2 miles) E of Oughterard.* Good views over lake. If this leaves you unsatisfied, follow minor road NW along lakeshore. This peters out 13 km (8 miles) from Oughterard, all the while giving excellent views of lake.

Cregg Castle, *Corandulla, 15 km (9 miles) N of Galway city:* restored 17th c castle, now guesthouse and traditional Irish music centre. Nearby old woods, nature reserve. ☎ *(091)91434.*

Derryhivenny Castle (NM), *5 km (3 miles) NE of Portumna, just E of T31:* this well-preserved castle, erected in 1653, was one of last built in Ireland.

Dooros Peninsula, fine views of N end of Lough Corrib. Minor road runs to end of peninsula.

Dooros House, *5 km (3 miles) NW of Kinvara on shores of Kinvara Bay:* mansion where Count de Basterot, traveller and writer, entertained friends, including Yeats and Lady Gregory on the occasion of the founding of Dublin's Abbey Theatre. Now Youth Hostel, ☎ *(091)37173.*

Dry Canal, *near Cong:* built during great famine 130 years ago. Hundreds of labourers toiled for over four years, but as soon as water was let into the canal, it drained off through porous limestone. Only small section near Lough Mask has any water. Best place to see it is on bridge to N of L101 to Clonbur.

Dunmore, *13 km (8 miles) NE of Tuam on N83:* numerous archaeological remains, mainly ring forts.

Furbo, *3 km (2 miles) E of An Spidéal:* fine, sandy beach.

Headford, *29 km (18 miles) N of Galway on T40.* Popular angling centre adjacent to Lough Corrib. Boats can be hired at Greenfield, 6 km (4 miles) W of Headford on E shore of lough.

Inchagoill Island, *N reaches of Lough Corrib, 8 km (5 miles) SW of Cong. Boats from Cong, Oughterard.* Beautifully wooded island, largest in lake, site of 5th c Teampall Pharaic church, the 9th/10th c Teampall na Naomh (Church of the Saints), and the Stone of Lugna, said to be oldest Christian inscription in Europe, with exception of Rome's catacombs.

Inverin, *29 km (18 miles) W of Galway on L100.* Ruined castle by shore, many sandy beaches nearby. Youth Hostel.

Keelhilla, *13 km (8 miles) SW of Kinvarra, in N Co. Clare:* was ancient hermitage of St Colman and scene of miracle wherein the feast laid for King Guaire and his nobles flew through the air for the hungry saint.

Kilcolgan, *3 km (2 miles) S of Clarenbridge:* Morans Oyster Cottage, old pub famous for its seafood, ☎ *(091)86113.*

Kilconnell, *13 km (8 miles) W of Ballinasloe on T4 to Athenry:* Franciscan Friary, founded in 1353, gothic style nave, choir, side aisles, S transept, cloisters, domestic apartments. Instructions for borrowing key on entrance gate. At W end of village 1682 Donnellan memorial cross. (NM).

Killeeneen, *5 km (3 miles) W of N6 at Craughwell:* church is burial place of Raftery, blind Mayo-born poet, who spent much of his life travelling Co. Galway.

Kilmacduagh, *5 km (3 miles) SW of Gort:* the monastery founded here in 600 has an impressive array of churches. The nearly round tower, restored a century ago, leans about 0.6 m (2 ft), Galway's answer to Pisa.

Kiltartan, *1.5 km (1 mile) N of Gort:* church of great antiquity. Interesting 15th c altar-tomb.

Kinvara: charming fishing village, on S shore of Galway Bay. Ideal base for exploring Gort area antiquities and Burren. Traught Strand, 7 km (4 miles) sandy beach. **Dunguaire Castle**, *16th c,* restored, strikingly set on rock at edge of Galway Bay. *Apr-Sept, daily, 9.30 a.m.-5.30 p.m.* Medieval banquets nightly. Entertainment includes Irish music, dancing, scenes from plays by writers with local connections, like Lady Gregory, W.B. Yeats, and readings from Raftery the poet, ☎ *(091)37108, TIO, Galway,* ☎ *(091)63081, Castle Banquets, Shannon Airport,* ☎ *(061)361555.*

Knockmaa Hill (Cnoc Má), *10 km (6 miles) E of Headford, just S of L98 to Tuam:* traditional home of King Finbarra and Connacht fairies. One legend says it is burial place of Maeve, mythological Queen of Connacht. Excellent views from top.

Knockmoy Abbey, *11 km (7 miles) SE of Tuam:* founded in 1189 by Cathal O'Connor, King of Connacht, whose tomb is preserved within the ruins. Traces of ancient murals decorate N wall of chancel. Attractively set by small lake.

Labane Church (C), *8 km (5 miles) N of Gort on N18 to Galway:* early examples of Dublin School of Stained Glass. The nearby private residence of Tullira Castle was the home of Edward Martyn, the school's founder.

Leaba Phadraig (Patrick's Bed), *between Tuam and Tulynadaly Hill:* altar set in pile of stones. The

two indentations have always been bare of grass: they mark where the saint's knees rested while he prayed.

Lisacormack Fort, *1.5 km (1 mile) E of Tuam:* largest of the area's many forts.

Loughpark Crannóg, *3 km (2 miles) E of Tuam on Ryehill road:* prehistoric lake dwelling.

Loughrea, *32 km (20 miles) E of Galway on N6, 81.* Delightfully set on N shore of Lough Rea. **St Brendan's Cathedral** (C): this somewhat dull-looking cathedral has fine stained glass windows by Sarah Purser, Evie Hone and embroideries designed by Jack B. Yeats. Magnificent repository of modern Irish ecclesiastical art. ♿ **Carmelite monastery**, founded by Richard de Burgo, 1300, in excellent repair. Adjacent modern abbey. Author Seamus O'Kelly was born in Loughrea in 1880. This fine but somewhat neglected writer of poetry and drama died in Dublin aged 38. All his books, including *The Weaver's Grave* are currently out of print. House marked with plaque, grave nearby.

Menlough Castle, *3 km (2 miles) N of Galway on E bank of River Corrib:* attractive ivy-covered ruin. From Menlough, follow progress of canal to Lough Corrib.

Milltown, *13 km (8 miles) NW of Tuam on N17:* admirable walks in pleasant wooded country. Brown trout fishing in River Clare.

Monivea, *10 km (6 miles) NE of Galway on L54:* noted for great lawns, once linen bleaching greens. Large estate grounds once belonged to Ffrench family. Key to Ffrench mausoleum from gate lodge. Nearby forest walk.

Oranmore, *8 km (5 miles) SE of Galway:* Galway Bay Sailing Centre, sailing, canoeing, wind surfing, ☎ *(091)64585.*

Oughterard, *27 km (17 miles) NW of Galway, on W side of Lough Corrib.* Noted angling resort, often called 'Gateway to Connemara'. V'Soske- Joyce, exquisite hand-made carpets, rugs, wallhangings. *By arr,* ☎ *(091)82113/82140.* Sections of the old Galway—Clifden railway are suitable for walks. Animal and bird farm, *Rosscahil,* ☎ *(091)80240.* Corrib Ferries, three trips daily in summer, *dep pier,* ☎ *(091)82644.* Pony trekking centre, ☎ *(091)82120.* Bicycles: T. Tuck, ☎ *(091)82335.* Golf Club, *Gurthreeva, 18 holes,* ☎ *(091)82131.* The 16 km (10 mile) drive along the N59 to Maam Cross has amazing variety of bog, lake, moorland, mountain scenery. Continue W from Maam Cross along shores of Loughs Shindilla and Oorid, with Maamturk peaks to N and Twelve Bens to W.

Pigeon Hole, *1.5 km (1 mile) N of Cong sawmill on L101 to Clonbur:* steps lead down to atmospheric cave, chasm, underground river. Forest walks in adjoining Pigeon Hole Wood. Car park, picnic area.

Portumna, *65 km (40 miles) SE of Galway.* Noted fishing centre for Shannon and Lough Derg. **Portumna Castle** (NM), dates from the 17th c; its walls are substantially intact. It is approached through two formal gardens, part of the fine demesne. The medieval Dominican friary is largely ruined, but worth seeing for its S and E windows.

Portumna Forest Park: this extensive wildlife sanctuary shelters many species of animal and bird life, including red and fallow deer. Well laid out nature trail, viewing stands, lakeside observation tower, car park picnic area, information centre. ♿ Cruisers: Emerald Star Line, ☎ *(092)41120.*

The Punchbowl, *1.5 km (1 mile) SW of Gort, just off N18:* almost perfect crater 30 m (100 ft) in diameter and almost 45 m (150 ft) deep. Beagh River flows from nearby Lough Cultra along floor of crater before disappearing. Many other nearby streams come to a similar end.

Rosmuck, *32 km (20 miles) SE of Clifden, just off L102.* Cottage where Patrick Pearse, leader of 1916 Easter Rising, stayed to improve his Irish, he also wrote most of his work here. Now a museum. Signposted. *Mid June-mid Sept, daily, 10 a.m.-6*

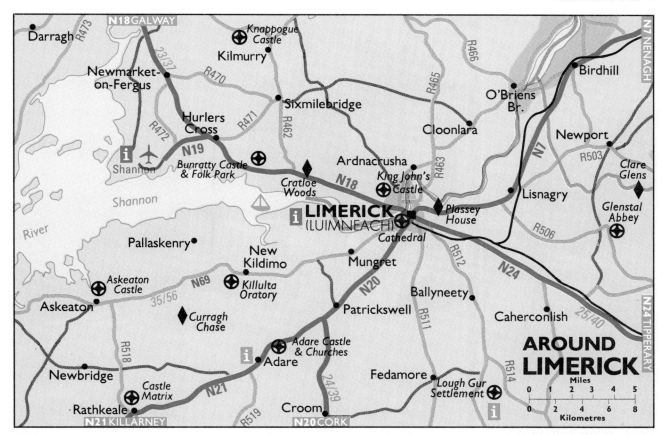

AROUND
LIMERICK

p.m., or key from house on main road, 90 m (100 yds) W of turn to cottage.

Ross Abbey, 3 km (2 miles) NW of Headford: Franciscan friary founded 1357, destroyed by Cromwellians in 1656. Remains of kitchen fish tank, mill, bakery.

Salthill, W suburb of Galway. TIO, Salthill, ☎ (091)63081, May-Sept. One of Ireland's leading seaside resorts, good walks along promenade. **Leisureland,** wide range of indoor sports facilities. Main complex, June-Sept, daily. Also special events. Pool, aft, eve, all year, except Mon, Tues, ☎ (091)21455. Galway Golf Club, 18 holes, ☎ (091)21827. Spiddal craft centre: workshops, art gallery, exhibitions, coffee shop. All year, Mon-Fri, 9 a.m.-5 p.m; Sun, 1 p.m.-6 p.m. ☎ (091)83355.

Thoor Ballylee, near Gort: once the home of W.B. Yeats, this castle has been refurbished, with the addition of audio-visual presentation, bookshop/craftshop, tea room, gardens and picnic area. Easter-Sept, daily,10 a.m.-6 p.m. ☎ (091)31436 (May-Sept), ☎ (091)63081 (Oct-Apr).

Tirneevin Church, just N of Kilmacduagh: exceptionally fine stained glass window by George Campbell, denoting Christ the Sower.

Tuam, 24 km (15 miles) NW of Galway. EC. Thurs. TIO, ☎ (093)24463 July-Aug. Bus enquiries, ☎ (091)62131. Small market town, formerly major ecclesiastical centre, home of renowned Sawdoctors' group. **Cathedral of the Assumption** (C), built in 1830s. Many fine carvings on windows and tower. In grounds, statue of illustrious 19th c cleric, John McHale, Archbishop of Tuam. ᴋ **St Mary's Cathedral** (CI), built in 1860s, incorporates windows and arch of late 12th c chancel, 14th c Chapter House at E end. ᴋ 12th c Cross in Town square. **Mill Museum,** Shop Street: this, the first industrial museum in West of Ireland, is built round fully operational cornmill and adjacent miller's house. Its kitchen and bedroom are just as they were when miller Mike Farrell and his wife lived here in first decade of century. Small exhibition hall, collection of folk items. Daily, June-Sept, 10.30 a.m.-12.30 p.m., 3 p.m.-5 p.m. Otherwise, Dr John A. Claffey, 5 Vicar Street; Jarlath Canney, Canney Bros, The

Square, ☎ (093)24141. **Tuam Arts Centre,** Town Hall, The Square: regular functions, including theatre. Details in local paper. Corrib Craft, The Mall: handcrafts, traditional Irish furniture. App. preferred, ☎ (093)24113. Swimming pool: indoor, heated, Mon-Sun, ☎ (093)24554. ᴋ Bicycles: Tony O'Neill Cycles, Dublin Road, ☎ (093)28365. Golf Club, Barnacurragh, 9 holes, ☎ (093)2435.

Tully, S Connemara: new church of St Colmcille.

Turoe Stone (NM), 5 km (3 miles) N of Loughrea, E of L11 to Bullaun: 1st c pillar stone, decorated with Celtic scrollwork.

Limerick

Pop. 65,000, 24 km (15 miles) E of Shannon, 198 km (123 miles) SW of Dublin. EC Thurs. TIO: Arthur's Quay, ☎ (061)317522. All year. Train and bus enquiries, ☎ (061)313333. Taxis: railway station.

The fourth largest city in Ireland, and an important market and manufacturing centre, Limerick's culture and 300 years of history will repay careful exploration, especially now that its wide range of monuments and art galleries have been enhanced by an impressive new city museum and the well-established Belltable Arts Centre.

St John's Cathedral (C), near St John's Square: 19th c Gothic building has the tallest spire in Ireland. Ask at Presbytery to see exquisite 15th c mitre and cross. ᴋ **St Mary's Cathedral** (CI), junction of Nicholas Street and Bridge Street: built 1172 by Donal O'Brien, last King of Munster. Many interesting monuments, 15th c choir stalls. Son et Lumière performances, early June-mid Sept, Mon, Wed, Fri, Sun, 9.30 p.m. ᴋ Old courthouse is being renovated to hold the **National Self-Portrait collection,** about 100 strong, now on the University of Limerick campus at Plassey. **Dominican Church** (C), Baker Place, Pery Street: early 19th c, has impressive 17th c statue. Our Lady of Limerick. Note modern fresco over chancel. ᴋ **Church of the Holy Rosary,** Ennis Road, 1 m (1.5 km) from

city centre: its stations of the cross were worked by the craftsmen of Oberammergau in Bavaria. Figure of Blessed Virgin on campanile carved by Oisín Kelly. ᴋ **Limerick Museum,** John's Square, ☎(061)47826. paintings and photographs of local scenes, personalities, archaeological finds, coins, many examples from the city's trade history, relics of 1919 Limerick Soviet. Fascinating collection, strongly recommended. Tues-Sat, 10 a.m.-1 p.m.: 2.15 p.m.-5 p.m., ☎ (061)47826. **University of Limerick,** 5 km (3 mile) E of Limerick on N7: **Hunt Museum** has about 1,000 items of Irish antiquities and medieval art, including Bronze Age implements and an interesting selection of early Christian brooches. May-Sept, Mon-Fri, 9.30 a.m.-5.30 p.m. Otherwise by app, ☎ (061)333644. **Belltable Arts Centre,** 69 O'Connell Street: art exhibitions, theatre, other cultural events. Gallery, daily except Sun, 9 a.m.-10 p.m., Coffee shops daily, except Sun, 10 a.m.-5.30 p.m. Theatre usually starts at 8 p.m., ☎ (061)319866. **National Self Portrait Collection,** University of Limerick. June-Sept, Mon-Fri, 9.30 a.m.-5 p.m. ☎ (061)333644. **Limerick city gallery of art,** Pery Square, People's Park: paintings by Keating, Jellett, Walter Osborne, Camille Souter, Percy French, Charles Lamb, etc. Special exhibitions. All year, Mon-Wed, 10 a.m.-1 p.m., 2 p.m.-6 p.m. Thurs, 2 p.m.-7 p.m., Fri, Sat, 10 a.m.-1 p.m., 2 p.m.-6 p.m. ☎ (061)310633.

Walls of Limerick, only portions remain. Best place to see them is at rear of Lelia Street. The two massive gateways at entrance to grounds of St John's hospital are town gate and outer gate of citadel. **Treaty Stone,** W end of Thomond Bridge: Treaty of Limerick said to have been signed here in 1691. **John's Square:** built over 200 years ago, it fell into disrepair. Recently, many of the houses have been restored. **Boru House,** Mulgrave Street, childhood home of magnificent and rather neglected writer Kate O'Brien. **King John's Castle,** restored to original 13th c splendour, with models, displays and audio-visual show telling Limerick's turbulent times. Battlement walkways give fine views of city and river. Tearoom, shop. Mid Apr-Oct, daily, 9.30 a.m.-5.30 p.m. Nov-Mar, Sat, Sun, 12 noon-5.30 p.m. ☎ (061)411201. **Limerick Market,** foot of

Bunratty Castle and 'Durty Nelly's' pub, Co. Clare

High Street: all kinds of bargains, best on *Sat.* **Good Shepherd Convent**, *Clare Street, on Dublin Road:* 150 year old tradition of lace-making, *viewing, Mon-Fri: 9.30 a.m.-1 p.m., 1 p.m.-5.30 p.m.,* ☎ *(061)45178.* Enjoyable walks along both banks of the Shannon and in Mary Street area. Guided walking tours: 1.5 hour duration, taking in most city sights, depart daily from Treaty Stone. SO. Details: TIO. **South's**, *Quinlan Street:* unchanged over many years, with remarkable antique mirror on wall behind bar. **Punch's**, *Punch's Cross, Dooradoyle:* popular haunt for racing fraternity, nightly sing-songs at the piano. **Hogan's Thomond House**, *O'Connell Place:* 200 years old, with tiny snug, two mahogany bars.

Leisure Activities: Limerick Racecourse, *Greenpark:* flat racing and steeplechases all year, ☎ *(061)29377/27961/29416/28972.* Greyhound racing: *Markets Field, Mulgrave Street: Mon, Fri, Sat eve,* ☎ *(061)45170.* Swimming pools: indoor heated, Roxboro Road, ☎ *(061)4 3303;* St Enda's Sports Complex, *Kilmallock Road, daily, closed Fri.* Outdoor: Ennis Road, *opp. Limerick Ryan Hotel and Corbally on River Shannon.* Bicycles: Babyworld, *25 Roche's Street,* ☎ *(061)415202,* Emerald Cycles, *1 Patrick Street,* ☎ *(061)416983,* The Bike Shop, *O'Connell Avenue,* ☎ *(061)315900.* Castletroy Golf Club, *18 holes,* ☎ *(061)45261.* Ballyclough, *18 holes,* ☎ *(061)44083.* Youth Hostel, *1 Pery Square,* ☎ *(061)44672.*

AROUND LIMERICK

Adare, *16 km (10 miles) SW of Limerick on N21. TIO:* ☎ *(061)396255 June-Aug.* Claimed to be the prettiest village in Ireland, set in wooded surroundings on W bank of River Maigue. Broad Main Street, thatched cottages, lichen-covered churches. The 15th c Franciscan friary, on slope overlooking river, is Adare's finest monastic ruin. **Church of the Most Holy Trinity** *(C)* and **Adare parish church** *(CI)* are historically fascinating. **Adare Manor** is fine 19th c baronial pile restored to its pristine glory and used as an hotel. Non-residents can explore the ground floor rooms and extensive gardens. ☎ *(061)86566.* To S is fine old Kilmallock Gate. Golf Club, *18 holes. Desmond Castle,* 13th c ruins overlooking river. Nearby are 11th c ruins of St Nicholas' church and 14th c Desmond Chapel. Adare Manor Golf Club, *9 holes,* ☎ *(061)94204.*

Askeaton, *26 km (16 miles) W of Limerick on N69.* Ruins of 15th c Desmond Castle on rocky islet in River Deel, well preserved tower and hall. Also fragments of 13th c St Mary's parish church next to Protestant church. Adjoining ruin is grave of poet Aubrey de Vere. Extensive remains of 15th c Franciscan friary on banks of River Deel.

Ballinagrane, *3 km (2 miles) S of Rathkeale:* Embury-Heck Memorial Church, named in honour of Philip Embury and Barbara Heck, who sailed with a group of Methodists from Limerick in 1760 and founded the Methodist church in America.

Barnagh Gap, *6 km (4 miles) SW of Newcastle West on N21:* magnificent views over four counties—Limerick, Clare, Tipperary and Kerry. Barnagh gardens: elevated, landscaped gardens also have wildlife, local folklore exhibition, cafe, shop. *Daily,* ☎ *(069)84122.*

Birdhill, *5 km (3 miles) S of Killaloe:* Matt the Thresher's pub full of antiquity.

Broadford, *E Clare, 16 km (10 miles) N of Limerick:* good coarse fishing in Doon Lake.

Bruree, *6 km (4 miles) W of Kilmallock on L28.* De Valera Museum. Old school, attended by the young Eamon de Valera, has been turned into a fascinating museum, with many relics of the leader and artefacts of the old rural way of life. *Sun, Thurs, church holidays, 2.30 p.m.-5 p.m.* Other times by arr: Mrs L. Cregan, caretaker, *in nearby house.* Also de Valera house in village. *Details,* ☎ *(063)91300.* Old royal forts, some dating from pre-Christian times. Also three 14th c de Lacy castles. Mill wheel near bridge over River Maigue, largest water wheel in the region, used to power adjoining mill.

Bunratty Castle and Folk Park, *13 km (8 miles) W of Limerick, off N18 to Shannon Airport.* Castle built 1460, now restored with one of best collections of 14th-17th c period furniture and furnishings in these islands. *Castle, all year, daily, 9.30 a.m.-5 p.m.* Folk park in castle grounds has examples of houses from every part of the region and 19th c Irish village street. Also demonstrations of basket making, farriery, candle and bread making in authentically reconstructed setting. Reconstructed smallholdings, complete with genuine farmyard smells. Bunratty House courtyard, *end of park,* exhibition of agricultural machines. *All year, daily, 9.30 a.m.-5 p.m. June-Aug, until 7 p.m.* ☎ *(061)361511.* **Bunratty Mead Factory** at back of folk park, ☎*(061)362222.* Durty Nelly's, nearby: very famous pub, very small, loads of atmosphere. Old ranges, open fires, súgán chairs, pianos, cages of live birds. Also seafood restaurant.

Carrigogunnell, *5 km (3 miles) W of Mungret:* ruins of large 14th c fort destroyed during second siege of Limerick, 1691.

Carrygerry House, *N side of Shannon airport* (signposted): guesthouse, restaurant in converted late 18th c house. Historical mementoes, books. ☎*(061)62339/62137.*

Castleconnell, *13 km (8 miles) NE of Limerick, near Falls of Doonass.* Enjoy walks along both banks of Shannon (nature trail signposted) in this famous salmon fishing village. **Pink Cottage:** local arts and crafts. Water skiing: *O'Brien's Bridge, 5 km (3 miles) N of Castleconnell. Details: Brian McCarthy, Shannon Water-Ski Club,* ☎ *(061)45540.*

Clare Glens, *just N of Glenstal:* Clare River flows through a gorge, making series of falls. Scenic walks signposted.

Craggaunowen Bronze Age Project, *Sixmile-bridge:* fascinating pre-history, recreated ring fort, medieval antiquities, *May-Oct, Mon-Sun, 10 a.m.-6 p.m.* ☎ *(061)72178.*

Cratloe/Woodcockhill, *11 km (7 miles) W of Limerick on N18:* extensive woodland walks, picnic area, car park. **Cratloe Woods House:** 17th c house. *June-Sept, Mon-Sat, 2 p.m.-6 p.m.* ☎ *(061)327028.*

Craggaunowen Project, near Sixmilebridge, Co. Clare

Croom, *11 km (7 miles) SE of Adare.* Pleasant town on banks of River Maigue. Remains of Croom Castle, 1190 Fitzgerald stronghold. From Tory Hill, 2 m (3 km) NW of town, good views.

Curraghchase, *18 km (11 miles) W of Limerick on N69.* Estate of 19th c poet and author Aubrey de Vere, now National Park. House, with priceless works of art, destroyed in accidental fire in 1941. Tombstone on site where de Vere buried his pets, also earth mound where he sat to write. Gardens and arboretum. Picnic area, car park, caravan park and nature trail. *All year, daily, 9 a.m.-9 p.m.,* ☎*(061)86558.*

Cush, *3 km (2 miles) N of Kilfinane:* extensive earthworks and burial mounds.

Daar River Gorge, *3 km (2 miles) SW of Ardagh:* fine views from ring fort.

Drumcollogher, *40 km (25 miles) SW of Limerick:* porcelain products, Dresden figurines, *all year, Mon-Fri, 9 a.m.-1 p.m., 2 p.m.-5 p.m. Closed first two weeks Aug and bank holidays.* ☎ *(063)9622.* **Dairy Co-op Museum**: The history of Ireland's first co-op creamery is on display. *May-Sept, Mon-Sun, 10 a.m.-6 p.m.* ☎ *(063)83113.*

Foynes, GPA Foynes Flying Boat Museum. During the late 1930s and early 1940s, Foynes was a base for flying boat era. *Apr-Oct, Mon-Sun, 10 a.m.-6 p.m.* ☎ *(069)65416.* Climb hill overlooking village to see huge limestone cross built in 19th c to commemorate one Stephen Rice. Foynes-Tarbert N69: fine coastal views along this 19 km (12 mile) stretch. Forest walks near village. Picnic area, lay-by, good Shannon views. Sailing: Sean Flynn, ☎ *(069) 65606.*

Gallows Hill, *3 km (2 miles) above Cratloe village off N18:* viewing point with fine vistas of Shannon estuary and airport 10 km (6 miles) W. Picnic area, car park.

Glenaster waterfall, *6 km (4 miles) NW of Newcastle West:* from lower Newcastle West-Glin road, cross fields and follow narrow paths to impressive fall on River Daar.

Glenstal Abbey, *14 km (9 miles) W of Limerick, near Murroe village on SW slopes of Slievefelim mountains:* Benedictine college, grounds very beautiful in early summer when rhododendrons flower. Monks work at variety of crafts, including beekeeping, sculpture, stonecutting, silver ware. *By arr,* ☎ *(061)81103.* ♿

The Graves of the Leinstermen, *6 km (4 miles) NE of Ballina:* on slopes of Touinna, highest peak in Arra mountains: a line of vast prehistoric slate slabs. Good views of Lough Derg.

Kilfinane, *10 km (6 miles) E of Kilmallock.* Attractively set in valley surrounded by forests. Rising in background are Ballyhoura and Galtee mountains. See Kilfinane motte, great flat-topped mound encircled by three earthen ramparts. Best views in district from Slieveragh, 467 m (1,531 ft) just NE of Kilfinane. Glenroe farm trail has guided tours of four working farms. *July-Sept, 11 a.m. and 2.30 p.m., or by arr.,* ☎ *(063)91300.*

Killaloe, *21 km (13 miles) NE of Limerick on L12.* TIO, ☎ *(061)376866, May-Sept.* **St Flannan's Cathedral** (CI), built 1182. Fine Romanesque doorway; in grounds, St Flannan's oratory. ♿ In the grounds of St Flannan's cathedral (C), perched on the town's height, St Molua's oratory, moved here in 1929 from Friar's Island in Shannon prior to flooding for hydro-electric scheme. ♿ New **Lough Derg visitor centre** traces history of Ireland's inland waterways, including the Shannon, and features the ESB hydroelectric power station at Ardnacrusha. Restaurant, TIO. Cross Shannon on 13 arch bridge to historic village of Ballina in Co. Tipperary. Cruisers: Derg Line Cruisers, ☎ *(061) 376364.*

Killmallock, *34 km (21 miles) S of Limerick on T50 A.* The town owes its origins to a monastery founded in the 7th c; it was fortified by the Fitzgeralds in the 14th c. Two of the town gates survive, as well as portions of the town walls. The Dominican friary is one of the best buildings of its type surviving in Ireland from around 1300. Kilmallock is attractively sited on the banks of the River Lubagh. *Town museum: all year, Sun-Fri, 1.30 p.m.-5 p.m.* ☎ *(063)91300.*

Lough Gur, *16 km (10 miles) SE of Limerick:* ringed with a remarkable variety of prehistoric remains: dolmens, stone circles, pillar stones, chamber stones, cairns, stone forts, 0.8 km (0.5 miles) N of Holycross Road, largest stone circle in Ireland. Ruins of two medieval Desmond castles, one E of lake, other S. Visitor interpretative centre, picnic areas, lakeside walks. During season, conducted walking tours. *Centre: May-Sept, Mon-Sun, 10 a.m.-6 p.m.* ☎ *(061)85186.*

Maghera Mountains, *SW of Lough Graney:* drives, walks. Minor road leads to Lough Ea, nearly 300 m (1,000 ft) up, while another minor road leads to TV mast. From vicinity, excellent views of E Clare, S Galway.

Manister, *5 km (3 miles) E of Croom:* ruins of Monasteranenagh, 12th c Cistercian abbey. Good carvings in church, remains of chapter house, abbey mill. Nearby, see remains of 14th c Rathmore Castle and ruins of ancient Rathmore ring fort.

Mountshannon, *8 km (5 miles) NE of Scariff on T41:* fine harbour and pier on SW shores of Lough Derg. From pier hire boat for holy island of Iniscealtra in Lough Derg, with five churches and other remains of early Christian settlement. Holy Island cultural exhibition centre planned for Mountshannon. Plaque on local post office denotes site of Ireland's last manually operated telephone exchange, closed 1987. Sailing: K. Simmons, Iniscealtra Sailing Club, Shore House, *Meelick, Whitegate.* Mountshannon Youth Hostel, ☎ *(0619)27209.*

Newcastle West: Desmond castle, interesting remains of 13th c fortress. Also tower house of Glenquin Castle, built 1462, in excellent state of preservation. *Key: W. Deeley, nearby farmhouse.* Pleasant walks in the extensive demesne, with wooded parkland open at all times. Monument near church dedicated to W Limerick men who died in War of Independence.

Rathkeale, *29 km (18 miles) SW of Limerick on N21.* Ruins of 13th c Augustinian priory. **Castle Matrix,** built in 1440 on site of ancient Celtic sanctuary to Matrix, their Mother Goddess. .Here Edmund Spenser and Walter Raleigh met for first time. Today, 12,000 volume library has rare first editions of some leading Elizabethan poets, including Spenser. In castle, authentic furnishings, objets d'art, historic documents. From 24 m (80 ft) tower, good view of surrounding counties. Home of Irish International Arts Centre, which holds seminars in graphic arts, poetry, drama. Medieval banquets for groups. *Castle and grounds, mid May-mid Sept, Mon, Tues, Sat, Sun, 1 p.m.-5 p.m.,* ℅ *(069)64284.*

Shannon Airport, viewing terrace, Hall of Fame listing of famous aviation personalities, shops, bars, restaurants, occ. exhibitions. *Details: Shannon airport TIO,* ☎ *(061)471664. All year.* **Ballycasey crafts centre.** Craftspeople produce a variety of items, including jewellery and pottery, all for sale. *Restaurant: all year, Mon-Sat, 9 a.m.-5.30 p.m.* Some workshops: *open Sun.* ☎ *(061)364115/ 362105.* Shannon Golf Club, Shannon Airport, 18 holes, ☎ *(061)61020.*

Tralee

Pop. 18,000, 32 km (20 miles) NE of Killarney, 102 km (64 miles) SW of Limerick, 300 km (187 miles) SW of Dublin. All day closing: Wed. TIO: ☎ *(066)21288. All year. Bus and train enquiries,* ☎ *(066)23566.*

A lively and attractively laid-out business centre and resort town; good food, good bookshops, and very handy for the Dingle peninsula.

Rose of Tralee Festival: a week of dancing and carousing, *end Aug-early Sept, details: TIO. Féile Pádraig: St Patrick's Week festivities, mid-Mar.* **Kerry the Kingdom,** *Ashe Memorial Hall, Denny Street:* three part interpretation of the kingdom of Kerry. **Geraldine Tralee** uses a "time car" to recreate life in Tralee in 1450, complete with sounds and smells. **Kerry in Colour** is a spectacular visual show. **Treasures of the Kingdom** is the new county museum, covering its history from the Stone age to the Computer age; includes priceless archaeological treasures. *All year, daily* ☎ *(066)27777.*

St John's, (C) *Castle Street:* built 1870. Stations of the Cross by late Sean Keating, 1959 statue of locally-born St Brendan the Navigator. ♿ **Holy Cross Church,** *Princes Street:* designed by Pugin in 19th c. Fine Michael Healy stained glass, sculptured stones from old Dominican abbey in priory. ♿ **Rathass church,** *12 km (1 mile) E of Tralee:* early Christian ruin. In adjoining cemetery, graves of those who died in War of Independence. **Siamsa Tíre theatre,** Ireland's lively and stimulating National Folk Theatre, in fine new setting. *May-Sept, daily performances,* ☎ *(066)23055.* **Ballyseedy Memorial,** *3 km (2 miles) E of Tralee:* fine bronze by Breton sculptor Jan Goulet, commemorating incident in Civil War.

Leisure Activities: Sports Centre, *Oakpark:* wide variety of sports, *all year, daily, 10 a.m.-10 p.m.,*

☎ *(066)22442.* ♿ Racing: five day meeting at Tralee Racecourse during Rose of Tralee festival. *Other races, Mar, June, Nov, details: TIO.* Greyhound racing, *Oakview : Tues, Wed, Fri, 8.15 p.m., closed winter,* ☎ *(066)21416.* Tralee Bay sailing: Len Breewood, *St Brendan's School of Sailing, Derrymore,* ☎ *(066)30132.* Riding: William J. Riding Centre, *Ballyard,* ☎ *(066)21840.* Bicycles: E. Caball, *15 Ashe Street,* ☎ *(066)22231.* Tralee Gas Supplies, *Strand Street,* ☎ *(066)22018.* Golf Club, *9 holes,* ☎ *(066)21150.*

AROUND TRALEE

Ardfert, *10 km (6 miles) NW of Tralee on L105.* St Brendan's Cathedral, 13th c ruins include nave and choir. **Ardfert Abbey,** *just E of St Brendan's,* Franciscan friary dating from 1253, now ruins. Teampall na nÓigh church ruins and Teampall Griffin, late Gothic church ruins, ogham stone in adjoining graveyard, *near W end of St Brendan's.*

Ballybunion, *34 km (21 miles) N of Tralee.* One of Ireland's top seaside resorts. Plenty of summer fun, highlight the Bachelor Festival, when eligible men meet eligible women, *usually June.* **Church of St Augustine,** built in 1877, transferred to present site from nearby Ballyduff in 1957. ♿ **Ballybunion Castle,** *on promontory:* built 1583, now ruins. The town has many attractive beaches and the caves in the cliffs to the N can be explored carefully at low tide. Seaweed baths: Collins' and Dalys', *mid-May-end Sept, daily.* Riding: Bennett's, ☎ *(068)27516.* Bicycles: The Cycle Centre, *Doon Road,* ☎ *(068)27258.* Ballybunion Golf Club, *18 holes,* ☎ *(068)27146.*

Ballyheigue Castle, *16 km (10 miles) NW of Tralee.* Striking 19th c ruins. The nearby beach stretches S for 13 km (8 miles) to Banna Strand, one of the country's finest beaches. There is a good walk 8 km (5 miles) NW of Kerry Head.

Ballylongford, *13 km (8 miles) N of Listowel.* Lislaughtin Abbey, *2 km (1 mile) N of village,* roofless Franciscan friary.

Barrow Harbour, *8 km (5 miles) NW of Fenit:* early 13th c round castle near harbour entrance, good views of Dingle peninsula and NW Kerry coastline.

Blennerville Windmill, *3 km (2 miles) S of Tralee:* 200 year old white, five storey **windmill** has been fully restored, with audio-visual show, emigration exhibition, craft workshops, pottery, restaurant. *May-Nov, daily, 9.30 a.m.-6 p.m.* ☎ *(066)21064.* **Steam railway:** narrow gauge track runs 2 km (1.5 miles) from Blennerville to Tralee. The last surviving engine from the old Tralee-Dingle railway has been restored, to pull two carriages. *Details: Tralee TIO.*

Casement's Fort, *2 km (1 mile) W of Ardfert:* Sir Roger Casement was arrested this earthen roadside fort after landing at nearby Banna Strand in 1916 with German arms for the Rising. 2 km (1 miles) further on, monument commemorates his execution.

Castleisland, *18 km (11 miles) E of Tralee on N21:* slight remains of castle built in 1226.

Crag Caves, *near Castleisland:* one of Ireland's largest cave systems has been opened as an exciting showcave. About 4 km (2.5 miles) of the system has been surveyed; about 400 m (400 yards) has been developed for visitors. Impressive stalactites. Craft shop, cafe. *Mar-Nov, daily, 10 a.m.-6 p.m. July, Aug, closes 7 p.m.* ☎ *(066)41244.*

Fenit, *13 km (8 miles) W of Tralee:* notable L-shaped pier, gives 1 km (0.5 mile) walk with fine views of Tralee Bay. The huge sandstone boulder by the water's edge is an Ice Age relic. Good sea angling and walks. **Fenit Island,** *approach by land from Fenit:* ruins of Fenit Castle, built to guard entrance to Barrow Harbour, which had thriving trade with Low Countries four centuries ago.

Glin Castle, *48 km (30 miles) NE of Tralee on S shore of Shannon.* Built 1780s, seat of Knight of Glin. Interior has fine neo-classical plasterwork. Drawing room, library and unique double flying staircase all have remarkable Adam-style ceilings. Good collection of mid-18th c furniture. Gate shop sells antiques, crafts and home-made food. *Tours by arr, with Mme Fitzgerald,* ☎ *(068)36230, shop manageress,* ☎ *(068)34188.* Hamilton's Tower, 19th c, good views of Shannon.

Knockanore Church, *6 km (4 miles) E of Ballybunion:* interestingly modern, built 1963-4, sculptures by Oisin Kelly. **Knockanore Hill,** *5 km (3 miles) E of Ballybunion:* breathtaking views of Shannon, as far as Limerick city.

Listowel, *27 km (17 miles) N of Tralee on N69. TIO,* ☎ *(068)22590. May-Sept.* Amazing plaster shop decorations executed by local man Patrick McAuliffe, who died in 1921. Local decorator Francis Chute and his son carry on tradition. Among most striking works are plaster lady on Central Hotel and lion and harp above P. M. Keane's. **St John's** literary, arts and heritage centre, in the converted CI church in the middle of the town's great square, has a theatre and frequent exhibitions. The centre traces the unique literary tradition of north Kerry. Poetry readings are among the regular events staged here. *Details: Listowel TIO.* On the outskirts of the town, on the Ballybunion road, the famine graveyard is a tragic reminder of one of the blackest periods of Irish history. **Writer's Week,** workshops, plays, exhibitions, book fair—a must for anyone with literary inclinations, *end June-early July.* Listowel Races, Harvest Festival, including All Ireland Wren Boys' Competition, *Sept.* **Castle,** *town centre:* ruin once belonged to Lords of Kerry, destroyed in 1600. **John B. Keane's pub,** *William Street:* here you may meet the great playwright and storyteller. Memory Lane Museum (near Crag Cave and Castleisland), 10 a.m.-dusk, ☎*(066)42158.* Antique cars, machinery, chinacraft.

North Kerry visitor farms: four are open for tours, including two cheese-making locations. *Details: Tralee TIO.* **Rattoo heritage centre,** *Ballyduff:* archaeology, folklore and history of area in museum and interpretative centre. *Details,* ☎*(066)31501.*

Tarbert, *6 km (4 miles) E of Ballylongford:* car ferry service to Killimer from Tarbert, departures on the half hour. *Apr-Sept., Mon-Sat, 7.30 a.m.-9.30 p.m.; Sun, 9.30 a.m.-9.30 p.m. Oct-Mar, Mon-Sat,*

Ballybunion, Co. Kerry

7.30 a.m.-7.30 p.m. Departures from Killimer on the hour, details, ☎ *(065)53124.*

Tarbert House. Built in 1690, it has fine Georgian interiors and furniture, which includes Ireland's best example of an Irish Chippendale mirror. Many family portraits. *May-Aug, daily, 10 a.m.-12 noon; 2 p.m.-4 p.m.* ☎ *(068)36198.*

Tralee Ship Canal, good 5 km (3 mile) walk from just S of Tralee to Tralee Bay, alongside canal. Return by minor road, starting where canal enters bay.

Westport

Pop. 3,500, 84 km (52 miles) N of Galway, EC Wed. TIO, ☎ *(098)25711.*

Set at head of Clew Bay, which is said to have an island for every day of the year, Westport is an attractive, hilly place with a very continental air. Designed by Georgian period architect James Wyatt the town is a good base for exploring S Mayo. See memorial in mall to Major John MacBride. **Clew Bay Heritage Centre,** genealogic research, *all year,* ☎*(098)26852.* Horse Show, *June. Details: TIO.*

Westport House, *2.5 km (1.5 miles) outside town:* stately home in beautiful demesne. Georgian house with fine family portraits, old Irish silver, Waterford glass, old furnishings and decorations. Narrow gauge steam railway, zoo, children's play facilities, shopping arcade, fishing, horse caravan holidays, holiday homes. *May-Sept, daily. Details,* ☎ *(098)25430.* Heritage centre being developed as part of Westport's new heritage town status. **The Mall,** tree-lined boulevard running each side of Carrowbeg River. **Westport Quay,** formerly a thriving port, now home of several nautically inclined pubs and restaurants, most notably perhaps the Asgard, an award-winning pub/restaurant with marine type decor and old boat fittings. Walking trails cover town and quays. Climb Tober Hill Street for an excellent view over town.

Leisure Activities: Sea Angling: Westport Sea Angling Centre, ☎ *(098)25280.* Horse Riding: Drummindoo Riding Centre, ☎ *(098)25616.* Cruises: *P. C. Marine,* ☎ *(098)25848.* Clew Bay Sea Tours, Club Atlantic Holiday Hostel ☎*(098)26367.* Bicycles: J.P. Breheny & Sons, *Castlebar Street,* ☎ *(098)25020.* Club Atlantic Holiday Hostel ☎*(098)26644.* Golf Club, *Ballyknock, Carrowholly, 18 holes,* ☎ *(098)25113.* Westport sports complex offers full range of facilities, including gym and squash courts. ☎ *(098)26341.*

AROUND WESTPORT

Aasleagh Waterfall, *32 km (20 miles) S of Westport:* peat-stained fall on Erriff River flanked by glorious mass of rhododendrons.

Balla, *11 km (7 miles) SE of Castlebar on N60.* Medieval altar, round tower from 7th c monastery founded by St Cronan, holy well and remains of shelter for blind and lame.

Ballinrobe: Ruins of Augustinian friary, built about 1313, at N end of town. Explore the old canal wharves that form Bowers Walk. In the 19th c there were great plans, never completed, to link Ballinrobe with Galway and the sea.

Horse racing: *June, Sept,* ☎*(092)41052/41071.* Burke Boats, trips on Loughs Carra and Mask, ☎ *(092)41100.* Riding facilities: Flannery's pub, ☎ *(092)41055.* Ballinrobe Golf Club, *9 holes.*

Ballintubber Abbey, *1.5 km (1 mile) E of T40 Castlebar-Ballinrobe road:* only church of kind in Ireland where Mass has been said for past 750 years. Founded, by St Patrick in 5th c, present abbey 13th c. Although Cromwell destroyed much of it in 1653, it survived and was restored between 1840 and 1966. Most impressive, well worth visiting. ♿ **Moore Hall,** *near abbey:* ruins of birthplace of George Moore, late 19th early 20th c writer. Fishing in nearby Lough Carra, forest walks, scenic views, car park, picnic area.

Ballycroy, *3 km (2 miles) N of Castlehill:* noted angling centre in desolate, largely uninhabited countryside.

Ballyhaunis Abbey: Set amid E Mayo lakes, abandoned during Dissolution, re-roofed early 19th c. Convent of Mercy (C), five Michael Healy windows. ♿ Golf club, *9 holes,* ☎ *(0907)30014.*

Burrishoole Friary, *3 km (2 miles) NW of Newport:* built about 1450, tower remains. Nearby, Carrigahooly Castle.

Caher Island, *S of Clare Island.* Holy Island. *Sailings by arr. from Roonagh Quay, details: Bay View Hotel,* ☎ *(098)26307 or (098)25380.*

Carrownisky Strand, *8 km (5 miles) SW of Louisburgh:* vast, empty, golden beach.

Castlebar, *18 km (11 miles) E of Westport on N60. EC Thurs, TIO,* ☎ *(094)21207. Enquiries: Castlebar station,* ☎ *(094)21222.* Situated where the Castlebar River flows into Castlebar Lough. Its pleasant tree-lined Mall, which once served as a cricket pitch for Lord Lucan and his family is an oasis of calm in a bustling, somewhat plain town. In the Imperial Hotel, at the Green, a plaque commemorates the founding of the late 19th c National Land League. Parts of the hotel's interior have remained unaltered for over 100 years. **Christ Church,** completed in 1739, is a major historical monument in the town.

International Walking Festival: *June.* **Exhibition Centre,** *Town Hall:* new venue stages regular arts, craft and historical exhibitions, *Daily.*

If you enjoy plaque spotting, the Mall is the birthplace of Margaret Burke-Sheridan, internationally famous prima donna; Main Street birthplace of Louis Brennan, inventor of torpedo and monorail. **Castlebar Airport,** pleasure flights, ☎ *(094)22853.* An Sportlann sports complex, *McHale Road,* wide range of indoor sports, ☎ (094)22983. Castlebar swimming pool, *the Mall,* ☎ *(094)21357.* Golf Club, Hawthorn Lodge, *18 holes,* ☎ *(094)21649.*

Castlehill, *N of Mulrany, via N59:* fine views of Bellacragher and Blacksod Bays.

Charlestown, *11 km (7 miles) NE of Swinford.* Town built by Lord Dillon in 1847. Western Rose Festival, *end July-early Aug.*

Clare Island, *mouth of Clew Bay.* Mail boat sailings from Roonagh Quay, 6 km (4 miles) W of Louisburgh, May-Sept, sailings twice daily. Details, Chris O'Grady, Bay View Hotel, ☎ (098)26307. Remote spot with 160 residents and one hotel, ideal for relaxing. *Clare Abbey,* 15th c, with frescoes. Doonagappul, promontory fort on S cliffs. From Knockmore, fine views of Clew Bay, Connemara and Mayo mountains. *Information: Aine O'Malley,* ☎*(098)26129.*

Claremorris, *E Mayo.* Three Aug events: Connacht Donkey Derby; All Ireland Pony Jumping Championship; Town Festival, including band recitals, agricultural show. *Details: Castlebar TIO.* **Claremorris Gallery,** *James Street,* ☎*(094)71348:* regular exhibitions by leading artists.

Bicycles: Cycle Centre, *Courthouse Road,* ☎ *(094)71573.*

Collanmore Island, *Clew Bay:* Glenans Sailing Centre, courses, ☎ *(098)26046.*

Corraun Peninsula, *near Mulrany:* very fine coastal views. Claggan Mountain, Cuchcamcarragh, Nephin Beg, each over 500 m (1,700 ft) high, all worth climbing.

Croagh Patrick, *8 km (5 miles) W of Westport.* Ireland's holy mountain, a little over an hour's climb from Murrisk on the Westport-Louisburgh road. To do it the hard way, join the mid-summer pilgrimage, *last Sun July.* Spectacular views on clear days.

Eochy's Cairn, *3 km (2 miles) E of Lough Mask, near Ballinrobe:* great prehistoric ruined cairn.

Gulf of Aille, *signposted lane from Westport-Partree road, 8 km (5 miles) SE of Westport, just W of Aille.* River Aille goes underground reappearing 4 km (2.5 miles) E. Caves in nearby cliffs have been partly explored: farmer's permission.

Inishturk Island, *13 km (8 miles) SW of Roonagh Quay:* interesting small harbour and beach at Portadoon. The whole island measures just 5 x 2.5 km (3 x 1.5 miles). Boats by arr. from Roonagh Quay. *Details: Mrs Therese O'Toole, Inishturk post office,* ☎ *(098)68640.*

Kilgeever Church, *3 km (2 miles) E of Louisburgh:* roofless ruins, holy well. Still used by some Croagh Patrick pilgrims. Magnificent views S of Sheeffry Hills.

Croagh Patrick, Co. Mayo

Killeen, *district 8 km (5 miles) S of Louisburgh:* many antiquities, including 37 arch clapper footbridge at Bunlahinch, 1.5 km (1 mile) W of Killeen Church.

Kiltimagh, *24 km (16 miles) E of Castlebar:* town museum set in old railway station has many artefacts from the locality. *SO, Mon-Sun, 2 p.m.-6 p.m.*

Knock, *11 km (7 miles) NE of Claremorris on N17. TIO: Knock,* ☎ *(094)67247. All year.* International airport served by flights from UK and North America. Major pilgrimage centre attracting over 2 million pilgrims yearly. Magnificent new basilica next to original church where famous apparition seen in 1879. Our Lady's Domain, to S, beautifully landscaped parklands with trees, shrubs, roses, ☎ *(094)88100, (01)775965.* ♿ *Knock Folk museum:* has many relics of old style life in Co Mayo, including a replica of a thatched cottage. *All year, Mon-Sun, 10 a.m.-7 p.m.*

Lecanvey, *3 km (2 miles) W of Murrisk:* excellent bathing beaches.

Lisnemonaghy, *1.5 km (1 mile) N of Kiltimagh in E Mayo:* Tobar na Cuimhne (Well of Memory), holy well whose waters said to improve memory.

Lough Nadirkmore, *10 km (6 miles) SW of Touramakeady on W shore of Lough Mask:* small, dramatically set lake surrounded by towering mountains. Start energetic three hour climb to lake at Cappanacreha, *8 km (5 miles) SW of Touramakeady.*

Louisburgh, *19 km (12 miles) W of Westport.* Quaint fishing village with good sandy beaches. Granuaile interpretative centre, *May-Sept,* ☎ *(098)66380.* Founded 1802, probably named after Louisburgh, Nova Scotia. Bicycles: Harneys Garage, ☎ *(098)26046.*

Moanbane Fort, *6 km (3.5 miles) SE of Ballyhaunis:* set on N slope of commanding height, good views.

Mulrany, *29 km (18 miles) NW of Westport on N59.* Attractive village on isthmus between Blacksod and Clew Bays. Sheltered from Atlantic winds, mild climate encourages giant fuchsias and rare plants, such as Mediterranean heather. Good bathing beach, sea fishing, boating. Youth Hostel.

Murrisk Abbey, *8 km (5 miles) W of Westport off T39:* 15th c ruins.

Mweelrea Mountains, *N shores of Killary Harbour:* three hour climb to Mweelrea summit, five routes to top, most popular from Delphi, just S of

Doo Lough on L100. Most dramatic approach by boat from Leenane across harbour. Superb views in clear weather.

Newport, *12 km (8 miles) N of Westport on N59.* Fronted by Clew Bay and sheltered to N by Nephin Beg mountain range. *St Patrick's church* has Harry Clarke windows showing the Last Judgement. An abandoned seven arch railway bridge, once part of the old Westport-Achill Island railway, spans the river and is now part of a linear park. Walking trail has been developed from Newport to Bangor. Letterkeen forest offers walks and picnic sites. Youth Hostel. Boat trips to Clew Bay islands, ☎ *(098)41524.* Hill climbing, orienteering, rock

On Clare Island, Co. Mayo

climbing available in vicinity, ☎ *(098)41500/41647.*

Old Head, *3 km (2 miles) NE of Louisburgh, off T39:* forest walks, spectacular views, car park, picnic area.

Rockfleet Castle, *6 km (4 miles) W of Newport, off N59:* 16th c tower house on shores of Clew Bay. When closed see caretaker.

Sheeffry, *22 km (14 miles) SW of Westport, on L100 from Louisburgh to Killary Harbour via Doo Lough:* viewing point, car park, picnic area. The two main peaks of the Sheeffry Hills are worth climbing for the views.

Straide, *on N5/N58 13 km (8 miles) NE of Castlebar.* Birthplace of Michael Davitt, founder of late 19th c Land League. Replica of house from which he and his parents were evicted. Davitt Museum, *June-Sept, daily.* Ruined 13th c Franciscan friary.

Touramakeady Demesne, *by Touramakeady village on W shore of Lough Mask:* forest walks, 3 km (2 mile) nature trail, waterfall, good views of lough, car park, picnic area. Boats: Martin Morrin, ☎ *(092)44034.*

Turlough, *6 km (4 miles) E of Castlebar on N5:* well-preserved round tower with ruined 17th c church.

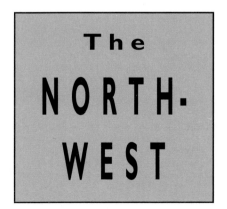

The NORTH-WEST

Bundoran

Pop. 1,500, 30 km (19 miles) S of Donegal, NW of Dublin. EC Thurs. TIO, ☎ (072)41350, June- *Sept. Bus enquiries: Bus Eireann, Sligo, ☎ (071)60066.*

The premier holiday resort in the North West, with a fine strand backed by a promenade. Salmon and trout fishing good in nearby Bunduff and Bundrowes River, as well as in nearby Lough Melvin. First-class sea angling in Donegal Bay.

Headlands, dramatic views from both, in clear weather, of S Donegal, Sligo and Mayo. Cliff walk: W of Bundoran, to small, roofless tower called Cassidy's Folly, standing by the sea's edge. Promenade to Rogey, along cliffs N to Aughrus Head with its fantastic rock formations, as far as magnificent Tullan Strand, backed by the Finner sandhills. Stracomer Horse riding ☎ *(072)41685. Bundoran Waterworld* is a complex with wave-making machine and water slides, incorporating the existing swimming pool at the shore front. *Daily.* ☎ *(072)41230.* Bicycles: Patrick McGloin, *East End,* ☎ *(072)41383.* Bundoran Golf Club, *18 holes.*

AROUND BUNDORAN

Ard Fothadh, *3 km (2 miles) SW of Ballintra:* ancient fort, believed to be the burial place of Hugh MacAinmire, a 6th c High King of Ireland.

Ballintra, *19 km (12 miles) NW of Bundoran on N15.* Attractive village set amid drumlins (small, rounded hills). In Brownhill demesne, beside village, River Blackwater flows through caves known as The Pullans. A few hundred yards E of village, at Aghadullagh Old Mill, the river forms a waterfall before flowing through a remarkable chasm.

Ballyshannon, *8 km (5 miles) NE of Bundoran on N15. Bus enquiries: (072)51101.* Town of great character built on banks of River Erne. Pleasant walks around older parts of town and by river. Lively Folk Festival, *early Aug, details: Bundoran TIO.* **The Mall,** William Allingham's birthplace. The cottage where the noted 19th c poet lived is in a decrepit state. In the Allied Irish Bank, you can see his bust, the tall desk at which he once kept accounts and the words he scratched on the windowpane. He is buried in the grave yard of St Anne's just N of the town. The Abbey mill wheels have been restored recently. *Assaroe Abbey,* 2 km (1 mile) NW of Ballyshannon. Mill buildings, legacy of Cistercian abbey founded in 1184. Audio-visual display. Just S, grotto-like Catsby Cave, where Mass was celebrated in penal times. *Easter and June-Sept, daily, 11 a.m.-9 p.m. Rest of year, Sun, 2.30 p.m.-7 p.m.* ☎ *(072)51580.* **Donegal Irish Parian China,** *Ballyshannon:* guided tours of factory, exhibition centre. *May-Sept, Mon-Sat, 9 a.m.-5 p.m.* ☎*(072)51826.* The ESB Station fish-pass allows fish to swim upstream - a fascinating sight. *By arr,* ☎*(072)51200.* Bicycles: P.B. Stephens, *4/6 Castle Street,* ☎ *(072)51178.* Swimming pool: indoor, heated, *daily, except Tues.*

Belleek, *6 km (4 miles) E of Ballyshannon on L24.* Pottery, begun in 1857. Its characteristically creamy porcelain products are renowned the world over. The work requires immense finesse and is absorbing to watch. Visitor centre, restaurant. *Guided tours all year, Mon-Fri, 9.30 a.m.-12.15 p.m.; 2.15 p.m.-4 .15 p.m. Phone first:* ☎ *(036565)501.*

Castle Caldwell, *between Boa Island and Belleek, off B136:* demesne and forest on two long peninsulas. By entrance is the Fiddler's Stone, set up in 1770 to commemorate a local fiddler Dennis McCabe. Marvellous lake views. Wildlife observation hides with identification pictures. Castle and chapel ruins, old quay and boathouse.

Kilbarron Castle, *3 km (2 miles) S of Rossnowlagh:* 14th c ruins stand majestically on rock promontory overlooking Donegal Bay. Nearby remains of 14th c Kilbarron church.

Kiltyclogher, *6 km (4 miles) SE of Lough Melvin:* Festival, mainly traditional events, *July, details:* Bundoran TIO. Seán MacDiarmada, one of 1916 Rising leaders, commemorated by memorial in village square. Route to his birthplace at Cormone

signposted. Megalithic tomb, known locally as Prince Connell's Grave. Between Lough Melvin and Upper Lough Macnean, a series of prehistoric earthworks once said to have divided Ulster from Connacht. Best place to view is just N of Kiltyclogher, where parts straddle the road.

Kinlough, *3 km (2 miles) S of Bundoran on T54:* pretty village. Site of interesting prehistoric remains. Forest walks, picnic area, car park. Attractive drive along S shores of Lough Melvin to Rossinver.

Castle Caldwell, Co. Fermanagh

Lurgan Carn, *6 km (4 miles) SW of Ballintra:* superb views.

Rossnowlagh, *16 km (10 miles) N of Bundoran, off N15.* Focal point is the magnificent strand, one of Donegal's finest. Surfing enthusiasts have been known to become addicted to the beach. Franciscan Friary, strikingly modern, with gardens, shrines. The friary houses, the Donegal Historical Society's museum. *All year, Mon-Sun, 10 a.m.-8 p.m.* ☎ *(072)51342.* Boats, canoes: Sand House Hotel, ☎ *(072)51777.*

Tullaghan, *5 km (3 miles) SW of Bundoran on N15.* Co Leitrim's only seaside village. Secluded sandy beaches nearby.

Donegal

Pop. 2,300, 30 km (19 miles) NE of Bundoran. EC Wed. TIO, ☎ (073)21148. May-Sept. Bus enquiries, ☎ (073)21101.

Pleasant, if bracing touring centre at the head of Donegal Bay. Many of the natural and historic attractions of S Donegal are within easy reach. *Donegal Castle:* 15th c ruins on banks of River Eske, *mid June-Sept, daily, 9.30 a.m.-6.30 p.m.* ☎*(073)22405. St Patrick's Church of the Four Masters* (C): modern, strikingly built with red granite, completed in 1935. *Donegal Abbey, just S of town:* slight ruins of Franciscan friary founded in 1474 on banks of River Eske. *Napoleonic anchor near TIO, quayside:* 4.5 m (15 ft) long. Believed to have been left by the French fleet which brought Wolfe Tone back from France for 1798 Rising. Quayside walk: along E bank of River Eske, in direction of abbey. Drumcliffe walk: about 1.5 km (1 mile) along W bank of River Eske. Excellent views of Donegal Bay, abbey ruins across river, surrounding woodlands.

Craft village at Ballyshannon road has a cluster of craft workshops. *Magee Tweed Factory:* century old tradition, visitors welcome, *conducted tours all year, Mon-Fri, 11.30 a.m.; 3.30 p.m.,* ☎ *(073)21100.* Donegal Social Club, *Water Street:* indoor sports, visitors welcome, *daily.* Bicycles: C.J. Doherty, *Main Street,* ☎ *(073)21119.* Donegal Town Golf Club, Tullycullion, *18 holes,* ☎ *(073)21108.*

Belleek Pottery, Co. Fermanagh

AROUND DONEGAL

Aghla Mountain, *8 km (5 miles) NE of Glenties:* worth climbing, superb views.

Ardara, *39 km (24 miles) NW of Donegal, EC, Wed.* One of most interesting towns in Donegal, with wide Main Street and several fascinating small shops in traditional Donegal style. **Church of the Holy Family (C),** masterly Evie Hone window in W nave depicting the 'Word of God', well worth seeing. **Caves of Maghera,** *short distance W of town:* signposted. The hour stroll from village past Drumbarron gives fine view of Loughros Bay and Ardara. Tweed weaving can be seen all year, *Mon-Fri, 9 a.m.-5 p.m.* at John McGill, *Maghera;* William McNelis, *Main Street,* ☎ *(075)41105.* Bicycles: Donal Byrne, *West End,* ☎ *(075)41156.*

Ball Hill, *3 km (2 miles) SW of Donegal:* Youth Hostel: ☎ *(073)21174.*

Barnesmore Gap, *11 km (7 miles) NE of Donegal on N15:* desolate stretch of about 5 km (3 miles) . Little imagination needed to relive the days of the highwaymen who once roamed here! And if you find the gap too bracing **Biddy O'Barnes pub** has an excellent atmosphere.

Blue Stack Mountains, *11 km (7 miles) N of Donegal:* very fine scenery, particularly in Eglish Glen.

Bruckless, *24 km (15 miles) W of Donegal on N56.* Linen village just before Killybegs.

Carntullagh Head, *near Killybegs:* can be reached by rowing across Killybegs Harbour. Not advised in winter! For boats, *contact Donegal Town TIO.*

Carrick, *5 km (3 miles) NW of Kilcar on T72A:* starting place for ascent of Slieve League, 600 m (1,972 ft). Beyond Teelin village, 3 km (2 miles) S of Carrick, mountain track leads over Carrigan Head to Bunglass cliffs, which rise sheer from water to height of just over 305 m (1,000 ft). View from Amharc Mor (literally 'great view') is among the most glorious in the county. After Croaghaun on Achill, these are the greatest sea cliffs in Ireland. Take care, many of the climbs are best left to experienced climbers. Bracing walk of about 16 km (10 miles) W as far as Malin Beg. If you wish, continue to Glencolumbkille and Maghera, about 32 km (20 miles) in all. Nearby Malinmore has fine strand. Youth Hostel.

Crownarad Mountain, *5 km (3 miles) W of Killybegs:* 500 m (1,621 ft), worth climbing, magnificent views.

Drumanoo Head, *5 km (3 miles) S of Killybegs:* minor road extends almost entire distance.

Dunmore Head, *1.5 km (1 mile) W of Portnoo:* good views of coast to SW, inc. Dawros Head and Crohy Head to NE.

Fintragh Strand, *3 km (2 miles) W of Killybegs:* vast, deserted stretch of sand.

Glencolumbkille, *56 km (35 miles) W of Donegal at end of T72A.* Fascinating self-help co-operative community, inspired by the late Fr James McDyer. As he said: 'If you like wild, rugged scenery, uncluttered beaches, a secluded area where you can unwind from modern city life, then Glencolumbkille is for you.' Fairies said to hold festive gatherings hereabouts. **Folk village and museum:** cottage dwellings from a three century span, shebeen, where poitín was sold,19th c schoolhouse. Craft shop, tea rooms. *Easter-Sept 30, Mon-Sat, 10 a.m.-6 p.m.; Sun, 12 noon-6 p.m.* ☎*(073)30017.* **Ulster Cultural Centre:** language courses, exhibitions. *St. Patrick's Day-Oct, daily.* The area is also rich in archaeological remains inc. 5,000 year old court cairns and line of dolmens. Many embossed standing stones, ruins of early Christian monastery, beautiful little church in centre of glen.

Glengesh Pass, *between Ardara and Glencolumbkille:* rises spectacularly to 274 m (900 ft) before plunging to valley. Forest walk, picnic area, car park. Excellent views.

Glenties, *30 km (19 miles) NW of Donegal.* Striking small town set amid woods where two glens meet. Nearby mountain landscapes offer desolate contrast. Fish Hatchery, *by arr,* ☎ *(075)51141.* Drive: take the Fintown road, skirting Lough Finn and Lough Muck, returning through Stracashel Glen. Most attractive 32 km (20 mile) route.

Inver Bay, *13 km (8 miles) W of Donegal:* excellent sandy bay near Inver village.

Kilcar, *13 km (8 miles) W of Killybegs on T72A:* picturesque weaving centre.

Killybegs, *27 km (17 miles) W of Donegal, just off N56.* One of Ireland's most important fishing ports, set on a fine natural harbour. **Maritime Centre:** historical material on fishing industry. Try and be

Killybegs harbour, Co. Donegal

there when the fishing fleet returns, the quaysides are a buzz of activity and the air is alive with gulls. Killybegs International Sea Angling Festival: *usually Aug, coinciding with annual regatta, details: Donegal TIO.*

Lough Derg, *16 km (10 miles) E of Donegal, access via L84 from Pettigo.* Car park 1.5 km (1 mile) from the pier for Station Island, lying just offshore. Picnic area, lakeshore drive, forest walks, viewing points, access to St Brigid's Well. Three day pilgrimage to Lough Derg one of most physically demanding in world, since only one meal a day of dry bread and black tea is permitted. During pilgrimage season, *June-mid-Aug,* pilgrims only allowed on Station Island. *Details, The Prior, Lough Derg, Co. Donegal.*

Lough Eske, *8 km (5 miles) NE of Donegal, off N15:* 24 km (15 mile) drive round lough shores gives splendid views of some of Ireland's most beautiful scenery. Forest walks.

Mountcharles, *6 km (4 miles) W of Donegal on N56.* Bleak but interesting one street village with excellent views of Donegal Bay from top of nearby hill. Sandy beach 1.5 km (1 mile) from village. Jack Furey's: hand embroidery, other hand crafts, *all year, Mon-Sat, 9.30 a.m.-6 p.m.*

Muckross Head, *4 km (2 miles) S of Kilcar:* cliffs and caves can be explored at low tide. Fine sandy beach at Traloar.

Narin and Portnoo, *13 km (8 miles) N of Ardara.* Twin villages on S shore of Gweebarra Bay. Chief attraction is Narin's wonderful 1.5 km (1 mile) strand. At low tide, you can walk to offshore island of Iniskeel. Golf Club, *18 holes.*

St John's Peninsula, *S of Dunkineely:* extends for about 8 km (5 miles) into Donegal Bay; a road covers almost entire distance. Exceptional views. Peninsula also has one of finest beaches in Donegal and that's saying something. On W shores, see remains of MacSwyne castle.

Dungloe

Pop. 900, 56 km (35 miles) NW of Donegal. TIO, ☎ *(075)21297. June-Aug. Bus enquiries: Londonderry and Lough Swilly Road Services, Letterkenny,* ☎ *(074)22863.*

Small town, virtually one street, set on the edge of the Atlantic, capital of The Rosses, a remarkable and extensive rock-strewn land crossed by innumerable streams and dotted with many lakes. Excellent brown trout, sea trout, salmon fishing. The warmth of the welcome you will receive is in direct contrast to the bleakness of the landscape. Mary of Dungloe Festival, *end July, early Aug. Details: Dungloe TIO.*

AROUND DUNGLOE

Arranmore, *5 km (3 miles) offshore from Burtonport.* Ferry: *all year, 11 a.m. daily, weather permitting. Summer, every 20 mins. Details of ferry, Tony Gallagher,* ☎ *(075)21521.* Largest island off W Donegal coast, with just over 700 inhabitants. One hotel, the Glen, ☎ *(075)21505.* Youth hostel. Magnificent trip in fine weather. Striking little villages, such as Illion, where houses rise up from chapel in strand. Magnificent cliffs and caves. **Leabgarrow,** island 'capital', a tiny village on E of island, with fine terraces, harbour, golden strand. Dermot and Mary Toland's craft shop, Gortar, has many island souvenirs, such as 'máirtins' a house slipper with knitted sock, ideal for Irish winters. **Lough Shure,** *N island,* is Ireland's only rainbow trout lake. **Aphort** on S has island's largest strand. Boats: Bridge House, ☎ *(075)21532.*

Bunbeg, tiny, restful fishing village facing Gweedore Bay and sheltered by cliffs. Extensive sandy Magheraclogher strand. Bunbeg drive: inland from village along L82, through village of Gweedore to Dunlewy. Return via Falcarragh, Bloody Foreland. Some of Donegal's most exciting lake and mountain scenery. About 56 km (35 miles).

Burtonport, *8 km (5 miles) NW of Dungloe on T72.* Fishing village noted for its lobster and salmon. Access to Arranmore and smaller islands such as Rutland, Inishfree, Inishmeal. Ask at harbour about boats.

Crohy Head, *6 km (4 miles) SW of Dungloe:* fine cliffs and coves. Martello Tower was built in Napoleonic times. Youth Hostel. Maghery Bay has perfect bathing strand.

Cruit Island, *near Kincasslagh:* popular resting point for visitors to W Donegal. Connected by bridge to mainland. Minor road runs to N tip of island.

Errigal Mountain, *near Dunlewy:* 751 m (2,466 ft), cone shaped, ascend from near Dunlewy Lake, the climb is not too arduous, even for a novice. Magnificent views of much of N Donegal. Errigal Youth Hostel: *Dunlewy,* ☎ *(075)31180.*

Gweedore-Falcarragh, *NW portion of Donegal,* a stronghold of the Donegal Gaeltacht, or Irish-speaking area.

Keadue Strand, *5 km (3 miles) N of Burtonport:* at low tide, short cut across to Kincasslagh village.

Poisoned Glen, *entrance 3 km (2 miles) SE of Dunlewy, near ruins of 19th c church.* Glen runs deep into Derryveagh Mountains; at head of glen, sheer cliffs. Name comes from the poisonous vegetation on the lake bank which makes the water unfit to drink.

Talamh Briste (broken earth): landslip near Crohy Head has left a chasm 400 m (400 yds) long, but only 3 m (9 ft) wide.

Enniskillen

Pop, 12,000, 43 km (27 miles) S of Omagh, 138 km (86 miles) SW of Belfast, EC Wed. TIO: Shore Road, ☎ *(0365)325050/323110, all year. Bus enquiries: bus station, Eden Street,* ☎ *(0365)22633.*

County town of Fermanagh, Ulster's lakeland, Enniskillen is attractively set on an island between two channels of the river connecting Upper and Lower Lough Erne. Nearly everywhere in the town you see water, and boats of all sizes may be hired for fishing and cruising.

St MacCartan's Cathedral (CI), *Church Street:* dates from 1842, but includes part of 17th c building. Old colours of Enniskillen regiments laid up here. ♿ *Convent Chapel* (C), *Belmore Street:* in Byzantine style, with remarkable nave windows by Michael Healy, Lady Glenavy, Sarah Purser. *St Michael's* (C), *Church Street:* completed 1875. Unusual sculpture of Resurrection above main door. ♿ *Methodist Church, Darling Street:* the bulges in the balcony were designed to accommodate crinolines.

Enniskillen Castle, houses two museums: County Museum, devoted mainly to pre-history, with models and dioramas showing lake dwellings and early life in Fermanagh; occasional exhibitions, an audio-visual presentation tells the story of the Maguires, who built the keep in the 15th c. *Watergate history and heritage centre. All year, Mon-Fri, 10 a.m.-1 p.m.; 2 p.m.-5 p.m. July, Aug, also Sat, Sun, 2 p.m.-5 p.m.* ☎ *(0365)25000.* Regimental Museum, relics of Royal Inniskilling Fusiliers and Inniskilling Dragoons. *Mon-Fri, 9.30 a.m.-12.30 p.m., 2 p.m.- 5 p.m. Weekend by arr.,* ☎ *(0365)323142. Fort Hill, E side of town:* good views and abundant walks. Victorian bandstand is rather delightful. Climb 108 steps to top of Cole monument for excellent panorama of Enniskillen and surrounding lakeland. There are walks along the varied length of Main Street, which has six changes of name between the bridges at each end. To N of Main Street, between Water Street and Market Street, a warren of alleys known as Boston conjures up the flavour of the old town. *Ardhowen Thea-*

tre and Arts Centre, Dublin Road: theatre, exhibition area, bar, restaurant. Events include dance, music, drama, films. Available for conferences and exhibitions, ☎ *(0365)25440.*

Leisure Activities: Lakeland Forum leisure centre, inc. pool, café: *Broad Meadow,* ☎ *(0365)24121.* ♿ Visitor Centre has details of local, expert cave explorers for those visitors wishing to see Fermanagh caves. ☎ *(0365)23110.* Lough Erne cruises: daily summer sailings from Round 'O' pier. *Details: Enniskillen TIO.* Enniskillen Golf Club, 18 holes, ☎ *(0365)25250.*

AROUND ENNISKILLEN

Ballyconnell Canal, *SE end of Upper Lough Erne:* designed 100 years ago to link Erne to Shannon. It silted up after eight boats made the journey. The canal is in the process of being reopened, in a major reconstruction project.

Bellanaleck, *6 km (4 miles) S of Enniskillen on A409:* picnic areas by shore of Lough Erne.

Boa Island, *N side of Lower Lough Erne.* Joined to mainland by bridge at each end. Near W side in ancient Caldragh cemetery, see two very strange old stone figures, called 'Janus' statues because they have face on each side. Near E end of Boa, on the jetty, tel. for a boat to Lusty Beg Island, a noted holiday spot.

Castle Archdale Forest, *just N of Rossigh, off B82.* Enchanting country park including ruins of Castle Archdale. Caravan park, fishing stands, picnic area, wildfowl observation base. Three offshore islands form nature reserve. *All year, daily.* Youth Hostel. ☎ *(03656)28118.* Boats for White island.

Castle Coole (NT), *3 km (2 miles) SE of Enniskillen on A4.* Great Palladian house started in 1790. No expense was spared in interior fittings and furniture, the house is considered Ireland's finest classical mansion. Parkland runs down to shores of Lough Coole; the park lake still has a flock of greylag geese established here 300 years ago. House open to general public. *April-Sept, weekends and also June-Aug, daily. Always access to grounds.* ☎ *(0365)22690.*

Correl Glen, *entrance nearly opp. that to Lough Navar Forest:* path from waterfall near entrance through woodlands to Carrick Lough.

Crevenish Castle, *3 km (2 miles) SW of Kesh:* two and a half storeys and square tower still stand. Good lakeside views.

Crom Estate, *3 m (5 km) W of Newtownbutler:* vast woodland, interspersed with lakes. Walks on the estate include the ruins of Crom Castle, burned down by accident in 1764. *Apr-Sept, daily, 2 p.m.-6 p.m.* ☎ *(03657)38174.* From the old boathouse, there are motor yacht trips on Upper Lough Erne. ☎ *(036 55)21221.*

Derrin Lough, *3 km (2 miles) NW of Tempo:* pleasant shore walks. Topped Mountain, 5 km (3 miles) SW has path to summit with Bronze Age cairn. Nearby picnic area and attractive lake with superb views.

Devenish Island, *5 km (3 miles) NW of Enniskillen:* best- known of 97 islands in Lower Lough Erne. Best-preserved round tower in Ireland can be climbed by internal ladders. Ruins of St Molaise's Oratory, Teampall Mór priory, Augustinian abbey of St Mary. *Museum.* Boats from Trory Point, Lower Lough Erne, *Easter-Sept, Tues-Sat, 10 a.m.-7 p.m.*

Ely Forest, *off Enniskillen-Belleek A46:* good walks, along S shores of Lower Lough Erne. At N end of forest, Carrickreagh and Blaney Bays are delightfully secluded and ideal for dropping in by cruiser, if this is your style. Nearby Carrickreagh hilltop viewpoint has good vistas of lake and islands.

Florence Court (NT), *13 km (8 miles) SW of Enniskillen on A32.* Three storey 18th c mansion of great charm, linked to flanking pavilions by open arched corridors. Fine paintings, plasterwork, furniture. Demesne has many specimen trees, includ-

ing the 221 years old yew tree said to have been the stock of all Irish yews. Pleasure gardens give landscaped views over adjoining mountains. Adjoins forest park. Walled garden and water-wheel. Tea room and shop. *Apr-Sept, weekends. Also June-Aug, daily, except Tues. Grounds open daily, 10 a.m. to 1 hour before dusk.* ☎ *(036582)249/788.* Scenic drive over Cuilcagh plateau to Lower Lough Macnean, about 16 km (10 miles).

Glenfarne, *24 km (15 miles) SW of Enniskillen on A4/T17.* Extensive forest walks, picnic areas, car parks. Excellent views of Upper and Lower Lough Macnean. Old railway station is poignant reminder of long-closed Enniskillen-Sligo railway.

Inishmacsaint, *W shore of Lower Lough Erne:* great sense of isolation. Unusual High Cross, ruins of 6th c monastery and early church, herd of wild goats. Boat hire at Killadeas for journey across.

Inver Lake, *SW of Rosslea:* good shore walks.

Kesh: *Ardress craft centre.* Many examples of craft work in fine Georgian house. Jacob sheep, poultry and peacocks roam the grounds. Craft shop. *All year, Mon-Sat, 10 a.m.-5 p.m., Sun, 2 p.m.-5 p.m.* ☎ *(036 56)31267.*

Kesh Forest, *5 km (3 miles) N of Kesh:* good views, walks.

Knockmore Cliffs, *5 km (3 miles) N of Derrygonnelly on S side of Lower Lough Erne:* superb views from the top (easily reached from Derrygonnelly road).

Knockninny Hill, *5 km (3 miles) N of Derrylin, midway between Enniskillen and Belturbet:* rises steep from the shore, tremendous view from cairn on summit.

Lisbellaw: *Old Barne family museum,* about 1,000 items collected over the years by the

Knockninny Hill, Co. Fermanagh

Carrothers family. Includes old bottles, newspapers and letters from the front, World War 1. *All year, Mon-Sat, 11 a.m.-9 p.m.* ☎ *(0365)87278.*

Lisnaskea, *EC, Thurs.* Castle Balfour, built early 17th c, Scottish features. Lisnaskea library has displays of rush and straw weaving, scythe stones, local customs. *All year, Mon-Sat, 11 a.m.-9 p.m.* ☎ *(03657)21222.* Bicycles: William Gannon, *Main Street, Lisnaskea,* ☎ *(03657)21280.*

Lough Navar, Blackslee, Big and Little Dog, Ballintempo, Belmore Forests all have good long distance walks.

Lough Navar Forest Park, *19 km (12 miles) NW of Enniskillen on A46:* vast expanse of woodland. Derrygonnelly is start of impressive 11 km (7 mile) forest scenic drive, culminating in 270 m (900 ft) viewpoint, from where you can see most of Lower Lough Erne, S Donegal, N Sligo. Footpaths, self-guiding nature trails. By entrance, two ancient sweat houses. *All year, 10 a.m.-dusk.* ☎ *(036564)256.*

Marble Arch Caves, *5 km (3 miles) W of Florence Court:* experienced cavers are still finding deep crevices, as well as exploring vast chambers with stalactites and stalagmites. See natural limestone Marble Arch, Marble Arch Glen. *Mar-Sept, daily from 11 a.m., depending on weather.* ☎*(036582)8855.*

Monea Castle, *7 km (4 miles) inland from Ely Forest:* well- preserved 17th c Plantation fortress. Abandoned in 1750 after a fire.

Pollahuna Cave, *Blacklion, near Belcoo:* recently discovered cave on Cavan-Fermanagh border, can be explored by experienced potholers.

Rossigh, *between Castle Archdale and Killadeas:* scenic footpath, fishing, car park, on the shores of Lower Lough Erne.

Upper Lough Erne, 57 islands, between Enniskillen and Galloon Bridge, worth exploring if you have a cruiser on the lake. Several interesting days can be spent island pottering. Cruises on Upper Lough Erne, *Easter-Aug.* Details: *TIO, Enniskillen.*

Upper Lough Macnean, B52 lakeside drive along N shores gives fine views across to Co. Leitrim mountains. Road continues to tiny hamlet of Garrison.

White Island, *Castle Archdale Bay, 16 km (10 miles) NW of Enniskillen.* Eight ancient, famous and inscrutable statues. The question of their origins continues to cause controversy. Ferry from Castle Archdale marina. *June-Sept, Tues-Sat, 10 a.m.-7 p.m., Sun, 2 p.m.-7 p.m.* ☎*(03656)21731.*

Falcarragh

Pop. 800, 19 km (12 miles) NE of Bunbeg, 35 km (22 miles) NW of Letterkenny. TIO: Letterkenny, ☎ (074)21160, all year. Bus enquiries: (074)22863.

The bilingual village near the E end of the NW Donegal Gaeltacht is an ideal centre for touring the area's rugged cliffs and mountains. Good trout and salmon fishing in the many streams and lakes; excellent sea fishing. **McKinley's Stone,** *1.5 km (1 mile) from village:* tradition says that when a local chieftain called McKinley was killed here by Balor of the Mighty Blows from Tory Island, his crystallised blood formed a red vein in the stone. Bicycles: Vincent Carton, ☎ (074)35150 after 6 p.m.

AROUND FALCARRAGH

Ards Forest Park, *3 km (2 miles) N of Cresslough on T72:* forest walks, scenic views, swimming, picnic area, car park. ♿ **Ards House,** *6 km (4 miles) NE of Creeslough:* now Capuchin Franciscan friary of Ard Mhuire. *By arr,* ☎ *(074)38013/38005.*

Ballyness pier, *1.5 km (1 mile) N of Falcarragh:* excellent beach in vicinity.

Bloody Foreland, takes its name from the warm reddish colour of the rocks in the setting sun. Fine views of Atlantic and offshore islands.

Carrigart, *at foot of Rosguill Peninsula on T72.* Quiet holiday resort with good fishing, excellent beach.

Creeslough, *10 km (6 miles) S of Dunfanaghy,* Interesting small village stands on high ground overlooking an inlet from Sheephaven Bay. Duntally Bridge and waterfall, just outside Creeslough, are most attractive. The path of the old Errigal Railway, 45 km (28 miles) across NW Donegal to Burtonport, makes a good walkway. Adventure Centre: wide range of outdoor sports, *all year.*

Doe Castle, *3 km (2 miles) NE of Creeslough:* built early 16th c, deserted 1843. Now a fascinating ruin, beautifully set on strip of land running into sea. Access by bridge across moat.

Downings, *5 km (3 miles) NW of Carrigart.* Well-known sea angling centre. Superb views of Ards Peninsula. Excellent beach. Tra na Rossan Youth Hostel.

Dunfanaghy: popular resort in inlet of Sheephaven Bay, near Horn Head. Strand is 5 km (3 miles) long. Nearby Port na Blagh and Marble Hill also have magnificent strands.

Eas Fhionain, *6 km (4 miles) E of Falcarragh:* waterfall issuing from rocks on coast. Associated with St Fionan, the waters are said to have medicinal properties.

Glenveagh National Park, *18 km (11 miles) SE of Falcarragh:* 10,000 ha (25,000 acre) nature preserve with splendid Scottish-style castle and 10 ha (25 acres) of gardens. Largest herd of red deer in Ireland. Visitor centre and audio-visual show. Restaurant at visitor centre and tearooms at castle.

Beach at Dunfanaghy, Co. Donegal

Easter-May, Mon-Thurs, 10 a.m.-6 .30 p.m., Sat, 10 a.m.-6.30 p.m., Sun, 10.30 a.m.-6.30 p.m. June-Aug, Mon-Sat, 10 a.m.-6.30 p.m., Sun, 10 a.m.-7.30 p.m. Sept, daily, 10 a.m.-6.30 p.m. Oct, Mon-Thurs, 10 a.m.-6.30 p.m., Sat, 10 a.m.-6.30 p.m., Sun, 10.30 a.m.-6.30 p.m. Fishing (sea-trout, salmon) by arr. ☎(074)37090.

Gortahork, *3 km (2 miles) SW of Falcarragh:* Art and Crafts Centre, *old technical school. July, Aug, daily.* Sub-aqua: McFadden's Hotel, ☎ (074)35267.

Horn Head, *16 km (10 miles) NE of Falcarragh:* cliffs rise out of the sea to height of over 180 m (600 ft). Splendid views of Atlantic and peaks of Errigal and Muckish. In clear weather, you can see the Paps of Jura in the Inner Hebrides, 160 km (100 miles) NE.

Inishbofin, *5 km (3 miles) offshore:* inhabited by about 150 people, a stronghold of Irish language, customs and traditions. Ask at Falcarragh about boats.

Lough Glen, *6 km (4 miles) E of Creeslough:* delightful lake with fine mountain backdrop.

Muckish Mountain, *8 km (5 miles) SE:* 670 m (2,197 ft), attracts many climbing enthusiasts.

Ray Old Church, *3 km (2 miles) E of Falcarragh on N56:* site of ancient celtic cross of St Colmcille. Tradition says that the saint hewed the cross from the top of Muckish Mountain and that bad weather stopped him taking it to Tory Island.

Rosapenna, *1.5 km (1 mile) from Downings:* fine strand. Golf Club, 18 holes.

Rosguill Peninsula, *between Sheephaven and Mulroy Bays:* part of Donegal Gaeltacht. Atlantic Drive round peninsula has some of the finest scenic views in Donegal. **Silver Strand,** *Drumnatinney, 5 km (3 miles) NE of Falcarragh:* good beach.

Tory Island, *15 km (9 miles) off coast.* A new boat connects Bunbeg, Downings and Magheraroarty on the mainland with the island. Tory's first hotel should be ready for the summer of 1993. Information about the island, ☎ (074)35502. Largest of four islands off this part of Donegal 5 km (3 miles) long and 1.5 km (1 mile) at its greatest breadth, it is largely barren, but its almost sheer cliffs are a fine sight. The permanent population of about 130, which rises to around 300 in summer, is often isolated for weeks on end by bad weather. A trip to the Island is an adventure; landing is not easy when the sea is rough and there is no guarantee you will be able to return the same day. Interesting remains: two churches, part of a round tower, 2 m (7 ft) high Tau Cross. Look out for the work of the island's untrained artists, considered seriously by critics of 'primitive' paintings. Handloomed sweaters, ships in bottles and miniature wooden boats are other Tory island specialities. Examples can be bought in new craft shop. See West Town, with one shop, one pub and walk along pier, as well as even smaller East Town. New Hotel. **Feile Torai,** *July.* Youth Hostel.

Tranarossan, *NE side of Rosguill Peninsula:* one of most picturesquely situated beaches in Co Donegal.

Glenveagh Valley, Co. Donegal

Letterkenny

Pop. 7,000, 34 km (21 miles) W of Derry, 51 km (32 miles) E of Dungloe. EC Wed. TIO, ☎ (074)21160, all year. Bus enquiries: Londonderry and Lough Swilly Road Services, ☎ (074)22863.

Situated on a hillside overlooking the River Swilly, it has one of the longest main streets in Ireland. Good touring centre for N Donegal. International Folk Festival, star-studded week long event, *Aug. Details, TIO.* Donegal International Motor Rally, *June. Details, TIO.*
Donegal County Museum, *High Road:* converted 19th c workhouse has exhibits on local archaeology, geology, history. *All year, Tues-Sat, 11 a.m.-1 p.m., 2 p.m.-5 p.m.* ☎*(074)24613.* ***Port Gallery,*** *86A Upper Main Street:* exhibitions by local artists. *All year, Mon-Sat, 10 a.m.-6 p.m.* ☎*(074)25073.* ***St Eunan's Cathedral*** *(C):* modern building in Gothic style with richly decorated ceilings and impressive windows. 65 m (212 ft) spire landmark for miles around. The CI Parish Church, *opp. St*

Eunan's is 300 years old. Churchyard obelisk in memory of Dr John Kinnean, local Presbyterian minister and 19th c champion of tenants' rights. Swimming pool: indoor, heated, *daily, except Tues,* ☎ *(074)25251.* Leisure centre, includes 25 m (25 yds) swimming pool. *Daily.* ☎*(074)25251.* Bicycles: Church Street Cycles, Church Street, ☎ *(074)25041.* Golf Club, Barnhill, *18 holes,* ☎ *(074)21150.*

AROUND LETTERKENNY

Ballybofey/Stranorlar, *19 km (12 miles) S of Letterkenny on N56.* 'Twin' towns connected by bridge over River Finn. Isaac Butt, founder of Home Rule Association, is buried in Stranorlar churchyard. Ballybofey drive: take L75 W, with a choice of routes, either taking the detour near Garranbane Hill, back to Altnapaste or continuing through to Fintown. Following the River Finn the road is quite dramatic and the countryside becomes very wild. From time to time, you may be able to see the old track bed of the late lamented County Donegal railway. Ballybofey and Stranorlar Golf Club, *18 holes,* ☎ *(074)31093.*

Beltany Stone Circle, *3 km (2 miles) S of Raphoe:* 64 standing stones, in place since the Bronze Age. Some claim it is older than Stonehenge.

Carn Hill, *6 km (4 miles) S of Ramelton:* excellent viewpoint.

Churchhill, *16 km (10 miles) W of Letterkenny:* angling centre near beautiful shores of Gartan Lough. ***Colmcille heritage centre:*** interpretative exhibition on St Colmcille. *Easter week, mid May-Sept 30, Mon-Sat, 10.30 a.m.-6.30 p.m., Sun, 1 p.m.-6.30 p.m.* ☎*(074)37306/21160.* Gartan outdoor adventure centre, *Churchill,* ☎ *(074)37932.*

Dunlewey Museum: agricultural museum based on life of a local weaver, Manus Ferry. His house has been reconstructed as an interpretative centre, to give the flavour of earlier 20th c Donegal home life. Farm animals, wool spinning, fabric design, weaving, crochet, basket weaving. Boat trips on lake. Tea room, craft shop. *Easter, June-Sept, Mon-Sat, 11.30 a.m.-6 p.m., Sun, 12.30 p.m.-7 p.m. Apr, May, Sat, Sun only.* ☎ *(075)31699.*

Glebe Gallery, *1.5 km (1 mile) beyond Churchill on shore of Lough Gartan.* Artist Derek Hill has given his house, gardens and splendid art collection to the State. Wonderfully eclectic selection of china, glass, original William Morris wallpaper and textiles. Art collection includes work by Landseer, Picasso, Evie Hone, Jack B. Yeats and the Tory Is-

past Knockalla Fort, which together with Leenan Fort on opp. side of Lough Swilly, was occupied by British garrisons until 1938.

Milford, *16 km (10 miles) N of Letterkenny, Lough Swilly bus from Letterkenny.* Tourist and angling centre attractively set at head of Mulroy Bay.

Murren Hill, Dargan Hill, *N Fanad Peninsula:* both worth climbing for excellent views across Mulroy Bay to W and Lough Swilly to E.

Portsalon, *40 km (25 miles) N of Letterkenny.* Charming, small seaside resort on E side of Fanad Peninsula, set on shores of Ballymastocker Bay. Rita's Bar, by the beach, is famous for its well-preserved traditional interior. Buy a length of tweed with your pint, if you wish. Portsalon Golf Course, *18 holes.* Bunnaton Youth Hostel.

Ramelton, *13 km (8 miles) N of Letterkenny on T72.* Noted angling centre. **The Old Meeting House:** Reverend Francis Makemie was rector here, emigrating to America in 1683 to found the first Presbyterian church in Virginia. Artefacts, displays, library. *July, Aug, daily, 9 a.m.-5 p.m., or by arr,* ☎*(074)51266.* The Pool, near the town, is famous for its salmon. Forest walks. Bicycles: H.P. Whoriskey, ☎ *(074)51022.*

Raphoe, *13 km (8 miles) SE of Letterkenny:* busy farming town with square called the Diamond, the pattern of many N towns in Ireland. Cathedral (CI) dates from 1702; alongside are ruins of former bishops' palace. Raphoe Horse Show: *first Mon, Aug.*

Rathmullan, *24 km (15 miles) NE of Letterkenny.* Historical town that was a main anchorage of the British Fleet during World War I. Town's villas are solid reminders of those far-off navy days. Pier, ruins of 15th c Carmelite friary on outskirts. The interpretative centre, open daily, has a display featuring the Flight of the Earls, who fled Ireland from here in the early 17th c. *Easter week, mid May-Sept, Mon-Sat, 10 a.m.-6 p.m., Sun, 12 noon-6.30 p.m.,* ☎ *(074)58178/58131.* Rathmullan Sea Angling Festival: *usually June.* Rathmullan Regatta: *early Aug.* Rathmullan Mountains: Croaghan and Crockanaffrin, both just over 300 m (1,000 ft) high and ideal for climbing. **Rathmullan Wood,** *1.5 km (1 mile) SW of Rathmullan on L77:* forest walks, fine views over Lough Swilly, picnic areas, car park. Golf Club, Otway, *9 holes.*

Seven Arches, *3 km (2 miles) N of Portsalon:* tunnels in the rock that are a striking sight. Further N at Doaghbeg cliffs rise to a great height, with natural Arch of Doaghbeg, big enough to take a boat.

Woodquarter, *3 km (2 miles) NW of Milford on T72:* forest walks, excellent views over Mulroy Bay, picnic area, car park.

land painters, over 300 works in total. *Easter week, daily, 11 a.m.-6.30 p.m., May-Sept, Mon-Thurs, 11 a.m.-6.30 p.m., Sat, 11 a.m.-6.30 p.m., Sun, 1 p.m.-6.30 p.m.* ☎ *(074)37071.*

Killydonnell Abbey, *6 km (4 miles) SE of Ramelton:* 16th c. Franciscan foundation by shores of Lough Swilly, still in reasonable repair.

Kilmacrenan, *11 km (7 miles) N of Letterkenny:* ruins of 15th c Franciscan friary. Lough Salt, near village, in very scenic area. **Lurgyvale thatched cottage.** The house is about 150 years old and is preserved in its original condition. There is a museum of domestic and farm appliances. Occ. demonstrations of traditional crafts. Walks in the vicinity include one to the wooded banks of the River Lurgy. *Easter week, May-Sept, Mon-Sat, 10 a.m.-7 p.m., Sun, 11 a.m.-7 p.m.* Traditional music: *8.30 p.m.* ☎ *(074)39216.*

Knockalla Ridge, *between Rathmullan and Portsalon:* good walking territory. Knockalla Coast Road Drive, round Fanad Peninsula, is one of the most spectacular drives in all Donegal. Completed in 1967, the road runs for 13 km (8 miles) to Portsalon, giving breathtaking views of Ballymastocker Bay, with its golden beaches. Road goes

Londonderry

Pop. 62,000, 117 km (73 miles) W of Belfast, 245 km (152 miles) NW of Dublin. EC Thurs. TIO: 8 Bishop Street, ☎*(0504)267284, all year. Bus enquiries: Ulsterbus, Foyle Street bus station,* ☎ *(0405)262261. Also: Londonderry and Lough Swilly Bus Co (for Co. Donegal), Great James Street,* ☎ *(0504)2620 17. Train enquiries: Waterside station,* ☎ *(0504)42228. Taxis: Waterside railway station.*

Perhaps more popularly known as Derry (the city's rightful title is a matter of political debate). Settlement began in the 6th c, and certain historical events, such as the lifting of the siege in 1689, are still recalled with passion. More recently, it has been wracked by some of the most serious disturbances in the present Troubles. A walk from Guildhall Square, through the William Street area as far as Free Derry Corner, with its internationally-known legend, "You are now entering Free Derry," will give a vivid illustration of this intensely Irish city's turmoil.

Guildhall, *Shipquay Place:* built 1912, fine stained glass windows. Corporation treasures include mag-nificent collection of Irish plate. *Business hours, Mon-Fri.* Venue for concerts and productions, including premières by Derry playwright, Brian Friel. **O'Doherty Tower:** near site of a 16th c O'Doherty tower in Magazine Street. Views over the city from roof platform. *Details:* ☎*(0504)365151.* **Ulster Science Centre,** *Foyle Street:* interactive exhibitions. *Details:* ☎ *(0504)370239.* **Amelia Earhart centre, Ballyarnet field,** *2 km (1.5 miles) beyond Foyle Bridge, off B194:* cottage exhibition on first woman aviator to fly the Atlantic solo. She landed in this field in 1932. Commemorative sculpture. *June-Sept, Tues, Sun, 2 p.m.-5 p.m. or by arr, (0504)353379.* **St Columb's Cathedral** (CI), *Bishop Street.* Memorial window depicts lifting of famous siege. Another window honours noted hymn writer Mrs Frances Alexander. Chapter House has historical objects, inc. padlocks and keys of gates closed by the apprentice boys in 1688. Audio-visual presentation. *All year, Mon-Sat, 9 a.m.-1 p.m.; 2 p.m.-5 p.m.* ☎ *(0504)262746.* Nearby Fountain Street has well-preserved wall murals of King William. **St Eugene's Cathedral** (C), *Infirmary Road:* Gothic style, late 19th c. Fine stained glass. Flamboyant, atmospheric building. *Daily.* &. **Long Tower Church** (C): built in 1784 just outside SW of city walls. Lavishly decorated interior. **Gordon Gallery,** *36 Ferryquay Street.* Works by prominent local artists. *Daily, except Thurs, 11 a.m.-5.30 p.m* ☎*(0504)266261.* **Orchard Gallery,** *Orchard Street:* regular exhibitions by local artists, also occ. Arts Council exhibitions. Also workshops, meetings, concerts. *Tues- Sat, 10 a.m.-6 p.m. Occ. eves.,* ☎ *(0504)269675.* **Magee College,** *Northland Road.* Occ. theatre, films, other events, ☎ *(0504)265621.* **Foyle Arts Centre,** *Lawrence Hill,* has art exhibitions and examples of the performing arts. ☎*(0504)363166.* **The Heritage Library** has exhibitions, ☎ *(0504)269792.*

Walls of Derry, only unbroken fortifications in either Ireland or Britain. Walk round open S sections for fine views of city. Also see various cannons facing Guildhall. New **Museum,** *beside O'Doherty Tower,* has impressive displays and audio-visual shows. *Tues-Sat, 10 a.m.-5 p.m.* Below W section of walls lie the Bogside and Creggan estates, internationally renowned during the present Troubles. *Shipquay Street:* walk up one of steepest

Folk Festival

main streets in world to Diamond with its impressive war memorial. **Craigavon Bridge,** invigorating walk from old city to E side, known as the Waterside, largely residential, good exercise climbing the steep streets. **Foyle Valley Railway Centre,** on W bank of river Foyle near Craigavon Bridge, relics of the old North-West railways, audio-visual presentations, trips on 1934 diesel railcar on adjoining section of track. *All year, Tues-Sat, 10 a.m.-5 p.m. Apr-Sept, Sun, 2 p.m.-6 p.m.* Train rides: *May-Sept, Sat, Sun aft.,* ☎ *(0504)265234.* **St Columb's Park,** *Waterside.* Fine views of Inishowen Peninsula on Co. Donegal site of Lough Foyle. There are also walks along the quays, through the Georgian-style Clarendon Street area, in Brooke Park and along Northland Road towards the city boundary.

Leisure Activities: Templemore Sports Complex, *Buncrana Road.* Wide range of indoor and outdoor sports, inc. pool, conference, function rooms, sauna, bar, restaurant, *Mon-Sun,* ☎ *(0504)265521.* St

Londonderry and River Foyle

Columb's Park Activity Centre, *Limavady road: Daily,* ☎ *(0504)43941* . Brooke Park Leisure Centre: *daily,* ☎ *(0504)262637.* Lisnagelvin Leisure Centre, inc. pool: *Richhill Park, daily,* ☎ *(0504)47695.* Brandywell sports centre, ☎*(0504)263902,* Pilot's Row centre, ☎*(0504)47695,* Rialto entertainment centre, ☎*(0504)260516.* Swimming pool: indoor, heated, *William Street, daily,* ☎ *(0504)264459.* City of Derry Golf Club, *18 holes,* ☎ *(0504)46369.* Greyhound racing, *Brandywell,* ☎ *(0504)265461.*

AROUND DERRY

Ballyliffen, *N Inishowen peninsula:* delightful small resort. Nearby, vast sandy stretches of Pollan Strand. Ballyliffen Golf Club, *18 holes,* ☎ *(077)76119.*

Banagher Church, *3 km (2 miles) SW of Dungiven:* impressive ruin; nave dates from about 1100.

Banagher Forest, *off Draperstown-Feeny B40:* largest in Co Derry, with large artificial Banagher Glen lake, nature reserve.

Buncrana, *W Inishowen, bus enquiries,* ☎ *(077)61340.* Seaside resort, fine beach, popular with folk from Derry 21 km (13 miles) down the road. The crack's good, especially in summer. *National Knitting Centre, Lisfannon:* details Donegal's cottage handknitting industry. *Jan-Sept, Mon-Fri, 9.30 a.m.-6 p.m., Sat, Sun, 2 p.m.-6 p.m. Oct-Dec, Mon-Fri, 9.30 a.m.-6 p.m. weekends by arr,* ☎*(077)62355. Tullyarvan Mill:* textile museum details over 250 years of production in the area. Wildlife display, craft and souvenir shop. *Easter-Sept, Mon-Sat, 10 a.m.-6 p.m. Sun, 12 noon-6 p.m.* ☎*(077)61613. Vintage Car & Carriage Museum:* vintage and classic cars, horse-drawn carriages, vintage bicycles and motor cycles, model cars and trains. *Summer, daily, 10 a.m.-8 p.m. Off season, weekdays, Sun, by arr.* ☎*(077)61130. Slieve Snaght Mountain,* just NE of the town, worth climbing if you're energetic — it's just over 600 m (2,000 ft) high. Rewarding views from summit. Walk: via Castle Bridge (O'Doherty's Castle) past Porthaw Bay to Friar Hegarty's Rock, where a local clergyman was executed in 1632. Riding: Bill Doherty, *Main Street.* Bicycles: Hegarty's, *Upper Main Street.* North West Golf Club, *18 holes, Fahan,* ☎ *(077)61027.*

Burt Church (C), *8 km (5 miles) W of the city:* striking circular church designed by Derry architect Liam McCormick, who drew his inspiration from the nearby Grianan of Aileach.

Carndonagh, *N Inishowen.* Donagh or St Patrick's Cross stands over 3 m (11 ft) high and is reputed to be the oldest of its kind in Ireland.

Culdaff, *on Malin-Moville T73:* Bocan church has 280 mm (11 inch) high bronze bell dating from 9th or 10th c.

Culmore Point, *5 km (3 miles) NE of Derry on A2.* Reconstructed Plantation fort next to lighthouse. Also ruins of old church used by Jacobite army in 1688-89.

Cumber House Riverside Park, *just outside Claudy, 13 km (8 miles) SE of Derry.* Nature reserve, picnic area on banks of River Faughan.

Dergalt, *5 km (3 miles) from Strabane on Plumbridge road:* birthplace of James Wilson, grandfather of U.S. president Woodrow Wilson.

Guildhall windows, Derry city

(NT) Original furnishings give good idea of late 18th c living conditions. *All year, call at farm for admittance.*

Donemana, *11 km (7 miles) NE of Strabane on B49. EC Wed.* Steep-streeted village on banks of Burn Dennet River. Just S of village is impressively modern St Patrick's church (C), with unusual fibreglass statue of the saint.

Dunaff Head, *6 km (4 miles) W of Clonmany:* spectacular sea views.

Dungiven Bawn, remains of early 17th c fortified mansion. Castle has gone, but the surrounding bawn can still be seen. *The Priory,* just S of town: founded in 1100 by the O'Cahans, now ruins attractively sited on rock overlooking River Roe.

Eglinton, *8 km (5 miles) NE of Derry.* Tree-lined village with very English air. Just S is *Muff Glen,* with woodland walks. *Eglinton airport.* Flights to Britain. ☎ *(0504)810784.*

Fahan, *6 km (4 miles) S of Buncrana on T73.* Attractive little village by shores of Lough Swilly. St

Mura's Cross in abbey graveyard. Nearby Inch island connected to mainland by bridge.

Fort Dunree Military Museum, Linsfort, Buncrana. Exhibition area, audio visual facilities with military memorabilia going back 180 years. The setting, once a coastal fort, is astounding. Café; *Easter-Sept, Tues-Sat, 10 a.m.-6 p.m., Sun, 12 noon-6 p.m. Also BH.* ☎ *(074)21160.*

Gap of Mamore, *8 km (5 miles) NE of Buncrana:* striking views over large part of Inishowen peninsula.

Greencastle, *5 km (3 miles) N of Moville.* Martello Tower ramparts give fine views over Lough Foyle. Bathing at nearby Shrove Strand. Golf course, *18 holes.*

Grianan of Aileach, *8 km (5 miles) W of Derry:* remarkable stone fort built about 1700 BC, yet virtually intact. Excellent views from top of the wall. Turn off main Derry-Buncrana road at Bridgend onto N13 towards Letterkenny. Track from this road runs right to fort.

Learmount Forest, *7 km (4 miles) SE of Claudy:* one of NI's most beautiful country parks. Caravanning facilities.

Lecamey, *7 km (4 miles) NW of Moville:* Sweat House, where in the bad old days, sick people sat amid turf fires and literally sweated it out. Have a look at any time.

Limavady, *27 km (17 miles) E of Derry on A2. EC Thurs.* Bus enquiries: Ulsterbus, Limavady, ☎ *(05047)62101.* Train enquiries, ☎ *(0504)42228.* Market town with lots of Georgian style. Six-arched Roe Bridge dates back to 1700. Monday market in main street good for bargains and banter. Riding: Mrs R. Smyth, *25 Dowland Road,* ☎ *(05047)62127.* Roe Valley Recreation Centre: *9 Greystone Road, Daily,* ☎ *(05047)66279.* Stradreagh Youth Hostel: *6 km (4 miles) NE of Limavady.*

Loughermore Forest, *8 km (5 miles) NE of Claudy off B69:* splendid walks through wild mountain scenery. At Ballyholly Hill, three stone circles that may have been used as a calendar in 2000 BC.

Magheramore Hill, *3 km (2 miles) E of Clonmany:* Bronze Age dolmen with massive capstone.

Malin, *N Inishowen, Lough Swilly bus from Derry.* Sited on Trawbreaga Bay with sandy beach and some of Europe's highest sand dunes, wins Tidy Towns contests with seemingly effortless ease. Museum.

Malin Head, *13 km (8 miles) N of Malin:* most N point in Ireland, with views and winds to match. The 8 km (5 mile) long Atlantic Circle drive gives the best views. Boats from harbour to deserted island of Inishtrahull, with lighthouse and ruins of former settlement.

Mount Hamilton, *or Sperrin, 15 km (9 miles) E of Plumbridge:* best starting-point for exploring lonely and rugged Sperrin Mountains, including Sawel Mountain, 680 m (2,240 ft). From the hamlet, minor roads run N and S across the mountains.

Moville: pleasant little seaside town on E shores of Inishowen peninsula. Moville Green is famous for its velvet-like turf; sandy beaches. Moville Regatta: feast of sporting events. *Usually first Mon Aug. Leisureland:* fun and entertainment for children of all ages. *Easter-Sept, daily,* ☎*(077)82306.*

Ness Country Park, *near Brackfield on A6:* Burntollet River forms highest waterfall in N. Ireland - about 12 m (39 ft). Narrow gorge above the fall is called Shane's Leap, after an 18th c highwayman who escaped from soldiers there. Nature trail, picnic area.

River Foyle, *S of Derry:* some 7 km (4 miles) of former railway track between bank of river and Letterkenny road has been turned into a pleasant riverside path. The city, on the hills, is very striking seen from the river.

Roe Valley Country Park, *just S of Limavady:* old water mills from great days of linen trade. The first hydro-electric power station in this part of Ireland, opened in 1896, is also preserved. Museum, craft shop, cafe. *Visitor centre open all year, daily, 9 a.m.-5 p.m., 9 p.m. in July, Aug. Access at all times to grounds.* ☎ *(050 47)22074.*

Sion Mills, *5 km (3 miles) S of Strabane on A5. EC Sat.* Originally a model linen village with an exceptionally broad main street, it still has great charm. *St Teresa's church* (C), designed in striking style by same architect (Patrick Haughey) as Catholic church in Donemana. There are pleasant walks to village of Carrigullin Lower across Bearney suspension footbridge over River Mourne.

Slievekirk Mountains, *5 km (3 miles) NE of Donemana:* old turf track runs up mountain from the Old Glen, Castlewarren, good views of Sperrin Mountains.

Strabane, *23 km (14 miles) S of Derry on A5, EC Thurs. TIO: Lifford Road,* ☎ *(0504)883735, June-Sept. Bus enquiries:* ☎ *(0504)382393.* Market town on the banks of the River Mourne. *Gray's Printing Press* (NT), *Main Street:* John Dunlap, who printed the first copies of the American Declaration of Independence in 1776, began his apprenticeship here 20 years earlier at the age of ten. Fine examples of old printing presses and type, including early 19th c Columbian press, topped by a golden eagle. *Apr-Sept, daily, except Thurs, Sun, 2 p.m.-6 p.m. or by arr. Knockavoe Hill, overlook-*

Malin Head, Co. Donegal

ing the town, is easy to climb and gives good views as far as Errigal and Muckish Mountains in Co. Donegal. *Strabane Glen: 1.5 km (1 mile) NE of the town,* has good River Foyle views and there are pleasant walks along the Water Mall and banks of River Mourne, also to Lifford, administrative capital of Donegal, literally on the other side of River Finn. Leisure centre: Lisnafin Park, ☎ *(0504)382672.* Strabane Golf Club, *18 holes,* ☎ *(0504)882271.*

Tullagh Bay, *3 km (2 miles) NW of Clonmany, N Inishowen:* good beach.

Omagh

Pop. 15,000, 55 km (34 miles) S of Derry, 117 km (73 miles) W of Belfast, 190 km (118 miles) NW of Dublin. EC Wed. Bus enquiries: bus station, Mountjoy Road, ☎ *(0662)42711.*

The county town of Co. Tyrone, Omagh is set where the Rivers Camowen and Drumragh meet to form the Strule. Its best view is perhaps along the steep and wide High Street, crowned by the

choicely-sited, classical style courthouse, behind which stands the modern C church, with Gothic style spires. Good salmon, trout, roach fishing in area. Agricultural Show: *first week July.*

Riverside walk: along the banks of the Camowen, past the 'lovers' retreat'. Nearby, see salmon leap 'stairs' in river. Scenic drive to Cookstown over Black Bog, about 27 m (43 km). Recreation and youth centre: *Old Mountfield Road, daily.* Dergmoney Riding School, ☎ *(0662)42336;* Omagh Golf Club, *18 holes,* ☎ *(0662)243160.*

AROUND OMAGH

Baronscourt, *5 km (3 miles) SW of Newtownstewart on B84:* seat of Duke and Duchess of Abercorn. Gardens and grounds open to organised parties by arr. Attractive deer park dating from 1770s—Japanese Sika deer. Self-catering chalets available all year. Good quality pike fishing. *Garden open Mon-Sat, 10 a.m.-4.30 p.m., Sun 2 p.m.-4.30 p.m. Details: Baronscourt Estate Office,* ☎ *(06626)61683. Baronscourt Forest:* set on slopes of Bessy Bell mountain. Nature trail adjacent to Hunting Lodge Hotel. *All year daily during daylight hours.*

Castlederg: ruins of Castlesessagh bawn (known locally as Derg Castle), built around 1610, on N bank of River Derg.

Clogher, *24 km (15 miles) SE of Omagh on B83. EC Thurs.* St MacCartan's Cathedral (CI), remodelled 1818. Porch has Clogh-cir, a pagan idol, as well as collection of portraits of former bishops. Good view of Clogher valley from top of tower. *By arr. the dean.*

Donaghmore heritage centre: a 19th c national school has been converted into a fascinating display centre for local history. Industrial history is included. *All year, Mon-Fri, 9 a.m.-1 p.m.; 2 p.m.-5 p.m. (Fri, 3.30 p.m.) or by arr.,* ☎ *(08687)67039.*

Fintona, *13 km (8 miles) S of Omagh on B122.* Pleasant walks in wooded park. Golf course next to Ecclesville Park has stone Cow Bridge over Quiggery Water River, all that remains of old coach road.

Fivemiletown display centre: old artefacts, including craftsmen's tools. *All year, Mon, Tues, Fri, 10 a.m.-1 p.m.; 2 p.m.-6 p.m., Thurs, 2 p.m.-8 p.m. Sat, 10 a.m.-5 p.m. Closed Sun, BH.* ☎ *(03655)21409. Fivemiletown Creamery:* cheese production. *Mon-Fri, by arr,* ☎*(03655)21209.*

Gortin Glen Forest Park, *8 km (5 miles) NW of Omagh on B48:* wildfowl enclosure and reserve with Sika deer, nature trails, natural history museum, café, children's play area. On E side of park, extensive views from Mullaghcarn Mountain. Near entrance on B48, the 'magnetic mile' effect will make your car appear to move uphill—leave the brake off, the road is quite flat! *All year, daily, 10 a.m.-sunset,* ☎ *(06626)48217.* Visit nearby Boorin Wood and Gortin Lakes. Youth Hostel in Gortin Village.

Knock-na-Moe Castle Hotel, *Cookstown Road, near Omagh:* Eisenhower and Montgomery Rooms are reminders of secret military planning meetings here involving the two leaders during World War II, ☎ *(0662)243131.*

Knockmany Forest, *20 km (12 miles) SE of Omagh on B83:* spread along slopes of Sperrins with good walks, waterfall, splendid viewpoints. On summit of 200 m (656 ft) hill, see Knockmany chambered cairn, with extraordinary surface designs, believed to date back five or six thousand years.

Lisahoppin open farm, *5 km (3 miles) SE of Omagh on B158:* includes working dairy farm, nature trail, riverside walk. *Mar-June, Sat, Sun, BH, 1 p.m.-6 p.m.; July-Aug, daily, 10 a.m.-6 p.m.* ☎*(0662)242502.*

Newtownstewart, *15 km (9 miles) NW of Omagh on A5.* Small town attractively set on River Strule. Ruin of Harry Avery's medieval castle is 0.8 km (0.4 miles) SW of village. The O'Neill chieftain who built the castle wasn't a nice man to know—he is

said to have hung 19 men who refused to marry his ugly sister. Ruins of castle, burned in 1689, behind shop at N end of Main Street. The Northern Bank is where Thomas Montgomery, a local policeman, murdered William Glass, a bank cashier, in 1871. *Mon-Fri, 10 a.m.-12.30 p.m.; 1.30 p.m.-3.30 p.m. Harry Avery's Castle.* Just SW of town: hilltop castle built in 14th/15th c. Newtownstewart Golf Club, *18 holes,* ☎ *(06626)61466.*

Seskinore Forest, *10 km (6 miles) S of Omagh on B83:* picnic sites, forest walks. Dept of Agriculture rears pheasants on game farm; see collection of ornamental birds.

Springtown, *3 km (2 miles) E of Augher.* William Carleton's cottage, where the famous 19th c Irish novelist spent his youth, is marked by a plaque.

Ulster-American Folk Park, *Camphill, 6 km (4 miles) N of Omagh on A5.* Endowed by Mellons, an American banking family. The cottage from which Thomas Mellon emigrated to America in 1818 is but one of many attractions on this site. Other reconstructed cottages, museum , audiovisual theatre, exhibition galleries detail Irish emigration to the U.S. Ship and dockside gallery. Farm museum, Old World and New World sections. Former includes meeting house, schoolhouse, forge, country shop. Latter includes log stockade, early Mellon log house at Turtle Creek, Pennsylvania. A full day out. Café, gifts and craft shop, picnic areas. *Easter-Sept, Mon-Sat, 11 a.m.-6.30 p.m. Sun, BH,11.30 a.m.- 7 p.m. Oct-Mar, Mon-Fri,10.30 a.m.-5 p.m.,* & ☎ *(0662)243292.*

Ulster History Park details the history of the province from 7,000 BC to the end of the 17th c. *Open daily,* ☎ *(06626)48188.*

Sligo

Pop. 18,000, 59 km (37 miles) NE of Ballina, 217 km (135 miles) NW of Dublin. EC Wed. TIO: Temple Street, ☎ *(071)61201, all year. Sligo airport: Strandhill,* ☎ *(071)68280/68318. Bus, train enquiries: CIE, MacDiarmada station,* ☎ *(071)60066. Coach tours: SO, details, TIO.*

The old and flourishing town of Sligo is one of the most attractively set in Ireland, with majestic mountains to the N and the vast, cone-shaped Knocknarea to the S. The town itself is an enticing mixture of modern commerce (complete with good bookshops), ancient history and relatively modern literature: a principal attraction is its connection with W. B. Yeats.

Cathedral of the Immaculate Conception (C), *John Street:* built in Norman style, 1870. *Calry Church,* (CI), *top of Mall:* Gothic style, attractively set above River Garavogue. *Sligo Abbey, Abbey Street:* founded in 1252 for Dominican Order. Finally destroyed in town's 1641 sacking. After restoration the cloisters are now almost perfect on three sides. Each has 18 beautifully worked arches and elaborately coupled pillars. Key from T. McLoughlin, *6 Abbey Street. Co Sligo museum and Yeats art gallery:* Ireland's largest collection of Jack B. Yeats' paintings, also works by his contemporaries. Museum and gallery: *June-Sept, Mon-Sat, 10.30 a.m.-12.30 p.m.; 2.30 p.m.-4.30 p.m.* ☎*(071)42212. County Library, Stephen Street* has special Yeats' section, including his complete poetical writings, first editions, his 1923 Nobel prize for literature. *Mon-Sat, 10.30 a.m.-12.30 p.m.; 2.30 p.m.-4.30 p.m.*

Hawk's Well Theatre, Temple Street: varied programme in impressive building which combines TIO, ☎ *(071)61518- 61526. Yeats Watch Tower, corner Adelaide Street, Wine Street:* tops an impressive stone building, once occupied by Pollexfen family, 19th c ship owners. William Pollexfen watched his ships from it and his grandson, W. B. Yeats, spent many happy hours in this eyrie.

Yeats International Summer School: full programme of events in and around Sligo. Lectures,

seminars on many aspects of the poet's life and work. *Yeats Memorial Building* has extensive library, audio-visual shows on life and times of W.B Yeats. *June-Aug, Mon-Fri, 10.30 a.m.-1 p.m.; 3 p.m.-5 p.m.* ☎ *(071)42693. Hargadon's bar, O'Connell Street:* unchanged for a century, with glass mirrors, mahogany counters, drawers, and atmosphere all of its own. Sligo Craft Pottery, *Market Yard:* original hand-made pottery. *Daily 10 a.m.-6 p.m. Doorly Park, upstream from town:* good walks and splendid views of Lough Gill and surrounding mountains. College Road: best views in Sligo of Ben Bulben and Knocknarea. Riverside walk: start just by Douglas Hyde bridge, go up pleasant Rockwood Parade alongside the river, continue across Thomas Street into Kennedy Parade, then back past Dominican Abbey. Guided tours, *July-Aug,* 11 a.m. and 7.30 p.m., leave tourist office, Temple Street, taking in Sligo Abbey, Yeats Museum, Art Gallery, St John's Cathedral, Sligo

Carrowmore Megaliths, *3 km (2 miles) SW of Sligo, at foot of Knocknarea:* over 60 Bronze Age tombs stretch over 3 km (2 miles) of striking countryside, making Carrowmore the largest concentration in Ireland of megalithic tombs and one of the largest in Europe. *Mid-June—mid-Sept, Mon-Sun, 9.30 a.m.-6.30 p.m.* ☎ *(071)61534.*

Coney Island, *near Rosses Point:* when tide is out, you can walk or drive to island from Strandhill side. Row of pillars marks route. Coney Island, New York, is believed to have been named after it.

Creevykeel Court Cairn, *near Cliffony, 24 km (15 miles) N of Sligo on N15.* Best megalithic remains in Ireland. Cairn enclosed by courtyard impressively sited with mountains to S and E.

Deerpark, *6 km (4 miles) E of Sligo on Colcagh road:* prehistoric cairn (NM) has galleries opening off each end of an oval court. Excellent views of Lough Gill, forest walks, picnic areas.

Ben Bulben, Co. Sligo

Cathedral. Bus tours of Yeats' country, summer eves by arr.

Leisure Activities: Sligo racecourse, *Cleveragh:* one of most beautifully set in Ireland, occ. races, *details:* TIO. Swimming pool: outdoor, Markievicz Road, *daily,* ☎ *(071)43003.* Bicycles: Garry's Cycles, Quay Street, ☎ *(071)45418,* Conway Bros, 6 High Street, ☎ *(071)61370.*

AROUND SLIGO

Abbey Court, *3 km (2 miles) NW of Achonry off N17:* ruins of Franciscan friary just outside Lavagh village. A wall vault has burst asunder and a nailed coffin protrudes. Don't come after dark.

Aughris Head, *24 km (15 miles) W of Sligo, off N59:* fine views of coast. Aughris is good surfing venue. Nearby Dunmoran Strand a vast, deserted beach.

Ballisodare: the Thatch is an old-style Irish pub, with thatched roof, regular Irish nights.

Ballymote, *24 km (15 miles) S of Sligo:* Ballymote Castle, by Richard de Burgh, Red Earl of Ulster, extensive ruins flanked by six towers. Remains of Franciscan friary. Remains of 14th c Knights of St John house on shores of Templehouse Lough, 3 km (2 miles) SW of village.

Bricklieve Mountains, *10 km (6 miles) SE of Ballymote, signposted road leaves L11 at Traveller's Rest:* five ridges have prehistoric cairns dating from 2000 BC, known as the Carrowkeel Passage Grave. Whole day can be spent exploring the ridges and cairns. Tremendous sunset views.

Lough Gill from Dooney Rock, Co. Sligo

Dooney Rock, *6 km (4 miles) E of Sligo on L117:* nature trail through woodlands, past shores of Lough Gill to top of rock. On site leaflets detail forest walks, viewing points. Nearby holy well, shrine.

Dromahaire, *16 km (10 miles) SE of Sligo:* ruins of Creevelea Franciscan abbey, built 1508. The 17th c Park's Castle is off the L16 just N of village, key at nearby farm.

Drumcliffe, *6 km (4 miles) N of Sligo on N15.* Churchyard (C) has impressive 11th c cross. On W side of main road, stump of 6th c round tower. W.B. Yeats is buried in churchyard of plain, square towered CI. Behind the churchyard are the steep cliffs of King's Mountain and the legendary Ben Bulben. Yeats heritage trail: starting at the TIO, *Stephen Street, Sligo,* a 170 km (105 mile) signposted trial suitable for cyclists and motorists follows the places associated with W.B. Yeats, the poet, and Jack B. Yeats, his painter brother. At each place, an explanatory narrative is illustrated with a poetic excerpt. Yeats died at Roquebrune in S France in 1939, and his remains were brought home in 1948. On his headstone are carved the immortal words:

> Cast a cold Eye
> On Life, on Death,
> Horseman, pass by!

Glencar Lake, *11 km (7 miles) NE of Sligo on N16, 282 bus from Sligo.* One waterfall has an impressive unbroken fall of 15 m (50 ft). Minor road along N shore has best views of upper waterfall.

Gleniff Horseshoe, *near Cliffony:* one of the most spectacular tours in the NW. Road runs round the glen, past Truskmore with its TV mast, giving fine views of towering limestone cliffs. Gleniff on the Horseshoe route has forest walks, picnic area. Turn

off at Cliffony, midway between Sligo and Bundoran on N15 in direction of Ballintrillick.

Grange, *10 km (6 miles) N of Sligo:* Sligo Irish Stone Cut Crystal. Factory and showrooms, *Oct-May, Mon-Sat, 9 a.m.-6 p.m., June-Sept, Mon-Fri, 9 a.m.-9 p.m., Sat, Sun, 10 a.m.-7 p.m.* ☎*(071)63251.*

Hazelwood, *5 km (3 miles) E of Sligo, 0.8 km (0.5 miles) off L116:* scenic views, although views from N shores of Lough Gill not as good as those on the S. Forest walks, picnic area, with Sculpture Trail of 13 wood sculptures en route.

Heapstown Cairn, *N end of Lough Arrow, 24 km (15 miles) SE of Sligo off N4:* over 61 m (200 ft) in diameter, said to have been built in one night. Labby Rock, an enormous dolmen, is 3 km (2 miles) E of cairn. Nearby Lough Nasool is said to drain dry every 100 years, the last time in 1933.

Innisfree Island, to find the place immortalised by W. B. Yeats, take L117 from Sligo towards Dromahaire, until the signpost for the island, 5 km (3 miles) from this point.

Inishmurray Island, *6 km (4 miles) off Streedagh Point:* 2 km (1 mile) long island, low-lying and bleak. Landing at pier on E side. Substantial ruins of St Molaise's monastery, plundered by Vikings in 807. 11 stations, wells, memorials dotted round island, which was abandoned in Oct 1947 when the 50 inhabitants moved to the mainland. Boats from Mullaghmore, Rosses Point, Streedagh.

Keshcorran Hill, *6 km (4 miles) SE of Ballymote, off L11:* caves of Kesh, in hillside, as well as summit, with breathtaking views, are reached by steep path from farmhouse on minor road to Kesh where it runs parallel to main L11.

Knocknarea, *6 km (4 miles) SW of Sligo:* huge limestone cone dominates whole area. Queen Maeve, whose likeness adorned the old Irish £1 note, reputed to be buried in great summit cairn, from where you can enjoy stupendous views. Easy climb on SE side, near Grange House.

Lady's Brae road, *24 km (15 miles) SW of Sligo:* spectacular views of Donegal, Mayo Mountains, as well as Ben Bulben, Knocknarea. At Skreen on N59, turn onto minor road up into Ox Mountains, signposted for Lady's Brae.

Lisnalurg, *3 km (2 miles) N of Sligo on N15:* one of largest earthwork enclosures in Ireland, covering about 0.8 ha (2 acres).

Lissadell House, *6 km (4 miles) NW of Drumcliffe.* 19th c Georgian house, childhood home of Countess Markievicz, a leader in the 1916 Rising, and her sister Eva Gore-Booth. W. B. Yeats regularly slept in bedroom above porch. Dining, music rooms particularly striking. Gardens with masses of daffodils in spring, nearby pine forests, picnic area, access to Drumcliffe Bay. *Jun 1-Sept 15. Mon-Sat, 10.30 a.m.-12 noon, 2 p.m.-4.30 p.m.* ☎ *(071)63150.* Ellen's Pub, Maugherow, full of atmosphere, very popular with Continental visitors.

Lough Gill, *3 km (2 miles) E of Sligo:* lake to rival Killarney, 22 islands. Silver bell from Sligo's ruined Dominican Abbey said to lie at bottom of lake. When it peals, only the perfect can hear. Lough Gill cruises depart from Riverside landing stage, near Blue Lagoon lounge, at Doorly Park entrance. *Apr-Dec, Daily departures, June, July, Aug. Details from Sligo TIO.*

Manorhamilton, *24 km (15 miles) E of Sligo on N16.* Attractive Co. Leitrim town with less than 1,000 inhabitants, nestling at the junction of four mountain valleys. Main object of interest is ruined mansion built by Sir Frederick Hamilton in 1638, just N. Wild Rose Festival: Wild Rose Colleen is chosen, various fringe events during week-long festivities, *Aug.*

Mullaghmore, *just off N15 between Sligo and Bundoran:* good, sheltered bathing in shadow of Classiebawn Castle. *Annie's bar* is over 200 years old, many fascinating mementoes (including photographs) left behind by visitors. No music, the pint is drawn slowly.

O'Rourke's Table, *5 km (3 miles) N of Dromahaire on Manorhamilton road:* prominent rock plateau

gives magnificent view of Lough Gill and Yeats Country.

Parke's Castle, *on Sligo-Dromahair road on NE side of Lough Gill:* 17th c fortified Plantation house has been thoroughly restored, as has the courtyard. Audio-visual presentation. Exhibitions. Tea room. *St Patrick's weekend, daily, 10 a.m.-5 p.m.; late Apr-May 30, Tues-Sun, 10 a.m.-5 p.m.; June-Sept, daily, 9.30 a.m.-6.30 p.m.; Oct, daily, 10 a.m.-5 p.m.* ☎ *(071)64149.*

Raghly, *on peninsula at entrance to Drumcliffe Bay:* quiet fishing village, nearby remains of 16th c Dunfore and Ardtermon castles. Just N of village, Tráigh Bhuí, or Yellow Strand, appropriately sandy. Raghly Promontory, excellent views of mountains encircling Sligo Bay.

Rathcarrick/Knocknarea, *3 km (2 miles) S of Sligo-Strandhill L132:* scenic views over Sligo Bay, forest walks, picnic area, car park.

Rosses Point, *8 km (5 miles) NW of Sligo on L16.* Cosy seaside resort with two splendid beaches good for swimming. Good views across Drumcliffe Bay. Rosses Point Golf Club, *18 holes,* ☎ *(071)77171.*

Sessue Gilroy, *32 km (20 miles) W of Sligo, turn S towards Lough Easkey at Dromore West: on N59:* fine forest walks and views.

Slish Wood, *S side of Lough Gill, just off L117:* forest, lakeside walks, paddling pool, picnic area. Fallow deer can sometimes be seen.

Strandhill, *6 km (4 miles) W of Sligo on L132.* Coastal resort with two sandy beaches. **Dolly's Cottage:** early 19th c rural house renovated by Strandhill Guild of Irish Countrywomen's Association. *July, Aug, daily, 3 p.m.-5 p.m. July, Aug, Wed aft. country markets. Wed eve, traditional entertainment. Details: Sligo TIO.* Strandhill Golf Club, *18 holes,* ☎ *(071)68188.*

Streedagh, *3 km (2 miles) W of Grange:* during spring tide low water, when wind is blowing strongly from S, you may see wreckage of three Spanish Armada galleons, wrecked in 1588 with only one survivor. Nearby ruins of 7th c Staid Abbey, Aghaharrow.

The NORTH

Antrim

Pop. 24,000, 27 km (17 miles) NE of Belfast, 180 km (112 miles) N of Dublin, via Lurgan. EC Wed. TIO, ☎ *(08494)64131, all year. Bus enquiries: Ulsterbus depot, Railway Street,* ☎ *(08494)28729.*

Slemish Mountain, Co. Antrim

Train enquiries: ☎ *(08494)29185.*

A pleasant if unremarkable town at the NE corner of Lough Neagh, founded on the site of an ancient monastery. Although Antrim is largely residential, it has points of interest and excellent sporting facilities.

Round Tower, About 1,000 years old, remarkably well preserved, **Steeple Park,** access at all times.

Armagh city from St Patrick's Cathedral

Antrim Castle Demesne, fine gardens W of town along Lough Neagh shore, laid out in late 17th c in similar style to Versailles, complete with ornamental waters. Only a tower remains of original castle, burned in 1922, during previous Troubles. Beside it, the Norman motte makes a fine viewpoint. Co. Antrim agricultural show held here in July. *Daily.* **Clotworthy House,** *castle grounds:* theatre, exhibitions, ☎ *(08494)67531.* **Alexander Irvine's cottage,** *Pogue's Entry, off Church Street:* 18th c cottage, childhood home of the author of the 19th c classic, *My Lady of the Chimney Corner.* Interior little changed. *All year, Mon-Fri, 10 a.m.-4 p.m. Closed lunch, BH. Key at adjacent TIO, Church Street,* ☎ *(08494)28331.*

Antrim Forum, *Lough Road:* impressive modern sports centre with extensive facilities, inc. pool, *daily,* ☎ *(08494)64131.* Lough Neagh cruises, *Antrim Marina, Sixmilewater, May-Sept, daily,* ☎ *(08494)64131.* Masserene Golf Club, *18 holes,* ☎ *(08494)62096.*

AROUND ANTRIM

Ballymena, *18 km (11 miles) NW of Antrim. All day closing Wed. Bus enquiries: bus station, Galgorm Road,* ☎ *(0266)652214. Railway enquiries: station,* ☎ *(0266)652277.* Prosperous town with a strong Scottish influence, which may account for it having been described, not entirely fairly, as the meanest town in Ireland. Excellent game fishing. **St Patrick's,** (CI), *Castle Street,* is noted for its rich interior and 19th c Art Nouveau windows. ♿ From Ballymena roads run through the Braid and Clogh valleys to Antrim moorlands. The coastal routes to Cushendun and Cushendall are very attractive. **Sentry Hill Sports Hall,** *Old Ballymoney Road,* ☎ *(0266)656101.* Seven towers leisure centre, *Trostan Avenue, Mon-Sat,* ☎ *(0266)41427.* Ballymena Golf Club, *18 holes,* ☎ *(022)861487.*

Broughshane, *5 km (3 miles) NE of Ballymena on A42.* Memorial in Rathcavan churchyard to the locally-born ancestors of General Sam Houston, who brought Texas into the United States. There is a pleasant walk near the village, across the Buttermilk Footbridge by River Braid.

Cullybackey, *5 km (3 miles) NW of Ballymena on B96.* Arthur Cottage, Dreen, home of the parents of Chester Alan Arthur, 21st President of the United States in early 1880s. Fully restored with typical 19th c furnishings, picture gallery, good view of the River Main. *Apr-Sept 30, Mon-Fri, 2 p.m.-6 p.m.* 1 m (2 km) N of village on B93 to Glarryford, there is a curious beehive-shaped thatched cottage.

Dunadry Inn, *5 km (3 miles) SE of Antrim.* Created from an 18th c linen mill and its cottages. Axles from the mill's beetling machinery were used to form the gallery's pillars.

Glarryford, *11 km (7 miles) NW of Ballymena on B62/B93:* small village on banks of the River Main. Attractive countryside deserving of wider recognition.

Gracehill, *3 km (2 miles) W of Ballymena on A42:* founded by Moravians in 18th c. German Christmas customs still observed in the village church. Ask rector to see Moravian church records.

Kells, *midway between Antrim and Ballymena.* Pleasant walk round Diamond and across the old bridge with views over the weir on the Kells Water River. Remains of ancient Augustinian abbey.

Portglenone: The Cistercian Monastery has its own printing press. *Male visitors only,* ☎ *(0266)821211.* **Portglenone Forest,** *13 km (8 miles) W of Ballymena:* Bannside oak woods, with Augustine Henry trail, in honour of the forestry pioneer born near by in 1857, and a memorial grove with some of the thousands of trees and shrubs he discovered. Two holy wells. Picnic sites, nature trails.

Shane's Castle Demesne, *3 km (2 miles) W of Antrim on A6T:* steam railway and nature reserve. Locos haul passenger trains on 3 km (2 mile) ride round demesne. Two hides by shore of Lough Neagh enable you to see many varieties of water birds. Café, small fairground, picnic sites. Excellent facilities for a full day out with the children. *Apr, May, Sun, BH, 12.30 p.m.-6.30 p.m.; June, Wed, Sun, 12.30 p.m.-6.30 p.m.; July, Aug, Tues-Thurs, Sat, Sun, BH, 12.30 p.m.-6.30 p.m.; Sept, Sun, 12.30 p.m.-6.30 p.m.* Steam locomotive *on all days except Wed in June and Tues-Thurs in July, Aug.* ☎ *(08494)63380.*

Slemish Mountain, *13 km (8 miles) E of Ballymena:* volcanic cone which dominates the whole area. Legend says that St Patrick, as a boy slave, herded swine here for his owner, Miluic. Road runs to near top of mountain.

Tardree Forest, *9 km (6 miles) N of Antrim:* forest walks give good views over Lough Neagh and Slemish. Nature trail, 3 km (2 miles) E of forest, Browndod Hill has a Neolithic cairn on summit.

Toomebridge, *16 km (10 miles) W of Antrim on A6T.* Eel fishery, run as a co-op. Spring is best time to visit, when about 20 million elvers, or baby eels, swim across Atlantic and up the River Bann.

Armagh

Pop, 13,000, 59 km (37 miles) SW of Belfast, 137 km (85 miles) NW of Dublin. All day closing Wed. TIO: ☎ *(0861)527808, all year. Bus enquiries: Ulsterbus depot, Mall West,* ☎ *(0861) 522266.*

Dominated by its two cathedrals, one Catholic, the other Protestant, for 1500 years Armagh has been the ecclesiastical capital of Ireland. Founded in the 5th c, when St Patrick established his Primatial See here, the city became an internationally renowned centre of learning during the middle ages. Today it retains much of its historic atmosphere and walks round the main sights are very rewarding.

St Patrick's Cathedral (C), set on a hilltop and reached by a fine flight of steps. 19th c Byzantine style, with lavish interior decoration. Red hats of four cardinals hang from Lady Chapel ceiling. **St Patrick's Cathedral** (CI), largely an early 19th c restoration on a 13th c building. Tablet outside N transept marks reputed grave of Brian Boru. **Palace Stables Heritage Centre,** *The Palace Demesne:* Georgian building with cobbled courtyard, in parkland of the Palace demesne. 18th c exhibition, A Day in the Life of Archbishop Robinson, Primate's chapel, 19th c coach, coachman's house, stables area, Hayloft gallery, restaurant, shop. *Apr-Aug, Mon-Sat, 10 a.m.-7 p.m., Sun, 1 p.m.-7 p.m. Sept-Mar, Mon-Sat, 10 a.m.-5 p.m., Sun, 2 p.m.-5 p.m.* ☎ *(0861)522722.* **Public Library,** *near CI cathedral:* remarkable institution, founded 1771, with interesting collection, inc. old manuscripts. *All year, Mon-Fri, 10 a.m.-12.30 p.m., 2 p.m.-4 p.m. or by arr,* ☎ *(0861)523142.* **Armagh Friary,** Franciscan, founded 1263-4, longest friary church in Ireland, now ruins. SE edge of city.

Planetarium, *College Hill:* public telescope, space equipment (inc. satellite), lectures, films, exhibitions. Astronomic instruments on display; visitors can explore the universe with hands-on computers in the hall of astronomy. Development plans for the planetarium include an extensive Astropark, with an Eartharium, showing the interior, surface and atmosphere of the earth. *All year, Mon-Sat, 2 p.m.-4.45 p.m. Shows every Sat, 2 p.m., 3 p.m. Extra shows, Easter, Christmas, BH. Daily shows, July, Aug, except July 13, Sun.* ☎ *(0861)523689.* Observatory grounds: see Robinson dome with telescope and sundial, video on observatory's work. Walks in grounds. *Apr-Sept, Mon-Fri, 9.30 a.m.-4.30 p.m.* ☎ *(0861)522928.* **Royal Irish Fusiliers Museum,** *Sovereign's House, East Mall:* tells story of regiment from 1793-1968. Exhibits include a 1943 Christmas card from Hitler. *All year, Mon-Fri, 10 a.m.-1 p.m.; 2 p.m.-4 p.m.* Telephone first ☎ *(0861)522911.* **County Museum,** *the Mall:* over 10,000 items, inc. prehistoric implements, local relics. Library, art gallery. Paintings by AE (writer and artist, George Russell, a Lurgan man). Occ. special exhibitions. *All year, Mon-Fri, 10 a.m.-12.30 p.m.; 2 p.m.-4 p.m.*

Apple-picking in Co. Armagh

or by arr, ☎ *(0861)523142.* **Adam Gallery,** *28 Linenhall Street,* ☎ *(0861)526908/523654.* In 1820s listed building, exhibitions of mainly Irish artists. *During exhibitions, 11 a.m.-5 p.m. daily, but closed Wed, Sun.* **The Mall,** attractive tree-lined green in the middle of Armagh, constructed on the old racecourse, a peaceful oasis. Jenny's Row, the Seven Houses, Market Square, Scotch Street, Dobbin Street or Castle Street. Folly Glen: pleasant streamside walk on S side of Armagh. Orchard leisure centre, *Folly Lane,* ☎ *(0861)522892.* ⅙ Armagh County Golf Club, *18 holes,* ☎ *(0861)522501.*

AROUND ARMAGH

Ardress House, *Annaghmore (NT), 8 km (5 miles) E of Moy on B28:* magnificent 17th c farmhouse with fine plasterwork and splendid collection of paintings. Small agricultural museum in farmyard. Garden, picnic area, adventure playground in woods. The Ladies Walk is a woodland walk around the estate. House, grounds, farmyard, *Easter, May, June, Sept, Sat, Sun, BH, 2 p.m.-6 p.m. July, Aug, daily, except Tues.* Farmyard, *May, June, Sept, also Mon-Fri, noon-4 p.m.* ☎ *(0762)851236.*

The Argory, (NT), *6 km (4 miles) NE of Moy on Derrycaw road:* fine early 19th c house set in over 300 acres of wooded countryside, overlooking River Blackwater. Rare herd of red Irish cattle, known as moile, being preserved here. Lit by an acetylene gas plant in stable yard, house little changed since turn of century. Contents include 1824 organ. Walks, shop, tea room. House, shop, tea room, *Easter, May, Sept, Sat, Sun, BH, 2 p.m.-6 p.m. July, Aug, daily, except Thurs.* ☎ *(08687)84753.*

Banbridge, *16 km (10 miles) SE of Portadown. EC Thurs. TIO:* ☎ *(08206)62799. Bus enquiries: 50 Newry Street,* ☎ *(08206)23633.* Unassuming market town, bisected by underpass in Main Street. Birthplace of Helen Waddell, the noted early 20th c writer. **Downshire Leisure Centre,** *Mon-Sat,* ☎ *(08206)62799.*

Benburb, *11 km (7 miles) NW of Armagh.* Servite Priory. Visitors are welcomed to the cheerful cloisters, setting for interdenominational meetings of all kinds. Art gallery, library. ☎ *(0861)548241.* **O'Neill Historical Centre** in basement of priory. ☎ *(0861)548187.*

Blackwater Forest Park, *on opp. bank of River Blackwater to Benburb:* extends for 5 km (3 miles), canoeing over weirs, deep pool for sub-aqua training, fossil hunting area, riverside walks.

Blackwatertown, *8 km (5 miles) NW of Armagh on A29/B128.* Good place to see road bowls, nicknamed 'bullets', being played. Rather like French *boules,* bowls are hurled along the road. Game is confined to counties Armagh and Cork. All-Ireland finals take place here in Aug.

Charlemont Fort, *opp. Moy on the River Blackwater, enter via S side of bridge:* the ruins of earthworks started in 1602 can be followed for most of their length.

Clare Glen, *runs SW from Tandragee for 5 km (3 miles).* Pleasant walks by River Cusher.

Craigavon, new town named after NI's first Prime Minister, set in wooded countryside S of Lough Neagh. Brownlow Recreation Centre, inc. pool, ☎ *(0762)341333.* Oxford Island: national nature reserve with 8 km (5 miles) of walks, bird hides, picnic areas. Wildlife exhibitions in visitor centre. Boats trips for bird watchers. *Always open.* ☎ *(0762)322205.* Craigavon Golf and Ski Centre, *Turmoyra, S of Oxford Island:* artificial ski slopes, golf putting. Refreshments. *Mon-Sat,* ☎ *(0762)326606.* Craigavon Lakes: rowing, sailing, canoeing, regular water sports events.

Fews Forest, *15 km (9 miles) S of Armagh on B31:* great walking country where you can stride for miles through forests and along moorland tracks. Fine views over countries Armagh and Down from picnic sites at Carrigatuke and Dead Man's Hill.

Gosford Forest Park, *near Markethill:* Gosford Castle closed, but see nearby round tower built by German prisoners-of-war held there during World War II. Traditional poultry breeds in paddocks, ornamental pigeons in dovecots. Walled garden, nature trail. *All year, Mon-Sun, 10 a.m.-dusk.* ☎ *(0861)551277.*

Loughgall, *8 km (5 miles) NW of Armagh on B77:* the apple growing centre of Ireland, rich with orchards. In May, follow signposted tour during apple blossom time. **Orange Order Museum,** *Main Street:* recalls founding of movement here in 1795. *By arr. with caretaker who lives next door. Mon-Sat, am & pm.* **Loughgall Presbyterian Church,** Ulster poet, W.R. Rodgers, was minister here before he devoted himself wholly to writing.

Lurgan, *34 km (21 miles) SE of Belfast on M1. All day closing Wed. TIO:* ☎ *(0762)323912, all year. Bus enquiries: Ulsterbus,* ☎*(0762)322724. Sureline coaches,* ☎ *(07622)324659. Train enquiries:* ☎ *(07622)322052.* Market town. Small lanes off main streets are remnants of 18th c linen weaving shops. In front of Brownlow House, see monument to Master McGrath, champion racing greyhound. Brownlow Park, boating, fishing. Swimming Pool: indoor, heated, *Robert Street, Mon- Sat,* ☎ *(07622)222906.* Lurgan Golf Club, *18 holes,* ☎ *(07622)322087.*

The Ould Lammas Fair, Ballycastle, Co. Antrim

Marlcoo Lake, *6 km (4 miles) E of Armagh on A51:* crannog or artificial islet, to which Hugh O'Neill, Earl of Tyrone, sent his family for safety at start of his 1595 rebellion. Attractive picnic area.

Middletown, *16 km (10 miles) SE of Armagh on A3:* enjoyable walk along rather overgrown towpath of long-derelict Ulster Canal.

Moy, *11 km (7 miles) N of Armagh on A29:* fine tree-lined square.

Navan Fort, *3 km (2 miles) W of Armagh on A28:* remains of Eamhain Macha, said to have been built about 300 BC and to have been the most important place in Ireland. No trace of buildings on site. The country's oldest legends, including the Ulster Cycle with its hero Cuchullain, are centred on this area. *Open at all times.*

Peatlands Country Park: Nature reserve, peat faces, small lakes, visitor centre, videos, outdoor exhibits on peat ecology, narrow gauge railway. Souvenir shop. Park *open all year, daily, 9 a.m.-*

White Park Bay, Co. Antrim

dusk. Railway: *Easter-Sept, Sat, Sun, BH, 2 p.m.-6 p.m., or groups by arr.,* ☎ *(0762)851102.*

Portadown, *43 km (27 miles) SW of Belfast. All day closing Thurs. TIO:* ☎*(0762)332499, all year. Bus enquiries: (0762)342511. Train enquiries: Portadown* station, ☎ *(0762)333501.* Market town on the River Bann, and a major coarse fishing centre. Swimming Pool: indoor, heated. Learner and competitive pools, *Thomas Street, Mon-Sat,* ☎*(0762)332802.* Portadown Golf Club, *18 holes,* ☎ *(0762)335356.*

Scarva Demesne, *near Banbridge:* Scarva Sham Fight (a traditional Orange v Green pageant) *July 13.*

Entrance hall, Mount Stewart, Co. Down

Seagahan Dam, *8 km (5 miles) W of Markethill:* the *edge of Fews Forest, encircled by scenic road with picnic sites. Pleasant, little-known spot.*

Tandragee, Golf Club, *18 holes,* ☎ *(0762)840727.*

Tandragee Castle: potato crisp processing at Tayto factory. *Daily, Tues-Thurs, 10 a.m.-3.30 p.m., or by arr,* ☎ *(0762)840249.*

Tannaghmore Garden, *N Craigavon:* Victorian garden, pleasures include an aviary and a children's farm with pony rides.

Tassagh, *3 km (2 miles) NW of Keady:* vast disused watermill on Callan River and 11 arches of disused railway viaduct.

Tullygiven Lough, *4 km (3 miles) W of Benburb:* popular for picnics and birdwatching.

Tullylish, *2 km (1 mile) E of Gilford off A50:* Birthplace of John Yeats, father of W.B. Yeats.

White Hill, *just N of Newtownhamilton, lane from B31:* reputed to have been site of palace of King Lir, whose children were turned into swans by a witch.

Ballycastle

Pop. 4,200, 30 km (19 miles) E of Coleraine, 108 km (67 miles) NE of Belfast via Antrim Road. EC Wed. TIO, ☎ *(02657)62024/62225. All year. Bus enquiries: Coleraine bus station,* ☎ *(0265)43334.*

An enormously attractive town on the N Antrim coast, completely unspoiled. Ballycastle proper is 3 km (2 miles) inland and connected to the smaller seaside part by a broad, tree-lined avenue. An ideal base for exploring the area's many natural attractions, and host to the lively, two day Ould Lammas Fair, *end of Aug:* many bargains, splendid banter.

Ballycastle Museum: the 18th c court-house has been transformed into a celebration of the folk culture and social history of the Glens of Antrim. Farm implements in the old jail at rear. *All year, Mon-Fri, 10 a.m.-1 p.m.; 2 p.m.-5 p.m. Closed Fri, 3.30 p.m. Telephone first for details,* ☎ *(02657)62024.* **Bonamargy Friary,** *(1 km) E of Ballycastle:* attractive ruins on banks of River Margy. Founded about 1500, burned by MacDonnells and Scots in 1584. Restored, but later fell into ruin. **Marconi Memorial,** *seafront:* marks the spot where the inventor of wireless telegraphy made his first successful transmission, between Ballycastle and Rathlin Island, in 1898. **Pans Rock,** *E end of Ballycastle beach:* old salt drying pan, reached by footbridge. Walks: around harbour area (boats leave from the pier for Rathlin) and in direction of Fair Head, E of beach. In the 18th c, there was extensive coal-mining in this area; occasional remnants may be seen. Cliffs stretch for 5 km (3 miles) W of Ballycastle to Kinbane Head, path for most of way. Loughareema Trekking Centre, ☎ *(02657)62576.* Golf Club, *18 holes,* ☎ *(02657)62536.* Youth Hostel: *34 North Street,* ☎ *(02657)62337.*

AROUND BALLYCASTLE

Ballintoy, *8 km (5 miles) NE of Ballycastle on B15.* North Antrim cliff path runs for 18 km (11 miles) from here to Runkerry, taking in Giant's Causeway, Dunseverick Castle, White Park Bay. The village has a most attractive harbour: white piers and white beach make fine contrast with black cliffs. Parish church with beautiful Resurrection window. Youth Hostel: *157 Whitepark Road,* ☎ *(02657)31745.*

Ballycastle Forest Park, *on slopes of Knocklayd Mountain 8 km (3 miles) S of Ballycastle:* scenic drive with splendid views, nature trail. Caravan and camping sites.

Carrick-a-Rede Rope Bridge, *8 km (5 miles) W of Ballycastle, near B15 coast road.* Crossing the

swaying bridge, made of planks and wires, from mainland to small offshore island, is an exhilarating experience. Magnificent coastal views if you dare look up. *Bridge erected early May, taken down mid-Sept.*

Fair Head, *6 km (4 miles) NE of Ballycastle:* one of most rugged spots on N coast with wonderful views of Rathlin Island and SW Scotland.

Kinbane Castle, *6 km (4 miles) NW of Ballycastle off B15:* from ruins on long narrow promontory, excellent sea and cliff views. Picnic area. **Grace Staples' Cave,** *below Kinbane Castle:* cuts through the entire cliff. Boat only, ask at Ballycastle Pier or Ballintoy Harbour.

Leslie Hill Historic Farm and Park, *1.5 km (1 mile) W of Ballymoney:* three centuries of farm history are displayed. Farm animals, museum, horse and trap rides through grounds, carriage display, adventure playground, picnic area. Crafts and tea shop. *Easter, May, Sun, BH, 2 p.m.-6 p.m. June, Sept, Sat, Sun, 2 p.m.-6 p.m. July, Aug, daily, 11 a.m.-6 p.m.* ☎ *(02656)668039.*

Loughareema, *vanishing lake on A2 from Ballycastle to Cushendun:* the lake can suddenly dry up, as quickly as if someone pulled the plug.

Murlough Bay, *just E of Fair Head:* unspoilt bay in National Trust care. Small, winding road runs down from Ballylucan, on main road; on way to shore, see monument to Sir Roger Casement.

Port Braddan, *W end of White Park Bay.* Tiny hamlet with smallest church in Ireland, 3 x 2 m (11 x 6 ft).

Rathlin Island, *13 km (8 miles) N of Ballycastle: between NI and Scotland's Mull of Kintyre:* visited by prehistoric man, and latterly by Robert the Bruce, who, while hiding in a cave here was inspired by a spider's persistence to recover the Scottish throne. Nearly all the coastline is formed by cliffs, but the island itself is almost flat, so walking is no hardship. Pop, about 100. Guesthouse. Crossings: *Daily service, weather permitting,* ☎ *(02657)63917/63934/63977 and 63907/63915. Minibus meets boats on arrival.* **Brockley,** remains of stoneage settlement and the prehistoric mound fort of Doonmore. **Knockanas,** *between Brockley and the harbour:* traces of an early Christian monastic settlement. The West Lighthouse is best place to see island's enormous bird population, and near the East Lighthouse, cement blocks with title 'Lloyds' mark the base of the wireless mast set up for Marconi in 1898. **Kebble national nature reserve,** West lighthouse.

Torr Head, *E end of Murlough Bay:* desolate spot with excellent views of North Channel. Scotland is only 19 km (12 miles) away. Narrow coastal road runs N from Cushendun or road from Murlough Bay.

Watertop Open Farm, *opposite entrance to Ballycastle forest park:* farm animals, poultry, game birds. Museum. Boating on lake, barbecue, shop, tea room. *Easter, June, Sat, Sun,10 a.m.-5.30 p.m. July, Aug, daily, 10 a.m.-5.30 p.m., or by arr.,* ☎ *(02657)62576/63785.*

White Park Bay, *3 km (2 miles) W of Ballintoy on B146.* The bay's half-moon beach is one of finest in the north. Youth Hostel, ☎ *(02657)31745.* Also has bicycles for hire.

Bangor

Pop. 50,000, 21 km (13 miles) NE of Belfast, 190 km (118 miles) N of Dublin, via Belfast, EC Thurs. TIO: Tower House, 34 Quay Street, ☎ *(0247)270069. All year. Bus enquiries: Abbey Street bus station,* ☎ *(0247)271143. Train enquiries: railway station,* ☎ *(0247)270141. Coach Tours: SO, details TIO.*

Originally the site of a rich and influential monastery founded in 559 by St Comgall and devas-

tated, three centuries later, by the Danes, Bangor today is a popular, pleasant and prosperous seaside town extending along the sandy bays of Bangor and Ballyholme. Plenty of indoor entertainments, with a number of nightspots, and excellent shopping.

Bangor Heritage Centre: exhibits include a 9th c handbell and the Ballycroghan swords, dating from 500 BC. Viking music, audio-visual shows. Tea room. *All year, Tues-Sat, 11 a.m.-4.30 p.m., Sun, 2 p.m.-4.30 p.m. July, Aug, 10.30 a.m.-5.30 p.m.* ☎ *(0247)271200.* **Bangor Abbey,** *at entrance to town, just off main Belfast road:* there are traces of the original monastery but most of its stone was used in the building of the present church, in 1617. **Town Hall,** *Castle Park:* ancient bell of Bangor Abbey and facsimile of Bangor Antiphonary, oldest datable document written in Irish 1,300 years ago, by arr., recreation officer. The town has a fine arboretum. ♿ **Ward Park,** *on Donaghadee side of Bangor:* attractions include nature trail, children's zoo, bowls, putting, *all year, daily.* **Promenade,** complete with traditional seaside amusements, sunken Gardens at E end, Marine Gardens at W. **Summer theatre,** *Central Avenue:* full range of entertainments, ☎ *(0247)271729.* Sea Cruises, *at intervals daily during summer, weather permitting. Fishing trips from harbour, daily during summer, weather permitting, at 10.30 a.m., 2.30 p.m., 7.30 p.m.* Golf Clubs: Carnalea, *18 holes,* ☎ *(0247)270922.* Clandeboye, *36 holes,* ☎ *(0247)271767.*

AROUND BANGOR

Ballycopeland Windmill, *2 km (1 mile) W of Millisle.* Late 18th c hilltop windmill is still in perfect working order. Miller's house is now a visitor centre. *Apr-Sept, Tues-Sat, 10 a.m.-7 p.m., Sun, 2 p.m.-7 p.m. Oct-Mar, Sat, 10 a.m.-4 p.m., Sun, 2 p.m.-4 p.m.* ☎ *(0247)861413.*

Ballyhalbert, *16 km (10 miles) S of Donaghadee.* Small fishing village on E coast of Ards peninsula: a string of cottages beside a beach, with small, attractive harbour and a shore walk 2 km (1 mile) SE to Burr Point, most E point in Ireland. Pass Celtic standing stone, ruins of old church.

Ballyholme beach, *2 km (1 mile) stretch on E side of Bangor,* with a promenade made for strolling.

Ballymacormick Point, pleasant shoreline walks at the entrance to Belfast Lough. Enter from the Ballyholme end of Bangor promenade or from the Watch House, Groomsport Harbour.

Ballywalter, *8 km (5 miles) S of Millisle.* Small seaside village with good beaches and harbour. The A2 coastal route offers excellent views and there is an attractive inland walk 2 km (1 mile) NW, as far as the 'White Church'.

Comber, *6 km (4 miles) SW of Newtownards on A21. EC Wed.* Fine central square and village green. Its renowned whiskey distillery closed down afte World War II, but some of the local pubs still have a few precious bottles. **Castle Espie Conservation Centre,** *78 Ballydrain Road.* Ireland's largest collection of ducks, geese and swans. Viewing from hides, waterfowl gardens or coffee room. Historical exhibits, craft shop. *All year, Mon-Sat, 10.30 a.m.-5 p.m., Sun, 2 p.m.-5 p.m.* ☎ *(0247)874146.*

Copeland Islands, *N of Donaghadee:* now deserted. Lighthouse Island (NT) is a bird sanctuary, boats from Donaghadee, *by arr. NT,* ☎ *(0238)510721.*

Crawfordsburn Country Park: beach, camp site, café, car park. Visitor centre, *open daily from 11 a.m.* Its shore path forms part of the 'Ulster Way' walk. ♿ The Crawfordsburn Inn: dates from 1614 and retains much of its old-world atmosphere. Clandeboye, Game and Country Fair, *June-July.*

Donaghadee, *10 km (6 miles) SE of Bangor on A2/B21, EC Thurs.* A most attractive and relaxing seaside town, full of character and characters, built around an imposing harbour. Good sea fishing. **Grace Neill's bar,** facing harbour, was built in

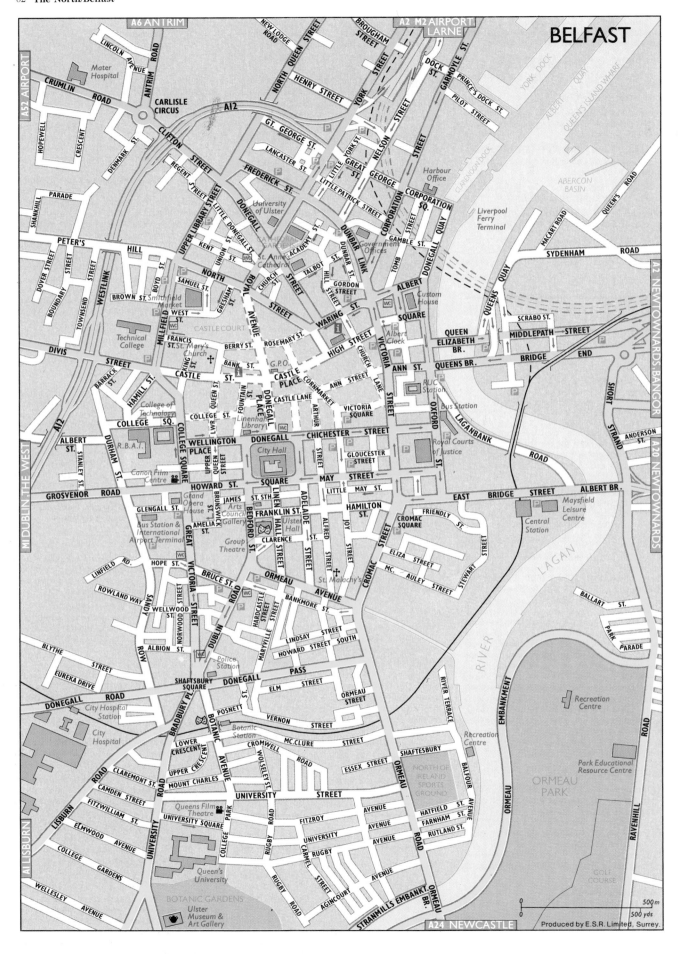

BELFAST

1611 and happily retains its historic atmosphere. Peter the Great of Russia was entertained here in the late 1690s during his Grand Tour of western Europe. It also sheltered Keats. The laneways in the town centre still have a little of the old French-style atmosphere and there are good views of the town and harbour from the castle-like moat, used for storing explosives during the harbour's construction. Short sea cruises: *10.30 a.m., 2.30 p.m., 7.30 p.m. daily, SO.* Donaghadee Golf Club, *18 holes,* ☎ *(0247)883624.*

Glastry Clay Ponds, *near Ballyhalbert:* educational nature reserve with work tables and informative displays. The site, created from old clay pits, is ideal for children. Access at all times.

Greyabbey, *11 km (7 miles) S of Newtownards on A20. EC Thurs.* Well-preserved ruins of Cistercian abbey founded in 1193. The grounds, filled with masses of trees and flowers are an equally striking sight. *Easter-Sept, Tues-Sat, 10 a.m.-7 p.m., Sun, 2 p.m.-7 p.m. Oct-Mar, Sat, 10 a.m.-4 p.m. Sun, 2 p.m.-4 p.m.*

Groomsport, *5 km (3 miles) E of Bangor, EC Thurs.* Old-world village with beach and promenade. Cockle Row has a summer exhibition of works by local artists.

Helen's Bay, *5 km (3 miles) W of Bangor. EC Thurs.* Small resort on S shore of Belfast Lough. Pleasant walk from the baronial-style railway station to the beach.

Mahee Island, *N end of Strangford Lough:* ruins of 1570 castle. Nendrum monastic site has impressive early Christian ruins and the elevated location gives fine views over the lough. Connected to Reagh Island (with bird observation hides) and mainland near Killinchy by a causeway.

Millisle, *3 km (2 miles) S of Donaghadee. EC Thurs.* Long, sandy beach.

Mount Stewart, and the **Temple of the Winds,** *8 km (5 miles) SE of Newtownards on A20.* Great 18th c house, Irish seat of the Londonderry family. House interiors most imposing, as are the formal and informal gardens, with lakes, woodlands, terraces. Temple built on lines of the temple of same name in Athens. House, with its stately interior plasterwork, is often described as the gem of Ulster architecture. House, shop and tea room, *House open, Easter, late April, daily,1 p.m.-6 p.m. May-Aug, daily, except Tues, 1 p.m.-6 p.m. Sept, Oct, Sat, Sun, 1 p.m.-6 p.m. Temple open as house, 2 p.m.-5 p.m. Details,* ☎ *(024774)387.*

Newtownards, *10 km (6 miles) S of Bangor on A21. EC Thurs. TIO:* ☎ *(0247)812215, all year. Bus enquiries: Regent Street bus station,* ☎ *(0247)812391.* Thriving manufacturing and market town, founded in the 17th c. **Gransha equestrian centre,** ☎ *(0247)813313.* **Movilla Abbey,** *2 km (1 mile) E of town on B172,* nothing remains of the original 6th c monastery; present ruins are of a 15th c church. Dominican friary ruins, near the old market cross, E end of High Street. Handsome 18th c Town Hall. **Ulster Flying Club,** *airfield just S off A21,* pleasure flights, ☎ *(0 247)813327.* The Ards Shopping Centre is the largest in Ireland. Swimming pool; indoor, heated, *daily,* ☎ *(0247)812837.*

Orlock Head, *3 km (2 miles) E of Groomsport:* marks entrance to Belfast Lough.

Ringhaddy, *just SW of Killinchy:* jetty, set in superb countryside, approached by a tiny, winding road.

Scrabo Tower, *set on a hilltop 3 km (2 miles) SW of Newtownards W of A21.* Built in 1857 as memorial to the third Marquis of Londonderry. There are 122 steps to the top of the tower. Displays tell story of the tower and surrounding countryside. The park has bluebell woods, old quarries and walks. *Tower, June-Sept, Tues-Sun, 12 noon-5.30 p.m., or by arr.,* ☎ *(0247)811491. Park always open.* Excellent views over the Ards peninsula and Strangford Lough. ☎ *(0247)811491.* Scrabo Golf Club, *18 holes,* ☎ *(0247)812355.*

City Hall, Belfast

Belfast

Pop, 330,000, 167 km (104 miles) N of Dublin. Six day shopping. TIO: Northern Ireland Tourist Board, North Street, ☎ *(0232)246609, all year. Irish Tourist Board. 53 Castle Street, Belfast,* ☎ *(0232)327888. Belfast Airport,* ☎ *(08494)22888, all year. Belfast city airport,* ☎*(0232)457745, all year. City Hall, (0232)320202, all year. If travelling within the city boundary always use Citybus (red). Ulsterbus (blue), runs no internal city service. Bus enquiries: Great Victoria Street bus station,* ☎ *(0232)320011. Train enquiries: Central Station,* ☎ *(0232)235282. Taxis: Donegall Square East, Central Station, York Road Station. Coach tours: SO, details: TIO / Ulsterbus,* ☎ *(0232)320011. Youth Hostel Association of Northern Ireland, 56 Bradbury Place,* ☎ *324733. Youth Hostel: 11 Saintfield Road,* ☎ *(0232)647865.*

Capital of Northern Ireland, attractively situated on the Lagan estuary at the foot of the Antrim plateau. Despite its relative decline as an industrial force, and more particularly the toll taken by The Troubles, Belfast is a vigorous city, much of which is extremely pleasing to the eye. It also has a fine cultural tradition which is not always recognised, and its museums and art galleries repay close inspection.

Major Festivals: Belfast Arts Festival: three week culture feast, with something for everyone. Local and international artists, enormous variety of music, theatre, film, *Nov, details: Festival House,* ☎ *(0232)667687 or Belfast TIO.* Circuit of Ireland international car rally: start and finish, Apr. Royal Ulster Agricultural Society, Kings Hall, Balmoral: annual agricultural show, *May.* July 12 Parades: marking the anniversary of the Battle of the Boyne in 1690. Ancient Order of Hibernians' parades, *Aug 15.*

CATHEDRALS & CHURCHES

St Anne's Cathedral (CI), *Donegall Street:* plain but impressive modern building. **St Malachy's Church** (C), *Alfred Street:* excellent fan-vaulted

ceiling. **Unitarian church,** *Rosemary Street:* fine plasterwork, woodwork. The city has many other fine religious buildings, mostly from the second half of the 19th c, when some seventy new churches were established. Perhaps the most notable are Fitzroy Presbyterian (1872), *University Street;* St Mary's (1869), *Crumlin Road;* St Thomas's (1870), *Lisburn Road;* Elmwood Hall, deconsecrated

Palm House, Botanic Gardens, Belfast

church, *by Botanic Gardens;* the small, delightful St Matthew's, *Woodvale Road,* which includes an imitation round tower; St Mark's, *Dundela,* completed in 1878 to design by William Butterfield.

NOTABLE BUILDINGS

City Hall, *Donegall Square:* handsome structure with a fine marble interior, wall murals, excellent city views from dome, *Guided tours,* ☎ *(0232)320202.* ♿ **Stormont,** *E Belfast.* Commanding building in 300 acres of gardens, seat of the NI parliament from 1921-72. Superb views from terrace, good walks. Stormont Castle, once the NI Prime Minister's official residence, is nearby. **Belfast Castle,** *N Belfast.* Attractive walks in extensive grounds. **Custom House,** *High Street:* majestically proportioned building set where the culverted Farset joins the Lagan. Anthony Trollope worked here as a surveyor's clerk in 1841. **Royal Courts of Justice,** *Chichester Street:* a substantial structure, in Portland Stone, opened in 1933 as a gift from Westminster. **Linen Hall Library,** *Donegall Square North:* late 18th c, now fully refurbished, very strong on Irish interest material, occasional exhibitions. *Mon-Fri, 9.30 a.m.-5.30 p.m. (Thurs, 8.30 p.m.); Sat, 9.30 a.m.-4 p.m.,* ☎ *(0232)321707.* **Queen's University,** *University Road:* founded 1849, attractive main building; library with over 750,000 books, various collections, including Hamilton Harty music. *By arr., librarian.* ⚹

MUSEUMS

Ulster Museum and Art Gallery, *Stranmillis Road.* Distinguished collection of art and antiquities, including treasure from the *Girona,* a Spanish Armada galleon wrecked off N Antrim coast. Coelacanth, rare preserved specimen of 'living fossil' fish. Permanent art collection featuring many fine modern works and such Irish artists as William Conor, Jack B Yeats, Colin Middleton, George Campbell. Sculpture by Henry Moore, Barbara Hepworth, F.E. McWilliam. Visiting exhibitions. Engineering hall has working examples of old machinery. Monthly poster lists all museum activities, *Café. Mon-Fri, 10 a.m.-5 p.m. Sat, 1 p.m.-5 p.m. Sun, 2 p.m.-5 p.m.,* ☎ *(0232)381251.* ⚹ **Malone House,** *Upper Malone.* Permanent exhibition on Belfast Parks, café. *All year, Tues-Sat, 10 a.m.-4 p.m.* ☎*(0232)681246.* **Transport Museum,** *Witham Street, off Newtownards Road.* Marvellous collection of railway rolling stock, cars, motor bicycles, trams, horse-drawn vehicles. Highlight is the 'Maeve' steam engine built for former Great Southern Railways. *All year, Mon-Sat, 10 a.m.-5 p.m.* ☎ *(0232)451519.* **Royal Ulster Rifles Museum,** *War Memorial building, 5 Waring Street:* relics of this famous regiment, 1793-1968. *All year, Mon-Fri, 10 a.m.-12.30 p.m.; 2 p.m.-4 p.m., or by arr,* ☎ *(0232)232086.* **Home Front heritage centre,** *War Memorial Building, Waring Street:* nostalgic exhibits from World War II. *All year, Mon-Fri, 10 a.m.-4 p.m.* ☎*(0232)310278.* **Dundonald Old Mill,** *231 Belfast Road, Quarry Corner, Dundonald:* 18th c corn-mill with huge water-wheel. Its 168 wooden buckets power three sets of millstones. *All year, Mon-Sat, 9.30 a.m.-5.15 p.m. Sun, 11 a.m.-6 p.m.* ☎ *480117.*

GALLERIES

Arts Council Gallery, *56-60 Dublin Road,* ☎*(0232)321402.* Frequent exhibitions by local and international artists. *Tues-Sat, 10 a.m.-6 p.m.* **Bell Gallery,** *13 Adelaide Park, Malone Road,* ☎*(0232)662998.* 18th, 19th and 29th c Irish art, *Mon-Fri, 9 a.m.-5 p.m. Sat, by arr.* **Tom Caldwell Gallery,** *40/42 Bradbury Place,* ☎*(0232)323226.* Regular shows of Irish and international artists. *Mon-Fri, 9.30 a.m.-5.30 p.m., Sat, 10 a.m.-1 p.m.* **Cavehill Gallery,** *18 Old Cavehill Road,* ☎*(0232)776784.* Exhibitions in all fine art media, mainly Northern Ireland artists. *Tues-Sat, 1 p.m.-6 p.m. Closed Jan, July-Sept.* **Crescent Arts Centre,** *2-4 University Road,* ☎*(0232)24233.* Exhibitions in all fine art media. *Mon-Fri, 10 a.m.-5 p.m., Sat, 11 a.m.-5 p.m. Closed July, Aug.* **Emer Gallery,** *110 Donegall Pass* ☎*(0232)231777.* Works by Irish artists; neglected artists a speciality. *Mon-Sat, 10 a.m.-5 p.m.* **Fenderesky Gallery at Queens,** *5-6 Upper Crescent,* ☎*(0232)235245.* Frequent exhibitions by contemporary Irish and international artists. *Tues-Fri, 11.30 a.m.-5.30 p.m., Sat, 12 noon-5 p.m.* **John Magee,** *455/457 Ormeau Road,* ☎*(0232)693830.* Regular shows, including work by emerging artists. *Mon-Sat, 9 a.m.-5 p.m.* **Old Museum Arts Centre,** *7 College Square North,* ☎*(0232)322912.* Regular exhibitions, including photographic. *Mon-Sat, 10 a.m.-6 p.m. during exhibitions.* **Orpheus Gallery,** *Orpheus Building, York Street,* ☎*(0232)246259.* Shows and other art events. *Tues-Fri, 11 a.m.-5 p.m. Closed July.* **Ulster Arts Club Gallery,** *56 Elmwood Avenue,* ☎*(0232)660644.* Regular events, including international exhibitions, on all forms of visual art. *Tues-Fri, 11 a.m.-4 p.m., Sat, 11 a.m.-1 p.m.*

Queen's University, Belfast

THEATRES

Grand Opera House, *Gt Victoria Street:* designed by 19th c theatre architect Frank Matcham, reopened in 1980 after a thorough refurbishing. Gloriously rococo interior complete with old-style stage safety curtain. Drama, opera, ballet, pantomime, ☎ *(0232)241919.* **Lyric Players' Theatre,** *Ridgeway Street, Stranmillis,* Fine, modern theatre offers modern and classical drama, with a generally Irish emphasis. Food bar, occasional lectures, recitals, ☎ *(0232)381081.* **Arts Theatre,** *Botanic Avenue.* Wide range of drama, seasonal childrens' shows, rock musicals, emphasis on entertainment, ☎ *(0232)324935.* **Group Theatre,** *Bedford Street:* amateur drama, ☎ *(0232)329685.*

ROUND & ABOUT

Cavehill and MacArt's Fort: easiest access for this panoramic viewpoint of the city is from the car park at Belfast Castle. **Belfast Zoo,** *Antrim Road:* superb collection of animals and birds, a magnet for children. Guided tours, film shows, lectures. *Apr-Sept, daily, 10 a.m.-5 p.m. Oct-Mar, daily, 10 a.m.-3.30 p.m. (Fri, 2.30 p.m.)* ☎ *(0232)776277.* ⚹ **Falls Road/Shankill Road,** *Belfast.* World famous, not to say notorious, the militantly Unionist Shankill, and Nationalist Falls are areas of considerable personality, and not without appeal. In the City centre the narrow passageways between Ann Street and High Street still have a little of their original 18th c atmosphere and at **Harland and Wolff**, where the 'Titanic' was built, you will find 'Goliath' and 'Samson', the world's 2nd and 3rd biggest cranes. *By arr,* PR Dept. University area: pleasant walks, including University Square, Upper and Lower Crescent, Gilnahirk Road, *E Belfast:* good 20 minute climb up into Castlereagh Hills, with superb views over N Co. Down, as far as Isle of Man in clear weather. **Streamvale Open Dairy Farm,** *38 Ballyhanwood Road, Dundonald:* watch the milking from a viewing gallery. Donkey rides, nature trail, picnic area, shop, cafe. *Feb-May, Sept, Oct, Wed, Sat, Sun, BH, 2.30 p.m.-6 p.m. Easter, daily, 10.30 a.m.-6 p.m June, daily, noon-6 p.m. July, Aug, daily, 10.30 a.m.-6 p.m.* ☎ *(0232)483244.* **Belmont Road,** *E Belfast:* invigorating walks into Holywood Hills. **Albert Clock,** *High Street,* built 1851.

St Georges Market, next to Law Courts, *Chichester Street.* All kinds of everything. *Every Tues and Fri.* ⚹ **Smithfield Market,** *West Street/ Winetavern Street (opp. Castle Court development):* new market modelled on original market, burnt down some years ago. *Open Mon-Sat 9 a.m.-5.30 p.m.* Range of new and secondhand goods.

The Crown Liquor Saloon (NT), *Great Victoria Street:* high Victorian style pub, snugs, gloriously over-the-top glass and tilework and a thoroughly distinctive atmosphere. **Robinsons,** *next door:* snugs, tile work, good Guinness and interesting old prints, **Kelly's Cellars,** *Bank Place, off Royal Avenue:* one of Belfast's oldest pubs, dating back some 200 years, with character to match. **Bass Ireland,** *Ulster Brewery, Glen Road:* audio-visual presentation on brewery's history. Viewing of production processes. By written application only, groups preferred. **Belfast Telegraph newspapers,** *124 Royal Avenue,* ☎*(0232)321242.* Video on newspaper production. Tours *all year, Wed, 1 p.m.* **Kings Hall,** *Balmoral.* Exhibition centre, *details TIO.* **Ulster Hall,** *Bedford Street:* regular Ulster Orchestra, rock and pop concerts. *Orchestral bookings:* Ulster orchestra shop, *Central Arcade, Cornmarket,* ☎ *(0232)233240/233219.*

PARKS

Botanic Gardens, *near Ulster Museum.* Acres of pleasant space, highlight is the Victorian palm house, an elegant structure in curved glass. Tropical ravine, also rose garden, herbaceous borders. Palm house and tropical ravine, *Apr-Sept, Mon-Fri, 10 a.m.-12 noon, 1 p.m.-5 p.m. Sat, Sun, BH, 2 p.m.-5 p.m. Oct-Mar, Mon-Fri, 10 a.m.-12 noon; 2 p.m.-4 p.m. Sat, Sun, BH, 2 p.m.-4 p.m.* ☎ *(0232)324902.* **Dixon Park,** *Upper Malone, S Belfast.* Setting for internationally renowned rose trials every summer. **Ormeau Park.** Fine expanse between Ormeau and Ravenhill Roads. **Old Waterworks,** *Antrim Road.* Now an attractive park with waterfalls and bridges. Minnowburn Beeches, *on S fringe of Belfast, in Lagan valley:* good walks in fields, woodland, open spaces, *best approached on B205 to Shaw's Bridge.* **Lagan Regional Park,** starts at Molly Ward locks on Stranmillis embankment, near Botanic gardens, and continues for 13 km (8 miles) to Lisburn; including Barnett's demesne: delightfully wooded park overlooking river Lagan. **Minnowburn Beeches:** woodlands, fields and open ground in Lagan River valley. **Hazelwood Park,** *next to zoo:* delightful setting with lake. Summer entertainment.

SPORT

Ravenhill Road, city's major rugby venue. **Windsor Park,** NI's main football stadium, ☎ *(0232)223703.* Greyhound racing: Dunmore Park, *Antrim Road, Tues, Thurs, Sat, 8 p.m.,* ☎ *(0232)776232.* **Belfast Bowl,** *4 Clarence Street West,* ☎ *242998.*

Leisure Centres, Andersonstown Road, ☎ *(0232)625211* (inc. pool); Avoniel Road, ☎ *(0232)451564;* Ballymacarrett, ☎ *(0232)458828;* Ballysillan Road, ☎ *(0232)391040* (inc. pool); Beechmount, *Falls Road,* ☎ *(0232)328631;* Divis Community Centre, Grosvenor Centre, *Grosvenor Road,* ☎ *(0232)242551;* Shaftesbury,

☎*(0232)329163;* Falls, ☎*(0232)324906;* Whiterock, ☎ *(0232)233239;* Loughside Centre, *Shore Road,* ☎ *(0232)781524/5;* Maysfield, *East Bridge Street,* ☎ *(0232)241633* (inc. pool); Olympia Centre, *Boucher Road,* ☎ *(0232)233369;* Ormeau Park Centre, ☎ *(0232)458024;* Queen's University Physical Education Centre, *Botanic Park,* ☎ *(0232)681126, extn. 4317;* Shankill Road, ☎ *(0232)241434* (inc. pool); Stadium Recreation Centre, *Shankill Road,* ☎ *(0232)322439. All daily.* Swimming pools: Falls Baths, ☎ *(0232)324906;* Grove Baths, ☎ *(0232)351599.* Templemore Avenue Baths, ☎ *(0232)457540. All daily.* Easthope Equestrian centre, *71 Killynure Road West, Carryduff,* ☎ *(0232)813186.*

Golf Clubs: Balmoral, *18 holes,* ☎ *(0232)668540,* Belvoir Park, *18 holes,* ☎ *(0232)491693,* Dunmurry, *18 holes,* ☎ *(0232)301172.* Fortwilliam, *18 holes,* ☎ *(0232)370770.* Knock, *18 holes,* ☎ *(02318)3251.* Knockbracken, 18 holes, ☎ *(0232)795666.* Malone, *18 and 9 holes,* ☎ *(0232)612758.* Shandon Park, *18 holes,* ☎ *(0232)794856.* Bicycles: Bikeit, *4 Belmont Road,* ☎*(0232)471141,* Coates, *104 Grand Parade,* ☎*(0232)471912,* McConvey Cycles, *476 Ormeau Road,* ☎*(0232)238602, Unit 10, Pottinger's Entry,* ☎*(0232)330322.*

AROUND BELFAST

Aghagallon, *near SE corner of Lough Neagh, turn off M1 motorway near Lurgan, B12 N of Aghagallon:* gardener's folly over 100 years old. Don't get lost in the maze! Nearby water-driven mill still in perfect working order.

Aghalee, *1.5 km (1 mile) NW of Aghagallon.* Neat little village with award-winning looks. ***Bartin's Bay,*** *just W of Aghalee:* see baskets being made from willows grown around nearby Lough Beg, *details: James Mulholland,* ☎ *(0846)651217.*

Belvoir Park, *Newtownbreda.* Norman motte, remains of 14th c Breda Old Church, golf course, forest caravan site.

Cairn Wood, *8 km (5 miles) E of Belfast just off B170:* forest high in Craigantlet Hills, nature trail, picnic area.

Colin Glen, *W of Belfast, at top of Glen Road:* wild woodland, with streams that run down from Black Mountain and Colin Mountain. Paradise of trees and wild flowers.

Crumlin, *16 km (10 miles) W of Belfast on A52, EC Tues or Sat.* Quiet, pleasant village at head of wooded Crumlin Glen. Good walks alongside tiny Crumlin River which forms cascades after the weir. The Glen has a 'Cockle House', a 19th c folly built partly as a house, partly as a cave. Largest opening faces Mecca! 13th c church ruins, by Pound bridge over river. ***Talnotry Cottage Bird Garden,*** *2 Crumlin Road, Crumlin.* Endangered species in 18th c walled garden. Craft shop, tea room. *Easter-Sept, daily, except Mon-Fri, also BH, 2 p.m.-6 p.m. Otherwise by arr.,* ☎ *(08494)22900.* ***Langford Lodge,*** *Gortnagallon Road:* a base for the US 8th Army Air Force during World War II. American war memorabilia.*All year, Sat, Sun, 12 noon-6 p.m. or by arr,* ☎*(0232)650451.* ***Nutts Corner*** motor cycle races, *details: Belfast TIO.*

Cultra, *13 km (8 miles) NE of Belfast.* Ulster Folk and Transport Museum will provide a very full day out in search of Ulster's social and economic history. The Manor House is in use as a conference centre. Gallery One houses displays of domestic objects, furniture and crafts, with 19th c photographs and William Conor paintings. Reference library. In surrounding park, reconstructed rural buildings, city streets, spade mill, linen scutch mill, blacksmith's forge, weaver's house. Transport section documents over 200 years of Irish transport, including the 1893 Carrickfergus-built 'Result' schooner, old aircraft, donkey creels and pony traps. *Apr-June, Sept, Mon-Fri, 9.30 a.m.-5 p.m., Sat, 10.30 a.m.-6 p.m. Sun, 12 noon-6 p.m. July, Aug, Mon-Sat, 10.30 a.m.-6 p.m., Sun, 12.30 p.m-4.30 p.m.* ☎ *(0232)428428.* ♿

Down Royal Racecourse, *the Maze, near Lisburn:* regular races including the Ulster Harp Derby, *July 13,* ☎ *(0846)621256.* ♿

Dromore, *27 km (17 miles) SW of Belfast on A1T. All day closing, Thurs.* Interesting market town, with ancient stocks in square; CI cathedral with 1613 Bible; Dromore Mound, a great Norman earthwork.

Dundonald, *just E of Belfast on A20. EC Thurs.* Striking Norman motte, by old village, surrounded by parkland. Dundonald Bowl, ten pin bowling, children's adventure playground, ☎ *(0232)482611.*

Giant's Ring, *Ballylesson, S of Edenderry:* neolithic earthwork, over 200 m (600 ft) in diameter. Most impressive, as is another ancient earthwork nearby, Fort Hill. From Farrell's Fort on hilltop, fine views of Belfast.

Hillsborough, *5 km (3 miles) S of Lisburn on A1T.* Charming village, steep main street, Northern Ireland's antiques and crafts centre. ***Fort,*** massive structure, 17th c. *Apr -Sept, Tues-Sat, 10 a.m.-7 p.m., Sun, 2 p.m.-7 p.m. Oct-Mar, Tues-Sat,10 a.m.-4 p.m. Sun, 2 p.m.-4 p.m. Closed 1 p.m.-1.30 p.m.* ☎*(0846)683285.* Custodian of fort will show visitors round pretty 1760 ***Market House.*** *Details,* ☎ *(0846)683285.* ***Hillsborough parish church*** (CI), *Belfast road:* imposing 1773 building. Composer and conductor Sir Hamilton Harty buried in churchyard. ***Fairfort House,*** *Ballynahinch Street:* plaque marks Harty's childhood home. ***Shambles Art Centre,*** summer exhibitions, specialising in sculpture. ☎ *(0846)682946.* Hillsborough park: ideal for walking. Ballyknock Riding School,*38 Ballyknock Road,* ☎ *(0846)692144.*

Holywood, *9 km (4 miles) NE of Belfast. EC Wed.* Pleasant seaside town on S shores of Belfast Lough, ***Old Priory Church,*** *High Street:* roofless ruins, partly dating from 13th c. Variety of good walks: around back of town, up into Holywood hills; along the esplanade, start of a 9 km (5.5 miles) coastal path to Bangor; from Redburn House, wooded walks, good views of Belfast hills. ***Seapark,*** by seashore, tennis courts and other sports facilities. Holywood Golf Club, *18 holes,* ☎ *(02317)3135.*

Knockbreda *just S of Belfast:* 18th c parish church (CI), Georgian, in delightfully sylvan surroundings.

Lisburn, *13 km (8 miles) SW of Belfast. All day closing Wed. Bus enquiries: Smithfield Square,* ☎ *(08462)2091/2092. Train enquiries:* ☎ *(08462) 662294.* Busy market town. ***Christ Church Cathedral,*** *Market Square:* early 18th c, a most interesting building. ***Lisburn Museum,*** *The Assembly Rooms, Market Square:* impressive new museum with material reflecting local archaeology and history. The story of the linen industry is told in graphic displays. Art gallery, exhibitions. *All year, Tues-Sat, 11 a.m.-5 p.m.* ☎ *(0846)672624.* Castle Gardens, between cathedral and River Lagan. Pleasant walks in delightful surroundings. Wallace Park, wooded area to N of town, ideal for walks and picnics. ***Grove Activity Centre,*** *15 Ballinderry Park, daily,* ☎ *(0846)671131.* Lisburn Recreation Centre, ☎ *674204.* Glenmore Activity Centre, *43 Glenmore Park, Hilden, daily,* ☎ *(0 846)662830.* Bicycles: Lisburn Cycle Shop, *Railway Street,* ☎ *(0846)662066. Swimming pool: indoor, heated, Market Place, Mon-Sun,* ☎ *(08462)662306.* ♿ Lisburn Golf Club, *18 holes,* ☎ *(08462)662186.* ♿

Magheraknock Fort, *5 km (3 miles) NW of Ballynahinch:* United Irishmen made their last stand here, late 18th c. Good views over N Down.

Moira, *11 km (7 miles) SW of Lisburn.* St John's parish church (CI) at head of imposing avenue from wooded park, which has foundations of castle of former Earls of Moira. Moira railway station, oldest in N. Ireland, Built 1841. *To view,* ☎*(0846)611439.*

Ram's Island, *off Sandy Bay, W of B12 near Glenavy.* Interesting Lough Neagh island, complete with stump of round tower. Wooded bird sanctuary. Ideal for a peaceful picnic.

Rowallane, (NT), *18 km (11 miles) SE of Belfast on A7.* Famous garden developed from wasteland over the past 100 years; 50 acres of gardens, shrubs and plants. Best date spring and autumn, although early summer most colourful. *Apr-Oct, Mon-Fri, 10.30 a.m.-6 p.m., Sat, Sun, 2 p.m.-6 p.m. Nov-Mar, Mon-Fri, 10.30 a.m.-5 p.m.* ☎ *(0238)510131.*

Carrickfergus

Pop. 17,000, 18 km (11 miles) NE of Belfast, 22 km (14 miles) S of Larne. EC Wed. Bus enquiries: Circular Road bus station, Larne, ☎ *(0574)72345. Train enquiries: Carrickfergus station,* ☎ *(09603)51286.*

Carrickfergus Castle, built 1180, in military occupation until 1928. Best preserved Norman castle in Ireland. Now magnificently set museum. Interesting relics of three local regiments and illustrations of numerous episodes in Irish history. Splendid Great Hall, chilling dungeons, fine views from battlements. *Apr-Sept, Mon-Sat, 10 a.m.-6 p.m., Sun, 2 p.m.-6 p.m. Oct-Mar, Mon-Sat, 10 a.m.-4 p.m., Sun, 2 p.m.-4 p.m.* ☎ *(09603)51273.* ***St Nicholas'*** (CI), *off Market Place:* Founded in 12th c, four interesting stained glass windows, by Lady Glenavy, Catherine O'Brien, Ethel Rhind. Near church, small section of old town wall. ***Andrew Jackson Centre,*** American Trail E *outskirts of town:* early 18th c Irish cottage. Adjacent to the site of the ancestral home of Andrew Jackson, 7th President of the USA 1829-37. Homestead and display gallery depicting the lifestyle of the area. *All year, daily, 10 a.m.-1 p.m., 2 p.m.-5 p.m. Also daily, 6 p.m.-8 p.m., Apr-Sept,* ☎ *(09603)64972.* ***Dobbin's Inn,*** *High Street:* 17th c pub has interesting relics of old town, inc. huge fireplace. Ask to see secret passage that runs to castle. ***Louis MacNeice Plaque,*** *North Road:* the distinguished poet lived in the town from two years of age until he went to Cambridge University. His father was rector of St Nicholas' church, commemorative plaque on rectory gate. Guided Walkabout Tours of town. *All year, by arr. Borough Council,* ☎ *(09603)51604.* Carrickfergus Festival *end July/early Aug.*

Harbour, *just W of castle:* plenty of seaborne activity. Rowing boats may be hired. Walks along the wide promenade and in Marine Gardens. Shaftesbury Park, walks, putting etc. ***Carrickfergus Marina,*** largest in Ireland, 300 berths with visitors berths available. Completely serviced by water, electricity and optional telephone; other amenities and services include boat sales and repairs, sail repairs, boat storage, chandlery supplies, showers and toilets, fuel berth, hoist, restaurant and tourist caravan park, ☎ *(09603)66666.* ***Leisure Centre*** offers a comprehensive range of indoor activities for all ages. Includes two swimming pools, squash courts and outdoor tennis courts. *Kennedy Drive, daily,* ☎ *(09603)51711.* Golf Club, *18 holes,* ☎ *(09603)63713.*

AROUND CARRICKFERGUS

Ballyboley Forest, *6 km (4 miles) N of Ballyclare off A36:* Dept of Agriculture caravan site, lake, viewpoint.

Ballycarry, *3 km (2 miles) N of Whitehead, just W of A2, EC Sat.* Quiet hilltop village. Ruins of Ireland's first Presbyterian church, built 1613; grave of James Orr (1770-1816), poet and United Irishman.

Ballyclare, *16 km (10 miles) SW of Larne, EC Thurs.* Annual fair, *end May.* Extensive pre-Christian settlements. Ballyclare Golf Club, *18 holes,* ☎ *(09603)22696.*

Ballyeaston, *2 km (1 mile) N of Ballyclare.* Attractive village on steep hill.

Ballygalley, *6 km (4 miles) N of Larne:* Youth Hostel, ☎*(0574)583377.*

Bellahill, *3 km (2 miles) W of Whitehead:* see exterior of Dalways' Bawn, built around 1609 and N. Ireland's best preserved plantation house.

Carrickfergus Castle, Co. Antrim

Carnfunnock Country Park, *5 km (3 miles) N of Larne:* walled garden, maze, picnic areas, walks, visitor centre with crafts exhibition. Cafe. Access at all times. ☎ *(0574)270541/272313.*

Glenoe, *on Ballycarry-Larne B149:* most attractive NT beauty spot, with woods, whitewashed houses and Glenoe Glen with four waterfalls.

Glynn, *foot of Glenoe Glen:* picturesque village with old corn mill and dam. From old church, footbridge spans River Glynn.

'Holestone', *3 km (2 miles) NW of Ballyclare:* Bronze Age megalith perched on a hill top. It has a small hole, through which a woman's hand may pass, but not a man's. In the past, couples plighted their troth by clasping hands through the hole.

Islandmagee, *peninsula 11 x 3 km (7 x 2 miles) .* Fine cliffs on the E side, with the Gobbins (about 60 m/200 ft) swarming with seabirds. Brown's Bay, Ferris Bay are popular bathing, picnic spots.

Giant's Causeway, Co. Antrim

Portmuck, *N tip of peninsula:* sandy cove and harbour reached by corkscrew road. Ruins of ancient castle, said to have been home of a Magee chief, on headland to E. Try your luck with a delicately poised **Rocking Stone,** a glacial boulder on the rocky shore E of Brown's Bay. Nearby **Druid's Altar** dolmen. **Ford Farm Park museum:** small country museum. Butter making demonstrations

and spinning, using wool from farm's sheep. *All year, daily, 2 p.m.-7 p.m.* ☎*(09603)53264.*

Kilroot, *6 km (4 miles) NE of Carrickfergus.* Ruins of church where youthful Jonathan Swift was 18th c incumbent.

Knockagh Monument, *3 km (2 miles) SW of Carrickfergus:* one of the best vantage points in area. Approach by path through golf course or by road on N side, which runs almost to the top of the cliffs.

Larne, *34 km (21 miles) NE of Belfast, EC Tues. Larne Harbour,* ☎ *(0574)74321, Easter-Sept 30. Bus enquiries:* ☎ *(0574)72345. Train enquiries:* ☎ *(0574)72347.* The gateway to the Glens of Antrim, with three interesting old churches: St Cedma's, *Inver* (16th c). First Presbyterian Church, *Bridge Street* (17th c). Unitarian Church, *Ballymena Road* (17th c). **District Historical Centre,** *Victoria Road,* ☎ *(0574)279482:* exhibits include 1900 country kitchen, with open peat hearth, dresser, grandfather clock; old smithy, with anvil, hand bellows, tools; photographs. *All year,* *Tues-Sat, 2 p.m.-5 p.m.* Walks: Chaine Memorial Park, seashore promontory, sickle-shaped Curran promontory S of harbour. Swimming pool: heated, indoor, *Tower Road, daily,* ☎ *(0574)60479.* Cairndhu Golf Club, 18 holes, ☎ *(0574)83248.* **Loughside open dairy farm,** *Ballycarry:* red deer, Jacob sheep vie with vixens in pets' corner. Bird sanctuary, adventure playground. *Apr-Sept, daily, 2 p.m.-7 p.m. Oct-Mar, Sat, Sun, BH, 2 p.m.-7 p.m.* ☎*(09603)53312.*

Dunluce Castle, Co. Antrim

Whitehead, *8 km (5 miles) NE of Carrickfergus on A2. EC Thurs. Bus enquiries:* ☎ *(09603)53345. Train enquiries:* ☎ *(09603)53377.* Attractive seaside town, with good walks along promenade E towards Black Head, from where you can enjoy fine views over Belfast Lough. The Irish Railway Preservation Society has preserved several old steam locos and carriages. For details of excursions and visits to display, ☎ *(09603) 53567.* Whitehead Golf Club, *18 holes,* ☎ *(09603) 53792.*

Coleraine

Pop. 20,000, 50 km (31 miles) NE of Derry, 87 km (54 miles) NW of Belfast. All day closing Thurs. Except July, Aug. TIO: (0265)52181, all year. Bus enquiries: bus station, ☎ *(0265)43334. Train enquiries,* ☎ *(0265)42263.*

Said to have been given its name by St Patrick in the 5th c, Coleraine became a small city during the Middle Ages, and though there are few remains from this period, there are a number from its second incarnation, as a plantation town, including remnants of the 1641 siege, also fine Georgian houses and streets. The University of Ulster main campus is sited here.

St Patrick's Church, *(CI), town centre:* see mark on N wall where cannon ball hit building during 1641. **Town Hall,** relics include sword presented by Irish Society in 1616. *Mon-Fri, by arr.* Walks: good along both banks of River Bann. Anderson Park *by river,* a quiet if windy oasis by the main shopping area. Ballysally, *on N side of University:* marina, caravan camp, café. **University of Ulster,** many arts events throughout the year. Concerts in Diamond Hall, smaller recitals and visual arts exhibitions in the Octogon. *Guided tours mid July-mid Aug, Wed, 11 a.m. Details and bookings, Cashier's Office,* ☎ *(0265)44141 extn 278.* Library of some 200,000 volumes inc. Denis Johnston manuscripts, much material relating to World Wars I and II. *Term time, Mon-Fri, 9 a.m.-10 p.m. Sat, 9 a.m.-1 p.m. Vacations, Mon-Fri, 9 a.m.-5 p.m.* **Riverside Gallery,** *University of Ulster campus,* ☎*(0265)44141:* shows in all media. *All year, Mon-Fri, 9 a.m.-6 p.m.* **Riverside Theatre,** amateur and professional productions, touring art exhibitions in foyer. *Details and bookings,* ☎ *(0265)51388.* **Guy Wilson Daffodil Garden,** with almost 1,500 varieties of daffodil, the world's most comprehensive collection. Access at all times, full bloom, *mid Apr.* Bicycles: Car & Home Supplies, *8-10 Queen Street,* ☎*(0265)42354,* Coleraine Motorcycles and Cycle Centre, *8 Newmarket Street,* ☎*(0265)52655.*

AROUND COLERAINE

Ballymoney, *12 km (8 miles) SE of Coleraine. All*

Glenelly Valley, Co. Tyrone

day closing Mon. All year. Bus and train enquiries: Ballymoney Railway Station, ☎ *(02656)63241.* Two interesting churches: Our Lady and St Patrick, (C), built of local basalt, fine stained glass windows.

Trinity Presbyterian Church, built 1884 by Home Rule advocate Rev. J.B. Armour. ***Bush Valley fish farm**, 55 Main Street, Stranocum, Ballymoney:* rainbow trout reared. *All year, Mon-Fri, 9 a.m.-12 noon, 2 p.m.-5 p.m. By arr,* ☎*(02657)41354/41463.* Riada Leisure Centre, inc. pool, *Charles Street, daily,* ☎ *(02656)65792.*

Bann Estuary Wildlife Sanctuary, *5 km (3 miles) E of Castlerock:* observation hide with illustrative panels. The River Bann is navigable by boats with draughts of up to 1 m (3 ft) all the way from sea to Portadown, crossing Lough Neagh. Unusual, little-used way of seeing a cross-section of Ulster life.

Bellarena, *8 km (5 miles) N of Limavady:* 'Miners' Marks', two small towers mark where first Ordnance Survey of Ireland and Britain was begun in 1834.

Bishop's Road, starts in Downhill village and climbs to Eagle Hill and Binevenagh. Excellent views of Donegal and Scottish coast from Gortmore picnic area.

Bushmills, *5 km (3 miles) S of Giant's Causeway. EC Thurs.* Old Bushmills Whiskey Distillery has world's oldest distillery licence dating from 1609. Attractively set by St Columb's Rill. *Mon-Thur, mid-morning and mid-afternoon; Fri, 10.30 a.m. only; tours at 10.30 a.m., 2.30 p.m.* Telephone in advance ☎ *(02657)31521.* Open-topped Bushmills bus runs from Coleraine to Giant's Causeway, *June-August, daily.* Bushfoot Golf Club, *9 holes,* ☎ *(02657)31317.*

Camus High Cross, *6 km (4 miles) S of Coleraine on A54:* weather-worn cross in Camus old graveyard on W bank of River Bann, site of former monastery. Camus Woods, by riverside, good picnic spot.

Castlerock, *13 km (8 miles) NW of Coleraine. EC Wed or Sat.* Bracing seaside village just W of Bann estuary. Good beach. Open air swimming pool. Castlerock Golf Club, *18 holes,* ☎ *(0265)848314.*

Causeway Safari Park, *Ballymoney:* lions and other wildlife roam free. Farmyard area, mini zoo, amusement park. Bar, restaurant, shops. *Apr-Aug, Mon-Sun, 10.30 a.m.-7 p.m.* ☎ *(02657)41474.*

Dervock, *7 km (5 miles) NE of Ballymoney. EC Sat.* Farm outhouse at Conagher was home of great-great-grandfather of US president William McKinley, assassinated in 1901.

Dundarave, *just N of Bushmills:* splendid Georgian house with sumptuous interior. *By arr. only. Details. Recreation Officer,* ☎ *(02657)62225/22565.*

Dunluce Castle, *midway between Giant's Causeway and Portrush.* Magnificent ruins on crag above sea, dating from about 1300. Part of the castle fell into the sea in 1639, taking with it several unfortunate servants who happened to be in the kitchen at the time. Two years later it was abandoned. Today it is one of the most massive and romantic ruins in Ireland, with spectacular views. Ruins of old church just S. *Apr-Sept, Mon-Sat, 10 a.m.- 1 p.m.; 1.30 p.m.-7 p.m. Sun, 2 p.m.-7 p.m. Oct-Mar, Tues-Sat, 10 a.m.-1 p.m.; 1. 30 p.m.-4 p.m. Sun, 2 p.m.-5 p.m.*

Dunseverick Castle, *E end of Giant's Causeway:* slight ruins of one of Ireland's earliest castles dating from about 500, perched on a high crag.

Giant's Causeway, *12 km (9 miles) E of Portrush on B146.* Ireland's best-known tourist attraction. A fascinating, often spectacular landscape of six-sided basalt columns. The tallest, in the Giant's Organ, are about 12 m (36 ft) high. Information centre, shop, visitor centre. Also picture boards telling the 'Girona' (Spanish Armada galleon) story. Café. Bus from car park to Windy Gap. Geological Walk: *5 km (3 miles),* signposted, illustrated information panels, an excellent way of seeing area's geology. ***Giant's Causeway Centre:*** displays on the flora, fauna and geology of the centre. Local history, including the tram that ran from Portrush

to the Giant's Causeway. Audio-visual presentations. Shop, tea room. *All year, Mon-Sun, 10 a.m.- 7 p.m. (July and Aug, otherwise closes earlier). Closed Christmas week.* ☎ *(02657)31582.*

Kilrea, *9 km (6 miles) SE of Garvagh:* Movanagher Fish Farm. *By arr,* ☎ *(02665)40533.*

Liffock, *just outside Castlerock.* 17th c Hezlett House built without foundations on flat rock. Unusual roof. *Easter, May, June, Sept, Sat, Sun, BH, 1 p.m.-5 p.m. July, Aug, daily, except Tues, 1 p.m.-5 p.m.* ☎*(0265)848567.*

Magilligan Strand, Ireland's longest strand runs from 10 km (6 miles), starting just W of Castlerock. Above the strand, ***Downhill Castle ruins, Mussenden Temple,*** glen walk, Downhill forest. Castle open *Easter, May, June, Sept, Sat, Sun, BH, 12 noon-6 p.m., July, Aug, daily, 12 noon-6 p.m.* ☎*(0265)848728.* ***Martello Tower,*** built during early 19th c Napoleonic wars. Key to tower during summer at nearby pub, Magilligan Field Centre, *Seacoast Road, during winter.* Nearby ***Portadvantage Cove*** is very quiet. ***Mount Sandel fort,*** *1.5 km (1 mile) SE of Coleraine:* large oval mound, site of Ireland's oldest house, inhabited 9,000 years ago, overlooks the River Bann.

Plaiskin Head, *to E of Giant's Causeway,* magnificent panorama of whole N Antrim coast and parts of SW Scottish coast in clear weather.

Portballintrae, *3 km (2 miles) SW of Giant's Causeway, loop road from A2. TIO,* ☎ *(02657)31672, July, Aug.* Pleasant, secluded seaside village with harbour and beach. Boat excursions from harbour, *SO.*

Portcoon Cave, *W end of Giant's Causeway cliffs:* beautiful internal colouring, enter from landward side.

Portnabo slipway, *near Giant's Causeway entrance:* boats to view Causeway coast caves from sea. *SO.*

Portrush, *19 km (12 miles) N of Coleraine on A29. EC Wed. TIO, Town Hall,* ☎ *(0265)823333, Easter-Sept.* Resort town set on a peninsula jutting into the ocean, with attractive terraces and a bustling, seaside atmosphere. Railway station of architectural interest. Many summer entertainments, including Town Hall theatre, fishing, bowling, swimming. Good beaches at east and west strand. Waterworld, indoor wet adventure playground for children.

Portrush Countryside Centre, *Bath Road:* Interpretative, information centre, ☎ *(0265)823600.* ☝ *June-Aug, daily, 1 p.m.-9 p.m. except Tues, or by arr.,* ☎ *(0265)823600.* Cliff walks W towards Portstewart. E to Dunluce. At E end of chalk White Rocks, car park, picnic area with fine coastal views. Walk to top of Ramore Head for invigorating views. Daily summer boat trips leaving from harbour, round offshore Skerry Islands. ***Barry's*** seafront: huge amusement arcade, ☎ *(0265)822340.* ***Royal Portrush Golf Club,*** Dunluce course, *18 holes;* Valley course, *18 holes,* ☎ *(0265)822311.* Rathmore Golf Club, *18 holes,* ☎ *(0265)822996.*

Portstewart, *6 km (4 miles) SW of Portrush. EC Thurs, except summer. TIO, Town Hall,* ☎ *(026583)2286, July, Aug.* Bus enquiries: Coleraine bus station, ☎ *(0265)43334. Train enquiries: Portrush Railway Station,* ☎ *(0265)822395.* The main streets of this attractive Victorian-style town form an Atlantic promenade, winding round rocky bays, with shore paths at each end. Magnificent 3 km (2 mile) long strand between town and River Bann. ***Flowerfield Arts Centre,*** regular exhibitions of local fine and applied art. *All year, Mon-Fri, 10 a.m.-1 p.m., 2 p.m.-5 p.m. or by arr,* ☎ *(0265)853959.* Boat excursions from harbour, *SO.* Two 18 holes golf courses, ☎ *(026583)2015.*

Slaghtaverty Dolmen, *on hill slope 5 km (3 miles) S of Garvagh:* legend has it that this is last resting place of Abhartach, a dwarf with magical powers who was killed by a neighbouring chieftain and buried upside down to silence his ghost.

Cookstown

Pop. 8,000, 74 km (46 miles) W of Belfast, 85 km (53 miles) SE of Derry. All day closing Wed. TIO: ☎*(06487)63359/63441. Bus enquiries: Dungannon bus office,* ☎ *(08687)22251.*

Renowned for its main street (two miles long and fifty metres wide) and its interesting old-fashioned pubs, which are particularly lively on market days; the River Ballinderry, just S of town, is one of best trout rivers in NI.

Killymoon Castle, *at golf club, SE of town:* fine exterior, built in 1803 to design of John Nash, architect of the extravagant Brighton Pavilion in S England. Derryloran Parish Church (CI), *S of end of Main Street:* also designed by Nash, Catholic church, *town centre:* spire of Gothic-style building is landmark for miles around. Adjoining convent chapel contains interesting modern church art. Swimming pool: heated, indoor, *Fountain Road, daily,* ☎ *(06487)63853.* ☝ Killymoon Golf Club, *18 holes,* ☎ *(06487)62254.*

AROUND COOKSTOWN

Ardboe Cross, *W shores of Lough Neagh, take B73 E from Cookstown for 16 km (10 miles) to lake shore, then turn R down minor road for 2 km (1 mile):* best preserved 10th c High Cross in NI; nearby, ruins of old churches, 6th c abbey.

Ballyronan, *6 km (4 miles) SE of Magherafelt:* popular sailing spot. Lough Neagh pleasure steamers call here. Walks along lake shore, bathing and picnic areas.

Beaghmore Stone Circles, *6 km (4 miles) NW of Drum Manor, approach by small road running N from Dunnamore hamlet:* six stone circles, also cairns, dating back 4,000 years. Their original purpose is obscure.

Benburb Valley Park: walks beside the Blackwater river. Ruins of Benburb Castle on cliffs above river. Interpretative centre. Access at all times. ☎ *(0861)548187.* ***O'Neill historical centre,*** Servite Priory basement: maps and exhibits. *May-Oct, 2 p.m.-5 p.m.* ☎*(0861)548187.*

Carndaisy Wood and Glen, *5 km (3 miles) NW of Moneymore:* many good picnic spots, to N road corkscrews almost to summit of Slieve Gallion. This is one of the most spectacular and least known drives in the entire North.

Castledawson, *5 km (3 miles) SE of village, at mouth of Moyola River. All day closing Mon.* Lough Neagh's best sandy beach. Due to commercial sand extraction, not suitable for swimming. Between Castledawson and river mouth, picturesque bridge. Nearby picnic area. Fishing. Moyola Park Golf Club, *18 holes,* ☎ *(0648)68468.*

Coagh, *8 km (5 miles) E of Cookstown on B73:* delightful crossroads village. From main Hanover Square, cross over bridge to enormous Clocktogle dolmen.

Davagh Forest Park, *13 km (8 miles) NW of Cookstown:* vaguely Wild Westish with gravelly bed of Broughderg River. From Beleevnamore Mountain, you can see most parts of NI on a clear day. Many nature trails, picnic areas.

Drum Manor Forest Park, *6 km (4 miles) W of Cookstown on A505:* butterfly gardens, delightful spot enclosed by old walls where rare species can be seen in summer. Wildfowl ponds. Nature trail, picnic area, camping, caravan sites, information centre, café. ☝

Dungannon, *18 km (11 miles) S of Cookstown. EC Wed. TIO:* ☎*(08687)25311, all year. Bus enquiries: Bus Office, Market Square, Dungannon,* ☎ *(08687)22251.* Walk up steep streets to Castle Hill, from where there are excellent views of the countryside between Lough Neagh and Sperrins . Tyrone Crystal makes a fine range of glassware. *Factory tours all year, Mon-Fri. By app. only. Groups preferred,* ☎ *(08687)25335.* Greyhound rac ing: Oak Park. *Regular weekly meetings,* ☎ *(08687)22023.* Swimming pool: indoor, heated, *Circular Road, daily,* ☎ *(08687)25310.* Dungannon Golf Club, *18 holes,* ☎ *(08687)22098.*

Glenshane Pass, *NW of Maghera on A6:* spectacular drive. Usually first road in Ireland to be snowed under in bad winter weather. Forest at top of pass for those interested in camping, orienteering.

Loughry Agricultural College, *5 km (3 miles) S of Cookstown:* plantation mansion much visited by Swift. He is said to have written part of *Gulliver's Travels* in the summerhouse. House has portraits of Stella, Vanessa. *By app. the principal,* ☎ *(06487)62491.*

Moneymore, *6 km (4 miles) NW of Cookstown on A29.* Pleasant Georgian-style village reconstructed in early l9th c. Go through archway in centre of village in broad market yard, surrounded by old corn stores with balconies.

Parkanaur Forest Park, *5 km (3 miles) W of Dungannon.* Woodland trails, deer park, camp and caravan sites, picnic places, car park. Farm buildings of original estate restored to initial character. *Details,* ☎ *(0232)650111, extn 456.*

Pomeroy, *11 km (7 miles) SW of Cookstown.* Tyrone's highest village, surrounded by fine moorland and mountain scenery. Market, *in Square, every second and fourth Tues.*

Springhill House, (NT) *2 km (1 mile) outside Moneymore on Coagh road.* Excellent example of settler's manor house, complete with furniture and one of Ulster's most regularly authenticated ghosts. Cottar's kitchen with bygone utensils. Costume museum. Gardens, woodland walks. *Easter, May, June, Sept, Sat, Sun, BH, 2 p.m.-6 p.m., July, Aug, daily, except Thurs, 2 p.m.-6 p.m.* ☎ *(06626)48142.* **Sperrin Heritage Centre,** *Gortin:* natural history and gold mining exhibits. Hire a gold pan and try your luck in the stream. Exhibition, craft shop, café. *Apr-Sept, Mon-Fri, 11 a.m.-6 p.m., Sat, 11.30 a.m.-6 p.m., Sun, 2 p.m.-7 p.m.* ☎ *(06626)48142.*

Stewartstown, *8 km (5 miles) SE of Cookstown on B520. EC Thurs.* Fine cobbled square with little shops and houses. Drumcairne Forest, 3 km (2 miles) E has Italian terrace, picnic sites. Old warehouses surround derelict canal basin. Other reminders of once prosperous Tyrone mining industry include coal workings to the S of the village. About 3 km (2 miles) NW, in Newmills direction, see ruined arches, remains of 'dry wherries', where the old canal barges had to be hauled over dry land.

Tobermore, *5 km (3 miles) SW of Maghera:* small village with delightfully 'unplanned' narrow streets, has won many best-kept village prizes. Several picnic areas.

Tullahogue Hill, *5 km (3 miles) S of Cookstown, just off B520:* from summit, fine view over much of Tyrone. Fine hilltop enclosure, the crowning place of the O'Neills, Ulster chiefs for five centuries until 17th c.

Wellbrook Beetling Mill (NT), *near Drum Manor Forest Park:* 18th c mill, with great wheel and sluices, on Ballinderry River, restored to full working order. Most impressive, if noisy, process. Nearby walks along river banks and mill race. *Easter, May, June, Sept, Sat, Sun, BH, 2 p.m.-6 p.m., July, Aug, daily, except Tues, 2 p.m.-6 p.m.* ☎ *(06487)51735.*

Cushendall

Pop. 1,000, 6 km (4 miles) S of Cushendun. TIO: ☎*(02667)71180, all year. EC Tues. Bus enquiries: Larne bus station,* ☎ *(0574)72345. Youth Hostel,* ☎*(02667)71344.*

Capital of the Glens of Antrim, and one of the most distinctively Irish parts of NI. The village, largely created by a wealthy l9th c landowner, Francis Turnly, is a charming little place, the ideal introduction to the scenic delights of the Glens. Game fishing.

Parish church (C), *riverbank:* built 1832, Michael Healy stained glass window. Mill Street: old corn mill, formerly powered by River Dall. Small, sandy beach.

AROUND CUSHENDALL

Antrim Coast Road (A21): from Larne to Cushendall, with some of the most impressive coastal scenery in Ireland. The mountain roads leading off the Cushendall—Cushendun A2 offer good views.

Ballygally, *8 km (5 miles) N of Larne.* Good beach. Well-preserved mill on inland side of village. Youth Hostel.

Carnlough, *5 km (3 miles) NW of Glenarm. TIO* ☎*(0574)85210, all year. EC Thurs, except July, Aug.* Pretty little Glens village with fine beach and harbour. Walk: up Waterfall Road to see old limekiln building with tall white chimneys, relic of a bygone era. Also see Cranny Falls. A track leads out onto the great expanse of Garron Moorland.

Cushendun, *8 km (5 miles) N of Cushendall on A2. TIO:* ☎*(026674)506, Apr-Sept. EC Tues.* Most N Glens village, and one of the most attractive, with cottages built in Cornish style to design of Clough Williams Ellis, who also designed the nearby 'Glenmona', home of Lord Cushendun. *Cave House, just S of village:* can only be approached by road through natural cave. Now a holiday retreat, but worth going to see, unusual entrance. *1.5 km (1 mile) N of Castle Carra ruins, on Torr Head road,* see modern cross on a cairn, commemorating a bloody 16th c clan feud. Next to it is a large monument to Sir Roger Casement. Sandstone cliffs to S of village have many caves. Boat from Cushendun Harbour. Just outside Cushendun, a path leads from Milltown houses alongside Brabla Burn to moors. Delightful walk, but it you want even more silence, head for Tornamoney Burn, 3.5 km (2 miles) N of Brabla.

Garron Point, *midway between Cushendall and Carnlough.* At its summit, an old earth fort, at foot of cliffs, a tiny harbour. Just N, White Lady, a chalk carving by the coastal road, from here, take lane to tiny hamlet of Galboly, set in Swiss-like scenery. Old quay, used for shipping limestone, is 0.8 km (0.5 miles) W of White Lady.

Glenaan, *5 km (3 miles) W of Cushendall:* where the road up the glen joins the road to Glendun, past Beagh's Forest. Splendidly desolate, open, wild countryside.

Glenariff Glen, *stretches inland for some 8 km (5 miles) from Waterfoot.* Known as the 'Queen of the Nine Glens', Glenariff was described by Thackeray as 'Switzerland in miniature'. Steep mountains rise on both sides of glen, which narrows to a deep, wooded gorge. Path winds along the river by means of rustic footbridges, enabling you to see the waterfalls. Also viewing places, but be careful in wet weather, when paths are very slippery. Glenariff Forest Park: charming walks at head of Glenariff, café, visitor centre. Look out for disused station, relic of the narrow gauge railway that once ran to Ballymena, and the flat slabs that once formed the ancient Black Causeway from the Bann Valley to the Antrim coast. A 42 km (26 mile) path, part of Ulster Way, runs from head of glen to Ballycastle. A good walk! Glenariff: Feis na nGleann, Community Carnival Week, *July.*

Glenarm, *EC Wed.* Most S village in Glens of Antrim has pleasing aspect. Quiet Sunday hide-away. The public park runs for some 7 km (4 miles) beside Glenarm River, up the glen, complete with waterfalls. Good salmon and trout river. The back roads W of the village make for interesting sorties into the mountains.

Glendun (C), *1.5 km (1 mile) beyond Knocknagarry Bridge:* St Patrick's Church, with Sweethearts' Stone. John McAlaster, who died in 1803 at the age of 18 after falling from a ship's rigging weeks before he was to marry, is buried here. His brokenhearted sweetheart was said to have cut the inscrip-

tions on the grave's flat headstone. **Glendun Viaduct,** *5 km (3 miles) E of Cushendun on A2:* most impressive structure on whole Antrim coast road. From the viaduct, good views down the glen. Fuchsia adds to the vista. Vicinity has good salmon and trout fishing.

Layde, *1.5 km (1 mile) N of Cushendall:* Layde Old Church ruins in a little valley overlooking the sea. Road to churchyard passes ornamental well that once provided the village's water supply. Walk: along cliff path down to beach.

Sallagh Braes, *5 km (3 miles) SW of Ballygally:* fine amphitheatre of crags, from which there are views as far as Ailsa Craig, the vast cone-shaped rock off the Ayrshire coast.

Tiveragh Hill, *1.5 km (1 mile) NW of Cushendall:* known locally as the 'fairy hill'. Good climbing.

Waterfoot, *1.5 km (1 mile) S of Cushendall.* Set at mouth of Glenariff River on Red Bay, so called because of the red sandstone washed down in nearby streams. 16th c ruins of Red Bay Castle are poised on cliffs above bay. Walks: starting at the White Arch, follow the course of the old railway track, once used for shipping iron ore to Cumberland and Scotland. Today, it's a pleasant walk along SE side of the glen.

White Bay, *3 km (2 miles) SE of Glenarm on A2:* see tiny fossilized marine creatures, as well as flints, in the rock. Car park, picnic area.

Monaghan

Pop. 6,000, 27 km (17 miles) SW of Armagh, 87 km (54 miles) SW of Belfast, 120 km (75 miles) NW of Dublin. EC Thurs. TIO, ☎ *(047)81122, all year. Bus enquiries,* ☎ *(047)82377.*

The county town of Monaghan has a distinctly Northern air, hardly surprising since it is in the historic province of Ulster. Surrounding area dotted with lakes, ideal coarse fishing country.

St. Macartan's Cathedral, (C) *S of town centre:* imposing l9th c structure in Gothic Revival style. ♿ **County Museum,** *The Courthouse:* many fascinating exhibits including prehistoric stone and metal weapons, pottery and ornaments, 18th c military material, Carrickmacross and Clones lace, police equipment, butter churns, baking irons, coins, maps, photographs. Canal, railway relics. Highlight is 14th c Cross of Clogher. Short term art, history exhibitions. *All year, Tues-Sat, 11 a.m.-l p.m.; 2 p.m.- 5 p.m.* ☎ *(047)82928.* ♿ **Heritage centre,** *St. Louis Convent:* displays and exhibitions tracing the history of the St. Louis Order in Monaghan and Ireland. *All year, Mon, Tues, Thurs, Fri, 10 a.m.-12 noon, 2 p.m.-4 p.m., Sat, Sun, 2 p.m.-4 p.m.* ☎*(047)82928.* **Ulster Canal,** good walks along disused banks. **Rossmore Forest Park,** *2 km (1 mile) S of town, off L44:* car park, picnic site, lakeside and forest walks, fishing, nature trails. From Rossmore Castle site, panoramic views. ♿ Canoeing, hill walking, rock climbing: Anne and Brendan Lillit, ☎ *(047)81721.* Swimming pool: indoor heated, Clones Road, *daily,* Bicycles: M & M Cycles, *North Road,* ☎ *(047)84244.* Patrick McCoy, *Dublin Street,* ☎ *(047)81283.* Rossmore Golf Club, *9 holes,* ☎ *(047)81316.*

AROUND MONAGHAN

Annaghmakerrig, *off L40, 8 km (5 miles) NW of Cootehill:* car park, picnic area, forest walks.

Ballybay, *14 km (9 miles) SE of Monaghan:* Billy Fox Memorial Park, picnic area, forest walks.

Black Island, *E outskirts of Castleblayney, 22 km (14 miles) SE of Monaghan on N2:* pleasant lakeside walks here and along shores of Lough Muckno.

Carrickmacross, *45 km (28 miles) SE of Monaghan on N2:* lacemaking displays at St Louis convent, *daily.* **Carrickmacross Lace Co-op,** *Main Street:* exhibition of locally-made lace items. *May-Oct, Mon-Sat, 9.30 a.m.-5.30 p.m., closed Wed.* ☎

View from Lurigethan, Co. Antrim

(042)62506. Carrickmacross Golf Club, *Nuremore, 9 holes.*

Castleblayney, Hope Castle and grounds have been developed as a leisure park. Lough Muckno regional park covers 37 ha (91 acres). The wooded park surrounding the lake is laid out with nature trails. Water ski-ing is a feature of the lake, which has many islets.

Castleshane, *8 km (5 miles) E of Monaghan on N2:* forest walks, attractive Castleshane Waterfall.

Clones, *19 km (12 miles) SW of Monaghan on N54.*

Ancient Celtic cross in Diamond, 22 m (75 ft) high round tower in graveyard near Cavan road and Early Bronze Age court cairn. Sarcophagus dates back to early Christian times. Exact origins unknown but worth a close look. Key from nearby Patton's pub. Lace making centre: details, Monaghan TIO. Derelict Ulster Canal skirts town. Bicycles: J. Reilly, *the Diamond.* Clones Golf Club, *Hilton Park, 9 holes,* ☎ *(047)56017.*

Dún a Rí Forest Park, *10 km (6 miles) SW of Carrickmacross, 2 km (1 mile) N of Kingscourt on L35:* numerous amenities include picnic site, planned walks, nature trails. 'Romantic Glen' of Cabra River runs full length of park, other features include ruins of military barracks, waterfall. Wishing Well. &

Kingscourt, St Mary's (C) has fine Evie Hone windows. The Ascension was one of her favourite works. &

Mannan Castle, *6 km (4 miles) N of Carrickmacross:* 12th c hilltop motte and bailey.

Tirgarvan, *3 km (2 miles) W of Carrickmacross:* interesting limestone caves.

Newcastle

Pop. 6,500, 21 km (13 miles) SE of Downpatrick, 50 km (31 miles) SE of Belfast. EC Thurs. TIO: 61 Central Promenade, ☎ *(03967)22222, all year. Bus enquiries: bus station,* ☎ *(03967)22296. Coach tours: SO, details TIO.*

One of Northern Ireland's top seaside resorts, beautifully situated, with the great sandy beaches of Dundrum Bay backed by the towering Slieve Donard Mountain. Plenty of sport, including fishing, golf, pony trekking.

Our Lady of the Assumption Church (C), *near N end of Downs Park:* circular, with striking

Newcastle, Co. Down

interior design, & **Grant Gallery,** Irish and international paintings, sculpture, *Mon-Sat, 2 p.m.-5 p.m. during exhibitions.* ☎ *(03967)22349.* **Newcastle Art Gallery,** *18-22 Main Street,* ☎*(03967)23555. Mon-Fri, 12 noon-5.30 p.m.; Sat, 12 noon-6 p.m., Sun, 3 p.m.-6 p.m.* **Newcastle Centre:** impressive range of indoor entertainments, sport, café, lounge. Ideal for when it rains, especially with children, *daily,* ☎ *(03967)22222.* & **Mourne Countryside Centre,** Central promenade: displays and maps on the Mourne country. *July-Aug, Mon-Sun, 9 a.m.-8 p.m. Sept-June, 9 a.m.-5 p.m., most days and by arr.,* ☎ *(03967)24059.* Promenade Gardens: see fountain commemorating Percy French, who wrote the song *The Mountains of Mourne.* Castle Park: wide range of sporting activities. Summer concerts, open air entertainment. **Donard Park,** rises up the slopes of Slieve Donard and Shanlieve. For an interesting walk, follow the Glen River from the town centre car park through Donard Park and forest up the path to the Saddle, a col between Slieve Donard and Slieve Commedagh. Above the second bridge is an old stone-built ice house. Newcastle Riding Centre, *35 Carnacavill Road,* ☎ *(03967)22694.* Royal County Down Golf Club, *18 holes,* ☎ *(03967)23314.* Youth Hostel: *30 Downs Road,* ☎ *(03967)22133.*

AROUND NEWCASTLE

Annalong, *13 km (8 miles) S of Newcastle on A2. EC Thurs.* Charming fishing village. Walk round harbour, often filled with fishing boats, before relaxing in a quayside pub. **Cornmill:** overlooks harbour. Watermills, water power exhibition. Visitor centre with cafe, antiques shop, herb garden. *June-Sept, daily, 2 p.m.-6 p.m.* ☎ *(03967)68736.*

Bloody Bridge, *4 km (2 miles) S of Newcastle, just W of A2.* Scene of 1641 massacre of Protestants. NT has provided car park, coastal walk. Nearby is Maggie's Leap, a narrow chasm so-called because a young lady of that name jumped across while carrying a basket of eggs to avoid a persistent suitor. Donard Cove is only accessible by boat from Newcastle.

Bronte Country, *between Rathfriland and Banbridge:* rolling hills and bushy dells, homeland of father and many uncles and aunts of the three novelist sisters. Bronte trail is signposted. Emdale, 5 km (3 miles) SE of Loughbrickland; ruin of cottage where Bronte's father, Patrick, was born is marked by plaque. Drumballyroney is 5 km (3 miles) NE of Rathfriland. On the hilltop can be seen church where Rev. Thomas Tighe coached Patrick for Cambridge and also school where he taught. In churchyard, graves of some six of his brothers and sisters. Magherally, 5 km (3 miles) NE of Banbridge: ruined church where grandparents of Bronte sisters were married. Also grave of novelist Helen Waddell, who wrote *Peter Abelard,* the touching story of Abelard and Heloise.

Castlewellan, *8 km (5 miles) NW of Newcastle on A50. All day closing Thurs.* Pleasant- looking market town; every second Mon, the town's fair takes place. May 1 and Nov 1, horse fairs in town centre. Walk the length of the broad Main Street, taking in both Upper and Lower Squares. **Castlewellan Forest Park,** *just N of Castlewellan:* outstanding wildlife. Signposted walks. Camping, caravan sites. Slievenaslat is a slight mountain that can be scaled on foot or horseback. Arboretum has many trees and plants from all over the world and is considered one of the finest in the world. 18th c farmstead, with courtyards, barns, belfries. Tropical birds kept in glasshouse. Trout fishing in lake. Café. ☎ *(03967)78664.* **Castlewellan Lakes,** *five within 8 km (5 mile) radius of town:* all good for fishing and lakeside walks: Castlewellan, Ballylough, Ballyward, Ballymagreehan, Lough Island Reavy. Last-named has easiest access; S end is alongside A25, about 6 km (4 miles) SW of Castlewellan. Near E end of this lake, Drumena Cashel is one of best-preserved ringforts (early defended homesteads) in N Ireland. Mount Pleasant Trekking Centre, *15 Bannanstown Road,* ☎ *(03967)78651.*

Annalong Harbour, Co. Down

Clough, *just S of Seaforde.* Crossroads village with well-preserved Norman motte and bailey, ruin of small castle.

Dromara, *8 km (5 miles) SW of Ballynahinch. EC Sat.* Lovely and secluded, with attractive old bridges over infant River Lagan. Good walks. Mossvale Riding Centre, *18 Church Road,* ☎ *(0238)532279.*

Drumkeeragh Forest, *16 km (10 miles) N of Newcastle, W of B175:* comparatively new, with outstanding views of Slieve Croob Mountain to S. Caravan site.

Dundrum, *5 km (3 miles) N of Newcastle. EC Thurs.* Attractive seaside village. Dundrum Castle: built by Normans, late 12th c, now substantial ruins. *Easter-Sept, Tues-Sat, 10 a.m.-7 p.m., Sun, 2 p.m.-7 p.m.; Oct-Mar, Sat, 10 a.m.-4 p.m., Sun, 2 p.m.-4 p.m.*

Katesbridge, *between Castlewellan and Banbridge on A50:* delightful little village on banks of Upper Bann River. Norman motte by river, also picnic area. Blacksmith's forge, by old bridge, has been run by Morgan family for five generations. See horseshoes being shaped on the anvil, amid clatter of sparks.

Legananny Dolmen, *7 km (4 miles) S of Dromara on slopes of Cratlieve Mountain:* considered the most graceful Stone Age monument in Northern Ireland.

Loughinisland, *11 km (7 miles) SE of Ballynahinch on A24T.* Ruins of three ancient churches on lake islet connected to mainland by causeway. Oldest church probably pre-dates 11th c.

Minerstown Beach, *E shores of Dundrum Bay:* splendidly situated. Tyrella Strand is W continuation of this beach, magnificent 6 km (4 mile) stretch, firm enough for driving.

Mountains of Mourne, rise up in spectacular fashion behind Annalong. Minor roads lead from village, but since no roads cross the centre of the range, you must walk to see main peaks at close quarters. **Slieve Donard,** *850 m (2,796 ft),* the highest mountain, is worth climbing, especially on clear day, when there are views to Donegal and Wicklow in Ireland, Isle of Man, NW England, N Wales mountains. Takes about 2 hours from Newcastle, following route of old tramway from near harbour. At summit, slight remains of 5th c oratory built by St Domhanghort, who gave the mountain its name. Mourne Coastal Path: runs S for 6 km (4 miles) along seashore from Bloody Bridge, at the foot of Slieve Donard. Most exhilarating: another path follows course of Bloody River into the mountains .

Murlough National Nature Reserve, *l.5 km (1 mile) S of Dundrum.* Impressive place where you may see badgers or find a Stone Age arrowhead. Illustrations of birds and flowers to guide walkers, special guided tours. For permits for restricted areas, contact the warden, ☎ *(039675)467.* Information centre has changing displays about the area. *Reserve always open. Visitor centre, June-mid Sept, daily, 10 a.m.-5 p.m.* ☎*(03967)24362.* &

Rathfriland, *6 km (4 miles) S of Katesbridge. EC Thurs.* Small plantation town set on a hill, steep streets rising to square. Old buildings include Quaker meeting house. Kinnahalla Youth Hostel: *Hilltown,* ☎ *(08206)30289.*

Rourke's Park, *3 km (2 miles) N of Annalong.* Forest recreation area in valley of Annalong River. Excellent starting point for mountain walks, taking in Slieve Binian, Blue Lough, great cave of Cove mountain, Brandy Pad. Car park.

Seaforde, *on Newcastle-Ballynahinch A24T.* Seaforde House demesne may be visited by prior arr. **Butterfly House** has many species of tropical butterflies and insects and reptiles from four continents. Nursery garden, playground, shop, tea room. *Easter-Sept, Mon-Sat, 10 a.m.-5 p.m., Sun, 2 p.m.-6 p.m.* ☎ *(039687)225.*

Slievenaman, *6 km (4 miles) W of Newcastle:* Youth Hostel. ☎ *(03967)22133.*

Slievenamoney Hill, *8 km (5 miles) N of Castlewellan:* granite cross on summit marks the fact that Franciscan friars found refuge nearby during 17th and 18th c Penal times.

Tollymore Forest Park, *near Bryansford:* impressive and enjoyable, with Gothic follies, arboretum, caravan, camping site, café, exhibition hall. Hermitage is random collection of stones forming cave-like room on banks of River Shimna. Wildlife and forestry exhibits in barn. Planned walks, varying in length from 1.5-13 km (1-8 miles). Fishing, pony trekking. ☎ *(03967)22428.*

Portaferry

Pop, 2,200, 40 km (25 miles) S of Belfast, EC Thurs, TIO, open June-Aug. Bus enquiries: Downpatrick bus station, ☎ *(0396)612384. Ferry enquiries:* ☎ *(039686)637. Ferry from Strangford.*

A most attractive seaside village near the S end of the Ards Peninsula, facing Strangford across the narrow waters at Strangford Lough entrance. The long waterfront has a mixture of Scots-style cottages and some Georgian houses, a most pleasing prospect enhanced by the charming old-world inns. Good sea angling centre, especially for giant skate.

Templecranny Old Church, *off Church Street:*

Murlough Sand Dunes, near Dundrum, Co. Down

belfry and one gable left. **Portaferry House,** ruins of 16th c castle in grounds. Aquarium and butterfly house, *Rope Walk.* About 70 marine species from Strangford Lough may be seen, also models of the seabed. Tea room. *Sept-Mar, Tues, Sat, 10.30 a.m.-5 p.m., Sun, 1 p.m.-5 p.m., Apr-Aug, Mon-Sat, 10 a.m.-6 p.m., Sun, 1 p.m.-6 p.m.* ☎ *(02477)28062.* Car ferry to Strangford: *daily at half hour intervals between about 7.30 a.m. and 10.30 p.m. 10 minute trip,* ☎ *(039686)637.* Boats: at quayside for trips round Strangford Lough and its innumerable islands.

AROUND PORTAFERRY

Ardglass, *11 km (7 miles) SE of Downpatrick. EC Thurs.* Main fishing port of this part of Co. Down. Walks around inner and outer harbour. **Ardtole Church,** *0.8 km (0.5 miles) N of town:* 15th c ruin on height overlooking sea. **Jordan's Castle,** 15th c structure by harbour. **Isabella's Tower,** *just N of town:* 19th c folly on a hilltop. Ardglass Golf Club, *18 holes,* ☎ *(0396)841219.*

Ardkeen Promontory, *E shore of Strangford Lough, 7 km (4 miles) N of Portaferry.* Foundations of 12th c Ardkeen Castle. 200 years ago the stones were used to build a nearby mansion, of which one large wall still stands.

Ballyhornan, *8 km (5 miles) S of Strangford on A2.* Growing coastal hamlet with two fine beaches in vicinity. Just S, you can walk over to Gun's Island. You may see seals on the coast here.

Ballynoe Stone Circle, *5 km (3 miles) S of Downpatrick:* large standing stones enclose a Neolithic burial mound, most impressive.

Ballywhite Hill, *4 km (2 miles) N of Portaferry:* highest point of Ards Peninsula, fine views.

Castle Ward (NT), *near Strangford:* most unusual house, part classical, part Strawberry Hill 'Gothic', apparently because Lord and Lady Bangor could not agree on the design of their new house. Lady Bangor's gothic boudoir is most eccentric and well worth seeing. Victorian laundry offers fascinating glimpse of great-grandma's wash day. Landscaped grounds include old Castle Ward, 15th c

tower house, formal garden, Temple Water with Greek temple folly, nature trails, tearooms, caravan park, wildfowl collection. Castleward theatre, regular performances. *House open, Easter, daily, 1 p.m.-6 p.m. May-Aug, daily, except Thurs,1 p.m.-6 p.m. Sept, Oct, Sat, Sun, 1 p.m.-6 p.m. Access to grounds all year, daily until dusk.* ☎ *(039686)204.* &

Cloughey, *3 km (2 miles) SW of Portavogie. EC Thurs.* Village set on shores of beautiful sandfringed bay. Just behind village is ruin of Kirkistown Castle, built 1622.

Downpatrick, *14 km (9 miles) W of Strangford. All day closing Wed. TIO:* ☎ *(0396)613426, all year. Bus enquiries: bus station,* ☎ *(0396)612384.* County town of Down. St Patrick said to be buried in churchyard of Down Cathedral at top of English Street. Fine walk along Georgian Mall beside cathedral. **Down County Museum:** Stone Age artefacts and Bronze Age gold ornaments found locally are on display in this converted jail. Ireland's patron saint is featured in the gatehouse, which is now St Patrick's heritage centre. *July—mid Sept, Mon-Fri, 11 a.m.-5 p.m., Sat, Sun, 2 p.m.-5 p.m. Mid Sept—June, Tues-Fri, 11 a.m.-5 p.m., Sat, 2 p.m.-5 p.m.* ☎ *(0396)615218.* **Downpatrick railway station:** steam train trips. *Details,* ☎*(0396)830141.* **Down Arts Centre,** *2/6 Irish Street:* ☎ *(0396)615283: fine and applied art exhibitions, arts events. All year, Tues-Fri, 10 a.m.-10.30 a.m., Mon, Sat, 10 a.m.-5 p.m. (June-Aug, Mon-Sat, 9 a.m.-5 p.m.)* **Quoile Pondage** is pleasant 5 km (3 mile) stretch of river turned into lake by barrage. Starting from the old stone bridge in the town, the winding lake side path gives pleasant views of Quoile Castle ruins and old quays. NT nature reserve. Exhibits in the Quoile Centre. Guided walks, trails, fishing, picnic areas. *Visitor centre, Apr-Aug, Tues-Sun, 10 a.m.-5 p.m., Sept-Mar, Sat, Sun, 1 p.m.-5 p.m.* ☎ *(0396)615520. Grounds always open.* **Downpatrick Racecourse:** *about six meetings a year,* ☎ *(0396)841125.* Leisure Centre, inc. pool: *Market Street,* ☎ *(0396)613426.* & Downpatrick Golf Club, *9 holes,* ☎ *(0396)612152.*

Inch Abbey, *3 km (2 miles) NW of Downpatrick:* founded by Cistercians about 1180, now impressive ruin. *Apr-Sept, Tues-Sat, 10 a.m.-7 p.m. Sun,*

2 p.m.-7 p.m. Oct-Mar, Sat, 10 a.m.-4 p.m. Sun, 2 p.m.-4 p.m. Closed 1 p.m.-1.30 p.m.

Kearney, *near 5 tip of Ards Peninsula:* delightful 19th c fishing village, restored by NT. Pleasant walks along rocky shore.

Killough, *4 km (2 miles) SW of Ardglass.* One long street lined with sycamore trees, has quite a continental air. Pleasant walk round harbour area, taking in partly 18th c parish church, old warehouses. On hilltop to S of village, tower of former windmill.

Killyleagh, *All day closing Thurs.* Delightful village on W shore of Strangford Lough, 6 km (4 miles) from Strangford as the crow flies, but 24 km (15 miles) by road via Downpatrick because of River Quoile estuary flowing into the lough. Pleasant walks around Killyleagh's broad streets and up to gates of the castle. Interesting harbour area.

Kirkistown, *just inland from Portavogie:* motor and motorcycle racing circuit, ☎ *(02477)71325.* &

Millin Bay, *just S of Kearney:* Tara Fort on hilltop overlooking bay is impressive Celtic defensive farmstead.

Mound of Downpatrick, *just NW of town:* hillock raised in 12th c for castle construction. Ideal for a light climb.

Portavogie, *11 km (7 miles) NE of Portaferry. EC Thurs.* Main fishing village of Ards Peninsula. Harbour often filled with fishing boats. Occasional evening quayside fish auctions, two beaches.

St John's Point, *just S of Killough:* rugged coastal walk, stretches for some 4 km (2 miles). See ruins of 10th c church.

Saul, *3 km (2 miles) NE of Downpatrick:* St Patrick landed here in 432 to begin his Irish mission and said to have died here in 493. Modern memorial church of St Patrick (CI) on height above village. 1.5 km (1 mile) W is Sliabh Padraig hill, topped by a huge granite figure of the Saint.

Strangford, *ferry enquiries:* ☎ *(039686)637. Ferry from Portaferry. EC Wed.* Attractive little harbour area facing Portaferry across the mouth of Strangford Lough. Strangford Castle: imposing 16th c edifice. *Open by arr. with caretaker.* Strangford Lough Wildlife Scheme: seven refuge areas around lough shores, also hides, for watching many varieties of water birds. Permits: A. Irvine, warden, *Castle Ward, Strangford,* ☎ *(039686)204.*

Struel Wells, *2.5 km (1.5 miles) S of Saul, near Downpatrick:* once a popular place of pilgrimage. St Patrick said to have blessed the wells. Site includes ruined church, drinking well, eye well, ruins of bathhouses for men and women (no mixed bathing!). *Open all year.*

Rostrevor

Pop. 2,100, 1.5 km (1 mile) by ferry from Omeath, 14 km (9 miles) SE of Newry. EC Wed. Bus enquiries: Edward Street bus depot, Newry, ☎ *(0693)63531.*

A small, delightfully nostalgic seaside town with a clear Victorian influence. An excellent centre for exploring Carlingford Lough and the Mountains of Mourne, just N behind the town.

Rostrevor Forest, *behind the town:* from car park, 0.8 km (0.5 mile) walk to viewpoint with panorama of lough. More strenuously, there is a walk to Cloghmore (Big Stone), perched at 820 m (900 ft), on a spur of Slievemartin. Another path to Cloghmore goes from shore level across the Oakwood and Fiddlers' Green. For a more leisurely stroll try the square, with its ancient trees and the area along the front.

AROUND ROSTREVOR

Ballykeel, *just N of Mullaghbawn:* fine Stone Age dolmen.

Castle Ward, near Strangford, Co. Down

Bessbrook, *5 km (3 miles) NW of Newry.* Good walks round main College and Charlemont squares. Also see huge old mill, with dam, sluices, weirs. As the town was founded just over 100 years ago by a Quaker linen manufacturer, there isn't a pub in sight. However, if you visit the nearby hamlet of Camlough, it has six to compensate. Walk: from old tramway depot, follow route of long closed track through woodlands and past several old mills into Newry.

'Bush Town', *5 km (3 miles) E of Hilltown on B27,* fairy thorn tree is largest in north of Ireland, in triangle formed by junction of Bryansford and Kilkeel roads.

Cairnhill House, *1.5 km (1 mile) NE of Newry on the B8/A25:* weeping wych elm tree in garden has greatest spread of foliage in Ireland, 71 m (232 ft).

Camlough Lake, *3 km (2 miles) SW of Bessbrook, off B30:* paths by NE shore, excellent climb to top of nearby Camlough Mountain, 420 m (1,389 ft).

Cassy Water Valley, *8 km (5 miles) E of Rostrevor:* one of the best walks in the Mournes. Kilfeaghan dolmen is W of lane leading up the valley.

Cloghoge, *5 km (3 miles) S of Newry:* start of fine walk to top of Flagstaff Hill, excellent views. Return through Newry Forest to canal side.

Cranfield Point, *6 km (4 miles) SW of Kilkeel:* fine beach and dunes popular with campers and caravanners.

Derrymore House, *1.5 km (1 mile) S of Bessbrook on A25:* late 18th c thatched manor house with interesting furnishings. 1800 Act of Union between Ireland and Britain said to have been drafted here. 19 ha (48 acre) park open daily. *House by arr, National Trust, Rowallane, Saintfield, Ballynahinch, Co. Down, BT24 7LM., ☎ (0238)510721.*

Fairy Glen, *3 km (2 miles) N of Rostrevor:* delightfully scenic, with small waterfalls on Kilbroney River and rustic paths, ideal for a quiet stroll.

Greencastle, *just NE of Cranfield Point:* well-preserved ruin of 13th c Norman castle, built at same time as Carlingford Castle, across the lough. *Apr-Sept, Tues-Sat, 10 a.m.-7 p.m., Sun, 2 p.m.-7 p.m.*

Hilltown, *13 km (8 miles) N of Rostrevor on B25.* Its numerous pubs are reminder of the village's brandy-smuggling past. Attractive tree-lined square.

Kilkeel, *16 km (10 miles) E of Rostrevor on A2. EC Thurs. Sept.-May, all day. TIO: Recreation Hall, Mourne Esplanade, all year.* Main fishing port of S Down. Winding streets, stepped footpaths, many old houses of great character, and an interesting harbour area. Water in granite trough at 14th c church ruins at town centre said to cure warts. Kilkeel Golf Club, *9 holes, ☎ (06937)62296.*

Killevy, *5 km (3 miles) S of Camlough:* site of one of Ireland's most important early nunneries, founded late 5th c.

Mount Norris, *on Bessbrook-Markethill B133:* attractive little village with good walks 3 km (2 miles) W of Shaw's Lake. NT wooded glen with trout stream and waterfall is 5 km (3 miles) SW. Just S of glen, in old burial ground of Ballymoyer, is the

grave of Florence MacMoyer, an informer who brought about the execution of St Oliver Plunkett and was so detested that her grave was heaped with stones. Sometimes a stone or two is still added.

Narrow Water Castle, *3 km (2 miles) on Newry side of Warrenpoint:* 16th c ruins on rock connected with shore by causeway. *July, Aug, Tues-Sat, 10 a.m.-7 p.m., Sun, 2 p.m.-7 p.m.*

Newry, *16 km (10 miles) NW of Rostrevor. EC Wed. TIO: Bank Parade, ☎ (0693)66232, all year. Bus enquiries: Edward Street bus depot, ☎ (0693)63531.* Though much scarred by the Troubles, the town has many interesting features and is a good shopping centre. The Clanrye River and canal cross the town, and the canal quaysides have interesting 18th c warehouses. **Cathedral of Ss. Patrick and Colman** (C), *Hill Street:* dates from 1825 with interesting mosaics and stained glass. **St Patrick's Church** (CI), *Church Street:* incorporates part of 16th c tower. **Newry Arts Centre Museum,** *Bank Parade:* range of artistic activities, also museum, with interesting local exhibits. Newry Museum, in the arts centre, has archaeological items, table used by Lord Nelson on HMS Victory. History of the 'Gap of the North'. Touring exhibitions. *All year, Mon-Fri, 11 a.m.-5 p.m., Sat, by arr. ☎(0693)66232.* **Newry Canal** *Kilmorey Park, between Stream Street and Cowan Street:* attractively wooded. Good coarse angling venue, boating, canalside walks. Newry sports complex, daily, ☎ *(0693)69214.* Newry Golf Club, *18 holes, ☎ (0693)63871.*

Poyntzpass, follow banks of canal 6 km (4 miles) S of Jerrettspass, passing hump-backed bridges and locks.

Silent Valley, *8 km (5 miles) N of Kilkeel, off B27:* reservoir and parkland; two huge reservoirs for supplying water to Belfast. Approach by 5 km (3 mile) long lakeside road to dam. Good park between entrance gates and Silent Valley dam. Coffee shop and information centre. *All year, daily. SO, bus tours.*

Slieve Gullion, *8 km (5 miles) SW of Newry:* massive 'whale-backed' mountain. Fine scenic drive. From summit, with its ancient passage grave and wild goats, you can see smoke of both Dublin and Belfast on a really clear day. Adjoining forest has caravan site, picnic areas, walks to viewpoints. SE side of mountain, Hawthorn Hill, has nature and crafts exhibition centre, *all year, daily, 10 a.m.-sunset.*

Spelga Dam, *6 km (4 miles) SW of Hilltown:* try the 'magnetic mile' effect similar to that at Gortin Forest Park in Tyrone. Your car will appear to go uphill when facing downhill and vice versa; breathtaking views. The road also runs N past Fofanny Reservoir, from where a loop road goes E across Trassey River, the start of the popular walk up the wide river valley to Hare's Gap.

Warrenpoint, *5 km (3 miles) W of Rostrevor. EC Wed, winter only. TIO: Information Office, Boating Pool, ☎ (0762)52256, July, Aug.* Spacious resort with fine square and tree-lined promenade, two piers ideal for fishing, walking. Summer events include open air art exhibition. Market in square, *Sun.* Summer boat excursions to Omeath. Warrenpoint Golf Club, *18 holes, ☎ (06937)53695.*

The
MIDLANDS

Carlow

Pop. 12,000, 84 km (52 miles) SW of Dublin, 40 km (25 miles) SE of Portlaoise, 38 km (24 miles) NE of

Kilkenny. *EC Thurs. TIO, ☎ (0503)31554, May-Sept. Bus and train enquiries, ☎ (0503)31633.*

A pleasant, modest town, a former Anglo-Norman stronghold, and 'capital' of the second smallest county in Ireland. Though recently industrialised, it retains a quiet air, and there are interesting walks to be had around older streets and along the River Barrow, where it is joined by the Burrin tributary, forming a four angled lake.

Cathedral of the Assumption, (C), *off Tullow Street:* consecrated in 1833, this Gothic-style edifice has Hogan marble monument to Bishop Doyle, a 19th c writer on politics and current affairs under the pen-name 'JKL', 'James of Kildare and Leighlin'. Stained glass windows by Harry Clarke. ♿ **Carlow Castle,** *near Barrow bridge:* ruins of Norman castle, W wall and two flanking towers. Captured by Cromwell in 1650 and later returned to Earl of Thomond. In 1814, Dr Middleton, a local physician, tried to convert it to a lunatic asylum and put explosives in walls to reduce their thickness. In the event, most of the castle had to be demolished for safety reasons. Access with permission, through adjacent Corcoran's Mineral Water factory, *Mon-Fri.* **Courthouse,** *junction of Dublin Street and Dublin Road:* design of this 19th c building 'lifted' from the Parthenon. **Museum,** *Haymarket:* old theatre full of fascinating local curios. Reconstructed forge and kitchen. Military and religious items, also relics of carpenter's and cooper's trades. Entrance from adjoining car park. *May-Sept, Mon-Fri, 11 a.m.-5.30 p.m. ☎ (0503)31532.* **Library,** *Dublin Street:* very interesting collection of local antiquarian books. *Mon-Fri, ☎ (0503)31126.* Technical College Library, Kilkenny Road: see equipment used by John Tyndall, 19th c founder of science of thermodynamics, *term time, Mon-Fri, 9 a.m.-5 p.m. Check with librarian first, ☎ (0503)31324.* See Ballinabranna. **Carlow Genealogical Centre** and **Carlow County Heritage Society,** *4 Kennedy Street:* genealogical information and the largest collection of local archival material in Ireland. ☎ *(0503)42399.* **Oak Park,** *3 km (2 miles) N of Carlow:* Agricultural Research Institute run by Teagasc. Extensive woodland lakes, wildfowl sanctuary, visitors welcome. *Mon-Fri, 9 a.m.-5 p m., ☎ (0503)31425.* Walks in vicinity of Haymarket, also S along Barrow towpath to Clogrennan or N along E bank of river. Swimming pool: outdoor, heated, *Athy Road Park, daily, June, July, Aug.* **Carlow Super Bowl** *Barrack Street, ☎ (0503)41555.* Bicycles: A. E. Coleman, *Dublin Street, ☎ (0503)31273.* Golf Club, *18 holes, ☎ (0503)31695.*

AROUND CARLOW

Altamont Gardens, *9 km (5 miles) of Tullow, off N16:* fine gardens set by the River Slaney, with views of the W side of Wicklow mountains. Ornamental lakes. Walks and nature paths. Home-made teas. *Easter-Oct, Sun, 2 p.m.-6 p.m. Otherwise by arr., ☎ (0503)59128.*

Ballinabranna, *near Carlow:* plaque on Old School to famous 19th c physicist, John Tyndall, who had primary education here.

Ballymoon Castle, *3 km (2 miles) E of Muine Bheag:* probably built between 1290 and 1310. According to local tradition, never finished. Although in ruins, doorways and fireplace of great hall in excellent condition.

Browne's Hill Demesne, *3 km (2 miles) E of Carlow on L7:* magnificent dolmen, the 100 tonne capstone is largest in Ireland.

Duckett's Grove Castle, *between Tullow and Castledermot on L31A:* built in 1830, burned down in 1933. Majestic ruins.

Killeshin, *5 km (3 miles) W of Carlow on L31:* magnificent Romanesque doorway, all that remains of 6th c monastery founded by St Diarmuid. Nearby is old rath called Castlequarter, with striking view of Barrow Valley. In clear weather, you will see nine counties.

Leighlinbridge, *11 km (7 miles) S of Carlow on N9:* W half of 16th c tower, access via nearby house. See Great Mound with circular moat, off *Kilkenny Road:* site of ancient palace of Kings of Leinster. Village set on banks of River Barrow marks edge of ancient 'pale'.

Muine Bheag, (Bagenalstown), *18 km (11 miles) S of Carlow.* The anglicised name comes from Walter Bagenal of Dunleckney, who tried to build a town of great architectural splendour, called Bersaille. Task never completed. Carrigbeg Riding Establishment, ☎ *(053)21157.*

St Mullins, *15 km (9 miles) S of Borris:* beautifully situated village on E bank of River Barrow. Monastic remains include St Mullins' Abbey and 7th c ruins of St Moling's monastery. Pleasant walks in village and nearby woodlands. Good coarse fishing.

Tullow, *12 km (7 miles) SE of Carlow:* annual show, *Aug 15,* horse and cattle competitions, goats' and pets' contests, trade displays, usually including a Bible society stand. Costumed riders take part in horse and trap competitions. All good, clean fun. *Tullow Museum, Bridge Street:* display includes the vestments of Fr John Murphy, the priest who led the insurrection at Vinegar Hill outside Enniscorthy in 1798. *All year, Sun aft, summer, also Wed aft.* ☎ *(0503)51337.*

Windy Gap, *on N80 between Carlow and Stradbally:* striking views.

Carrick-on-Shannon

Pop. 2,000, 48 km (30 miles) SE of Sligo, 162 km (101 miles) NW of Dublin. EC Wed. TIO, ☎ (078)20170, May-Sept. Bus and train enquiries, ☎ (078)20036.

Leitrim has the smallest population of any county in Ireland and Carrick-on-Shannon is the smallest county town. A noted angling centre, and the mecca of Shannon cruising. Attractive walk from river banks to town centre. Shannon Boat Rally: *late July, details: TIO.*

Costelloe Chapel, reputed to be the second smallest in the world. No interior fittings, apart from altar and stained glass window. *Open daily.* **Old Barrel Store** *beside the bridge* has art and craft shows.

Leisure Activities: Canoes: Kennedys, Jamestown Bridge. Cruisers: Athlone Cruisers; Carrick Craft, *The Marina,* ☎ *(078)20236;* Emerald Star Line, ☎ *(078)20234;* Flagline (1972), *The Marina,* ☎ *(078)20172;* Weaver Boats, *St Patrick's Park,* ☎ *(078)20204.* Swimming pool: outdoor, heated, *summer, daily,* Bicycles: Fred Holt, *Bridge Street,* ☎ *(078)20184.*

AROUND CARRICK-ON-SHANNON

Aghrane, *16 km (10 miles) SW of Roscommon, near Ballygar on N63:* forest walks, picnic area, lay-by parking.

Arigna Mountains, *W of Lough Allen:* route round mountains clearly signposted, superb views of Leitrim countryside.

Ballinamore, *24 km (15 miles) NE of Carrick.* Pleasantly set amid hills and near Garadice Lake, ideal centre for angling, golfing, horse riding. Boats: *details: TIO,* ☎ *(078)44021. June-Sept.* Tully Farm Riding Centre, ☎ *(078) 44177.* Rent-a-Bike, *High street,* ☎ *(078)44091.*

Boyle, *14 km (9 miles) W of Carrick on N4. EC Wed, July, Aug; rest of year, all day. TIO,* ☎ *(079)62145, June-Aug. Bus, train enquiries,* ☎ *(079)62027.* Cistercian Abbey, founded 1161, ruins near river on N side of town. Nave, choir, transepts still in good repair. Among domestic buildings, kitchen and hospitium are best preserved. *Mid June-mid Sept, daily, 9.30 a.m.-6.30 p.m. Rest of year, key with*

Boyle Abbey, Co, Roscommon

caretaker. ☎ *(079)62604.* Boats: Peter Blishen, Lakeshore Restaurant, ☎ *(079)62214;* M. Burke, Knockvicar, ☎ *(079)67012;* Mrs A. Harrington, Glencarne House, *Ardcarne,* ☎ *(079)67013;* Mrs K. Mattimoe, *Lakeview, Shannon Cruisers,* ☎ *(079)67007;* Bicycles: M. E. Sheerin, *Main Street,* ☎ *(079)62010.*

Castlerea, *30 km (19 miles) NW of Roscommon on N60. Train enquiries,* ☎ *(0907)20031.* Attractive town on wooded reach of River Suck. People's Park has sports facilities, inc. swimming pool. *Clonalis, just W of town:* great 19th c manor, unique among great houses of Ireland in being owned by a Gaelic family. Drawing room is comfortably Victorian, library has 19th c portraits and many fine books. Private chapel. Museum, inc. Carolan's harp and portrait, Gaelic manuscripts, glass porcelain, Victorian costumes, Sheraton furniture. *June-Sept, Mon-Sat, 11 a.m.-5.30 p.m., Sun, 2 p.m.-6 p.m.* ☎ *(0907)20014.*

Clooneyquin, *5 km (3 miles) SW of Elphin on N61:* birthplace of Percy French, noted song writer and entertainer.

Derrycarne, *just N of N4 at Dromod:* attractive picnic area with access to Shannon.

Dromonona, *4 km (2 miles) W of Boyle on L133:* site of one of largest dolmens in Ireland, measuring 4.5 x 3.3 m (14 x 11 ft).

Drumshanbo, *13 km (8 miles) N of Carrick on T54.* Angling centre near S end of Lough Allen, reputed to have best pike in N Europe. An Tostal Festival: everything Irish, dancing, music, singing, *June, details: Carrick TIO.* Swimming pool: outdoor, heated. *All year, daily.*

Drumsna, *8 km (5 miles) SE of Carrick.* Huge ancient earthworks of Doon just S of village.

Elphin, *13 km (8 miles) SW of Carrick-on-Shannon:* cathedral town. Smith Hill, *1.5 km (1 mile) NW,* held to be birthplace of Oliver Goldsmith.

Fenagh abbey, *5 km (3 miles) S of Ballinamore:* ruins of Gothic church, only remains of monastery founded by St Columba.

Frenchpark, *13 km (8 miles) SW of Boyle on L11:* Douglas Hyde, founder of the Gaelic League and first president of Ireland was born at Ratra House 5 km (3 miles) to W, now a shell in the middle of a field. His grave is in the old Protestant churchyard about 1.5 km (1 mile) W, on S side of N5. Interpretative centre, *details: Roscommon TIO.* Remains of 13th c Dominican Cloonshanville Abbey.

Hill of Rathcroghan, *10 km (6 miles) SE of French-park:* ancient palace of Kings of Connacht once stood here. 0.8 km (0.5 miles) SW is cave of Owneygrat, The Cave of the Cats, in ancient times considered to be the entrance to the Other World.

Kilronan Forest, *turn L 1.5 km (1 mile) NW of Keadue:* attractive walks midway between Lough Allen and Lough Key.

Lough Allen, the 48 km (30 mile) lakeside road gives fine if sometimes bleak views of lake.

Lough Key Forest Park, *3 km (2 miles) E of Boyle on N4:* one of Ireland's most beautiful. Walks through extensive forest area, with detailed and most interesting nature trail. Bog Gardens, a mass of rhododendrons and azaleas in early summer, feature many peat-loving plants and shrubs. Deer enclosure. Attractive gazebo gives excellent views of lake and islands. Fine views from Moylurg Tower, on hill where mansion once stood—destroyed by accidental fire in 1957. One of house's subterranean passageways has been restored and lit. Restaurant and shop open during summer. Picnic area, caravan park, camping site, fishing, swimming, water sports. Boats from the shop, ☎ *(079)62214.* Lake cruises, ☎ *(079)67007.*

Lough Rynn demesne, *near Roosky:* estate with three walled gardens, arboretum, coach yard, dairy yard, farm yard. Craft shop, restaurant. *May-mid Sept, daily, 10 a.m.-7 p.m.* ☎ *(078)31427.*

Oran, *14 km (9 miles) NW of Roscommon on N60.* Stump of round tower, meagre remains of pre-Romanesque church, all that is left of early monastery.

Roscommon, *43 km (27 miles) S of Carrick. EC Thurs. TIO,* ☎ *(0903)26342, June-Sept. Bus, train enquiries,* ☎ *(0903)26201.* County town of Co Roscommon, several interesting ruins. Indoor heated swimming pool. Horse- racing. **Roscommon Castle,** 13th c, attractively set on hillside. Dominican Friary, founded 1253, main ruins, church with N transept. The old jail, town square, once had a female hangman (hangperson?).

Slieve Bawn Hills, *E of Strokestown:* worth climbing for views over plains of Roscommon and River Shannon.

Source of the Shannon, *from Dowra, at N end of Lough Allen, take L43 N for about 6 km (4 miles), turn R for about 3 km (2 miles).* Source signposted; 0.8 km (0.5 mile) climb.

Strokestown, *19 km (12 miles) S of Carrick.* **Strokestown Park House:** at the end of Ireland's widest main street, an avenue leads to the house, built in the Palladian style in the 1730s. The house includes Ireland's last galleried kitchen, where the lady of the house could look down on the culinary activity without taking part. Fully restored, the house includes reception rooms, a school room and a nursery. In the study, documents deal with the great famine of the late 1840s. The vast parkland surrounding the house has been replanted. Also see stables. Famine museum planned. *June-Sept, Tues-Sun, 12 noon-5 p.m.* ☎ *(078)33013.* **St John's Heritage Centre:** photographic exhibitions, audio-visual presentations, genealogical research service. *All year, Tues-Fri, 9.30 a.m.-5.30 a.m., Sat, Sun, 2 p.m.-6 p.m.* ☎ *(078)33380.*

Cavan

Pop. 3,300, 114 km (71 miles) NW of Dublin, 30 km (19 miles) SW of Clones. All day closing Mon. TIO, ☎ (049)31942, all year. Bus enquiries: Bus Eireann. Cavan, ☎ (049)31353.

A delightful small town, attractively set among low hills. Its many nearby lakes offer excellent coarse fishing.

St Mary's Franciscan Abbey, Abbey street (rear of Post Office): founded by Giolla losa O'Reilly in 1300, only belfry tower remains. Adjacent park. Cavan Crystal, *Dublin Road:* see fascinating spectacle of blowing and handcutting glass, *closed first two weeks Aug. details,* ☎ *(049)31800.* Sports Centre: special events, *details, TIO.* Bicycles: Wheels, *Farnham Street,* ☎ *(049)31831.* Golf Club, *18 holes,* ☎ *(049)31283.* Cavan Equestrian Centre, ☎ *(049)32017.*

AROUND CAVAN

Baileborough, *30 km (18 miles) SW of Cavan on L24.* Excellent coarse fishing in five neighbouring lakes. *Castle Lake,* car park, picnic place, forest walks.

Cohaw, *5 km (3 miles) SE of Cootehill on L46 to Shercock:* good example of prehistoric double court cairn, which looks as if two single cairns were placed back to back.

Cornafean, *13 km (8 miles) SW of Cavan and 3 km (2 miles) off L15 Cavan-Killeshandra road:* Corr House, the Pighouse Collection, housed in a converted pighouse, a fascinating collection of local curios including three legged pots, wooden porringers and cow bells. *All year, by arr.,* Mrs Phyllis Faris, ☎ *(049)37248.*

Cuilcagh House, *5 km (3 miles) NE of Virginia, beside Cuileagh Lough:* site of house and mound called Stella's Bower, where Jonathan Swift had inspiration for *Gulliver's Travels.*

Headford/Deerpark, *2 km (1 mile) W of Virginia off L49:* pleasant walks through broadleaf and conifer woodland.

St Canice's Cathedral, Kilkenny

Kilmore, *5 km (3 miles) W of Cavan on old Killeshandra Road:* 12th c Romanesque door built into cathedral, (NM).

Killykeen Forest Park, *3 km (2 miles) E of Killeshandra and 13 km (8 miles) W of Cavan turn NW off L15:* attractively set by shores of River Erne and Lough Oughter. Excellent coarse fishing area. Car park, picnic area, boating, swimming, forest walks, nature trails, shop, restaurant, marina.

Loughcrew Hills, *13 km (8 miles) S of Virginia:* about 30 prehistoric passages graves. Excellent views across central plain to western mountains.

Mulrick, *3 km (2 miles) SW of Gowna village in S Cavan:* forest walks with fine views of Lough Gowna.

Murmod Hill, *3 km (2 miles) N of Virginia:* fine vantage point Lough Ramor.

Oldcastle, local parish church with relic of St Oliver Plunkett. &

Rann Ford, *6 km (4 miles) W of Cavan on River Erne system:* Cloughhoughter Castle, well preserved 13th/14th c circular tower castle, attractive picnic site.

St Colmcille's Abbey, *8 km (5 miles) SW of Belturbet, T52 Milltown, minor road to N shore of Derrybrick Lake:* although founded in 6th c, present ruins are 14th c, also round tower, in exceptionally beautiful setting.

Shantemon Hill, *6 km (4 miles) NE of Cavan:* row of pillars on N slope of hill marks inauguration place of O'Reillys, ancient Lords of east Breifne.

Slieve Rushen Mountain, *3 km (2 miles) NW of Ballyconnell:* from summit excellent views of much of Erne system.

Virginia, *31 km (19 miles) SW of Cavan.* Excellent coarse fishing in adjacent Lough Ramor and neighbouring lakes and rivers.

Kilkenny

Pop. 10,000, 117 km (73 miles) SW of Dublin, 101 km (63 miles) NW of Rosslare, 193 km (120 miles) NE of Killarney. TIO: Rose Inn Street, ☎ *(056)21755, all year. Bus and train enquiries,* ☎ *(056)64933.*

This ancient city, set attractively on the banks of the river Nore, has a distinguished and colourful past, and is now designated as one of Ireland's major heritage towns. The Confederate Irish Parliament regularly sat here, the Lord Lieutenant had a residence in the town and during the 17th c it came close to upstaging Dublin as an administrative centre. It wears its history well however, the atmosphere is relaxed and peaceful, and though the town really ought to be lingered over, it can be explored in a day. Arts Week: multi-media arts event, including music in St Canice's Cathedral, exhibitions in Kilkenny Castle Modern Art Gallery, readings, theatre, fringe performances. *End Aug, early Sept,* ☎ *(056)22118.*

St Canice's Cathedral (CI): 13th c, one of most beautiful in Ireland. From tower, magnificent views of city and much of county. Tower *by arr. only.* *Black Abbey, Abbey Street:* built 1225, nave and transept restored as Dominican church. & Museum: *next door to abbey, in presbytery.* Probably smallest museum in Ireland, with many religious items, such as a liturgical directory printed in Paris

Kilkenny Castle, Kilkenny

in 1475 and one of oldest books in existence. Ring Presbytery doorbell. *St Francis' abbey, 14th c, is in grounds of Smithwick's Brewery.* Video of brewery and tour of abbey ruins, *all year, Mon-Fri,* ☎*(056)21021.* *Kilkenny Castle,* built in 12th c and remodelled since, notably in Victorian times. Rooms restored and open to view in the east wing include the Long Gallery, the castle kitchen and the modern Butler art gallery, where regular exhibitions are held. Work is under way on restoring the rest of the castle. The grounds, with their woodland walks, lake and formal terraced garden, have also been restored. *Apr, May, daily, 10.30 a.m.-5 p.m.*

June-Sept, daily, 10 a.m.-7 p.m., Oct-Mar, Tues-Sat, 10.30 a.m.-12.45 p.m., 2 p.m.-5 p.m., Sat, 2 p.m.-5 p.m., Sun, 11 a.m.-12.45 p.m., 2 p.m.-5 p.m. Times may change due to restoration work; telephone first, ☎ *(056)21450.* & *Black Freren Gate, near Black Abbey:* only remaining medieval gate. *St Canice's Library, just N of Cathedral:* some 3,000 books, many 16th and 17th c, *by arr. with librarian.* *Tholsel, High Street:* Corporation regalia, including 1609 Mayor's sword and 1677 Mace, old records and charters. *By arr. with Town Clerk.*

Kilkenny Design Workshops, opp. Castle: permanent display of glassware, jewellery, woven goods. Workshops not open. *Mon-Sat, 9 a.m.-1 p.m.; 2 p.m.-6 p.m.,* ☎ *(056)22118.* Rudolf Heltzel, *Lower Patrick Street,* makes gold, silver jewellery. *Mon-Fri, 9 a.m.-5.30 p.m.,* ☎ *(056)21497.* Michael Rafter, silversmith, *John Street.* **Rothe House,** *Parliament Street:* 1594 Tudor merchant's house, meticulously restored. Museum, with many items of local historical and cultural interest, such as old pikes, old picture postcards and 1850 Kilkenny-made double bass. On top floor, see amazingly restored ceiling, held together by dowels. Not a single nail was used. The third of the three houses which make up Rothe House has been restored, for an extension of the *museum,* an *interpretative centre,* and the *genealogy centre* for Co Kilkenny. *Apr-Oct, daily,10 a.m.-12.30 p.m., 3 p.m.-5 p.m. Oct-Apr, Sat, Sun, 3 p.m.-5 p.m.* ☎ *(056)22893.* Cityscope exhibition on first floor of tourist information office in Rose Inn Street is a vast model of Kilkenny as it was in 1642, down to the very last detail. The presentation, complete with computer-controlled lighting, takes 20 mins. *Kyteler's Inn, St Kieran's Street:* Dame Alice Kyteler, a noted witch, said to have been born here 1280. Building has been an inn since 1324. Restored, with restaurant and bar, so you can contemplate the magical happenings of old in modern comfort, ☎ *(056)21064/21888.* Walking tours of Kilkenny's pubs leave from Kilkenny Castle: *May-mid-October, Mon, Wed, Fri, 8 p.m. For groups only, details, TIO.* *Tynan's Bridge House Bar, near Castle:*

authentic Edwardian interior, with marble counter, gas-lights. Outstanding traditional front looks onto river. *High Street,* the slips (alleys) and lanes between here and St Kieran's Street are worth exploring, as are lanes off far side of Parliament Street and High Street. Interesting walks from John's Bridge, below castle walls, along riverside path into open country. In opp. direction, along John's Quay towards St Canice's. Walking tours of Kilkenny leave from the TIO, four times daily. *Watergate Theatre*: Kilkenny's latest cultural venue, due to open spring 1993.

Leisure Activities: Greyhound racing: *St James's Park,* regular meetings, ☎ *(056)21214.* Swimming pool: indoor, heated, *Michael Street, daily, except Mon, Fri,* ☎ *(056)21380.* Bicycles: John Wall, *88 Maudlin Street,* ☎ *(05 6)21236.* Raleigh Cycle Centre, *5 John Street,* ☎*(056)62037.* Golf Club, *Glendine, 18 holes,* ☎ *(056)22125.*

AROUND KILKENNY

Abbeyleix, *35 km (22 miles) N of Kilkenny:* attractive town with broad main street, de Vesci demesne (open daily in summer) and CI church on demesne. Abbeyleix has been designated a heritage town, and a heritage centre is planned. *Morrissey's Pub* in the town centre has been preserved just as it was 80 years ago, full of old artefacts. *Heywood Gardens, Ballinakill, 8 km (5 miles) SE of Abbeyleix:* the manor house was destroyed by fire in 1950, but the extensive gardens, with lawns, pergola and terraces, designed by Edwin Lutyens, have been restored. *By arr, Midlands and East Tourism, Mullingar,* ☎ *(044)48761.*

Ballyragget, *11 km (7 miles) W of Castlecomer on L110:* attractively set on upper reaches of River Nore. Remains of large 15th c Ormonde castle.

Barrow River, *near Graiguenamanagh:* riverside walks, car park, picnic area.

Bennettsbridge, *8 km (5 miles) SE of Kilkenny on T20.* Attractively set on banks of River Nore. Fine stone bridge across river. Craft workshops.

Bishopswood, *3 km (2 miles) SW of Durrow on N8:* forest walks, picnic area, car park.

Brandon Hill, *near Graiguenamanagh:* well worth climbing for the patchwork views of Barrow valley, also forest walks.

Baunriach Summit, *13 km (8 miles) SE of Castlecomer:* dizzy views of Barrow valley from Carlow to New Ross.

Callan, *16 km (10 miles) SW of Kilkenny.* Birthplace of Edmund Ignatius Rice, founder of Irish Christian Brothers. The preserved 17th c farm house at Westcourt, where he was born in 1847, and adjacent monastery and chapel, are open to visitors. *Daily, 9.30 a.m.-6 p.m.* ☎ Br Nixon, *CBS, Callan,* ☎ *(056)25141.* ⓑ Kilkenny Crystal Company: glass cutting. *All year, Mon-Fri, 8.30 a.m.-5.30 p.m. Weekends by arr,* ☎ *(056)25132.* Callan Golf Club, *9 holes,* ☎ *(056)25136.*

Castlecomer, *20 km (12 miles) N of Kilkenny on N78.* Attractive town, once coalmining centre. Planned and built to classical design about 1636, it retains its good looks and handsome boulevard of lime trees. Pleasant walks in vicinity. *Reddy's pub,* coal miners museum, with helmets, tools, photographs.

Clara Castle, *10 km (6 miles) NE of Kilkenny, turn off N10 before Coolgrange:* 15th c fortified residence impressively set below mountains. Huge six storey tower, secret chambers and a 'murder hole'. *Key from cottage opp.*

Clashganny, *5 km (3 miles) S of Borris on L184:* walks by River Barrow and canal, car park, picnic area.

Dunmore Cave, *11 km (7 miles) N of Kilkenny on N78.* One of finest limestone caves in Ireland, with a number of large chambers and magnificent dripstone formations. Most striking is 'Market Cross' stalagmite, over 6 m (20 ft) high. Equipped with lighting and viewing galleries, full guide service. *Mid Mar-June, Tues-Sat, 10 a.m.-5 p.m., July-Sept, daily, 10 a.m.-6.30 p.m., Oct-Feb, Sat, Sun, BH, 10 a.m.-5 p.m.* ☎ *(056)67726.*

Foulksrath Castle, *13 km (8 miles) NW of Kilkenny on N77:* an Anglo-Norman foundation, now an extravagant Youth Hostel, ☎ *(056)27674.*

Gowran, *13 km (8 miles) E of Kilkenny, on N10.* Parish church built about 1225. Many interesting monuments. Gowran marble workshops: Jim Harding, ☎ *(056)26177;* Kilkenny Stone and Marble, ☎ *(056)26233.* Gowran race-course: ☎ *(056)26126.*

Graignamanagh, *32 km (20 miles) SE of Kilkenny.* Attractive village set on banks of River Barrow by

Brandon Hill, amid beautiful wood-lands. *Duiske Abbey,* the largest Cistercian foundation in Ireland, built between 1207 and 1240. Restored to its original glory and now used as parish church. ⓑ Walking tours of the town, by arr., Kilkenny TIO. Forest walks by canal bank. Youth Hostel.

Inistioge, *8 km (5 miles) SE of Thomastown on T20.* Thoroughly attractive village set in striking part of Nore valley. Tree-lined square, faced by adjoining C and CI churches; short walk to riverside. Excellent walks through surrounding countryside. Norman castle remains on rock above river. *Augustinian priory,* founded 1210, nave, tower, Lady Chapel remain. Island View, just S of village on New Ross road, as attractive as its name implies.

Jerpoint Abbey, *3 km (2 miles) SW of Thomastown, on N9:* Cistercian foundation dating from 12th c and one of finest monastic ruins in Ireland. Visitor centre. *Apr-mid June, mid Sept-mid Oct,Tues-Sun, 10 a.m.-1 p.m., 2 p.m.-5 p.m. Mid June-mid Sept, daily, 9.30 a.m.-6.30 p.m.*

Kells Priory, *13 km (8 miles) S of Kilkenny on L26:* founded 12th c. Ruins cover 2 ha (5 acres), running down to King's River. Car park, picnic area. 800 year old walled village.

Killamery, *8 km (5 miles) SW of Callan:* outstanding 8th c High Cross. Although much bruised by the weather, carvings can be clearly seen.

Thomastown, *18 km (11 miles) S of Kilkenny.* Busy market town on banks of River Nore. Ballylynch and Mountjuliet demesne, ideal for walks. Riverbank, with imposing castle ruin and flowers, excellent for stroll. The *Water Garden,* small but utterly peaceful garden, with trees, shrubs, aquatic plants. *Café. May 1-Sept 30, daily, 10 a.m.-6 p.m.,* ☎ *(056)24478.*

Tincashel crossroads, *3 km (2 miles) SE of Urlingford:* see a grand total of 12 castles from here.

Ullard, *5 km (3 miles) N of Graiguenamanagh:* attractive site near River Barrow with ancient church ruins, tall, sculptured cross.

Woodstock Park, *1 .5 km (1 mile) S of Inistioge, turn R off T20:* forest walks, arboretum, car park, picnic area.

Mullingar

Pop. 8,000, 80 km (50 miles) NW of Dublin, 51 km (32 miles) SE of Longford. EC Wed. TIO, ☎ *(044)48650, all year.*

The county town of Westmeath and centre of Ireland's top cattle raising area, so the steaks are normally good! Too often, visitors rush through the Midlands, convinced there are no sights on offer, however the quiet, unpretentious countryside around Mullingar deserves closer study.

Cathedral of Christ the King, striking structure built in 1936. See Mosaics of Ss. Patrick and Anne by Russian artist Boris Anrep, near high altar. Ecclesiastical museum above sacristy normally closed: sacristan for permission. *Town Museum* in 18th c Market House has many local history relics. *Late June-mid Sept, Mon-Fri, 2.30 p.m.-5.30 p.m. Military Museum, Columb Barracks,* has mementoes of the Army in Mullingar and UN service. *By arr,* ☎*(044)48391. Mullingar Pewter, 46 Dominick Street:* renowned pewter maker, *Mon-Fri, 9 a.m.-5.30 p.m.,* ☎*(044)48791.*

Library, Dublin Road: world's largest collection of Goldsmith first editions. *Mon-Fri, 9.30 a.m.-5.30 p.m. Closed 1 p.m.-2 p.m. Canton Casey's,* claimed to be the oldest pub in Midlands, dating back 200 years. Little changed interior, with old order books and ancient mirrors. *Greville Arms Hotel,* see realistic likeness of James Joyce, who had Mullingar connections, in the hotel reception area. Royal Canal: good walks along towpath. Town park: enjoyable walks just off town centre.

Leisure Activities: Greyhound track, *Kilbeggan Road: Tues, Sat, 8.30 p.m.,* ☎ *(044)48348.* Swim-

ming Pool: indoor, heated, Annebrook, *off Austin Friar Street, daily,* ☎ *(044)40262.* Golf Club, *Belvedere, 18 holes,* ☎ *(044)48366.*

AROUND MULLINGAR

Abbeyshrule Airfield, *24 km (15 miles) W of Mullingar on L18:* pleasure flights. Annual air show, early Aug, ☎ *(044) 57424.*

Abbeyshrule Cistercian Abbey, *6 km (4 miles) NE of Ballymahon, Co. Longford:* founded about 1200. Remains include choir and part of church nave.

Ardagh, *near Edgeworthstown:* delightfully neat little 19th c estate village, now given heritage designation. New heritage centre, details: *Longford TIO.*

Athlone, *EC Thurs. TIO,* ☎ *(0902)94630, Apr-Nov. Bus and train enquiries, (0902)72651.*

Historic town on Shannon banks, at the boundary between provinces of Leinster and Connacht. Good fishing and cruising centre. *Church of Ss. Peter and Paul,* (C) renaissance twin spires and dome, on W bank of river. ⓑ Ruins of 13th c Franciscan abbey, *Abbey Road. Athlone Castle, (NM) W bank of Shannon:* 13th c, from loopholes in curtain wall, good town views. Museum has many interesting items relating to town and district, *Apr-Oct, daily, 9.30 a.m.-6.30 p.m. Museum, June-mid Sept, Mon-Sat, 11.30 a.m.-1 p.m., 3 p.m.-6 p.m.* ☎ *(0902)94630. New interpretative centre* features John McCormack, world-famous tenor, born in Athlone. *Library,* by bridge over Shannon: many fine volumes of local interest, including books on McCormack and Goldsmith. Occasional exhibitions, art shows, ☎ *(0902)92166.* Parts of old town walls can be seen at Railway View on E side of river. *Glendeer Pet Farm, all year, Mon-Sat, 10 a.m.-6 p.m., Sun, 12 noon-6 p.m.* ☎*(0902)37147.* Good riverside walks. Shannon boat trips: *details from Athlone TIO.*

Leisure Activities: Swimming pool: indoor, heated, *Retreat Heights, daily.* Outdoor swimming in Lough Ree. Athlone Golf Club, *Hodson's Bay, 18 holes,* ☎ *(0902)92073.*

Auburn, *13 km (8 miles) NW of Athlone on N55;* ruins of Oliver Goldsmith's boyhood residence.

Barley Harbour, *near Newtowncashel, on E shore of Lough Ree:* home of Michael Casey, artist in bog oak. It takes several years from when he fishes pieces of oak from bog until they dry and are suitable for working. Worth a call. *Mon-Sat, 9 a.m.-5 p.m., all year.* ☎*(043)25297. Newtowncashel heritage centre, June-Sept, daily, 2.30 p.m.-6.30 p.m.*

Belvedere, *3 km (2 miles) S of Lynn, on NE shore of Lough Ennell:* great Gothic 'jealous wall' built by former Lord Belvedere to prevent his wife seeing her brother-in-law's mansion nearby. He believed his wife was having an affair with his brother. Gardens open to public: *May-Oct, daily, 12 noon-6 p.m.,* ☎ *(044)40861.*

Carrick Wood, *the shore of Lough Ennell, 10 km (6 miles) SE of Mullingar, take T9 Kilbeggan road:* forest walks by the shores of Lough Ennell.

Castlepollard, *21 km (13 miles) N of Mullingar on T10.* Tullynally Castle: seat of Pakenhams, Earls of Longford, for over 300 years. 12 ha (30 acres) of lawns, woods and walled garden set above Lough Derra'aragh. In castle courtyard, Victorian kitchens and laundries now 'life below stairs' museum. *Gardens open June -Sept, daily, 10 a.m.-6 p.m. Castle, July, Aug, daily, 2 p.m.-6 p.m.* ☎ *(044)61159.*

Centre of Ireland, at least two claimants! One spot round tower-like structure on hill, *3 km (2 miles) NE of Glasson,* the other a pillar stone on island off W shore of Lough Ree, *6 km (4 miles) NE of Athlone* and directly opposite Hodson Bay Hotel.

Clonmellon, *31 km (19 miles) NE of Mullingar:* ruins of 18th c castle, home of Sir Benjamin Chapman who designed the village. Obelisk next to castle commemorates a relative, Sir Walter Raleigh, who introduced the potato to Ireland.

Cloondara, *6 km (4 miles) W of Longford on N5 to Strokestown:* site of forgotten Richmond Harbour, where Royal Canal joins Camlin River and thence the Shannon. Tall warehouses and derelict locks create atmospheric setting. In Cloondara, delightful village of many bridges, Teach Cheoil (Irish music house) stages performances of Irish music during summer. Visitors cordially welcomed. SO. Details: Longford, TIO , ☎ *(043)46566.* ♿

Delvin, *21 km (13 miles) NE of Mullingar:* ruins of 12th c Delvin Castle (NM), built by Hugh de Lacy, Lord of Meath.

Edgeworthstown, (Mostrim), *13 km (8 miles) E of Longford on N4.* Long association with Edgeworth family, whose best-known member was novelist Maria.

Fore, *5 km (3 miles) E of Castlepollard:* Seven Wonders of Fore. Monastery in a bog: 13th c Benedictine Abbey of Ss. Feichin and Taurin more like a castle. Mill without a race: now in ruins, it had miraculous underground water supply, so no need for millrace (counts as two miracles). Tree with three branches: said never to have had more than three branches, in honour of Holy Trinity. Water that never boils: from spring by three branch tree. Never boils, ill luck said to overtake anyone who tries. Stone raised by St Feichin's prayer: huge lintel stone on low W door of St Feichin's church said to have been raised by him. Anchorite in stone: just outside village, on Castlepollard road, anchorite's cell by partly restored 6th c St Feichin's church. Also large motte, to E of village, on lower slopes of Ben of Fore. Abbey pub, paintings of seven wonders of Fore. Owners Michael and Beatrice Coffey mines of information.

Granard, *26 km (16 miles) NE of Longford.* Prominent motte on SW side of town topped by statue of St Patrick.

Hill of Ardagh, *6 km (4 miles) SW of Edgeworthstown:* good views across Lough Ree.

Levingston, *3 km (2 miles) N of Mullingar:* St Bridget's Well, stations and small oratory, signposted.

Lilliput House, *SW shores of Lough Ennell:* ruins of house once visited by Jonathan Swift; said to have helped inspire *Gulliver's Travels.*

Longford, *43 km (27 miles) NW of Mullingar.* All day closing Thurs. TIO, ☎ *(043)46566, June-Aug.* Bus and train enquiries, ☎ *(043)45208.*

County and market town on S bank of Camlin River. Lough Forbes, good for perch and pike, and the River Shannon, are within reach. See ruined Harbour Row home and printing works of *Vincent Gill,* great eccentric who ran *Longford News* newspaper from start in 1936 until not long before his death in 1976. *St Mel's Cathedral* (C), a striking 19th c renaissance building, with ecclesiastical museum, inc. vestments and objects dating to before penal days, *June-Sept, Mon, Wed, Fri, Sat, 11 a.m.-1 p.m.* **Longford museum heritage centre:** history of Co Longford, including noted writers Oliver Goldsmith, Maria Edgeworth, Padraic Colum and Leo Casey. Artefacts include tools used since the Stone Age. Typical old Longford folk kitchen. *All year, daily, 12 noon-2 p.m., 3 p.m.-6 p.m. By arr,* ☎*(043)46735.* **Carrigglas Manor:** romantic Tudor house with beautifully restored interiors. Costume and lace museum, Victorian gift shop, tea room. *Mid June-early Sept, weekdays, 1 p.m.-5.30 p.m. Aug, Suns, 1 p.m.-6 p.m. Closed, Tues, Wed. Or by arr,* ☎ *(043)45165.* Greyhound racing: Longford Park, ☎ *(043)46441.* Swimming pool: indoor, heated, *Market Square, daily all year,* ☎ *(043)46536.* Longford Golf Club, Glack, 18 holes, ☎ *(043)46310.*

Lough Ree, major recreational amenity area, offering fishing, boating, water-skiing. Lakeside picnic places.

Multyfarnham Abbey, (C), *11 km (7 miles) N of Mullingar:* Franciscan, largely 15th c, restored in recent years. In grounds of adjoining college, elaborate life-size stations of the cross.

Rathconnell Hill, *3 km (2 miles) NE of Mullingar off N52 to Delvin:* fine views. Nearby ruins of Rathconnell Court. Four small, attractive lakes to W and NW.

Rinndown Peninsula, *13 km (8 miles) N of Athlone on W shore of Lough Ree, just E of Lecarrow:* minor road from Lecarrow continues as track to lakeside where ruins of castle, church and other 13th c buildings combine to make one of the most eerie places in Ireland. Don't go at nightfall.

Ross, *turn left 7 km (5 miles) E of Finea on Mountnugent road:* forest walks along the S shore of Lough Sheelin.

St Munna's Church (NM), *9 km (6 miles) NE of Mullingar:* 15th c structure with four storey, castle-like tower and battlements. Caretaker in house opp. graveyard.

Slanemore Hill, *6 km (4 miles) NW of Mullingar:* 152 m (499 ft), three tumuli on summit, fine views of locality, including nearby Lough Owel.

Tang, *on N55 Athlone-Ballymahon road:* in heart of Goldsmith country. Flagstone of 'Busy Mill' that once stood nearby, mentioned by Goldsmith, is now doorstep of the Three Jolly Pigeons pub.

Uisneach Hill, (NM), *20 km (12 miles) W of Mullingar off to Ballymore:* ancient seat of High Kings of Ireland. Burial mounds and fort on hilltop. From here, on clear day, you can see 20 of Ireland's 32 counties. Large limestone boulder to W, the Catstone, was common centre of Ireland's five early provinces.

Naas

Pop. 10,100, 34 km (21 miles) SW of Dublin on the N7. No EC. Bus enquiries: Bus Eireann, Dublin, ☎ *(01)366111.*

In early times, Naas was the seat of the Kings of Leinster, and the North Mote, off Main Street, was the site of the ancient royal palace—indeed St Patrick is said to have camped on the site of the present Church of Ireland. Today Naas, county town of Co Kildare, is peaceful and prosperous.

Walks: behind courthouse in Main Street and around the canal harbour basin. You can also walk along Grand Canal towpath. Just SE of Naas, see park, with lake, between Blessington and Ballymore Eustace roads.

Leisure Activities: Mondello Park, *9 km (6 miles) NE of Naas:* motor racing, ☎ *(045)60200.* Naas Racecourse, ☎ *(045)97391.* Swimming pool: indoor, heated. Fair Green, *all year, Tues-Thur, Sat, Sun.* Golf Club, Kerdiffstown, 9 holes, ☎ *(045)97509.*

AROUND NAAS

Athy, *21 km (13 miles) SW of Naas,* market town, set on formerly strategic ford. **Town Hall heritage centre:** dating back to 1740, the market house has been renovated to include a museum with old photographs and memorabilia, material on the town during World War I and an 1802 marriage chalice. Also resource centre for the arts. *Details (045)31486/31109.* **Dominican church** (C), built near River Barrow in 1963-5. Pentagon shape with striking interior design. Impact heightened by George Campbell's stations of the cross and Bríd Ní Rinn's statues, high altar crucifix. ♿ **Woodstock Castle,** *just N of town:* 13th c ruins on W bank of River Barrow. Bicycles: Duthie Large Ltd, ☎ *(0507)31594.* Athy Golf Club, *9 holes,* ☎ *(0507)31729*

Ballitore, *4 km (3 miles) N of Moone, off T51:* old meeting house of once flourishing Quaker settlement now library and museum with interesting collection of mainly Quaker material. *All year, Wed, 7 p.m.-9 p.m., Fri, 4 p.m.-6 p.m., Sat, 11 a.m-1 p.m. Details,* ☎ *(01)683684.* **Crookstown Mill** has many fascinating artefacts from milling industry and old social order. *All year, daily, 10 a.m.-7 p.m. (5 p.m. in winter)* ☎*(0507)23222.*

Baltinglass, *30 km (19 miles) SW of Blessington on T42.* See impressive ruins of 12th c Baltinglass Abbey on banks of River Slaney. Abbey was sister foundation of Mellifont, Co. Louth. **Baltinglass Hill,** *2 km (1 mile) E of Baltinglass:* Remains of large Bronze Age cairn, good views.

Baltyboys, *near Blessington Lakes:* Youth Hostel.

Blessington: pleasant strolls from this tree-lined village to shores of Poulaphouca Reservoir.

Brittas, Slade Valley Golf Club,*18 holes,* ☎ *(01)582207.*

Carbury Hill, *6 km (4 miles) E of Edenderry:* fine views of Midland plain from where the T41 to Enfield crosses the shoulder of the hill.

Carnalway Church, (C), *3 km (2 miles) NE of Kilcullen:* 1922 window of St Hubert by Harry Clarke.

Castletown House, 18th c mansion fully restored by Irish Georgian Society. Splendid approach along 800 metre lime tree avenue. In house, see Long Gallery (with Venetian chandeliers), main hall and staircase (with Italian plasterwork), Print Room and Red Drawing Room. Festival of Music in Great Irish Houses held here, *Apr-Sept, Mon-Fri, 10 a.m.-6 p.m., Sat, 11 a.m.-6 p.m., Sun, BH, 2 p.m.-6 p.m. Oct-Mar, Mon-Fri, 10 a.m.-5 p.m., Sun, BH, 2 p.m.-5 p.m.* ☎ *(01)628 8252.*

Celbridge: Celbridge Abbey once home of Esther Van Homrigh, Swift's Vanessa, now residence of Hospitaller Brothers of St John of God, who run it as St Raphael's School for Mentally Handicapped Children. The brothers will be happy to show you over house; also see Vanessa's pleasure grounds along banks of Liffey, ☎ *(01)6288161.* ♿

Connolly's Folly, *3 km (2 miles) NW of Castletown House:* 40 m (140 ft) triumphal arch built in 1740 to provide relief work.

Curragh, *E of Kildare.* Curragh Racecourse: several meetings during year. Best-known is Irish Sweeps Derby, *June,* ☎ *(045)41205.* Curragh Camp ask to see marvellous 1920 armoured car, the 'Slievenamon', used by Michael Collins on his way to Béal-na-mBláth in 1922. Permission: Officer Commanding, ☎ *(045)41301.* Curragh Golf Club, *18 holes,* ☎ *(045)41714.*

Donadea Forest Park, *8 km (5 miles) SW of Kilcock on L181:* car park, picnic place, castle ruins, lake, forest walks. Nature trails inc. for disabled. Information centre, shop. *Sat, Sun, 12 p.m.-6 p.m.*

Donard, *16 km (11 miles) S of Naas:* Ballinclea Youth Hostel, ☎ *(045)53657.* ♿

Donnelly's Hollow, *4 km (3 miles) NW of Kilcullen, beside Ll9:* here the famous boxer beat English champion George Cooper in December, 1815. Long line of footprints said to have been made by Donnelly.

Glen of Imaal, *10 km (6 miles) S of Poulaphouca Lake:* walks in four forests, Leitrim, Knickeen, Knockamunnion, Stranahely. Five entrances to these forests on roads from Seskin Bridge and Ballinaclea to Knickeen Ford. Parts of glen used as army firing ranges—watch for the 'Danger' signs.

Hill of Allen, *13 km (8 miles) NE of Kildare Town, off L180:* famous in Irish legend as the otherworld seat of Fionn MacCumhail. Tower, 206 m (676 ft) summit, built by Sir George Aylmer in mid-19th c. Path to top of hill, good views.

Hollywood Glen, *S of Poulaphouca:* 3 km (2 miles) of natural delights. Fine views from top of nearby Church Mountain. At far end of glen, at Woodenboley, car park, forest walks, picnic area.

Jigginstown House, *2 km (1 mile) SW of Naas, by N7 to Kildare:* begun in 1632. If it had been finished, this would have been Ireland's largest private residence.

Kilcock. Kilcock Art Gallery, *School Street:* work by contemporary Irish artists. *All year, Mon-Sat, 10 a.m.-5 p.m.,* ☎ *(01)628 7619.* ♿

Japanese Gardens, near Kildare

Kilcullen, *13 km (8 miles) SW of Naas on N9.* If you're of a mind to, see arm of early 19th c prize fighter, Dan Donnelly, in glass case at Hide-Out bar by crossroads. They serve good lunches, ☎ *(045)81232.* W Attractive walk by Liffeyside, picnic area. Bicycles: T. J. Kelly, *Naas Road,* ☎ *(045)81388.*

Kildare, *13 km (8 miles) SE of Naas:* **St Brigid's Cathedral** (CI), 19th c restoration of 13th c structure. Round tower; climb to the top. Opening times posted in window of verger's house, beside church yard gate. **Kildare Way,** *37 km (22 mile)* walkway from Kildare to Edenderry. Flat for entire distance.

Leinster Aqueduct, *5 km (3 miles) N of Naas and just W of Sallins:* late 18th c engineering feat carries Grand Canal over River Liffey in great style. Long sections of towpath in this area are ideal for walking.

Lyons Hill, *4 km (3 miles) S of Celbridge:* one of early seats of Kings of Leinster, tremendous views.

Maynooth, *14 km (9 miles) N of Naas.* **St Patrick's College,** chapel, library, sacristy, museum, with ecclesiastical and scientific sections. 15th c chalices, induction coil horse shoeing machine and Maynooth battery, invented by Rev. Dr Nicholas Callan, 19th c professor of science here. *By arr,* ☎ *(01)628 5222.* College and grounds, *mid June-mid Sept,* ☎ *(01)628 5222.* **Maynooth Castle,** *near St Patrick's College gates:* see 12th c ruins, including gate house, keep, great hall.

Michael O'Dwyer's cottage, *SW side of Glen of Imaal at Derrynamuck on Rathdangan road:* furnished just as it was when he escaped from British forces in 1799. Key at entrance on main road.

Monasterevin, *10 km (6 miles) W of Kildare:* walks along Grand Canal towpath.

Moone, *12 km (8 miles) E of Athy:* high cross with 51 sculptured panels showing biblical scenes, one of most famous in Ireland. Timolin Pewter Works, *open daily.*

Moore Abbey, *just S of Monasterevin on L18:* car park, forest walks, picnic place. Mansion was once home of famous tenor, Count John McCormack. Now a convent; closed to public.

National Stud, *2 km (1 mile) E of Kildare:* ideal for half-day out. National Stud: *Easter Sun-Oct.* **Irish Horse Museum,** in grounds of National Stud: traces evolution of horse in Ireland. Highlight is Arkle's skeleton. *All year, Mon-Fri, 10 a.m.-5 p.m., Sat, 10 a.m.-6 p.m., Sun, 2 p.m.-6 p.m.* ☎ *(045)21617.* **Japanese Gardens,** laid out in 1906, they symbolise life of man from cradle to

grave. Also plant souvenir shop, selling bonsai trees. *Opening details as horse museum,* ☎ *(045)21251* &

Oughterard Hill, *9 km (6 miles) NE of Naas:* ruins of ancient monastery and stump of round tower. Fine views over Kildare plain.

Poulaphouca, *10 km (6 miles) SE of Naas.* Liffey cataracts, not quite Niagara, but some good falls near bridge.

Punchestown Standing Stone, *5 km (3 miles) E of Naas:* one of finest examples in Ireland. Race course, ☎ *(045)97704.*

Reban Castle, *5 km (3 miles) NW of Athy:* ruins of 13th c fortress on a yet more ancient site, marked on Ptolemy's 2nd c map of Ireland.

Russborough, *near Blessington.* Beit art collection includes works by Goya, Rubens, Velasquez, Vermeer. Guided tours round Palladian house, built 1740-1750 to see Irish silver, magnificent Francini plasterwork. Woodland gardens open when rhododendrons are in bloom. Craft shop, tea room. Special events, including Festival of Music in great Irish Houses, *June. Easter-Oct, Sun, BH, 2.30 p.m.-5.30 p.m., June, July, Aug, 10.30 a.m.-5.30 p.m.* ☎*(045)65239.*

Straffan, *near Naas: turn off main Dublin-Naas N7 at Kill.* **Steam museum:** marvellous collection of steam locomotives and steam engines. One steam engine came from the original whiskey distillery at Midleton, Co Cork, another from the old Jameson brewery in Dublin, and a third from Smithwick's brewery in Kilkenny. On live steam days, models and engines make a highly impressive sight. The main building housing the museum was a church at the Inchicore railway works, Dublin. Shop, tearoom. *All year, Sun, BH, 11.30 a.m.-5.30 p.m., except Dec 24-Jan 2; June, July, Aug, daily, times as above.* ☎*(01)628 8412.* **Butterfly farm:** tropical butterflies, tarantulas, scorpions and other creepy crawlies, all safely behind glass. *May 1-Aug BH, daily, 12 noon-5.30 p.m.* ☎*(01)627 1109.*

Stratford-on-Slaney, *6 km (4 miles) NE of Baltinglass,* 18th c weaving village on W side of Little Slaney River.

Valleymount, *8 km (5 miles) S of Blessington:* Glenbride Youth Hostel, ☎ *(045)67266.*

Wicklow Gap, follow L107 through magnificent mountain scenery to Laragh, near Glendalough.

Wolfe Tone's grave, *near Clane, 6 km (4 miles) N of Naas:* evocative location in beautiful countryside.

Wonderful Barn, *2 km (1 mile) SW of Leixlip.* 1743 five storey building built for Lady Conolly of nearby Castletown House, conical in shape, tapering to top, outside staircase.

Navan

Pop. 6,000, 48 km (30 miles) NW of Dublin and 127 km (17 miles) W of Drogheda. EC Thurs. TIO: Drogheda or Dublin. Bus enquiries, ☎ *(041)35023.*

This hilly town, set at the confluence of the Boyne and the Blackwater, was once a walled and fortified outpost of the Pale. Today, thanks to mining developments, it enjoys a new prosperity. Good fishing.

Athlumney House, *3 km (2 miles) S of Navan, by River Boyne:* impressive remains of four storey 15th c castle with attached 17th c Tudor house. Tradition has it that the last occupier, Sir Launcelot Dowdall, set it on fire rather than have it shelter William of Orange. *Key from convent opp.* **Dunmoe Castle,** *5 km (3 miles) NE of Navan:* 16th c ruin, burned down in 1799. Good views of the Boyne. **Navan motte,** *on W side of town:* excellent vantage point.**Donaghmore Round Tower,** *3 km (2 miles) NE of Navan on Slane road:* on early Christian site, reputedly founded by St Patrick. Nearby remains of 15th c church, Fair Green (C), Blackcastle and St Mary's (CI) are also worth exploring. Navan Trade Centre, *Trim Road:* frequent exhibitions and other events, ☎ *(046)23377/23388.*

Leisure Activities: Navan Racecourse, ☎ *(046)21350.* Greyhound racing: *Trim Road, every Wed, Thurs eve.* Swimming pool: indoor, heated. *Commons Road, all year, daily, details. (046)23001* &. Bicycles: Clarke's Sports Den, Londis Shopping Centre, ☎ *(046)21130.* Royal Tara Golf Club, *18 holes,* ☎ *(046)25244.*

AROUND NAVAN

Athboy, *13 km (8 miles) NW of Trim on L3.* Protestant church has 15th c tomb with effigies of armoured knight and wife.

Bective Abbey, *8 km (5 miles) S of Navan on T26:* founded as a Cistercian house in 12th c. Ruins of original chapter house and church, also remnants of fortified house into which abbey was converted after the Dissolution.

Castlerickard, *14 km (8 miles) SW of Trim, just off T26:* see Swift Mausoleum, large, pyramid-shaped structure next to church.

Corronaugh, *turn N off T35 5 km (3 miles) S of Virginia or E off L49 5 km (3 miles) SW of Virginia:* walks along the S shore of Lough Ramor, car park, picnic area.

Donore Castle, *13 km (8 miles) SW of Trim on T26 to Kinnegad:* said to have been built in early 15th c to qualify for £10 grant from Henry VI. Nothing new about housing subsidies! In good condition. Key from cottage opp.

Hill of Lloyd, *3 km (2 miles) W of Kells along L142 to Crossakeel:* the hill's lighthouse-shaped tower was built in 1791 in memory of Sir Thomas Taylor by the first Earl of Bective, his son. Pleasant walk through fields; views over Co. Meath are excellent.

Hill of Tailte, *near Donaghpatrick village, just off N3 road:* site of one of four ancient palaces built by King Tuathal. Venue of Aonach Tailteann, Olympic Games of ancient Ireland which were founded in prehistoric times and lasted until 12th c.

Hill of Tara, *10 km (6 miles) S of Navan, 1.5 km (1 mile) W of N3 Dublin-Navan road.* One of the most historic places in Ireland, formerly cultural and religious capital. Although only simple earthworks remain, it's worth walking to the top to sense the history and sample the stunning view.Interpretative centre details hill's history. Details, OPW, ☎ *(01)613111.*

Hill of Ward, *1.5 km (1 mile) E of Athboy, just off L14 in Navan direction:* reputed location of Palace of Tiachtga, site of famous ancient festival. In 1168, on occasion of national synod of prelates and kings, 13,000 horsemen said to have thronged nearby roads. Fine views from summit.

Rock of Cashel, Cashel, Co. Tipperary

Kells (Ceanannus Mór), *16 km (10 miles) NW of Navan. EC Wed.* Ancient town in River Blackwater valley. Designated a Heritage Town. Originally, the site of an important 6th c monastic settlement founded by St Colmcille. Pleasant and interesting walks up and down hilly central streets. *St Columba's Church, top of Market Street:* most impressive building in the town, built on site of original settlement. The magnificent Book of Kells was written here and in the church gallery there are facsimiles of the Book, reproduction pages from the Book of Durrow and large scale photographs of the Columban site. In the grounds, a round tower, self-standing spire and four High Crosses. The town's fifth, Market Cross, is in centre of Kells. St Colmcille's House, a high roofed monastic building similar to St Kevin's Church, Glendalough, is just outside the churchyard. *Key from house opp.* Swimming pool: indoor, heated, *Navan Road, daily,* ☎ *(046)40551.*

Laracor *3 km (2 miles) S of Trim on L25:* Jonathan Swift was once rector here. The present CI is said to occupy the site of Swift's church; the communion silver he used is preserved. Nearby, on Trim road, remains of cottage occupied by Swift's 'Stella' (Esther Johnson).

Mount Oriel *3 km (2 miles) NW of Collon on N2 Slane Ardee road:* worthwhile views from 246 m (810 ft) hill.

Moynalty, *6 km (4 miles) N of Kells:* Field Day, with steam-driven agricultural machinery, old agricultural implements on show, *mid-Aug.*

Newtown Trim, *1.5 km (1 mile) E of Trim on N bank of River Boyne:* vast ruin, once the abbeys of Ss. Peter and Paul. Stand at the gate in the hedge facing the ruin and shout; a flawless echo will return from the ruins.

Skreen Hill, *11 km (7 miles) S of Navan, 1.5 km (1 mile) E of N3 Dublin-Navan road:* climb to ruined tower on summit for good views.

Slane, *Ledwidge museum:* the cottage birthplace of poet Francis Ledwidge killed at Ypres in 1917. *Mar-Oct, Mon, Tues, Wed, 10 a.m.-1 p.m., 2 p.m.-6 p.m.* ☎ *(041)24285/24244.* **Slane Castle demesne:** fine walks, including one beside the River Boyne.

Slane Hill, *1.5 km (1 miles) N of Slane:* 152 m (500 ft) hill where St Patrick lit historic Paschal Fire in 5th c, proclaiming Christianity throughout Ireland. Remains of 16th c church and school on site of an ancient church founded by St Patrick. Excellent views take in whole Boyne valley from Trim to Drogheda.

Trim, *14 km (9 miles) SW of Navan on T26. EC Thurs.* Rich in history, contains perhaps more antiquities than any other town in Ireland. Heritage town; fine new folk theatre, heritage centre. *St Patrick's Cathedral (CI),* with fine baptismal font, 11th c tower and medieval gravestones. ॐ *Yellow Steeple, opp. Castle:* part of 13th c St Mary's Abbey, destroyed in 1649 to prevent it falling to Cromwell. *Trim Castle,* built by Hugh de Lacy in 1172, largest Anglo-Irish fortress in country, well preserved ruins cover large area. *Town Hall, Castle Street:* ask to see the interesting Corporation records; they date from 1659. *Mon-Fri, business hours,* ☎ *(046)31238.* **Exhibition Centre,** *Castle Street:* regular exhibitions of historic and local interest material. *All year, Mon-Fri, 10 a.m.-1 p.m., 2.30 p.m.-5 p.m.,* ☎ *(046)31158.* ॐ Swimming pool: indoor, heated, *daily,* ☎ *(046)31140.*

Thurles

Pop. 7,500, 21 km (13 miles) N of Cashel, 40 km (25 miles) NE of Tipperary, 148 km (92 miles) SW of Dublin. EC Wed, TIO, Nenagh, ☎ *(067)31610, May-Sept.*

Market town pleasantly situated on the banks of the River Suir. Once an Anglo-Norman town, you can see the remnants of two castles at the main bridge and near Liberty Square. Interesting shopfronts, including Sweeney, Baker and Grocer, Mitchel Street, good town and riverside walks.

Cathedral (C): interior richly decorated with marble. Its campanile is a landmark for miles around. ॐ Interesting modern Church of St Joseph and St Brigid at *Bothar na Naomh, near railway station. EC Wed, TIO,* ☎ *(067)31610, May-Sept.* **Hayes Hotel,** *Liberty Square:* historic building where Gaelic Athletic Association was founded in 1884. Library: fine collection of Co Tipperary historical material, *Mon-Sat.* GAA theme museum: *details, TIO, Nenagh.*

Leisure Activities: Racing, *3 km (2 miles) NW of Thurles, off T21:* regular meetings, *details: Nenagh TIO.* Greyhound racing, Thurles track: *Tues, Sat, eves,* ☎ *(0504)21003.* Swimming pool: indoor, heated, *Mon-Sun,* ☎ *(0504)22349.* Golf Club, *18 holes,* ☎ *(0504)222426.* Shamrock Bus Service, ☎ *(0504)21622;* coach tours of area.

AROUND THURLES

Athassel Abbey, *3 km (2 miles) SE of Thomastown:* 12th c Augustinian foundation on W banks of River Suir, ruins consist of church, cloister, monastic buildings.

Ballinacourty, *on Tipperary-Lisuernane scenic route, 2 km (1 mile) from Christ the King statue:* forest walks, viewing points over Glen of Aherlow, car park, picnic area.

Ballinahow Castle, *5 km (3 miles) from Thurles on Newport road:* 16th c fortress of rare circular design. Signposted access via farmyard.

Ballydavid Wood, *6 km (4 miles) SE of Tipperary on N24:* forest walks, picnic area, car park. Ballydavid Wood Youth Hostel, ☎ *(062)54148.*

Barna Castle, *3 km (2 miles) SW of Templemore:* circular five storey keep, 18 m (60 ft) high. Spiral staircase to battlements. View from top outstanding.

Brittas Castle, *3 km (2 miles) N of Thurles:* 19th c structure begun as copy of Warwick Castle. Work stopped after owner killed by lump of falling masonry. A house has since been built within the foundations.

Cahir, *S. Tipperary. EC Thurs. TIO :* Cahir Castle, *TIO,* ☎ *(052)41453, May-Sept.*

Small, quiet town with many outstanding Georgian buildings. Good salmon and trout fish ing. Excellent centre for climbing the Galtee Mountains. *Cahir Castle,* magnificent structure, built 1142, excellently restored. Massive keep, spacious courtyard and hall, high enclosing walls. Now architectural interpretative centre. *Apr-June, daily, 10 a.m.-6 p.m., June-Sept, daily, 9 a.m.-7.30 p.m., Oct, daily, 10 a.m.-6 p.m., Nov-Mar, daily, 10 a.m.-1 p.m., 2 p.m.-4.30 p.m.* ☎ *(052)41011.* 13th c abbey ruins in attractive setting beside River Suir. *Cahir Park, 2 km (1.5 miles) S of Cahir on L184:* forest and riverside walks by River Suir (very beautiful here and spanned by cast iron bridge), scenic views, car park, picnic area. *Swiss cottage,* early 19th c building like an Alpine chalet, with thatched roof and verandahs, has been thoroughly renovated. *Mar, Apr, Oct, Tues-Sat, 1 p.m.-5 p.m., Sun, 10 a.m.-5 p.m., May-Sept, Tues-Sun, 10 a.m.-6 p.m., Nov-Sat, 1 p.m.-4.30 p.m., Sun, 10 a.m.-4 p.m.* ☎ *(052)41144.* Cahir Park Golf Club, *9 holes,* ☎ *(052)41474.*

Cashel, *21 km (13 miles) S of Thurles, TIO ,* ☎ *(062)61333, Mar-Sept.* Small but attractive country heritage town with points of interest other than the Rock of Cashel. Also see outstanding traditional shopfronts, inc Meany's pub. Variety of craft workshops. Cashel Folk Village, *Chapel Lane, Dominic Street, May-Sept, Mon-Sun, 9.30 a.m.-8 p.m.* Brú Ború complex: New heritage venue. Activities include traditional music entertainment. Shop, restaurant. *All year, daily,* ☎ *(062)61122.* Padraig O Mathuna, *Main Street:* exquisite jewellery with Celtic themes, paintings and sculptures. Good centre for exploring historical riches of Co. Tipperary. Salmon and trout fishing centre. *Hore Abbey, just W of Rock of Cashel:* Cistercian foundation. Dominican friary ruins, *Chapel Lane, near base of Rock.* **Cashel Palace Hotel:** formerly palace of Church of Ireland archbishops, built in Queen Anne style in 1730. Splendid interiors, magnificent lounge hall with original panelling and carving, spacious Adam drawing room. Hotel's food and wine match sumptuous interiors. *Diocesan Library, in precincts of CI cathedral:* one of the finest collection of 16th and 17th c books in Ireland, as well as ancient maps. *All year, Mon-Sat, 9.30 a.m.-5.30 p.m., Sun, 2.30 p.m.-5.30 p.m.* ☎ *(062)61944.* **Bothan Scoir,** *Clonmel Road:* totally authentic single room 17th c thatched cottage. *By arr,* ☎ *(062)61360.* **Rock of Cashel,** this magnificent rock is one of Ireland's great historic sites. Main features are 12th c round tower, in good condition; Cormac's Chapel, styled as miniature cathedral; St Patrick's Cross; the cathedral of St Patrick and the Hall of Vicars Choral, which you pass through on entering the grounds, and where there are many fascinating replicas and relics of this historic site. It is easy to spend hours scrambling round these fascinating ruins. Full guide service. *Mid Sept-mid Mar, daily, 9.30 a.m.-4.30 p.m., mid Mar-*

Damer House, Roscrea, Co. Tipperary

early June, daily, 9.30 a.m.-5.30 p.m., June-mid Sept, daily, 9 a.m.-7.30 p.m. ☎ (062)61437.

Derrynaflan, *3 km (2 miles) SE of Horse and Jockey on N8:* impressive ruins of 13th c church on grassy mound in middle of peat bog. From near Heathview House, follow track across the bog. Outstanding archaeological treasures unearthed here in 1980.

Devil's Bit Mountain, *6 km (4 miles) NW of Templemore:* take the road to near summit for splendid views over N Tipperary. Legend says that the nearby gap in range was formed when the Devil spat out the Rock of Cashel, to S.

Dromineer, *10 km (6 miles) NW of Nenagh:* Lough Derg's finest resort. Sail Inn has great nautical atmosphere. Boats for hire, *details, Nenagh TIO.*

Dundrum, *12 km (8 miles) NE of Tipperary town on L119:* 1.5 km (1 mile) SW of village forest walks, nature trail, game sanctuary at Marl Bog.

Durrow, *32 km (20 miles) NE of Thurles:* attractive setting on banks of Erkina River. Ruins of village's early monastic foundation are in churchyard.

Fethard, *14 km (9 miles) NW of Clonmel:* an agreeable village full of historical atmosphere. A detailed walk round the entire village is rewarding. Historic remains include a priory on site of Augustinian foundation, keeps of three castles. Most of the medieval town walls and flanking towers survive and are now being restored. The farm, folk and transport museum, housed in the old railway station has over 1,000 items, from a Victorian hearse to a forge and country kitchen. There are many old craft tools and implements and old farm machinery. *May-Sept, daily, 10 a.m.-6 p.m., or by arr,* ☎ (052)31516.

Glen of Aherlow, *immediately S of Tipperary:* noted beauty spot. On N side of glen, minor road runs across wooded slopes of Sliabh na Muc: the views here are tremendous.

Glengarra, *13 km (8 miles) SW of Cahir on N8:* forest and riverside walks alongside Burncourt River. Nature trail, note unusual tree and shrub species. Picnic area, car park.

Gortavoher, *6 km (4 miles) S of Tipperary, on Tipperary-Lisuernane road:* forest walks, car park. Picnic area offers extensive views over Glen of Aherlow.

Holy Cross Abbey, *6 km (4 miles) S of Thurles on W bank of River Suir.* Founded in 1168 by the Benedictines and shortly afterwards transferred to the Cistercians. After standing roofless for generations, it was completely restored (1975) and is now used as a parish church. *All year, daily, 10 a.m.-6 p.m.,* ☎ (0504)43241.

Horse and Jockey, *12 km (8 miles) NE of Cashel on N8:* interesting painting of Horse with jockey on gable wall of pub.

Kilcash Castle, *follow N76 12 km (8 miles) NE of Clonmel, turn L to Ballypatrick, 2 km (1 mile) N of Ballypatrick crossroads, turn R and continue for about 2 km (1 mile):* set on the SE slopes of Slievenamon, striking views from ivy-covered ruins.

Knockelly Castle, *5 km (3 miles) NE of Fethard:* magnificent ruins, including a tower and walled bawn, set on a high hill.

Limerick Junction Racecourse: regular races, ☎ (062)51357

Mona Incha Abbey, *3 km (2 miles) E of Roscrea:* dates 1,300 years, now fashionable as a pilgrimage centre. 12th c church remains, interesting High Cross.

Mount St Joseph's, Cistercian monastery, *3 km (2 miles) W of Roscrea, just off L34:* daughter house of Mount Melleray, Co. Waterford and charmingly set on banks of Little Brosna River. Ireland's only silk farm. By arr, ☎ (0505)21711.

Mountain Lodge, *13 km (8 miles) SW of Cahir:* Youth Hostel.

Mullinahone, *16 km (10 miles) NE of Fethard:* see house in Fethard Street where 19th c novelist Charles Joseph Kickham lived. Celtic Cross over his grave in local C church.

Nenagh, *39 km (24 miles) NE of Thurles.* EC Wed. TIO, ☎ (067)31610, May-Sept. Chief town of N Tipperary and bustling centre of rich agricultural district. **Nenagh District Heritage Centre,** house of governor of old county gaol has been turned into fascinating reconstruction of area's history. Also temporary exhibitions. *Apr-Nov, Mon-Fri, 10 a.m.-5 p.m., Sat, Sun: 2.30 p.m.-5 p.m* ☎ (067)32633. **Nenagh Castle,** impressive circular keep which formed part of larger castle built around 1200. Keep, *all year, key: caretaker, Ballyartella Woollen Mills. Mon-Fri, 9.30 a.m.-1 p.m.; 2 p.m.-5.30 p.m. Sat, 9.30 a.m.-12.30 p.m.,* ☎ (067)331055. Swimming pool: indoor, heated, *Tues-Sun.,* ☎ (067)331788. Bicycles: J. Moynan & Co, 61 Pearse Street, ☎ (067)31293.

Rockwell College, *6 km (4 miles) S of Cashel on N8, near New Inn village:* visitors are welcome in the beautiful grounds and will be shown over the college, ☎ (062)61444.

Roscrea, *34 km (21 miles) N of Thurles.* EC Wed. Pleasant market heritage town with interesting historical ruins, good centre for walking and climbing in Slieve Bloom Mountains. *Damer House,* neglected early 18th c building saved from demolition in 1975 and since completely restored. Richly decorated and carved staircase, much good furniture, fine paintings, relics of life in old Roscrea. Heritage Centre, guided tours, slide shows. Delightful Georgian formal garden at rear of house gives fine views over town. *All year, Mon-Fri, 10 a.m.-5 p.m. June-Sept, also open Sat, 11 a.m.-5 p.m., Sun, 2 p.m.-5 p.m.* ☎ (0505)21850. *Roscrea Castle, near Damer House:* built 1281, reconstructed 1332. Gate tower, two other towers, parts of walls remain. Now restored, *opening hours same as house.* **St Cronan's Monastery,** divided in two by main road. Round tower can be seen to full advantage, following improvements to its surrounding location.

There are remains of a 15th c *Franciscan friary* partly incorporated into St Cronan's Church. Opp. Glebe View Garage see ruins of primitive Methodists' meeting place. Pleasant walk along the Mall, on opp. site of Moneen river. ***Cistercian College,*** fine museum, items on folk life, archaeology, history, natural history. *Not usually open, but ask the monks,* ☎ *(0505)21061.* Bicycles: Michael England, ☎ *(0505)21776.* Roscrea Golf Club, *9 holes,* ☎ *(0505)21130.*

Silvermine Mountains, *S of Nenagh:* many fine climbs. For panoramic views, visit Step viewing point near Silvermines village, car park, picnic area.

Slievenamon Mountain, *10 km (6 miles) SE of Fethard:* superb views from summit reward for energetic climb.

Soloheadbeg, *6 km (4 miles) N of Tipperary:* first shots in War of Independence fired here, January 1919. Memorial to event at Solohead Cross.

Templemore Park, *14 km (9 miles) N of Thurles on N62, train from Dublin, Limerick.* Remains of Templemore Abbey and Black Castle. Swimming pool, nature trail.

Terryglass, *NE shores of Lough Derg:* village of great character, with century-old stone church and 13th c Old Court castle. Picnic area, boating facilities.

Timoney Standing Stones, *6 km (4 miles) SE of Roscrea in townlands of Timoney Hills and Cullaun:* nearly 300 scattered over wide area.

Tipperary, *40 km (25 miles) SW of Thurles, EC Wed . TIO* ☎ *(062)51457, all year. Bus and train enquiries,* ☎ *(062)51555.* Farming town with interesting historical remains. Heritage town designation. Fine old shopfronts in Church Street, Main Street, O'Brien Street. Brown trout fishing. Good centre for climbing and hill walking on Slievenamuck and Galtee Mountains. ***St Michael's Church (C).*** Impressive Gothic style with a number of distinctive architectural features, including W door. Chancel arch of 13th c Augustinian abbey in grounds of Christian Brothers' school. Also ruins of 17th c Abbey Schools Motte of Norman motte-and-bailey castle on sandhill just N of town. Monument to Charles Kickham, 19th c patriot, poet, novelist. Also Manchester Martyrs' memorial. Sean Treacy Memorial Pool, *Bank Place, daily,* ☎ *(062)51806/51817.* Bicycles: J. J. O'Carroll, *10 James's Street,* ☎ *(062)51229.* Tipperary Golf Club, *9 holes,* ☎ *(062)51119.*

Toomevara Folk Museum, *16 km (10 miles) E of Nenagh on N7.* Many items used in rural Ireland over the centuries. *Daily, at all reasonable times. Key next door.*

Tullamore

Pop. 9,500, 40 km (25 miles) SE of Athlone, 45 km (28 miles) NE of Roscrea, 96 km (60 miles) W of Dublin, EC Mon. TIO: ☎ *(0506)52141, June-Aug.*

A quiet, modest town, with heritage town designation, whose development owes much to the laying out of the Grand Canal in 1798. Probably the single most exciting event in Tullamore's history occurred in May 1785, when a hot air balloon caught fire during its ascent and crashed, setting fire to a third of the town.

St Catherine's, *Hop Hill, Portarlington Road:* fine 1818 Gothic church on impressive hill site. ***Irish Mist*** has its origins in the town: video presentation and product sampling, *Mon-Fri, 3 p.m.-5.30 p.m.,* ☎ *(0506)21586.* Walks: There is an interesting walk from Chapel Street to Convent Road, on S bank of Grand Canal; Chapel Street has the town's last farmyard. Also Harbour Street, round the old canal harbour and back by canalside Convent Road. S bank of canal continues past Irish Mist factory to Kilbride Street. If you are in the SE outskirts, walk along the Clonminch Road, to see the site of the old 1854 railway station, never popular because of its distance from town and only used for ten years. ***Charleville House:*** 1798 Gothic House. Conducted tours of interior. *Nov-Mar, by app; Apr, May, Sat, Sun, BH; Jun-Sept, Wed-Sun, 11 a.m.-5 p.m.* Restaurants. ☎ *(0506)21279.*

Leisure Activities: *Grand Canal, Shannon cruises:* Celtic Canal Cruisers Ltd, 24th Lock, ☎ *(0506)21861.* Swimming pool, *daily,* ☎ *(0506)21867.* Bicycles: C. McCabe, *Church Street,* ☎ *(0506)21717. Golf Club, 18 holes,* ☎ *(0506)21439.* Buckley's Riding Centre, ☎ *(0506)43507.*

AROUND TULLAMORE

Ballaghmore Castle, *Borris-in-Ossory:* built in 1480, features a Sheela-na-Gig on the front S wall. Restored in 1836 and more recently in 1990. *All year, daily, details:* ☎ *(0505)21453.*

Banagher, *25 km (12 miles) SW of Tullamore. 51 bus from Tullamore.* Remains of 17th c English-built batteries which commanded crossing of River Shannon. ***Cloghan Castle,*** *5 km (3 miles) S of Banagher:* 800 year old castle restored after 19 years' work. Interesting interior. Surrounding parkland has large flock of Jacob sheep. *All year, Wed, Thurs, Fri, Sat, Sun, 2 p.m.-6 p.m.*

Birr, *37 km (23 miles) SW of Tullamore. All day closing: Thurs. TIO,* ☎ *(0509)20110. May-Sept.* Attractive heritage town full of graceful Georgian architecture. Spend a day exploring town and castle grounds. Birr Vintage Festival: great festivities, *Aug, details: TIO.*

Birr Castle, home of Earl and Countess of Rosse, gardens open to the public. Ornamental lake, arboretum, displays of trees, shrubs, flowers, inc. 200 year old box hedges, claimed to be tallest in world. See walls and tube of great mid-19th c Birr telescope, for 80 years, largest in the world. Museum, section on scientific discoveries of Sir Charles Parsons; *demesne: all year, daily, 9 a.m.-1 p.m.; 2 p.m.-6 p.m., or dusk in winter.* Theme exhibitions in castle, *May-Sept, aft, details,* ☎ *(0509)20056.* ♿ ***Slieve Bloom display centre,*** *Railway Road:* archaeology, geology, history, wildlife of Slieve Bloom mountains. *July-Sept, Mon-Fri, 10 a.m.-6 p.m., Sat, Sun, 2.30 p.m.-6 p.m.* ☎ *(0509)20029.* ***Crottys' Church,*** *Castle Street:* relic of early 19th c Catholic schism, when Fr Michael Crotty set up an independent church. ***Seffin Stone,*** *John's Mall:* believed to be Megalithic; also Crimean Gun, presented to Birr in 1858 for services rendered in Crimean War. Riverside walk along banks of Camcor, also Mill Island mid-river park.

Pleasure flights: Midland Flying Club, Birr Air field. Swimming pool: indoor, heated, *Wilmer Road, Tues-Sat, all year,* ☎ *(0509)20343.* C W Bicycles: P. L. Dolan and Sons, *Main Street,* ☎ *(0509)20006.* Birr Golf Club, *The Glens, 18 holes,* ☎ *(0509)20082.*

Bunreagh, *11 km (7 miles) NW of Mountrath on Kinnity road:* car park, picnic place, forest walks, viewing points, scenic route over Slieve Bloom Mountains.

Cadamstown, *5 km (3 miles) NE of Kinnity on T9:* Silver River ravines, old mill, bridge of Ardara, ruins of St Luna's Abbey. Just NE of village, megalithic Giant's Grave, *by arr. local forestry officials,* ☎ *(0509)37005/37020.*

Clonenagh, *3 km (1.5 miles) E of Mountrath on N7 to Portlaoise:* St Fintan's Well, embedded in trunk of large roadside tree, said to have arrived there miraculously.

Clonmacnois, *6 km (4 miles) N of Shannonbridge on Offaly bank of River Shannon;* one of Ireland's great holy places, monastery founded in 548 and for nearly 1,000 years, renowned as centre of piety and learning. Raided many times and finally abandoned in 1552. Cathedral, seven church ruins, two round towers, castle ruins. Ancient Pilgrim's Road, fragments of 11th c causeway to cemetery still in use. Interpretative centre. Jetty for cruisers. *Nov-mid Mar, daily, 10 a.m.-5 p.m., mid Mar-May,*

Clonmacnoise and River Shannon, Co. Offaly

daily, 10 a.m.-6 p.m., June-early Sept, daily, 9 a.m.-7 p.m., Sept, Oct, daily,10 a.m.-6 p.m. ☎ *(0905)74195.*

Clonmacnois and West Offaly railway: narrow gauge railway trundles through bogland for 8 km (5.5 miles) in a fascinating trip lasting about 1 hour, with plenty of sights of flora and fauna. *Mar-Oct, guided tour every hour on the hour, 10 a.m.-5 p.m.,* ☎ *(0905)74114/74172.*

Coolbanagher Church, *9 km (6 miles) NE of Portlaoise, near Emo on L26:* very striking late 18th c interior by Gandon, who also designed Custom House, Dublin. *By arr.,* ☎ *(0502)24143.*

Croghan Hill, *16 km (10 miles) NE of Tullamore:* good views, nearby village of Tyrellspass has a most attractive semi-circular green, backed by village church and the Village Hotel, part of a Georgian style crescent built in 1800.

Donaghmore Museum, *12 km (8 miles) S of Borris-in-Ossory.* Agricultural and social artefacts; ☎ *(0505)46315.*

Durrow Abbey, *6 km (4 miles) N of Tullamore on T9 to Kilbeggan:* little remains of St Colmcille's monastery, origin of 7th c Book of Durrow (now in Trinity College), but see holy well and Durrow High Cross, with panels showing Biblical themes.

Emo Court Garden, *3 km (2 miles) NE of Coolbanagher church:* specimen trees, shrubs, imposing lake. Late 18th c Gandon house only open to special interest groups. Gardens: *Apr-Oct, daily, 10.30 a.m.-5.30 p.m. House, Apr-Oct, Mon, 2 p.m.-4 p.m.* ☎ *(0502)26110.*

Emo Park, *7 km (4 miles) S of Portarlington:* forest walks.

Glenbarrow, *19 km (12 miles) S of Tullamore:* six waterfalls, riverside walk by exuberant River Barrow. Car park, picnic area. Good climbers can tackle nearby Ridge of Capard, superb views.

Glendine East, *N of Camross village on S side of Slieve Bloom Mountains:* attractive natural site by Killeen River, car park. If you feel energetic, it's an hour's climb to Glendine Gap, 600 m (2,000 ft). On far side, the open glen of Glendine West.

Glendineoregan, *3 km (2 miles) S of Clonaslee:* car park, viewing point, forest walks, scenic route over Slieve Bloom mountains. Just SE, at the Cut and Glen Bordowin (car park and viewing point), impressive mountain pass.

Glenletter, *8 km (5 miles) SE of Kinnitty on Kinnitty Mountrath road:* car park, picnic area, viewing point, forest walks. Source of Silver River, attractive viewing points along Hogan's Road.

Gloster, *11 km (7 miles) SE of Birr off T32:* pleasant lakeside forest walks here and at Goldengrove, 5 km (3 miles) further along T32.

Heywood House, *2 km (1 mile) NE of Ballinakill, on Abbeyleix-Ballyragget road.* Magnificent Italianate gardens designed by Sir Edward Lutyens. Now a Salesian missionary college; grounds by arr, ☎ *(0502)33334.*

Kilbeggan, *11 km (7 miles) N of Tullamore.* Horse racing. ☎ *(0506)32176/32125.* ***Locke's Distillery:*** distillery established in 1757, closed down in 1954, has been restored as a fascinating industrial museum, complete with old stills, beam engine and waterwheel. Craftspeople make the whiskey casks in the traditional way. Visitors can try the new generation of Locke's whiskey. Folk museum, shops, art gallery, "Distillery Kitchen" restaurant. *Apr-Oct, daily, 9 a.m.-6 p.m., Nov-Mar, Mon-Sat, 10 a.m.-4.30 p.m., Sun, 2 p.m.-6 p.m.* ☎ *(0506)32134/32115/32183.*

Kilcormac, *16 km (10 miles) NE of Birr:* C church with carved wooden 16th c Pieta, buried in bog for 60 years during Penal times, in order to keep it safe.

Kinnitty, *13 km (8 miles) E of Birr on L116.* Charming village at foot of Slieve Bloom

Mountains. As William Bulfin, in the l9th c Rambles in Erin, wrote; 'Kinnitty is probably the most beautifully situated village I have ever seen, embowered in woods, a sheltered Eden in the hills.' The L116 over the mountains is a most striking route into Co. Laois.

Leap Castle, *9 km (6 miles) SE of Birr on T9 Kinnitty Roscrea road:* remains of 16th c stronghold of the Ely O'Carrolls—said to be most haunted in Ireland, with 24 ghosts.

Monicknew, *11 km (7 miles) N of Mountrath on Mountrath-Clonaslee road:* forest walks, viewing points, scenic route over Slieve Bloom mountains, 2 km (1 mile) nature trail taking in Monicknew bridge, built as Roman arch. From car park at the Cut, direct climb to summit of Wolftrap mountain.

Mountmellick Business Park - exhibitions and tourist information point.

Portarlington, *27 km (17 miles) SW of Tullamore:* once home of a strong French-speaking Huguenot community. French Week, *Sept,* celebrates Portarlington's colourful history, events include snail eating. *All day closing Mon.* **'French' Church of Ireland,** *just off town square:* interesting graveyard, Huguenot records, French silver. Viewing by arr., ☎ *(0502)23144.* Swimming pool: indoor, heated, *daily, except Tues,* ☎ *(0502)23149.* Golf club ☎ *(0502)23115.*

Portlaoise, *28 km (17 miles) SE of Tullamore:* **Gash gardens:** young, small garden with fine trees, shrubs and plants in riverside setting. *Easter-Sept, daily, by arr,* ☎ *(0502)32247.* Portlaoise Sports Centre, *daily.* Moneyballytyrell swimming pool, *daily,* ☎ *(0502)21710.* Bicycles: M. Kavanagh, *Railway Street,* ☎ *(0502)21357. Heath Golf Club, 18 holes,* ☎ *(0502)26533*

Rahan, *8 km (5 miles) W of Tullamore:* remains of 6th c monastery, three ruined churches, roofed church with fine rose window.

Rahugh, *8 km (5 miles) NE of Tullamore on Grand Canal banks:* holy well, nearby St Hugh's tombstone is said to be good for headaches.

Rock of Dunamase, *6 km (3.5 miles) E of Portlaoise:* ruined fortress perched atop 46 m (150 ft) rock is magnificent in its desolation. Great views over Midland plain.

Rosenallis, *6 km (4 miles) NW of Mountmellick:* oldest Quaker burial ground in Ireland.

Shannon Harbour, *32 km (20 miles) W of Tullamore:* a forlorn sight, with deserted quaysides, empty warehouses, facade of once lavish canal hotel: loads of atmosphere. Alternatively, the Grand Canal area is usually thick with craft.

Stradbally, *10 km (6 miles) E of Portlaoise on T16.* Most attractive village with steep Main Street. Narrow gauge railway in grounds of Stradbally Hall, *SO,* Steam Rally, *Aug BH.*

Timahoe Round Tower, *13 km (8 miles) SE of Portlaoise:* built in 1100, one of finest in Ireland. Nearby ruins of castle and abbey.

Gazetteer Index

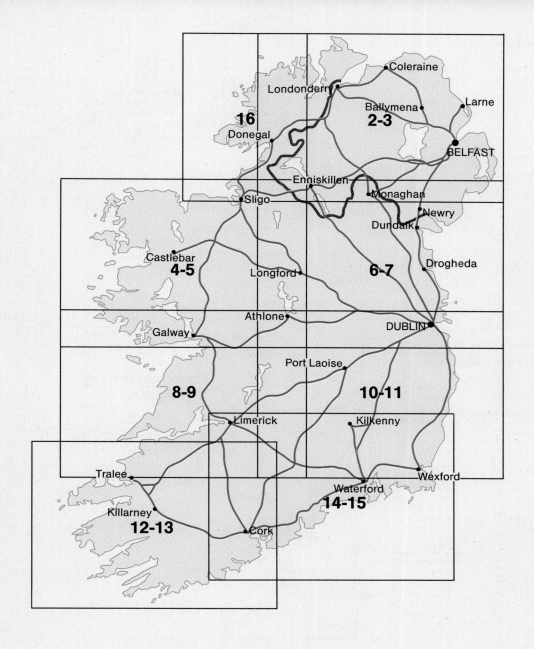

Legend of Map Symbols

Motorway with interchange		Boating	
Primary road		Viewpoint	
'A' and 'B' roads		Place of general interest	
Unclassified road		Place of historic interest	
Distance in miles/kilometres	*18/29*	Tourist information office:	
Passenger railway with station		– open all year	
Approved border crossing point	★	– open summer only	
Car ferry		Area of outstanding natural beauty	
Airport		Spot height (in feet)	•2788
Sandy beach		Border	
Major golf courses	▶	County boundary	

0 5 10 15 20 25 Miles

0 10 20 30 40 Kilometres

Scale 1:443 520

© ESR

Cartography by E.S.R. Ltd., West Byfleet, Surrey, England.

1

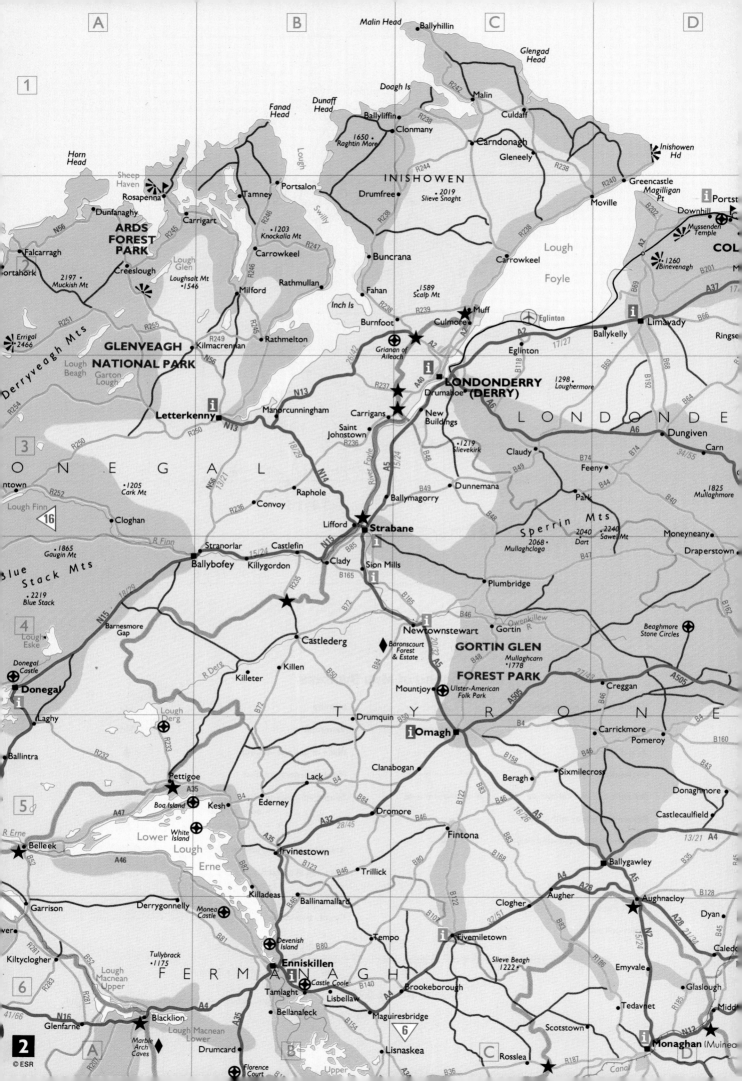

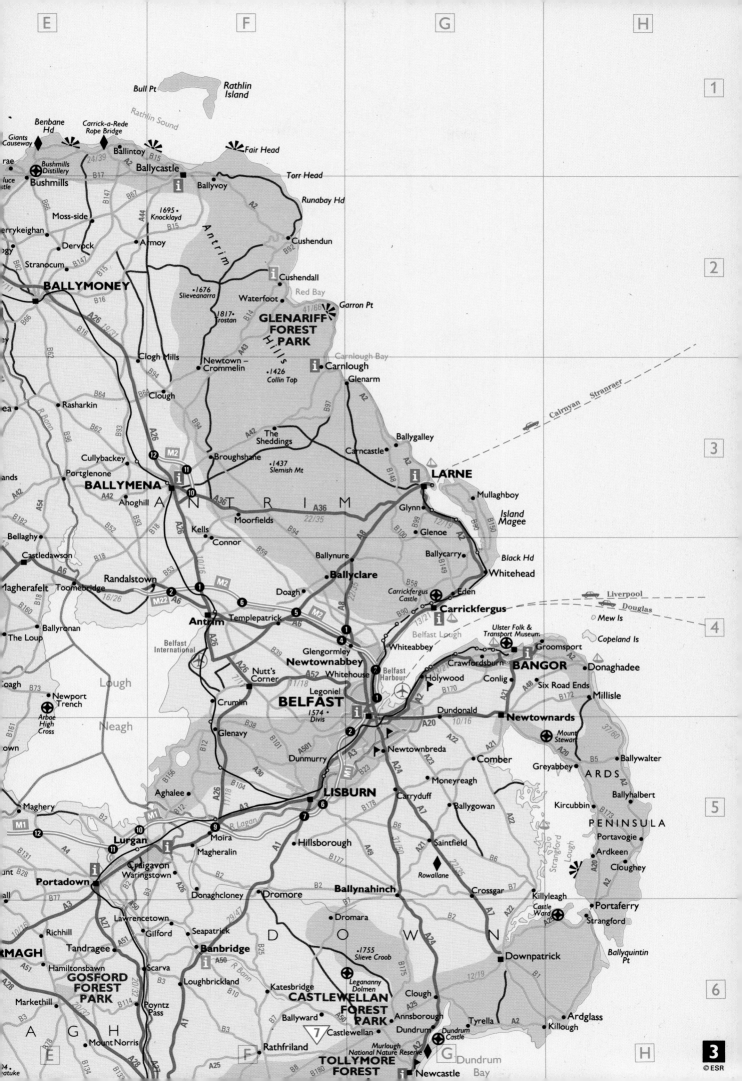

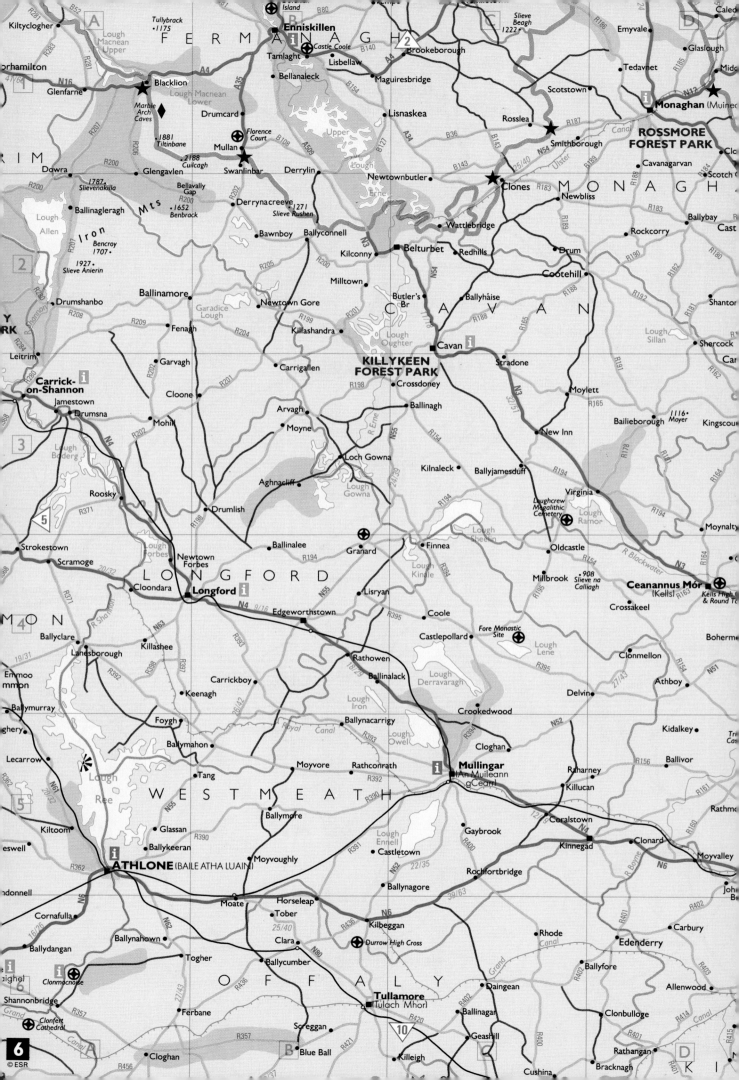

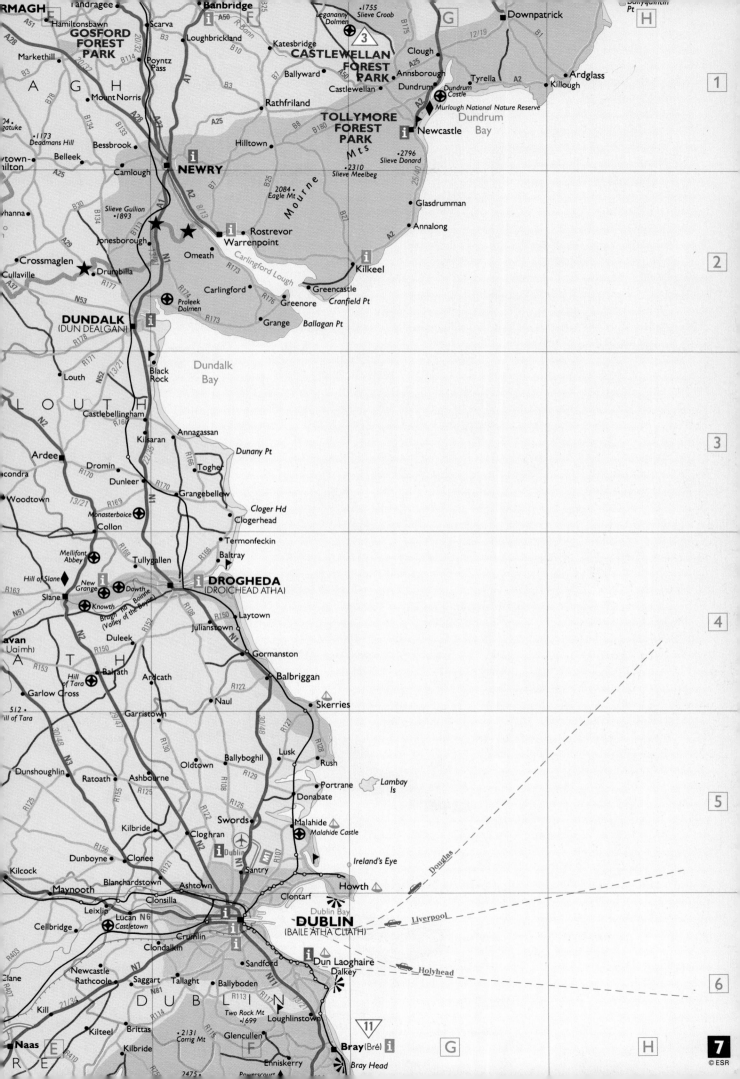

Grid references: A, B, C, D (columns); 1–6 (rows)

A1
Slyne Head

B1
Ballyconneely
Toombeola
Roundstone
Glinsk
R341
R342
R340
Moyrus
Carna
Kilkieran
Mweenish Is
Kilkieran Bay
Gorumna Is
Lettermullan
Golam Hd
R340

C1
4
Derryrush
Screeb
R336
LAR CONNAGHT
R343
Costelloe
Carraroe
Cashla Bay
Inveran
R336

D1
Castle
Corrib
Oughterard
G
Rosscahill
A

Galway Bay
Spiddal

B2 / C2
North Sound
Kitmurvy
Inishmore
i Kilronan
Aran Islands
Inishmaan
Inisheer
South Sound

D2
Black Head
Murroogh
Blackh or Ballyva B
Ballyvaughan
R477

C3 / D3
1109 Slieve Elva
Poulnabro Dolmen
N67
i Lisdoonvarna
R479
R478
R476
Kilfeno
Leamaneh Castle
Doolin Pt
Cliffs of Moher
i
Hags Head
Liscannor
R478
Ennistymon
Lahinch
Liscannor Bay
N67
N85

C4 / D4
C
Milltown Malbay
R460
1282 Slievecallan
Shanavogh
R474
Mutton Is
Mullagh
Donegal Pt
Doonbeg
N67
Creegh
Lissycasey
Kilmihil
R484
34/55
Cooraclare
R485
Kikee i
Moyasta
R483
Kilmurry McMahon
Ki
N68

B5 / C5 / D5
R487
Kilrush
R473
Knock
Labasheeda
Carrigaholt
Scattery Is
Killimer
Lo
Carrig Is
Tarbert
Glin
Loop Head
Kibaha
Carrigafoyle Castle
R551
N69
Glin Castle & Gate Shop
Ballyha
Mouth of the Shannon
Ballylongford
R524
i
Ballybunion
Ahafone
R551
Athea

B6 / C6 / D6
Ballyduff
Listowel
R523
R524
Kerry Head
Causeway
Finuge
Duagh
R Fede
R555
Lixnaw
R557
Abbeyfeale
Ballyheige
R551
R552
N69
36/58
N21
Kilkinlea
Ballyheige Bay
Lyracrumpane
Mullag
The Seven Hogs or Magharee Islands
1062 Beenageeha
Knocknagashel
Mountcollin
Ardfert
Ardfert Cathedral
12
Kilflynn
Stack Mts
Reanagowan
R556

A lower / B lower
Brandon Hd
Rough Pt
Tralee Bay
Fenit
R558
Spa
i Tralee (Trá Li)
Brandon
Brandon Bay

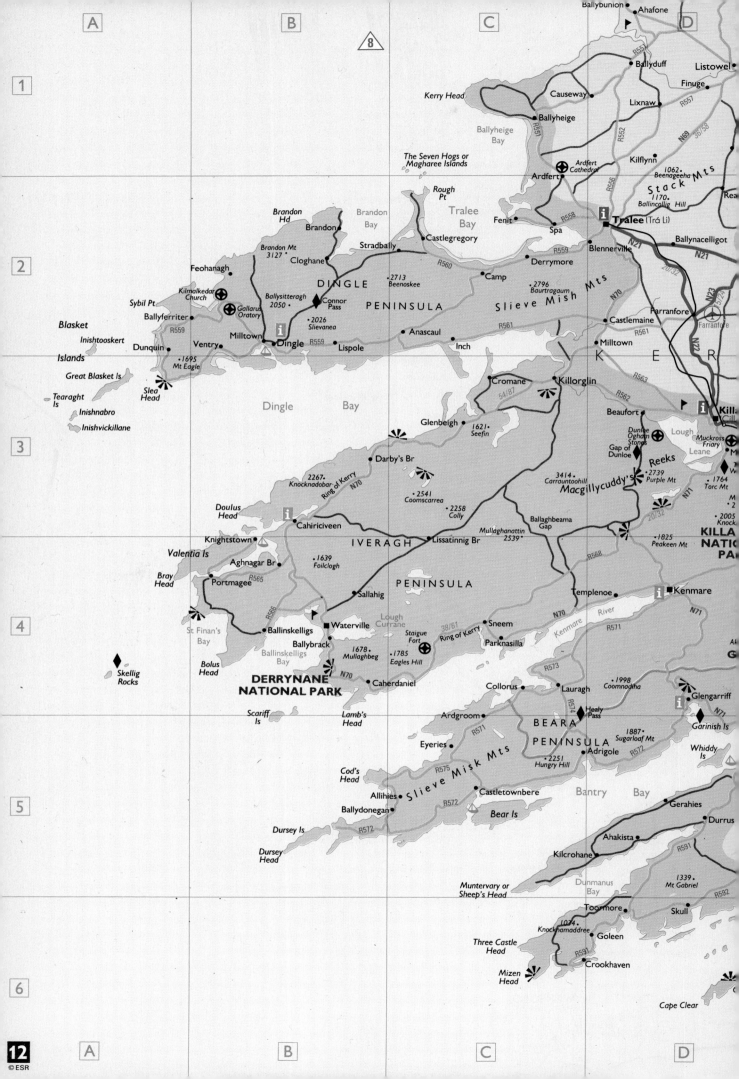

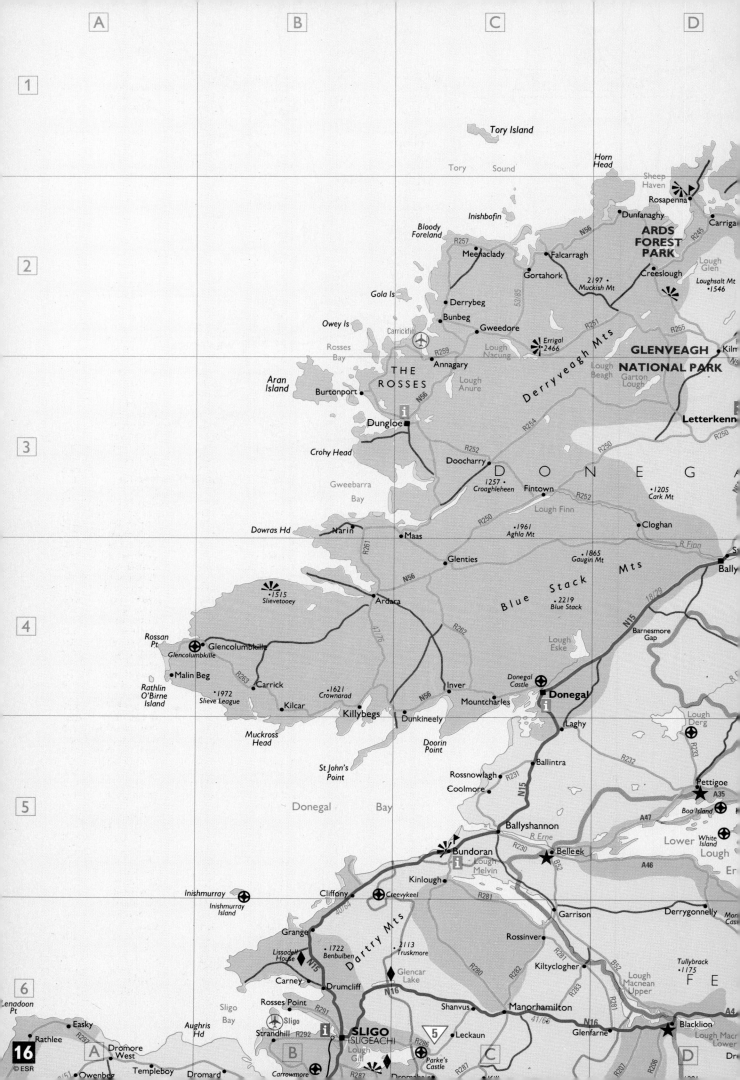

Road Atlas Index